DEVELOPMENTAL BEHAVIORAL NEUROSCIENCE

The Minnesota Symposia on Child Psychology

Volume 24

DEVELOPMENTAL BEHAVIORAL NEUROSCIENCE

The Minnesota Symposia on Child Psychology

Volume 24

edited by
MEGAN R. GUNNAR
CHARLES A. NELSON
University of Minnesota

LAWRENCE ERLBAUM ASSOCIATES, PUBLISHERS
1992 Hillsdale, New Jersey Hove and London

Lawrence Erlbaum Associates, Inc., Publishers
365 Broadway
Hillsdale, New Jersey 07642

Library of Congress Cataloging-in-Publication Data

Developmental behavioral neuroscience / edited by Megan R. Gunnar, Charles A. Nelson.
p. cm. — (The Minnesota symposia on child psychology : v. 24)
"Contains the papers presented at the 24th Minnesota Symposium on Child Psychology, held 19–21 October 1989, at the University of Minnesota, Minneapolis"—Pref.
Includes bibliographical references and index.
ISBN 0-8058-0977-5
1. Developmental psychobiology—Congresses. 2. Developmental neurology—Congresses. 3. Child psychology—Congresses. I. Gunnar, Megan R. II. Nelson, Charles A. III. Minnesota Symposium of Child Psychology (24th : 1989 : University of Minnesota) IV. Series: Minnesota symposia on child psychology (Series) ; v. 24.
QP356.25.D48 1991
155.4—dc20 91-25000
CIP

Printed in the United States of America
10 9 8 7 6 5 4 3 2 1

Contents

Preface

Charles A. Nelson
University of Minnesota

This volume contains the papers presented at the 24th Minnesota Symposium on Child Psychology, held 19–21 October 1989, at the University of Minnesota, Minneapolis. As has been the tradition for this annual series, the faculty of the Institute of Child Development invited internationally eminent researchers to present their work and to consider problems of mutual concern.

The topic for discussion of the 24th Minnesota Symposium was developmental behavioral neuroscience. The title is certainly ambitious, suggesting as it does the melding of three separate disciplines. Furthermore, the discipline of developmental psychology is itself interdisciplinary. To focus on development means to focus on change or ontogeny. The term "developmental" is impartial and unprejudiced to the processes promoting change. The process may involve the changing expression of a genetic blueprint, the cumulative effects of experience, the factors determining how migrating neuroblasts find their target destination in the cortex, or the interaction of all of the above. The study of "behavior" focuses concern on the *actions* as opposed to the neurological make-up of the organism. Finally, the discipline of neuroscience deals with the physiological and anatomical substrata of the brain that underlie behavior. Neuroscience is a broad discipline, involving many levels of analysis, from the biochemical makeup of individual cells to the functioning of vast areas of the cortex. It has in common with developmental psychology an enormous spectrum of questions it investigates and perhaps an even more enormous methodological repertoire.

"Developmental behavioral neuroscience" represents, then, a marriage of disciplines and levels of analysis. Its very complexity is an attempt to bring the organism together, linking the behavioral with the neurological, and at the same time attempting to trace these linkages within the framework of development. It is a monumental and formidable undertaking, and represented herein is a set of chapters written by investigators working at the cutting edge of this endeavor.

One question frequently heard by those who work in this discipline is, "why bother?" What can or does the attempt to assemble these linkages promise to tell us about development, behavior, or neuroscience? For example, to a developmental psychologist, what is there to learn about Piaget's concept of "schema" if we are able to identify where in the brain schemata reside; what their neural characteristics are, and how such characteristics change as the child assimilates and accommodates new information? Some might argue that such an endeavor is too reductionistic, and that in so being it treats the organism as "abehavioral." To those who use the term pejoratively, "reductionism" implies a simplicity that underrepresents the complexity of the phenomenon. I stress, to the contrary, that the more we know about the brain, the less it seems that searching for the neural mechanisms that underlie behavior has anything to do with reducing the phenomenon to something simple. The brain, simply, is not simple, and our developing understanding of its complexity presents no danger of oversimplification of complex psychological or behavioral phenomena.

Stated in these terms, I think most would agree that developmental behavioral neuroscience should, in principal, have far-reaching implications for our understanding of human development. If this is so, you might ask, why has it taken 24 Minnesota symposia to arrive at a symposium on this topic?

The concern with reductionism provides a partial answer. Another has to do with attitudes and philosophy. For example, as Patricia Goldman-Rakic has suggested (1987), for the first half of this century an antinativistic and "empty organism" cult permeated many departments of Psychology. Although the empty organism has since been filled with intentionality and information-processing skills, it has not necessarily been filled with a central nervous system. As a result, relatively little attention was paid to role of the brain in mediating behavior.

Another answer to this question concerns the training involved in becoming either a behavioral scientist or a neuroscientist. The training in both fields is long and protracted. There is, generally speaking, more than enough theoretical and empirical literature in both disciplines to keep a student going forever. As a result, researchers tend not to become familiar with the complement to their own discipline (i.e., behavior to the neuroscientist, the brain to the behavioral scientist), however relevant such familiarity might be. The information overload is only enhanced by adding the developmental slant.

As if the foregoing were not enough, there is one additional reason to consider. This concerns the unique challenge of studying the relation between brain and behavior in an organism that, over its first one or two decades, changes more rapidly than at any other point in the life span. As a result, the armamentarium of the developmental behavioral neuroscientist must be considerably more vast than that of those who study the mature organism.

Fortunately, we have witnessed in the last several years movement towards understanding the psychological and neural mechanisms that underlie behavior, and have begun to convince ourselves and our students of the need to adopt an interdisciplinary approach to the study of brain and behavior. More importantly, the methodological limitations that once constrained the developmental behavioral neuroscientist have begun to be lifted. Advances on all three fronts are very much in evidence in the chapters presented in this volume.

In the opening chapter by Herbert Vaughan Jr. and Diane Kurtzberg (*Electrophysiological Indices of Human Brain Maturation and Cognitive Development*), two related problems are addressed: First, what is the link between behavioral development and neural development? Second, how does one study this link? After providing a precis to some of the principles of brain organization, the authors describe how event-related potentials (ERPs) have been used to draw inferences about the neural events that underlie cognition. This, in turn, is related to an examination of the interface between brain maturation and cognitive development. This last theme is illustrated by the authors' research program, which has aimed to develop dynamic or "real-time" methods for studying the maturation of the brain, and linking this maturation to changes in behavior.

Having provided an overview to the relation between brain development in general and some specific cognitive abilities (e.g., attention, discrimination), the next chapter by Forssberg, Stokes, and Hirschfeld (*Basic Mechanisms of Human Locomotor Development*) examines an often-neglected part of the nervous system (the spinal cord and lower brain stem) and its relation to locomotor development. In work that is remarkable in its detail, Forssberg and colleagues go a long way toward elucidating the neurobiological contribution to locomotor development. Cut from similar cloth as Arnold Gessel, these authors pave the way for a richer understanding of both normal and aberrant patterns of development, and in so doing also provide a model for other behavioral domains.

Don Tucker covers the next topic, that of the relation between brain and emotion (*Developing Emotions and Cortical Networks*). Tremendous inroads have been paved in the field of emotional development over the past 20 years. We now have a wealth of information on at least three facets of the behavioral expression of emotional development: the child's inner affective life, and how this life influences the child's interactions with family and peers; how the child conveys emotion to others; and how the child recognizes and interprets emotion in others. Turning now to the "brain" side of this issue, we have *some* information on the neural operations involved in selected aspects of emotional development, such as laterality differences in recognizing emotion. The work discussed in Tucker's chapter does not focus narrowly on one neural structure and its relation to one aspect of emotion. In this respect his approach is unorthodox, in that he seeks to consider the relation of the whole brain to all of emotion. He accomplishes this by considering that a multitude of brain functions and brain structures are involved in regulating emotion. In so doing he puts forth a compelling view of brain/emotion relations.

Having ambitiously set the stage for tackling a problem as large as brain and emotion, Jocelyn Bachevalier seeks to examine the relation between brain and memory development, and to make tractable the historically intractable problem of infantile amnesia (*Cortical versus Limbic Immaturity: Relationship to Infantile Amnesia*). Bachevalier's work can best be viewed in the context of a relatively new field of inquiry called *cognitive neuroscience*. Cognitive neuroscience is concerned with explicating the relation between brain and cognition by merging the tools of the neuroscientist with those of the cognitive scientist. Bachevalier begins by proposing that there are multiple memory systems, each of which is responsible for performing different operations, and each of which has a different developmental course. These systems are actually comprised of distinct neural circuits, which, like the behaviors they subserve, also have different developmental histories. By describing the interface between these circuits and the behaviors they subserve, Bachevalier offers up a very attractive view of the ontogeny of memory, including why we are unable to remember our earliest experiences.

The next chapter in this volume (*Induction of Brain Structure by Experience: Substrates for Cognitive Development*) takes on the formidable task of considering the role of early experience on later development. The effects of early experience have of course been discussed for centuries, as the question itself is at the heart of the often touted "controversy" between genes and environment. Rather than take a behavioral genetics approach to this question, William Greenough and James Black instead manipulate the environment and observe what effect such a manipulation has on behavior. They then go a step further and, after specifying both the environment *and* behavior, look at the impact both have on the brain. This search has led to the cellular level of the nervous system, and revealed to the reader are some fundamental principles that account for why enriched environments versus impoverished environments impact as they do on the developing brain.

The closing chapter, by Ursula Bellugi and colleagues, concerns the link between thought, language and the brain (*Language, Cognition, and Brain Organization in a Neurodevelopmental Disorder*). This ambitious quest has drawn Bellugi to examine the methods and theories of neurology, neuropsychology, cognitive psychophysiology, developmental psychology and psycholinguistics. The knowledge accrued from these areas is then applied to both normative and "special" populations, including the very unusual population of children suffering from Williams' syndrome. The result is what most would consider extraordinary insight into the relation between thought and language. Indeed, although much work remains to be done on this problem, a rich and imposing set of data are described in the chapter.

In closing, it should be evident that the chapters comprising this volume represent emergent trends in developmental behavioral neuroscience. These trends concern elucidating the relation between brain and the development of cognitive, linguistic, emotional and locomotor abilities, as well as examining how experience impacts on the developing brain. Although much of the "neurologizing" that goes on in these chapters may be unfamiliar to many behavioral scientists, the authors have taken great pains to make their contributions accessible to a wide audience.

In closing, along with my co-editor, Megan Gunnar, I would like to acknowledge the various individuals who made the 24th Minnesota Symposium on Child Psychology a rich and rewarding experience. Thanks are due the speakers, of course, who provided an exciting introduction to their various research programs, and to Adele Diamond, who did a splendid job as discussant. I would also like to thank the graduate students of the Institute of Child Development, both for their enthusiasm for this topic, and for their help with many of the administrative details of the symposium. Helen Dickison and LuJean Huffman-Nordberg are due special thanks for all of their efforts. The symposium went smoothly largely due to their able organizational abilities. Finally, I would like to acknowledge financial support for the symposium from the General Mills Foundation and the National Institute of Child Health and Human Development (R13 HD21906).

REFERENCES

Goldman-Rakic, P. S. (1987). Development of cortical circuitry and cognitive function. *Child Development, 58,* 601–622.

1 Electrophysiologic Indices of Human Brain Maturation and Cognitive Development

Herbert G. Vaughan, Jr.
Diane Kurtzberg
Albert Einstein College of Medicine

Human developmental psychobiology seeks to link emerging psychological and behavioral functions with their underlying neural mechanisms. The development of perception, cognition, emotion and motor performance involves the interaction of environmental experience with the maturing brain (see Greenough, chapter 5). However, maturational changes in the neural substrates that underlie these psychological phenomena are as yet not well defined. There is substantially more information on the facts of psychological development than on their biological underpinnings. Although in principle the relations between brain maturation and psychological development can be addressed at many levels in experimental animals, these investigations are limited in the range of cognitive processes that can be examined. Specifically, language and the cognitive operations it supports can only be studied in humans (see Bellugi, chapter 6).

We have incomplete information on cerebral structure during early human development and data on neuronal interconnections and synaptic density are fragmentary (e.g., Purpura, 1975a, 1975b; Huttenlocher, 1984; Marin-Padilla, 1988). We have even less information on the developmental expression of neurotransmitters and modulators that are thought to control the establishment of neural connections and to mediate the cellular modifications associated with learning (see Parnavelas, Papadopoulos, & Cavanagh, 1988; Johnston, 1988 for reviews).

Studies of human developmental psychobiology must rely primarily on the use of non-invasive techniques to obtain information on brain maturation. It is currently possible to obtain detailed information on the gross anatomical status of brain development using computerized axial tomography and, with finer resolution, through magnetic resonance imaging. Metabolic techniques, such as regional blood flow and positron emission tomography, are invasive and therefore not applicable to normal infants and children. Furthermore, despite the functional localization provided by measures of local cerebral metabolism, these methods are inherently incapable of providing real time information on the neural mechanisms that underlie psychological processes.

In principle, the most valuable information on brain function should be provided by the electrical activity generated by neurons within the functioning brain. In humans, this neural activity is manifested in the electroencephalogram (EEG), and in the electrical signals related to sensory, motor and cognitive processes, called "event related potentials" or ERPs (Vaughan, 1969). ERPs provide unique real time indices of specific brain processes that can be monitored throughout the course of development. In the past, the interpretation of developmental EEG and ERP changes has been hampered by the uncertain neural origins of these scalp-recorded signals. During the past two decades, however, both the brain mechanisms (Vaughan & Arezzo, 1988) and the psychological correlates (Picton & Hillyard, 1988) of ERPs have become increasingly better defined. Although much remains to be learned about the neurophysiological basis and psychophysiological relations of the numerous ERP components that have been identified, these real time physiological indices of specific psychological processes can serve as powerful indices of the psychobiology of human development.

In this chapter we show how ERPs, employed as indices of regional brain maturation and of the spatiotemporal patterns of neural processing within the brain, can begin to elucidate some key aspects of developmental psychobiology in infants and children. Before we consider these possibilities, we will outline the conceptual and empirical framework within which this work is placed. We briefly consider the regional anatomical substrate of brain maturation, and relate that to the neuronal network architecture that underlies brain function.

PRINCIPLES OF BRAIN ORGANIZATION

It is a basic premise of human developmental psychobiology that psychological phenomena are manifestations of brain processes, and that psychological changes during development reflect alterations in brain organization and function. Although the neurobiological substrate of psychological processes is obscure and difficult to delineate in detail, we must nevertheless endeavor to learn as much as possible about human brain maturation in order to understand the neural basis of psychological development.

We take as the starting point for this paper, certain principles of brain organization that guide our research. A central feature of human cerebral organization is its parcellation into regions, each having specific features of intrinsic cellular organization and of connectivity with other brain regions (Braak, 1980; Eccles, 1984; Jones, 1984).

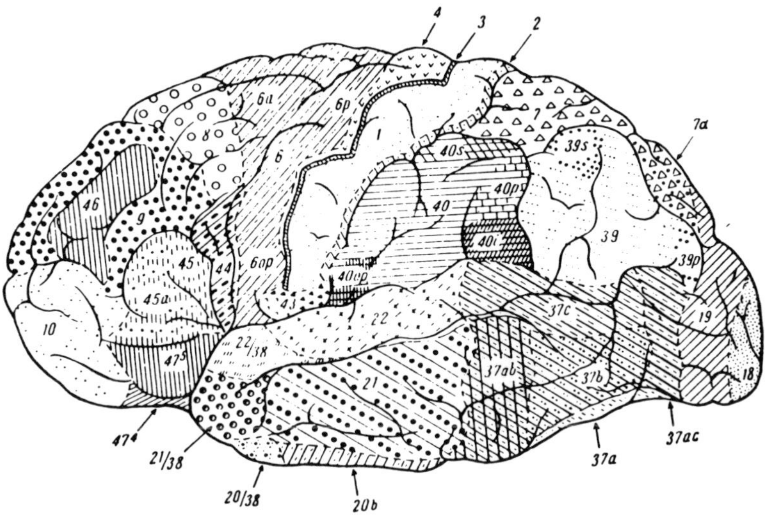

FIG. 1.1. A cytoarchitectonic map of the lateral surface of the human cerebral cortex with areas numbered according to the scheme introduced by Brodman (1909). The cortical areas differ not only in their characteristic laminar patterns of cell body distribution, that are the criterion for the cytoarchitectonic method of parcellation, but also in their patterns of intracortical circuitry and their connectivity with other brain regions. These latter features are the basis for functional differences across cortical regions.

Despite more than a century of controversy, the parcellation of cerebral cortex on the basis of cytoarchitectonics (Fig. 1.1), intrinsic neuronal organization, external connectivity and physiological properties forms the foundation of contemporary cognitive neuroscience (see Peters and Jones, *Cerebral Cortex,* Vols. 1–7 for detailed reviews of cortical organization). Although there are no isolated "organs of the mind," there is much to be said for a "modular" approach to understanding the organization of the brain. It is convenient to segregate cortical regions as subcomponents of larger brain systems. Anatomists and physiologists typically select one brain region, and possibly some of the structures with which it connects, for intensive analysis. Nevertheless, even the simplest psychological processes are not limited to a particular patch of brain, as was emphasized by Luria (1973). We accept the idea that psychological processes represent the coordinated interaction of a number of brain regions, each of which has its specialized intrinsic organization and modes of operation (see e.g., Pandya & Yeterian, 1985; Goldman-Rakic, 1988 for further discussion).

A complementary way of looking at brain organization focuses on its network properties. Inasmuch as the brain comprises neurons and their connections, and operates through the activation and modification of these connections, the brain is in fact a neural network. The anatomical organization of these neural networks and the principles that govern modifications in the functional effectiveness of their synaptic connections are key issues to be addressed in order to understand the neurobiological basis of psychological development.

The formulation of "neural network" models has become a prominent area in cognitive neuroscience in recent years, following a long period of development by a small group of pioneering theorists. The basic ideas that underlie contemporary neural network theory were set forth by Donald Hebb in his seminal work *The Organization of Behavior* (Hebb, 1949). Hebb postulated that brain circuitry comprises two kinds of neuronal networks, which he called "cell assemblies" and "phase sequences." Cell assemblies are groups of neurons, which through a combination of genetic determinants and repeated exposure to specific external inputs, come to respond to particular stimuli with characteristic, relatively stereotyped patterns of activation. Phase sequences, by contrast, represent more flexible dynamic network activation patterns, comprising linkages of cell assemblies directed by the particular processing demands of the perceptual-cognitive task at hand. Hebb's theory is a developmental one, in which the establishment of cell assemblies and phase sequences is conditioned by changes in synaptic efficiency, due to repeated associations of a presynaptic input pattern with concurrent activation of the postsynaptic neuron. This associative mechanism for the modification of synaptic efficiency has come to be known as the "Hebbian synapse" and represents a major, although probably not the sole determinant of synaptic changes that occur during learning.

Hebb's ideas were revolutionary and did not immediately lead to efforts to develop them into formal theory. The work of McCulloch and Pitts (1943) was probably more influential among early mathematical network modelers, including Rosenblatt (1958), whose "perceptron" represented the first attempt to model a specific sensory system, and other workers who incorporated learning into network models. (See Anderson and Rosenfeld, 1989 for a compendium of seminal papers on neural network modeling.)

A competing, and for a time dominant, model of brain mechanisms was proposed by John von Neumann (1958). This model was the serial processing digital computer. At the time, digital computers seemed to provide the nearest analogy to the powerful computational abilities of the human brain. Models of perceptual and cognitive operations that employed serial models similar to the logical structure of digital computers have been especially popular in cognitive psychology, in which the concepts of "processing stages" and "serial search of memory" has been the topic of much experimental work and theory (e.g., Sternberg, 1969). In serial models, memory storage is generally viewed as distinct from the brain structures responsible for sensory, perceptual and cognitive operations. These operations would *access* memory, much as discrete memory locations are addressed in a computer.

The development of parallel distributed processing (PDP) models, which are essentially Hebbian in their main features, has radically altered our conceptualization of the brain operations that underlie perceptual and cognitive processes (Rumelhart, McClelland et al., 1986; McClelland & Rumelhart et al., 1986). The most important differences include, first, an emphasis on the massive parallelism of brain operations, which is hardly surprising to anyone who knows anything about neuroanatomy; and second, the localization of mnemonic mechanisms within the processing networks themselves, so that memory is an intrinsic property of the network, residing in the efficiency of a synaptic transmission among the neural elements that comprise it. A third key feature of network models is the presence of feedback from later levels of the network to earlier ones. This feature is anatomically embodied in the recurrent projections that are ubiquitous within the brain, and which may form the basis for so-called "top down" processing in cognitive psychology, and "back propagation" in PDP network models. These recurrent connections can modulate the responses of brain regions that process sensory input at earlier stages according to the presumed significance of the input, either filtering out unimportant inputs or selecting information deemed to be of significance for further processing. Recurrent projections can also participate in the operation of "comparator" mechanisms that serve to detect novel or deviant stimulus patterns.

We emphasize that characterization of the brain as a neural network does not imply either that the brain is diffusely organized, with every neuron connected to every other, or that the organization of the networks is similar in all brain regions. Neither of these circumstances is likely to be the case. For example, the manner in which visual and auditory information is processed by the brain differs substantially, as reflected in major differences in the anatomy and physiology of these sensory systems. It is necessary to consider these specialized features of regional brain organization as well as interactions among brain regions when we examine the changes in brain organization that underlie psychological development.

Having briefly mentioned some aspects of contemporary models of brain processes, we now consider how the electrophysiologic study of human brain dynamics may shed light on certain aspects of the development of brain organization.

EVENT RELATED BRAIN POTENTIALS

Event related potentials (ERPs) are manifestations of the activity of large numbers of neurons that are closely synchronized with some externally observable event, such as a stimulus or motor response. ERPs can be extracted from the ongoing spontaneous neuroelectric potentials by averaging a number of EEG samples time-locked to the synchronizing event. The averaged ERPs are enhanced with respect to the amplitude of the random background EEG in proportion to the square root of the number of averaged samples. Thus, even very tiny synchronous brain signals can be resolved, given a sufficiently large number of samples. For example, the extremely small electrical signals generated within the subcortical auditory pathways, which are in the order of tenths of a microvolt at the surface of the scalp, can be recorded by averaging the responses to 1000 or more stimuli. ERPs generated within cerebral cortex, which are usually several microvolts in amplitude at the scalp, can often be satisfactorily recorded with averages of less than 100 trials.

Over the past 2 decades ERPs have been described that represent the cortical and subcortical responses to sensory stimuli, brain activity associated with voluntary movements, and with various cognitive processes (see Picton, 1988 for reviews). The sensory evoked potentials (EPs) represent more or less obligatory responses to the physical properties of the sensory stimuli. Movement related potentials (MRPs) are observed in recordings time-locked to quick extremity or eye movements. MRPs include not only the endogenous brain activity that precedes the movements, but also reafferent activity associated with the movements and changes in sensory input that are a consequence of the movements. A third class of ERPs are those associated with active processing of sensory input and with various cognitive operations. These ERP components are often called "endogenous" potentials to contrast them with the obligatory, "exogenous" EPs. We use the term "processing contingent components" (PCCs), to emphasize that these components represent the processing of sensory input beyond the obligatory responses elicited by the repetitive presentation of a nonsignificant stimulus, and also to distinguish them from MRPs which are also "endogenous." PCCs are elicited in a variety of tasks requiring active sensory or other cognitive processes, including linguistic processing. PCCs, however, can also be elicited automatically by unexpected stimuli or unexpected changes in the physical properties or the timing of stimuli. This latter class of PCCs is especially important in studying the discriminative capacities of infants and young children who are unable to perform active discrimination tasks.

We advance the idea that certain of the major features of network activation during sensory, perceptual, cognitive and motoric processes can be spatially and temporally localized within the brain employing ERP analysis. The realization of this prospect requires knowledge of brain anatomy and physiology in order to interpret the patterns of scalp recorded electrical activity. Despite limitations of our detailed knowledge of the relevant brain microphysiology, we have a fairly good grasp of the main features of intracortical and corticocortical connectivity that underlie the sequential activation of the brain regions involved in perceptual and cognitive processes. A critical advance in the utility of ERPs for directly observing specific brain processes has been afforded by techniques that use topographic ERP data to localize the intracranial sources of specific portions of the ERP waveform. The spatiotemporal dipole method (Brain Electrical Source Activity or BESA) of Scherg (Scherg & Von Cramon, 1986; Scherg, 1989;

Scherg, Vajsar, & Picton, 1989) has made it possible to dissect ERPs into constituent source waveforms that reflect the moment by moment activity of localized brain regions (Fig. 1.2). This capability makes it possible to examine not only the activation pattern of individual cortical areas, but also to evaluate the interactions among several active regions.

The basic premise is that brain network activation during psychological processes has a characteristic sequential activation pattern of successive levels within the network. Thus, if large numbers of neurons are responding more or less in synchrony within one network level of a particular brain region, their summed electrical discharge can provide an externally recordable ERP component that indexes the magnitude and timing of this activation. Synchronous activation of brain networks may not generally occur in the psychological processes of ordinary life. Nevertheless, under circumstances in which such synchronization occurs, it can be possible to identify some of the spatiotemporal features of network activation by their neuroelectric manifestations. Thus, the brain processes under examination must either be naturally or experimentally synchronized to achieve the massive summation of concurrent neural activity that is required to generate recordable ERP components.

There are several aspects of normal brain operation that facilitate such synchronization. The nervous system responds best to transient signals or to changes in input, thus providing a built-in mechanism for synchronization of the parallel input that is ordinarily elicited by a stimulus. For example, visual scanning comprises sequences of saccades and fixations which serve to synchronize visual input with each saccade. In the perception of speech, syllables and words have a temporal energy structure that emphasizes neural responses to distinct features such as stop consonants and the onset of syllables and words. Even cognitively salient aspects of language, such as semantic classification or incongruity can have a significant synchronizing effect upon network responses, as manifested by the appearance of specific ERP manifestations of semantic processing (Kutas & Van Petten, 1988; Novick, Lovrich, & Vaughan, 1985).

It is more difficult to be sure that a significant degree of synchrony persists during prolonged perceptual and cognitive operations. Indeed, it is known that temporal variability, as well as mean response latency increases in successive processing stages. Thus, we can anticipate a temporal dispersion of brain network activation with increasing distance from the input stage. This dispersion is seen in human ERPs, in that longer latency ERP components are more variable in amplitude and latency than earlier ones. For example, the "N2" ERP component, which reflects the selection of the target stimuli in sensory discrimination tasks, exhibits latency variability that is highly correlated with reaction time (Ritter, Simson, Vaughan, & Friedman, 1979). Thus, movement-related brain potentials are most clearly visualized either when motor response latency variability is minimal, as in simple reaction time tasks (Vaughan, Costa, Gilden, &

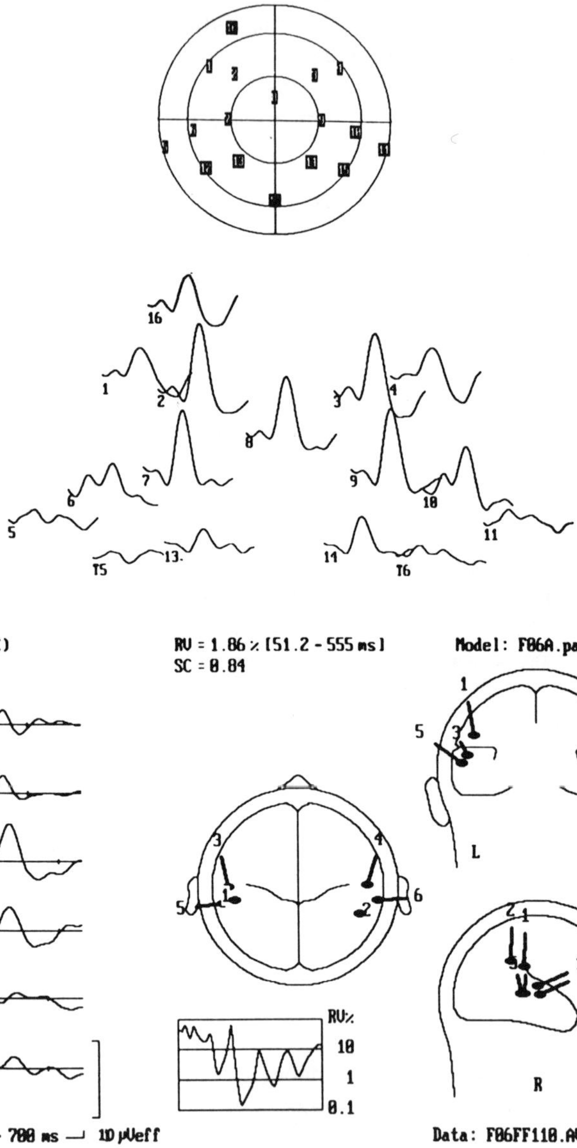
BESA (C)
RV = 1.86 % [51.2 - 555 ms]
SC = 0.84
Model: F06A.par
L
R
RV%
10
1
0.1
└ 0 - 700 ms ┘ 10 μVeff
Data: F06FF110.AVR

FIG. 1.2

Schimmel, 1965), or when brain activity is averaged in synchrony with the motor responses rather than the stimuli (Friedman, Vaughan, & Erlenmeyer-Kimling, 1978; Gilden, Vaughan, & Costa, 1966).

Despite the increasing temporal dispersion of neural activity as brain networks are traversed, the basic activation sequence persists. Synchronization of all stages of network activation can be experimentally maximized by selectively averaging the ERP signals from those trials that have similar motor response latencies. By comparing these ERPs that are associated with a range of behavioral response latencies, the timing of activity related to a specific stage of network activation can be systematically varied and observed (e.g., Ritter, Simson, Vaughan, & Macht, 1982; Ritter, Vaughan, & Simson, 1983).

Although ERP components can be utilized as indices of the synchronous excitation or inhibition of large numbers of neurons, it remains to be determined what neural elements are involved and how they are related to the sequential activation of the network. This information can only be derived from animal experimentation. The search for such information is the principal focus of experimental work in monkeys by Arezzo and associates in our laboratory. In these studies, detailed intracortical recordings of ERPs and multiple unit activity are taken from multicontact electrodes. An example of this type of data, recorded from the visual cortex of an alert monkey in response to a visual stimulus is shown in Fig. 1.3. This recording depicts the laminar profile of visual evoked potentials, current source density (CSD) derived from the intracortical field potential distribution, and summed multiple unit activity (MUA) recorded simultaneously from a 16 contact electrode. CSD, which is proportional to the second spatial derivative of the field potentials, provides an estimate of net transmembrane current flow at each recording site (Nicholson & Freeman, 1975). These inward and outward current flows are due primarily to synaptic activation, both excitatory and inhibitory, and generate the extracellular volume current flows that ultimately produce the ERP recorded from scalp electrodes. By visualizing the magnitude and direction of the synaptic currents, and comparing them

---

FIG. 1.2. Brain Electrical Source Analysis (BESA) showing the location, orientation and time varying strength of the computed equivalent dipoles that provide a model of intracranial generators of the surface recorded ERP topography. In this example, AEPs to tone are recorded in a group of 6 month old infants. The electrode recording sites and AEP waveforms are depicted in the upper part of the figure. The right lower portion of the figure depicts the six dipolar generators within a spherical model of the head, and on the left are depicted the strength of each source over the course of the AEP. Note that two bilateral pairs of dipoles are located in the auditory areas within the superior temporal plane, and two additional dipoles are located in the position of secondary auditory cortex on the lateral surface of the temporal lobe. The posterior dipole is located in the approximate location of primary auditory cortex and has the earliest onset source waveform.

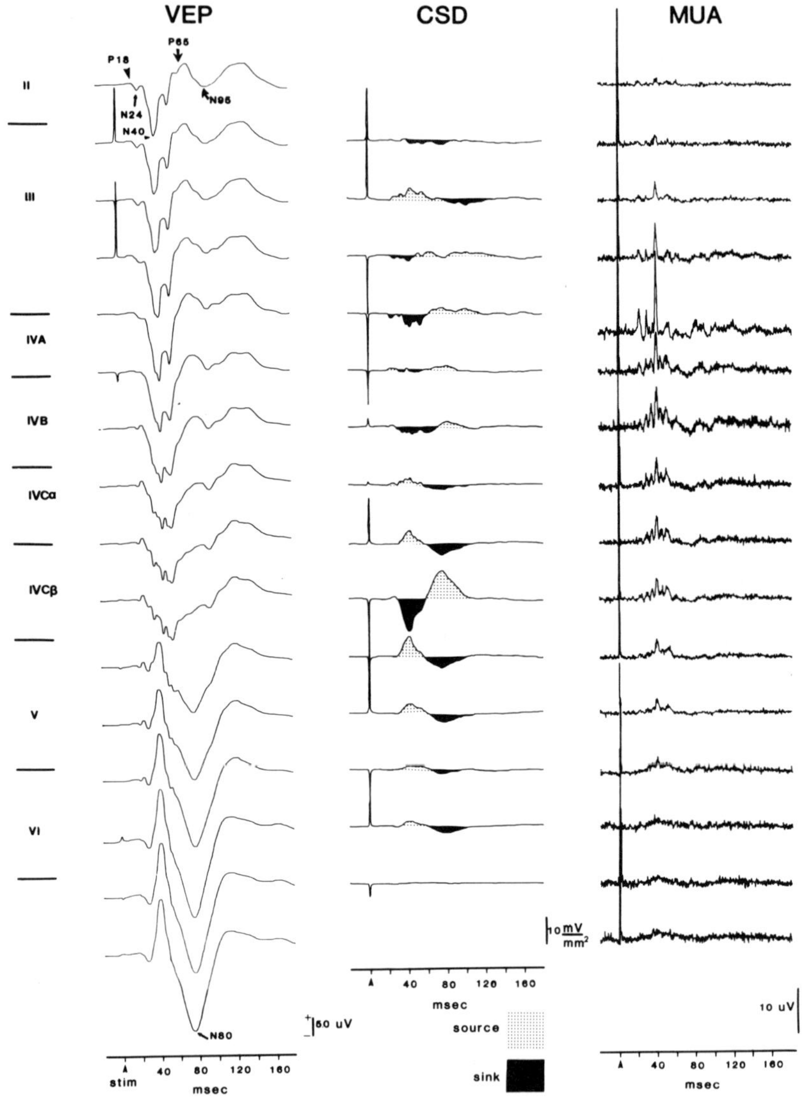
VEP
CSD
MUA
P18
P65
N24
N40
N95
N80
II
III
IVA
IVB
IVCα
IVCβ
V
VI
50 uV
stim
40
80
120
160
msec
10 mV/mm²
source
sink
10 uV

FIG. 1.3

with the concurrent changes in cellular firing patterns seen in the multiple unit activity, we can infer the locations of net cellular excitation and inhibition at each intracortical level. These data, taken together with surface recordings of the visual evoked potential, allow us to characterize the intracortical synaptic events that generate the surface recorded potentials (Kraut, Arezzo, & Vaughan 1985; Schroeder, Tenke, Givre, Arezzo, & Vaughan, in press). In some instances, it is possible to identify individual surface recorded ERP components with excitation or inhibition of neuronal populations at a single intracortical level, although ERP components often represent the summation of synaptic events within more than one intracortical lamina. When combined with knowledge of the cellular anatomy, local circuitry and the identity of the neurotransmitters that elicit the synaptic potentials, it is possible to draw inferences regarding the neural mechanisms that generate specific ERP components.

This experimental work, which has been applied to the obligatory evoked potentials in visual, somatosensory and auditory cortex, and to movement related potentials in sensorimotor cortex and hippocampus (Arezzo, Vaughan, Kraut, Steinschneider, & Legatt, 1986), is currently being extended to studies of task-related potentials in neocortex and limbic system structures. The data derived from these analyses provide information on the specific intracortical patterns of population synaptic activity that contribute to the surface recorded ERP components. In those instances in which these contributions can be localized to specific intracortical cell populations, we approach the goal of identifying specific synchronous network activation stages. As yet, these data are insufficient to provide

---

FIG. 1.3. Laminar patterns of intracortical visual evoked potentials (VEP-left column), transmembrane current flow estimated by current source density (CSD-middle column) and multiple unit activity (MUA-right column) recorded from the striate cortex of an alert monkey in response to flash stimulation. Cortical laminar boundaries are indicated by Roman numerals at the left. Note the prominent early excitation in lamina IVCb, depicted by the current sink, followed by inhibitory post synaptic activity. Excitation and inhibition are reflected in an initial increase in MUA succeeded by a small reduction in overall neural firing level, concurrent with the CSD sinks and sources. The active sources and sinks are flanked by complementary outward and inward current flows that represent passive current return. An additional excitatory input to visual cortex is seen in lamina IVA, which also receives thalamocortical projections from the lateral geniculate nucleus (see Kraut, Arezzo, & Vaughan, 1985 for detailed description). The components of the VEP waveform recorded in superficial cortex are labelled in polarity and latency. This waveform is essentially identical to that recorded at lower amplitude from the overlying cortical surface and scalp. Note that N40 can be attributed largely to the lamina IVCb excitation and P65 to the later inhibitory process at the same level. Under these stimulus conditions, activation of supragranular and infragranular laminae is not prominent.

a general interpretation of scalp-recorded ERP waveforms in terms of their cellular correlates, but the approaches we are using give promise of providing such information.

Of particular importance for interpretation of human ERPs is the fact that surface recorded potentials more strongly reflect activity in the granular and supragranular cortical laminae. The granular laminae receive cortical input from the thalamus, whereas the supragranular laminae contain the main local circuits that govern corticocortical interactions. The supragranular laminae also receive the recurrent corticocortical feedback inputs. Thus, ERPs tend to provide more information on sensory input and corticocortical interactions than on efferent cortical-subcortical activity. This is a limitation that we can live with, inasmuch as feedforward and feedback corticocortical operations are presumably the most significant component of network operations associated with perceptual and cognitive processes.

REGIONAL BRAIN MATURATION

A major issue in human developmental psychobiology is the timing of the emergence of functional competence within specific brain regions and systems. Early studies of human brain maturation examined the ontogenetic pattern of cortical myelination as an anatomical indicator of the sequence of maturation of the cortex. This early work, especially that of Flechsig (1920) and C. and O. Vogt (1919), supplemented by the more recent studies of Yakovlev and Lecours (1967) delineated a myelinogenetic sequence beginning in sensorimotor systems, followed by secondary cortical regions and latest in frontal, parietal and temporal association cortex, as depicted in Fig. 1.4. These observations led to developmental neuropsychological formulations that envisaged a direct relationship between the myelinogenetic sequence and the early developmental emergence of sensorimotor processes, followed by more complex perceptual and cognitive operations. Myelination principally influences the speed of transmission along neural processes, so the density of myelination does not provide a direct marker of functionally significant aspects of cortical architecture and connectivity. Thus, the interpretation of the myelinogenetic studies as markers of functional competence is problematic. Since myelination of cortical neuropil and certain corticocortical fiber tracts continues into adolescence, inferences were made regarding the prolonged physiological immaturity and functional incompetence of association cortex. This idea has influenced thinking in developmental and educational psychology, and has led to the notion of inherent maturational limits upon the development of perceptual and cognitive capacities during infancy and childhood. Despite the fact that the extent of myelination does not directly index the functional status of cortical networks, the sequence of regional cortical myelination does appear to reflect some maturational feature that is consistent with

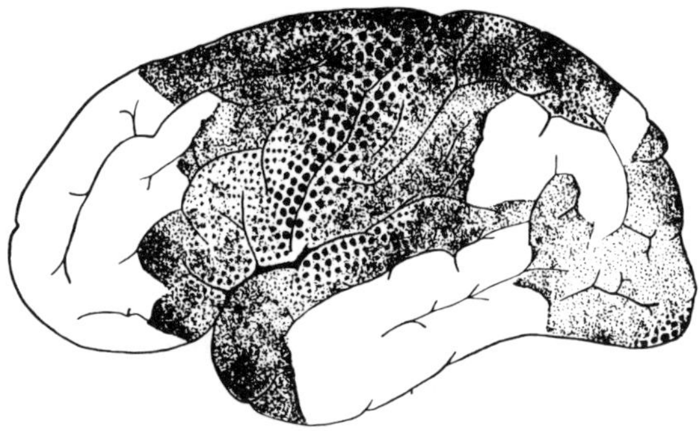

FIG. 1.4. Myelinoarchitectonic mapping of the developmental sequence within the human cerebral cortex after Vogt (1906). Primary sensorimotor areas (large dots) are the first to myelinate, followed by secondary areas indicated by smaller dots and stipple. The latest development of myelination occurs in the "nonspecific association" areas of parietal, temporal and frontal cortex (blank areas).

what is known about maturational changes in the plasticity of cortical areas. Thus, the sensorimotor regions that are thought to establish their basic intrinsic organization early in life during the so called "critical periods" are those that exhibit the earliest myelinogenesis, whereas the nonspecific association areas of frontal, parietal and temporal cortex are the last to myelinate. We do not as yet know what aspect of neural plasticity might be indexed by myelination of the cortical neuropil.

Equally influential in delineating the maturational pattern of sensorimotor and association cortex were the monumental studies of cortical cellular maturation by Conel (1939–1963) using the Golgi technique. The Golgi data provide a more useful correlate of neuronal function than does myelination, in that the Golgi stain discloses the developmental state of dendritic branching patterns and the development of dendritic spines. Conel's work has until recently been the sole source of information on neuronal maturation in human cortex. However, his data were somewhat deficient from a technical standpoint, and suggested a greater degree of neural immaturity at birth than has been observed in more recent studies. These later studies of sensory and motor cortex in human neonates have served to correct the notion of extreme neonatal neuronal immaturity to a large degree (Marin-Padilla, 1970a, 1970b; 1972; Huttenlocher, 1979, 1984; Huttenlocher, de Courten, Garey, & Van Der Loos, 1982; Purpura, 1961; 1975a, 1975b). Nevertheless, the idea that the infant brain is so immature at birth as to be incapable of sophisticated processing of sensory input has died hard, and still exhibits occasional postmortem spasms. Furthermore, the occurrence of postnatal cell death and synaptic pruning was unknown to the earlier investigators, so that some contortions were required to fit Conel's data into a presumed monotonic sequence of maturational complexity.

The single most significant anatomical correlate of functional cortical maturation is the status of synaptic connections. Their presence can be inferred to some extent from the appearance of dendritic spines, which are presumptive sites of excitatory synaptic connections, and can be seen in Golgi-stained tissue. However, quantitative analysis of synaptic density and examination of the proportion of presumptive excitatory and inhibitory synapses requires electron microscopic studies in conjunction with Golgi staining to identify the cellular location of the synapses. These laborious studies have rarely been done in humans, but have been a key technique in experimental studies of cortical development in animals. (e.g., Greenough, Black, & Wallace, 1987). The work of Huttenlocher and colleagues has provided some information on maturational changes in synaptic density in human visual and frontal cortex (Huttenlocher, 1979; Huttenlocher, de Courten, Garey, & Van Der Loos, 1982). Although these data are limited, they provide critical information on the timing of synaptic development in these two cortical areas, one sensory and the other association, in human infants. The key facts are that synaptic density in striate cortex, an early maturing sensory region, reaches its maximum at about eight months of age, and in prefrontal cortex, presumably one of the latest maturing cortical areas, by two years of age. In both areas, synaptic density declines during the first decade of life to reach adult values during adolescence.

Since striate cortex reaches its adult volume by about 4 months, the greatest total number of synapses in visual cortex must be achieved at about the same age as the maximum synaptic density. It should be noted that from birth through the first 2 months of life, synaptic density in striate cortex is greater than two thirds that of the adult. In frontal association cortex, the maximum synaptic density is achieved by the end of the first year. Total brain size approaches adult values by about 2 years of age, so the total number of synapses within frontal cortex presumably also reaches its maximum at around 2 years. More detailed data from several cortical areas of monkeys (Rakic, Bourgeois, Eckenhoff, Zecevic, & Goldman-Rakic, 1986) exhibit a developmental pattern of synaptogenesis that is somewhat more precocious than that of human cortex. These data have led Goldman-Rakic to suggest that neocortical areas develop more or less in synchrony (Goldman-Rakic, 1987, 1988). As we shall see in the course of this paper, there appear to be differences in the rates of functional development of human cortical areas, but these differences are relatively small in comparison with earlier ideas about the relative pace of regional cortical maturation based on myelinogenetic patterns.

The newer observations on neural morphology and synaptic density within human and monkey cortex, suggest that the basic cerebral cellular architecture is present at birth or shortly thereafter, and that postnatal loss of neurons and synapses is a prominent feature of normal cortical development. By 2 years of age, from a quantitative standpoint, all of the synapses necessary for emerging perceptual and cognitive processes appear to be present. What is not as yet present is the specific *patterning* of synaptic connections that is the neural substrate of emerging psychological processes. It can be presumed that the sculpturing of synaptic connectivity and efficiency is the critical process underlying perceptual and cognitive development.

With the ideas in hand that the basic neuronal architecture is present to a large degree at birth and the quantity of synaptic connections develops rapidly to its apogee during the first year of life, we now consider how these developmental characteristics of the infant are manifested in the electrical responses of the brain to sensory stimulation.

REGIONAL MATURATION OF SENSORY EVOKED POTENTIALS

Early work on EPs in preterm infants established that obligatory cortical responses to sensory stimulation are present in the visual, auditory and somatosensory modality by 26 weeks postconception (Vaughan & Kurtzberg, 1989). A uniform sequence of changes in the waveshape of sensory EPs has been observed, with a surface negative potential in the youngest preterm infants becoming predominantly surface positive by term (Weitzman & Graziani, 1968; Kurtzberg, Hilpert, Kreuzer, & Vaughan, 1984; Vaughan & Kurtzberg, 1989). We made two main observations in these developmental ERP studies of premature infants. First, even in the EPs recorded from the youngest preterm infants, responses that differed in their timing and waveshape were recorded overlying primary, secondary and association cortical regions (Vaughan, 1975; Vaughan & Kurtzberg, 1989). This observation indicated that by 3 months before term, when cortical neurons are extremely immature in their morphology (e.g., Purpura, 1975a, 1975b; Rabinowicz, 1984), functioning synaptic connections are present not only in primary sensory cortex but in secondary and association cortex as well. There are obvious implications of such precocious cortical responsiveness to stimulation for possible environmental modulation of cortical connectivity during late intrauterine development and in the premature infant.

A second key finding is the fact that the characteristic sequential changes in EP morphology seen in primary cortex precede a similar maturational sequence of the EP generated in secondary visual and auditory cortical areas (Kurtzberg, Hilpert, Kreuzer, & Vaughan, 1984; Vaughan & Kurtzberg, 1989; Novak, Kurtzberg, Kreuzer, & Vaughan, 1989). These observations suggest that EPs can provide an objective index of regional cortical maturation that reflects the developmental status of neural connectivity and synaptic function within each cortical area.

Subsequent studies of the maturation of obligatory EPs to visual and auditory stimulation provide support for the idea that EP component magnitude during development may provide a dynamic index of the magnitude of net population

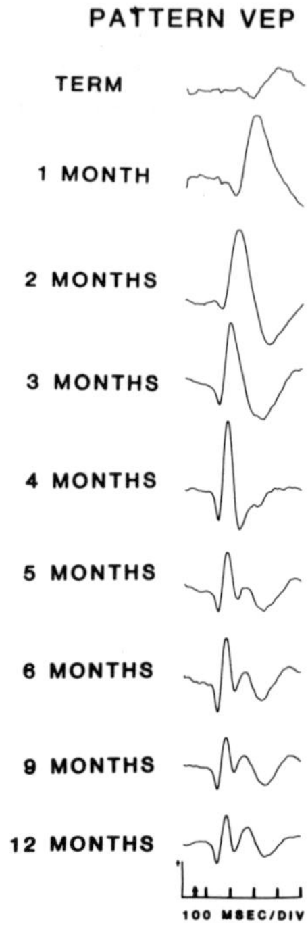

FIG. 1.5A. Grand mean visual evoked potentials (VEP) recorded overlying occipital cortex in a group of healthy full term infants from birth through the first year of life. Stimulus is reversal of a black and white checkerboard, with each check subtending 40′ of visual angle. The positive component decreases in latency and duration, particularly during the first 4 months of life. Pattern reversal at arrow. Calibration: 2.5 uV for term through 2 months and 5 uV thereafter.

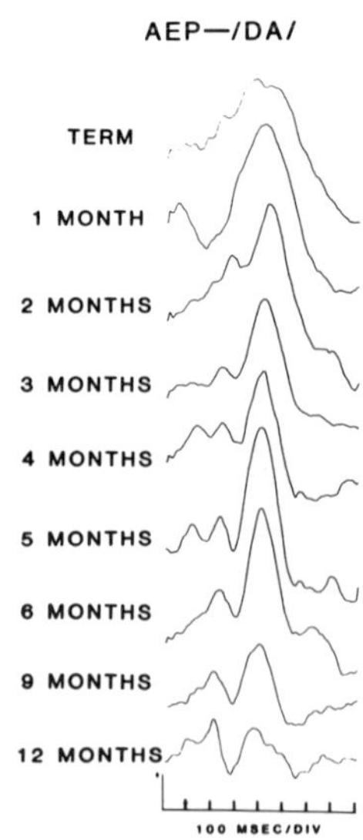

FIG. 1.5B. Grand mean auditory evoked potentials (AEP) to the synthesized speech sound /da/ recorded over the midline central region in a group of healthy full term infants from birth through the first year of life. The morphology of the response becomes better defined and shorter in latency during the first 6 months of life. More complex changes in waveshape occur between nine and twelve of age. Stimulus onset at arrow. Calibration: 2.5 uV for term through 4 months and 5 uV thereafter.

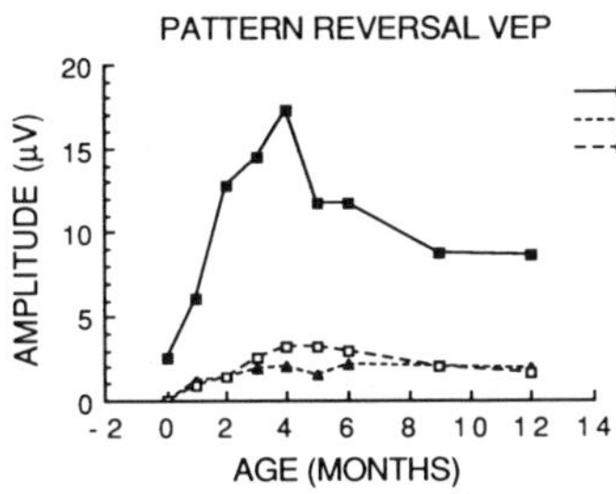

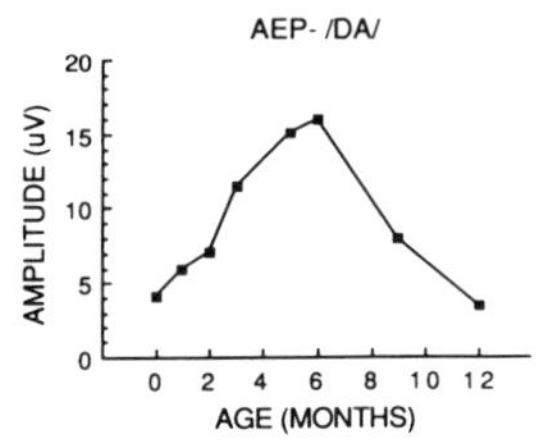

FIG. 1.6A. Peak to peak amplitudes of the negative-positive complex of the pattern reversal VEP recorded from electrodes overlying occipital, parietal and posterior temporal cortex. Measurements were derived from data recorded from the group of healthy full term infants studied longitudinally from birth depicted in Fig. 1.5A. Occipital response amplitude increases rapidly to a maximum between two and four months of age and then diminishes. Response amplitude from parietal and posterior temporal cortex gradually increases until 4 to 5 months, thus lagging behind primary visual cortex by 1 to 2 months.

FIG. 1.6B. Baseline to peak amplitudes of the major positive component of the AEP to the speech sound /da/ recorded from the midline central region. This peak represents activity of primary auditory cortex. (See Figs. 1.2 and 1.5B). Amplitude steadily increases, reaching a maximum at 5 to 6 months and then rapidly diminishes in the latter 6 months of the first year of life.

synaptic potentials elicited by sensory input. As illustrated in Figs. 1.5A and B, visual and auditory EPs recorded from electrodes placed so as to record mainly from the generators in primary cortex exhibit striking changes in waveshape ampliutude and timing over the first year of life. The amplitude of the EPs recorded overlying primary visual cortex in response to patterned stimulation rapidly increase in amplitude to reach their maximum by 2- to 4-months-of-age and then diminish (Fig. 1.6A). Similar amplitude changes are observed in the responses from auditory cortex, but the maximum amplitude is achieved somewhat later, usually at 5 to 6 months (Fig. 1.6B).

It is, of course, not possible to precisely equate EP amplitude to synaptic density, or even with the number of synapses activated by the sensory input. Nevertheless, EP amplitude is proportional to the magnitude of intracerebral volume currents that generate the EP. These volume currents are driven by the transmembrane currents generated by synaptic activation. Therefore, despite the complexities and uncertainties involved in the quantitative relation of synaptic activity to EP amplitude, ERPs provide us with the best available noninvasive estimate of the magnitude of synaptic activation in humans. Thus, using ERP amplitude as the criterion, it appears that synaptic activation within the primary visual and auditory cortex elicited by passively presented visual or auditory stimulation reaches a maximum by 2- to 4-months-of-age for the former and 5 to 6 months for the latter.

Response amplitudes from secondary cortical areas exhibit maturational patterns that differ from those of primary cortex. In the visual modality, pattern reversal stimulation elicits responses from the posterior temporal and parietal region that gradually increase in amplitude until 4 to 5 months (see Fig. 6.1A). Thus, there is a 1- to 2-month lag in achieving maximum response amplitude between primary and secondary visual cortical areas. In the auditory modality, there is a similar developmental lag reflected in response morphology between primary and secondary cortical areas (Kurtzberg, Hilpert, Kreuzer, & Vaughan, 1984).

The obligatory cortical responses elicited by sensory input within primary and secondary sensory cortex can, we propose, be identified with the activation of cell assemblies in the Hebbian sense, and perhaps with the developing neural substrate that has been designated "experience expectant" by Greenough and colleagues (1987 and this volume). The developmental changes in component amplitude, which are presumed to index the magnitude of synaptic activation, permits some inferences on maturational status of the primary and secondary sensory cortical regions. The data now at hand suggest that the magnitude of synaptic activation reaches its maximum in both primary and secondary cortex within the first few months of life, that maturation in secondary cortex lags about a month behind that of primary cortex, and also that maturation of both primary and secondary visual areas precedes that of auditory cortical areas by a similar interval.

The developmental sequence of maximal synaptic activation varies not only for different cortical regions but for different ERP components within a given cortical area. We shall see in a moment that the magnitude and maturational course of maximum synaptic activation also depends upon the processing required of the stimuli, so the time course of developmental maxima can differ if stimuli are actively processed. These differential effects may reflect variations in the degree of activation within successive levels of the neural networks within each cortical region. Thus, it seems possible to gain from the analysis of developmental changes in the amplitude, timing and topographic distribution of ERP components, information on the dynamics of human brain development that cannot be disclosed by anatomical methods.

In tracing the maturation of the obligatory EP through infancy and early childhood, the main changes consist of progressive shortening of component latency and concurrent sharpening of EP component morphology, together with an increase in complexity of the EP waveform with the emergence of new components. These developmental EP changes reflect increased speed of neural processing, greater synchronization of network processing levels, and an increasing complexity of intrinsic cortical processing during the course of early development. Detailed knowledge of these changes in EP morphology during early development is still incomplete, and their interpretation in terms of specific developmental changes in intracortical circuitry has yet to be attempted.

We now turn to a consideration of more complicated, but even more interesting manifestations of ERP maturation, namely developmental changes in the ERP components that reflect processing beyond the obligatory responses to the physical properties of the stimuli. These processing contingent components (PCCs) have been a prominent focus of ERP research in adults, in which the principal objective has been to define the nature of the psychological processes of which these ERP components are neurophysiological manifestations.

Process-contingent ERPs provide indices of at least three more or less distinct types of brain processes. These include (1) automatic mismatch detection and consequent orienting responses, (2) attention-dependent stimulus processing, and (3) a large and heterogeneous class of active or "controlled" cognitive operations, including linguistic processes. PCCs have been most extensively studied in adults, for whom a large body of experimental data exists on ERP components related to stimulus encoding and selection, effects of selective attention, phonetic and verbal discrimination, semantic classification, scanning of short term memory, and motor response selection, to name some of the major foci of current ERP investigations (see Picton, 1988 for review).

There are, by contrast, relatively few studies of PCCs during infancy and childhood (see review by Friedman, 1991). The pursuit of such studies, however, provides major opportunities for gaining insight into the physiological basis for emerging perceptual and cognitive functions employing process contingent ERPs as indices of their underlying brain mechanisms.

MATURATION OF PCCs: I. AUTOMATIC PROCESSES

Processing is considered automatic or involuntary when it is elicited by an unexpected change in sensory input without an explicit processing requirement. These automatic processes include dishabituation, mismatch detection, and orienting to novel stimuli, which have in common their elicitation by a change in sensory input, without the mediation of active attention or intentional discriminative processing. These automatic brain responses are of considerable importance during early development when environmental changes impinge upon the infant, often without his active participation in eliciting them. Thus, early experience consists of various sensory experiences that include many surprises, which gradually become incorporated into a body of sensory memories and expectations that are necessary for active selective attention, perception and cognitive processing.

ERPs, like certain autonomic and behavioral responses, exhibit characteristic changes in response to novel or unexpected stimuli. These "discriminative responses" were initially identified in 4- to 7-month-old infants presented novel visual stimuli (Courchesne, Ganz, & Norcia, 1981). Kurtzberg (1985) found similar responses in newborn infants in response to unexpected changes in auditory stimuli, including speech sounds.

A major issue in early infant development is the extent to which various stimuli can be processed by infants at a given age. Behavioral techniques have shown that the sensory capacities of newborn and young infants for visual and auditory discrimination are substantial, but at least with regard to visual abilities, well below the discriminative capacities attained during the first few months of life (e.g., Dobson & Teller, 1978). The use of ERPs to examine the discriminative capacities of the infant bypasses the requirement for an overt motor response that restricts the application of behavioral approaches to infant sensory discriminative ability in very young infants. In principle, the brain's discriminative response can be used to examine the difference threshold between stimuli that vary along any dimension that one wishes to study. This approach has important diagnostic applications, in that it permits the detection of sensory discriminative impairments, even in the newborn period. We have found that neonatal impairment in discrimination of speech sounds as indexed by ERPs provides a surprisingly robust predictor of later delay in language development (Kurtzberg, Stapells, & Wallace, 1989). Thus, we already have some indications of the practical value of being able to assess discriminative capacity in the newborn by electrophysiologic methods.

From the perspective of our interest in the development of perceptual and cognitive abilities, these passively elicited, automatic discriminative responses may be an important adjunct to the learning of associations between environmental stimuli, possibly through the mediation of long term potentiation of synaptic efficiency. As discussed later, the automatic discriminative responses observed in the newborn and very young infant differ substantially from ERPs elicited under similar circumstances in older infants, children and adults.

In the adult, ERPs associated with automatic mismatch detection has been most thoroughly studied in the auditory modality. A negative ERP component designated "mismatch negativity" (Naatanen, 1982) is elicited by auditory stimuli that change unexpectedly in physical characteristics such as pitch or duration, when presented within a train of identical stimuli. Mismatch negativity is generated in or near primary auditory cortex (Hari, Hamalainen, Ilmoniemi, Kaukoranta, Reinikainen, Salminen, Alho, Naatanen, & Sams, 1984; Sams, Hamalainen, Antervo, Kaukoranta, Reinikainen, & Hari, 1985; Scherg, Vajsar, & Picton, 1989). It occurs as early as 25 msec after the arrival at auditory cortex of the information required for the brain to detect the stimulus change (Novak, Ritter, Vaughan, & Wiznitzer, 1990). The elicitation of mismatch negativity does not require attention to the stimuli so it is considered to be an automatic brain response to the occurrence of discrepant input. Mismatch negativity is, however, clearly dependent upon some short term, rapidly decaying trace of the anticipated stimuli. A manifestation of this trace can be directly observed in ERPs when a stimulus is unexpectedly deleted from a regular train of identical stimuli. The "missing stimulus potential" that appears when the stimulus would have occurred exhibits an extremely short latency negative deflection that may represent the template or trace of the anticipated but absent stimulus (Simson, Vaughan, & Ritter, 1976). Both the mismatch negativity and the presumed stimulus template are small, so the obligatory EPs that occur concurrent with the PCCs are only slightly modified in amplitude, with positive components being diminished and negative ones enhanced. Mismatch negativity is usually revealed by waveform subtraction in which the ERP to the regular "standard" stimuli are subtracted from those elicited by the unexpected stimulus changes or "deviants."

By contrast to the situation in adults, young infants exhibit a striking *increase* in the amplitude of the obligatory positive auditory EP components in response to deviant stimuli, that during the first few months is twice the amplitude of the response to the repetitive standard stimuli. The evolution of this differential amplitude effect is depicted in Fig. 1.7. It can be seen that the response amplitudes to the standard and deviant stimuli equalize by the end of the first year.

The most likely mechanism for the early disparity in amplitude of the EPs to the standard and deviant stimuli is that of simple refractoriness or adaptation of the response to repetitive stimulation, which reduces the obligatory EP amplitude. Refractoriness is a particularly prominent feature of the infant EP, in that EP amplitudes are even more sharply reduced by decreasing interstimulus interval than in adults. The striking EP enhancement when a physically different stimulus is presented presumably represents responses of neural elements that were not stimulated by the standard stimuli (Butler, 1972).

The relative equalization of the EP to standard and deviant stimuli that occurs

FIG. 1.7. Amplitudes of the positive component of the AEP to /da/ recorded over the midline central region in a group of healthy full term infants studied longitudinally through the first 2 years of life. Baseline to peak measurements were derived from data recorded in response to the stimuli /da/ and /ta/ in the oddball paradigm. /Da/, when the standard stimulus, occurred 86% of the time and, when the deviant stimulus, it occurred 14% of the time. Note the larger amplitude of this component to the deviant stimulus through 9 months of age, after which the responses equalize.

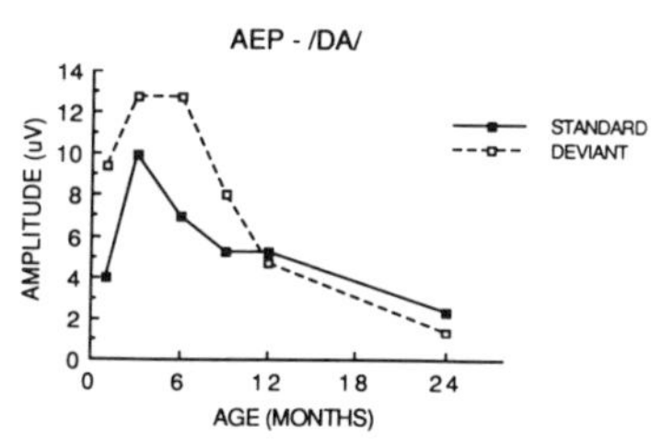

during the latter half of the first year poses an intriguing question as to its mechanism. Refractoriness certainly does not disappear at this time, as there is still a prominent effect of interstimulus interval on EP amplitude in adults (Ritter, Vaughan, & Costa, 1968). Thus, it is necessary to invoke some other mechanism, possibly the development of mismatch negativity, which reduces the apparent amplitude of the concurrent obligatory EP to physically deviant stimuli.[1]

Following the obligatory response components, a large long latency frontal negative wave (Nc) followed by a positive wave (Pc) occurs, most prominently in response to the deviant stimuli. These potentials, which we call "discriminative potentials" are largest at frontal electrode sites to both visual (Courchesne, Ganz, & Norcia, 1981) and auditory (Kurtzberg, 1985) stimuli, and may represent a nonspecific "orienting" response of frontal cortex to novel or infrequent stimuli. In adults, unexpected auditory stimuli often generate, in addition to mismatch negativity, a sequence of later negative and positive components, designated N2 and P3a, that might be analogous to the Nc and Pc components seen in infants. It should be mentioned that "P3-like" potentials at around 300 msec in latency in young infants (Hofmann & Salapatek, 1981; Hofman, Salapatek, & Kuskowski, 1981; Nelson & Salapatek, 1986) are unlikely to be equivalent to the complex processing contingent late positive potentials seen in adults and older children (Courchesne, 1979; Kurtzberg, Vaughan, & Kreuzer, 1979). As shown in Fig. 1.5, the latencies of the obligatory auditory and visual EP components are in the range of 200–300 msec during the first year, so the latencies of "automatic" PCCs in infants must be longer than those of comparable components in older subjects.

From the standpoint of cerebral network development and activation in early infancy, it seems likely that the marked enhancement of both obligatory and discriminative components of ERPs to the deviant stimuli would provide a powerful input to the extended brain systems involved in short term retention of sensory input and in changes related to more permanent storage of sensory information. It is tempting to propose differential effects on network formation of repetitive as contrasted with novel or unexpected stimuli. Repetitive stimulation would exercise existing sensory networks and strengthen the cell assemblies within sensory cortex by a feedforward Hebbian mechanism. By contrast, the enhanced and more extensive, but less frequent brain activation elicited by deviant stimuli might play a role in the development of mnemonic traces that involve attention-sensitive brain systems, including frontal cortex and limbic structures. The emergence of mismatch negativity during the latter portion of the first year could be a manifestation of an automatic short term storage mechanism that serves to signal the occurrence of a deviant stimulus. In speculating on the

---

[1]A recent report (Alho, Sainio, Sajaniemi, Reinikainen, & Naatanen, 1990) suggests that mismatch negativity may be present in sleeping newborn infants. This observation needs to be replicated in awake infants.

possible neural mechanisms of the mismatch negativity, we note that surface negative potentials have traditionally been viewed as evidence of superficial cortical activation. Since the major recurrent corticocortical projections are to the superficial cortical laminae, the electrophysiological manifestations of the activation of feedback corticocortical network connections would exhibit a negative polarity.

MATURATION OF PCCs: II. ATTENTION DEPENDENT PROCESSES

The role of attention in learning is well recognized. However, even in the adult subject, the measurement and manipulation of attention poses significant experimental difficulties. These difficulties are amplified in the infant, whose attentiveness and level of arousal constantly varies in a manner most frustrating to the student of infant perception and cognition. There is, however, an infant behavior that fortuitously optimizes the level and stability of attention, namely active visual scanning. Full term infants, and even preterm infants as young as 34 weeks postconceptional age, exhibit patterns of saccades and fixational pauses while looking at visual stimuli that are similar to those of older children and adults. Infant scanning differs mainly in longer fixation durations and less frequent saccades (Kurtzberg & Vaughan, 1979). Saccadic eye movements may be the most sophisticated behavioral capability of the neonate, in that they permit the infant to actively control the acquisition of information about the visual environment, long before other purposeful behaviors such as active reaching and grasping emerge. It is possible to record the cortical potentials associated with the onset of each saccade while the infant is actively scanning a visual stimulus. It is also possible, both by observing the infant's appearance while scanning and the quantitative patterns of saccade intervals and fixation durations to be sure that the infant is alert and actively searching the visual stimulus.

As shown in Fig. 1.8, the occipital potentials recorded in synchrony with the onset of saccades during visual scanning resemble in waveshape the potentials evoked by passive pattern reversal stimulation. Work in adults has shown that the post saccadic potentials, called "lambda waves" largely reflect visual input that occurs at the initiation of the fixation following each saccade (Kurtzberg & Vaughan, 1977). There are, however, differences in response amplitude between visual EP to passive pattern stimulation and the eye movement potentials during active scanning. The maximum amplitude of both the pattern reversal visual EP and the eye movement potential recorded over occipital cortex is reached by 4 months of age and is similar for both passive and active stimulation. By contrast, the amplitude of the eye movement potentials recorded over parietal and temporal regions exceed those of the passively elicited pattern visual EP (Fig. 1.9). In addition, changes in morphology of the responses begin to emerge at four

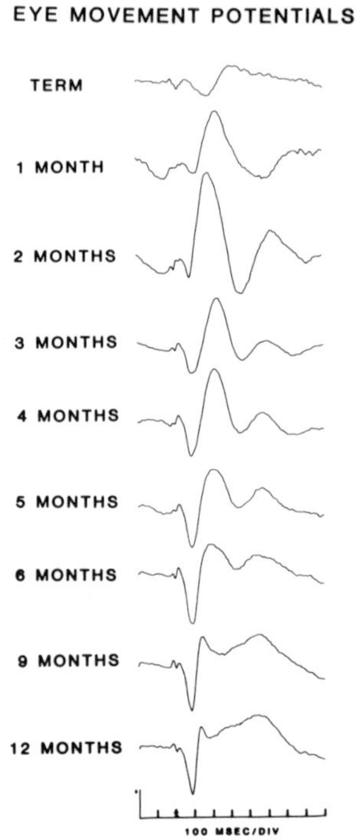

FIG. 1.8. Eye movement potentials recorded over the occipital region from a group of healthy full term infants while scanning simple black and white stimuli such as checks, stripes, and a bulls-eye pattern. The occipital response, called the "lambda wave," resembles the pattern reversal VEP and mainly reflects visual input at the initiation of the fixation following each eye movement. Arrow indicates onset of saccadic eye movement. Calibration: 2.5 uV for term through 2 months and 5 uV thereafter.

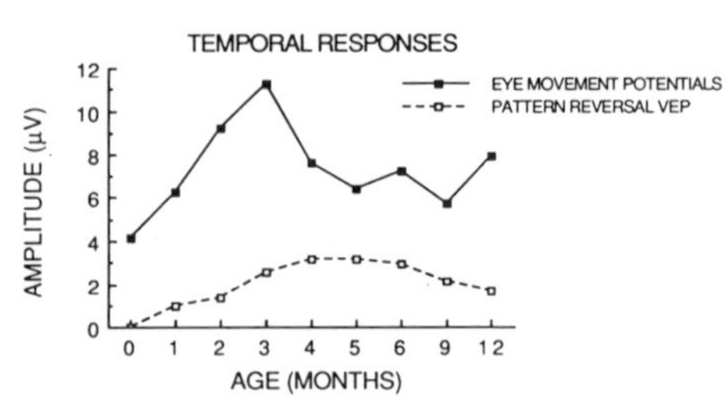

FIG. 1.9. Maturational changes in amplitude of potentials elicited by passive pattern reversal stimulation compared with those associated with spontaneous saccadic eye movements during active scanning of a patterned field. Peak to peak amplitude measurements were made of the distinct positive components overlying the posterior temporal cortex for the VEP and EMP. The latter are consistently larger throughout the first year of life and reach their maximum at 3 months of age. These differences in response of a secondary cortical area involved in pattern vision presumably reflect enhanced processing during active looking.

months of age. Evidently, the active acquisition of visual information elicits a different and more robust response from secondary visual areas than does the passive reception of patterned visual stimulation.

PCC III: ACTIVE DISCRIMINATION AND SELECTIVE ATTENTION

During the past several years a large body of experimental work has examined PCC in tasks involving selective attention and various sensory and linguistic discriminations. Despite the large number of different experimental paradigms and somewhat varied conceptual frameworks within which this work has been carried out, a coherent picture of the PCC observed in active discriminative processing has begun to emerge. It is now possible to propose a general schema that encompasses the increasingly large number of PCC observed in discrimination and selective attention tasks. From a phenomenological standpoint, it is possible to divide the PCC into two broad classes, namely the "processing negativities" and the "late positive components." In most discrimination paradigms one or more processing negativity is observed, followed by a complex positive wave. Several names have been used to designate the various processing negativities, whereas the late positivity is generally called P3, P300 or the late positive complex (LPC).

The earliest processing negativity, which we call NA (Ritter, Simson, & Vaughan, 1983), appears whenever the subject is required to attend to a stimulus in order to perform a sensory discrimination. It is present in both the non-target and target ERP waveforms and is thought to reflect, in part, processes involved in encoding the physical properties of the stimulus. It is usually visualized by subtracting the ERPs recorded in a condition wherein no discrimination among the stimuli is required from the non-target ERP in a discrimination condition. NA is observed both in visual and auditory discrimination tasks, and has a modality specific scalp topography. NA is a complex waveform, having both early and late segments with differential scalp topography. The initial portion of the wave is thought to be related to stimulus encoding, but the later portions have as yet no clear functional interpretation. NA differs from mismatch negativity, in that the latter is not attention dependent. Both of these components can be seen in the same experimental condition (Novak, Ritter, Vaughan, & Wiznitzer, 1990), with mismatch negativity signalling an automatic detection of a stimulus difference and NA reflecting active processing of the stimulus attributes.

Other processing negativities have been observed in semantic classification tasks, employing either visual or auditory stimuli (Ritter, Simson, & Vaughan, 1983; Novick, Lovrich, & Vaughan, 1985). These processing negativities may be considered analogous to the NA elicited in physical discriminations in that they are present in both target and non-target ERP waveforms, and thus appear to represent some aspect of the discriminative process itself, rather than the outcome of the discrimination. By contrast, a later negativity, N2, is seen only in the target waveform (Ritter, Simson Vaughan, & Friedman, 1979). Thus N2, like mismatch negativity, reflects the output of a processing stage that differentiates the stimuli in a discrimination task. Another negativity, N400, has been observed in conditions of incongruity or low semantic probability (Kutas & Hillyard, 1980), but this component, like N2, may not represent the semantic processing itself, but some consequence of the process. Thus, it is necessary to differentiate negativities that represent discriminative processing from those that reflect an output of a discriminative mechanism such as mismatch negativity, N2 and N400. Inasmuch as processing negativities are attention dependent, they are present in selective attention tasks, being larger in the attended channel. A comparison between ERP in attended and nonattended channels has led to the description of a difference waveform, Nd, which is a manifestation of the differences in processing negativities elicited by stimuli in the attended and nonattended channels (Hanson & Hillyard, 1980; Naatanen, 1982, 1990).

The neurophysiological substrates of the processing negativities are not known. Some of the processing negativities are modality specific in scalp distribution, and thus are likely to be generated within sensory cortical areas, but some may also be generated in association cortex and limbic system structures. A prominent negative component can be recorded intracranially in humans in the vicinity of the amygdala during tasks in which surface negative components such as N2 and N400 are also recorded (McCarthy, Wood, Williamson, & Spencer, 1989). This observation indicates that an extensive brain system is activated in association with these PCC.

We have suggested that the processing negativities of cortical origin may represent the activation of recurrent corticocortical connections, and thus index feedback in cortical networks (Vaughan, Ritter, & Simson, 1983). This postulated mechanism for the processing negativities has important developmental implications, in that these PCCs should emerge concurrently with the development of corticocortical feedback mechanisms, which are presumably to a large extent dependent upon learning. These feedback connections could subserve top-down processing mechanisms, such as input selection or filtering based on perceptual and cognitive expectancies.

There are as yet no developmental data on the attention-dependent processing negativities. Although we are currently carrying out studies of auditory discrimination and linguistic processing in young children that will yield such data, we do not know as yet whether processing negativities similar to those obtained in adults during similar tasks will be found in young children.

Complementing the catalog of negative PCCs, is a set of later positive ERP components. The prototypic P3 or P300 is elicited in an "oddball paradigm" in which the infrequent stimuli are usually designated the targets, which are either counted or require a motor response from the subject. Squires, Squires, & Hillyard (1975) differentiated a late positivity (P3b) elicited by attended stimuli from another positive component (P3a) elicited by unattended stimuli, on the basis of their differential timing and topography. Other studies have identified additional late positive components in various kinds of discriminative tasks (e.g., Friedman, Vaughan, & Erlenmeyer-Kimling, 1979). Although few detailed topographic studies of the late positive components have been done, there are variations in the temporal patterns and scalp distribution of LPC in different tasks (Simson, Vaughan, & Ritter, 1976, 1977a, 1977b). Topographic analyses of the LPCs recorded during linguistic tasks provide additional evidence of the multiplicity and task related regional specificity of human late positive components (e.g., Lovrich, Simson, Vaughan, & Ritter, 1986; Lovrich, Novick, & Vaughan, 1988).

Task related positive components have been reported in children as young as four or five years (Kurtzberg, Vaughan, & Kreuzer, 1979; Courchesne, 1979, 1983). In a longitudinal study of children from $4\frac{1}{2}$ years to $8\frac{1}{2}$ years of age, ERPs recorded during in a visual discrimination task exhibited a topographically complex series of long latency positive potentials in response to the target stimuli. These data were recorded from ten electrodes, which permitted only a crude topographic mapping and comparison of interhemispheral ERP amplitudes. The most striking developmental change was the emergence of a large parietal maximum positive component peaking at about 400 msec in the youngest children, that gradually diminished in latency to about 325 msec by 8 years of age. Reaction times to the target stimuli decreased concurrently, from 340 to 280 msec. The parietal focus and correlation of its peak latency with reaction time identifies this component with the adult P3b component. A longer latency frontal maximum component was also seen that may be the Pc of Courchesne. Another positive peak at still a different latency was seen over the posterior temporal region. These potentials were also averaged in synchrony with the motor responses, which yielded two movement related potentials, one occurring about 200 msec prior to the motor response and the other roughly concurrent with it. Both of these response related potentials were larger over the left central region, consistent with the use of the right hand for the motor response, whereas the stimulus synchronized P3b was largest over the right parietal region. Similar stimulus and response synchronized late positive components have also been described in adults by Friedman, Vaughan, and Erlenmeyer-Kimling (1978). A recent developmental study that included children as young as 7 years of age (Johnson, in press), has shown differences in scalp topography of auditory as compared to visual P3 in simple oddball discrimination tasks. The complexity of these late positive task related potentials contrasts with the traditional view that P3 comprises no more than two peaks, one predominantly frontal and the other parietal, called P3a and P3b in the adult literature, and Pc and P3b in the developmental studies of Courchesne. Although other late components, including the so called slow wave, have often been observed, a comprehensive classification of late positive components is lacking.

From a neurophysiological standpoint, the late positive components are at least as poorly understood as the processing contingent negativities. Human intracranial recordings targeting the hippocampal formation have shown positive components that have approximately the same timing and behavior in relation to experimental manipulations as the scalp recorded late positive components (McCarthy, Wood, Williamson, & Spencer, 1989). It is currently being debated as to what contribution this long latency hippocampal activity contributes to the scalp recorded late positive components, but a consensus is beginning to emerge that this contribution is likely to be limited to potentials recorded from the lateral temporal scalp (McCarthy, Wood, Williamson, & Spencer, 1989). Human intracranial data on other possible cortical contributions to scalp recorded late positive components are sparse, but there is some suggestion that both frontal and parietal association cortex might contribute to the scalp recorded late positive components as has been inferred from their scalp topography (Vaughan & Arezzo, 1988).

It is increasingly clear that late positive components represent the activation of extensive brain systems that include not only frontal and parietal association cortex and limbic structures, but probably other neocortical areas as well, as determined by the processing requirements of specific tasks. Future studies of ERP associated with cognitive tasks must examine the scalp topography of the PCC in greater detail so as to permit the differentiation of potentials generated within the various cortical structures that are active in a given task.

CONCLUSIONS AND PROSPECTS

In this chapter we have suggested that the dynamic spatiotemporal picture of brain activity provided by event related potentials can offer insights into the development of the neural mechanisms that underlie perceptual and cognitive functions during infancy and childhood. It is possible to identify from this preliminary overview of ERP maturation some questions and issues that can guide future research into the development of brain systems that underlie cognitive development. These prospects will be presented as speculations on the development of cortical connectivity during early development.

The electrophysiologic data confirm the precocious development of cortical neural architecture disclosed by recent anatomical studies. We have seen that the cortical responses to sound and light of even the youngest viable preterm infants (as early as 3 months before term) manifest a clear regional differentiation in response to sensory input that reflects the presence of functioning connections from primary to secondary visual and auditory cortex, and probably to frontal cortex as well.

The obligatory cortical responses to sensory input reach their maximum amplitude within the first few months of life, with the primary cortical areas achieving their maxima shortly before the secondary cortical responses. These obligatory responses reflect a summation of synaptic activity within sensory cortex, and the time course of their maturation is consistent with the few available data on synaptic density in human cortex during postnatal development. Thus, sensory EPs may provide a dynamic indicator of the magnitude of synaptic activation within specific cortical areas during early development.

Differential cortical responses to unexpected or novel stimuli are prominent during the first few months of life. These differential responses initially appear to be primarily due to refractoriness or habituation to repetitive stimuli, in that the potentials elicited by the infrequent deviant stimuli are much larger than those elicited by repetitive stimulation. The larger response in sensory cortex to deviant stimuli elicits a later response in frontal cortex that signifies stimulus change or novelty. This mechanism is precocious, being present in the normal full term infant, and evidently demonstrates the competence of long range corticocortical connections between sensory and association cortex. Thus, extensive functional corticocortical networks involving primary, secondary and association cortex must be present at birth.

The possible emergence of the mismatch negativity toward the end of the first year of life reflects the development of a mechanism for detection of stimulus change that is more sophisticated than simple refractoriness. In adults, MMN has been shown to occur in response to various physical differences between stimuli, and could therefore represent a mechanism for detecting changes in a wide variety of sensory inputs (Naatanen, 1990).

The frontal discriminative ERP components elicited by deviant visual or auditory stimuli may be an early manifestation of the short term registration of deviant events in an association area that is thought to be implicated in mechanisms of working memory. Inasmuch as novelty is a condition for learning that is especially important in the infant, these cortical responses to unexpected changes in stimulus characteristics could index one condition for the learning of new information.

Inasmuch as these discriminative cortical responses provide an objective indication that the infant's brain has differentiated between two stimuli, they afford the possibility for examining the limits of an infant's ability to detect stimulus differences. The application of cortical discriminative responses for clinical testing of auditory discrimination thresholds appears promising.

Evidence for active processing of sensory input is provided by the enhanced amplitude of potentials following saccadic eye movements during active visual scanning, in contrast to passively elicited VEP to patterned stimulation. This enhancement is present in secondary cortical areas at or shortly after birth, providing evidence for an early development of active visual attentional process within these areas.

Identification of corticocortical feedback mechanisms is more speculative. We have suggested that the relative reduction in amplitude of responses to deviant stimuli that occurs late in the first year reflects the emergence of the "mismatch negativity" that is considered to represent the output of an automatic comparator mechanism signalling the occurrence of stimulus change. The operation of a comparator implies the presence of a transient memory for the repeated stimuli. Any deviation from this memory trace would trigger an error signal, namely the mismatch negativity. In some neural network models such error signals are fed back into the earlier levels of the network in order to modify the transmission of information through the network. Mismatch negativity could represent a cortical feedback mechanism, based on a temporary memory store. It seems likely that one of the consequences of early perceptual learning might also be the activation of recurrent corticocortical connections that serve to filter or enhance sensory inputs at earlier stages of cortical processing, in accordance with stored information on the possible significance of a given sensory input. This mechanism could underlie the process of selective attention and other active discriminative processes.

One of the most important contributions of ERPs to the understanding of human cognitive development is the information they can provide on the spatiotemporal sequence of cortical processing during well defined sensorimotor and cognitive operations. These processes involve the coordinated operation of a number of brain structures, each of which is specialized to perform certain operations. Framed in the context of neural networks, several processing levels exist within each cortical area. Each level comprises large numbers of neurons located within specific intracortical lamina that have parallel input and output connections. Activation of these intracortical processing levels or stages, in association with a particular perceptual or cognitive operation, has a characteristic temporal sequence of synaptic activation.

It is the parallel organization of neural mechanisms within each brain region that permits relatively slow neural elements that perform no more than a few hundred operations per second to process massive quantities of sensory data or stored information, often in substantially less than a second. For example, saccadic eye movements occur two to four times each second, so the processing of visual information from each fixation must require only a quarter to half a second. Transmission time through retina to visual cortex, and the efferent processes involved in oculomotor control take up a substantial portion of this time, so the cortical processing of visual input required to program each successive eye movement probably takes no more than 100 msec or so. Intracranial recordings in monkeys using the current source density technique (Arezzo, Vaughan, Kraut,

Steinschneider, & Legatt, 1986) show that temporally cohesive periods of excitation or inhibition within a particular lamina generally range from 10–50 msec or more in duration. The duration of these periods provides an indication of the time course of activity within one layer of an intracortical network. Judging from the spatiotemporal configuration of intracortical transmembrane current flows observed in response to pattern stimulation, it appears that visual processing within a particular cortical region involves only a small number of network levels. Thus, the entire sequence of cortical visual processing is likely to proceed largely in parallel with relatively few serial stages across the several cortical visual areas. Semantic classification in adults requires only about 200 msec more than the response to a simple auditory stimulus (Novick, Lovrich, & Vaughan, 1985), so even this complex cognitive operation probably involves a small number of sequential levels of network activation.

Current knowledge of brain anatomy and physiology supports the idea that individual cortical regions subserve specific processing mechanisms, and that each cortical area exhibits a substantially parallel architecture, with only a limited number of successive intracortical processing levels. Thus, it is possible that even the most complicated mental processes can be carried out as a sequence of modular network operations, each of which involves a parallel distributed processing network that contains only a small number of serial processing levels. With this idea in mind, we can see how the study of human brain potentials during the performance of cognitive operations can shed light on both the identity of the active modules and the main temporal features of the processing within each module.

Using the new technical capacities provided by BESA for resolving the spatiotemporal distribution of scalp recorded ERPs into estimates of the time-varying strength of their several intracranial generators (as shown in Fig. 1.2), we can begin to examine the dynamic sequential properties of the activation of network levels within each active cortical region. Current source density analysis of intracortical responses to visual stimuli in the monkey manifest a spatiotemporal pattern of current sources and sinks (shown in Fig. 1.3) that reflect laminar patterns of temporal synaptic activity that can at least partially be seen in the potentials recorded from the surface of the active cortex. By combining source analysis of human ERP with insights gained from simian intracranial recordings we may be in a position to trace out spatial and temporal patterns of network activation within the human brain in the course of psychological processes. With the application of such approaches to developmental studies, we can anticipate the acquisition of a rich body of information on dynamic brain function as it relates to human perceptual and cognitive development. When combined with the rapidly expanding body of knowledge on the cellular and biochemical mechanisms that operate during brain maturation, we can come to grips with the neurobiology of human psychological development.

ACKNOWLEDGMENTS

Preparation of this chapter was supported in part by grants from the United States Public Health Service (HD01799, DC00224, DC00223, and NS20489). We wish to thank many colleagues for their collaborative efforts and assistance, especially Joseph C. Arezzo, Anna Brattson, Ana M. Cioffi, Chester Freeman, Judith A. Kreuzer, Cecelia M. McCarton, Ashesh Mehta, Gerald P. Novak, Walter Ritter, Gregory V. Simpson, Charles L. Stone, Jr., Maria Tschernkowitsch, Bonnie Vogeler, and Candace Wood.

REFERENCES

Alho, K., Sainio, K., Sajaniemi, N., Reinikainen, K., & Naatanen, R. (1990). Event-related brain potential of human newborns to pitch change of an acoustic stimulus. *Electroencephalography and Clinical Neurophysiology, 77,* 151–155.

Anderson, A., & Rosenfeld, E. (Eds.). (1989). *Neurocomputing,* Cambridge, MA: MIT Press.

Arezzo, J. C., Vaughan, H. G., Jr., Kraut, M. A., Steinschneider, M., & Legatt, A. D. (1986). Intracranial generators of event-related potentials in the monkey. In R. Q. Cracco & I. Bodis-Wollner (Eds.), *Frontiers of clinical neuroscience. Vol. 3–Evoked potentials,* New York: Alan R. Liss.

Braak, H. (1980). *Architectonics of the human telencephalic cortex. Studies of brain function, Vol. 4,* Berlin: Springer-Verlag.

Butler, R. A. (1972). Frequency specificity of the auditory evoked response to simultaneously and successively presented stimuli. *Electroencephalography & Clinical Neurophysiology, 33,* 277–282.

Conel, J. L. (1939–1963). *The postnatal development of the human cerebral cortex.* Cambridge, MA: Harvard University Press.

Courchesne, E. (1979). Neurophysiological correlates of cognitive development: Changes in long-latency event-related potentials from childhood to adulthood. *Electroencephalography and Clinical Neurophysiology, 45,* 468–482.

Courchesne, E. (1983). Cognitive components of the event-related brain potential: Changes associated with development. In A. W. K. Gaillard & W. Ritter (Eds.), *Tutorials in ERP research: Endogenous components* (pp. 329–344). Amsterdam: North Holland.

Courchesne, E., Ganz, L., & Norcia, M. (1981). Event-related brain potentials to human faces in infants. *Child Development, 52,* 804.811.

Dobson, V. & Teller, D. Y. (1978). Visual acuity in human infants: a review and comparison of behavioral and electrophysiological studies. *Vision Research, 18,* 1469–1483.

Eccles, J. C. (1984). The cerebral neocortex: A theory of its operation. In E. G. Jones & A. Peters (Eds.), *Cerebral cortex, Vol. 2. Functional properties of cortical cells* (pp. 1–36). New York: Plenum Press.

Flechsig, P. (1920). *Anatomie des menschiden Gerins und Ruckenmarks auf myelogenetischer Grundlage.* Leipzig: George Thieme.

Friedman, D. (1991). The endogenous scalp-recorded brain potentials and their relationship to cognitive development. In J. R. Jennings & M. G. H. Coles (Eds.), *Handbook of Cognitive Psychophysiology.* New York: Wiley.

Friedman, D. Vaughan, Jr., H. G., & Erlenmeyer-Kimling, L. (1978). Stimulus and response related components of the late positive complex in visual discrimination tasks. *Electroencephalography and Clinical Neurophysiology, 45,* 319–330.

Gilden, L., Vaughan, H. G., Jr., & Costa, L. D. (1966). Summated human EEG potentials with voluntary movement. *Electroencephalography and Clinical Neurophysiology, 20,* 433–438.

Goldman-Rakic, P. S. (1987). Development of cortical circuitry and cognitive function. *Child Development, 58,* 601–622.

Goldman-Rakic, P. S. (1988). Topography of cognition: parallel distributed networks in primate association cortex. *Annual Review of Neuroscience, 11,* 137–156.

Greenough, W. T., Black, J. E., & Wallace, C. S. (1987). Experience and brain development. *Child Development, 58,* 539–559.

Hansen, J. C., & Hillyard, S. A. (1980). Endogenous brain potentials associated with selective auditory attention. *Electroencephalography and Clinical Neurophysiology, 49,* 277–290.

Hari, R., Hamalainen, M., Ilmoniemi, R., Kaukoranta, E., Reinikainen, K., Salminen, J., Alho, K., Naatanen, R., & Sams, M. (1984). Responses of the primary auditory cortex to pitch changes in a sequence of tone pips: neuromagnetic recordings in man. *Neuroscience Letters, 26,* 31–43.

Hebb, D. O. (1949). *The organization of behavior.* New York: Wiley.

Hofmann, M. J., & Salapatek, P. (1981). Young infants' event-related potentials (ERPs) to familiar and unfamiliar visual and auditory events in a recognition memory task. *Electroencephalography and Clinical Neurophysiology, 52,* 405–417.

Hofmann, M. J., Salapatek, P., & Kuskowski, M. (1981). Evidence for visual memory in the averaged and single trial evoked potentials in human infants. *Infant Behavior and Development, 4,* 401–421.

Huttenlocher, P. R. (1979). Synaptic density in human frontal cortex-developmental changes and effects of aging. *Brain Research, 163,* 195–205.

Huttenlocher, P. R. (1984). Synapse elimination and plasticity in developing human cerebral cortex. *American Journal of Mental Deficiency, 88*(5), 488–496.

Huttenlocher, P. R., de Courten, C., Garey, L. J., & Van Der Loos, H. (1982). Synaptogenesis in human visual cortex—Evidence for synapse elimination during normal development. *Neuroscience Letters, 33,* 247–252.

Johnson, Jr., R. (in press). Developmental evidence for modality-dependent P300 generators: a normative study. *Psychophysiology.*

Johnston, M. V. (1988). Biochemistry of neurotransmitters in cortical development. *Cerebral cortex, Vol. 7. Development and maturation of cerebral cortex* (pp. 211–236). New York: Plenum Press.

Jones, E. G. (1984). History of cortical cytology. In A. Peters & A. G. Jones (Eds.), *Cerebral cortex, Vol. 1, Cellular components of the cerebral cortex* (pp. 1–32). New York: Plenum Press.

Kraut, M. A., Arezzo, J. C., & Vaughan, H. G., Jr. (1985). Intracortical generators of the flash VEP in monkeys. *Electroencephalography & Clinical Neurophysiology, 62,* 300–312.

Kurtzberg, D. (1985). Late auditory evoked potentials and speech sound discrimination in newborns. Paper presented at Symposium "Event-Related Potentials of the Brain and Perceptual/Cognitive Processing of Infants." *Society for Research in Child Development.* Toronto, Canada.

Kurtzberg, D., Hilpert, P. L., Kreuzer, J. A., & Vaughan, Jr., H. G. (1984). Differential maturation of cortical auditory evoked potentials to speech sounds in normal full term and very low-birthweight infants. *Developmental Medicine and Child Neurology, 24,* 466–475.

Kurtzberg, D., Stapells, D. R., & Wallace, I. F. (1988). Event-related potential assessment of auditory system integrity: Implications for language development. In P. Vietze & H. G. Vaughan, Jr. (Eds.), *Early identification of infants with development disabilities* (pp. 160–180). Philadelphia, PA: Grune & Stratton.

Kurtzberg, D., & Vaughan, H. G., Jr. (1977). Electrophysiological observations on the visuomotor system and visual neurosensorium. In J. E. Desmedt (Ed.), *Visual evoked potentials in man: New developments* (pp. 314–331). Oxford: Clarendon Press.

Kurtzberg, D., & Vaughan, H. R., Jr. (1979). Maturation and task specificity of cortical potentials associated with visual scanning. In D. Lehmann & E. Callaway (Eds.), *Human evoked potentials—Applications and problems* (pp. 185–199). New York: Plenum Press.

Kurtzberg, D., Vaughan, H. G., Jr., & Kreuzer, J. (1979). Task-related cortical potentials in children. In, J. E. Desmedt (Ed.), *Progress in clinical neurophysiology. Vol. 6—Cognitive components in cerebral event-related potentials and selective attention* (pp. 216–223). Basel, Karger.

Kutas, M., & Hillyard (1980). Reading senseless sentences: Brain potentials reflect semantic incongruity. *Science, 207,* 203–205.

Kutas, M., & Van Petten, C. (1988). Event related brain potential studies of language. In, P. K. Ackles, J. R. Jennings, & M. G. H., Coles (Eds.), *Advances in psychophysiology, Vol. 3* (pp. 139–187). Greenwich, CT: JAI Press.

Lovrich, D., Novick, B., & Vaughan, Jr., H. G. (1988). Topographic analysis of auditory event-related potentials associated with acoustic and semantic processing. *Electroencephalography and Clinical Neurophysiology, 71,* 40–54.

Lovrich, D., Simson, R., Vaughan, H. G., Jr., & Ritter, W. (1986). Topography of visual event-related potentials during geometric and phonetic discriminations. *Electroencephalography & Clinical Neurophysiology, 65,* 1–12.

Luria, A. R. (1973). *The working brain.* New York: Basic Books.

Marin-Padilla, M. (1970a). Prenatal and early postnatal ontogenesis of the human motor cortex: A Golgi study. I. The sequential development of the cortical layers. *Brain Research, 23,* 167–183.

Marin-Padilla, M. (1970b). Prenatal and early postnatal ontogenesis of the human motor cortex: A Golgi study. II. The basket-pyramidal system. *Brain Research, 23,* 185–191.

Marin-Padilla, M. (1972). Double origin of the pericellular baskets of the pyramidal cells of the human motor cortex: A Golgi study. *Brain Research, 38,* 1–12.

Marin-Padilla, M. (1988). Early ontogenesis of the human cerebral cortex. In A. Peters & A. G. Jones (Eds.), *Cerebral cortex, Vol. 7, Development and maturation of cerebral cortex* (pp. 1–34). New York: Plenum Press.

McCarthy, G., Wood, C. C., Williamson, P. D., & Spencer, D. D. (1989). Task-dependent field potentials in human hippocampal formation. *Journal of Neuroscience, 9,* 4253–4268.

McClelland, J. L., & Rumelhart, D. E., & the PDP Research Group (1986). *Parallel distributed processing: Explorations in the microstructure of cognition, Vol. 2: Psychological and biological models.* Cambridge, MA: MIT Press.

McCulloch, W. S., & Pitts, W. (1943). A logical calculus of the ideas immanent in nervous activity. *Bulletin of Mathematical Biophysics, 5,* 115–133.

Naatanen, R. (1982). Processing negativity: An evoked-potential reflection of selective attention. *Psychological Bulletin, 92*(3), 605–640.

Naatanen, R. (1990). The role of attention in auditory information processing as revealed by event-related potentials and other brain measures of cognitive function. *Behavioral and Brain Sciences, 13*(2), 201–233.

Nelson, C. A., & Salapatek, P. (1986). Electrophysiological correlates of infant recognition memory. *Child Development, 57,* 1483–1497.

Nicholson, C. & Freeman, J. A. (1975). Theory of current source-density analysis and determination of conductivity tensor for Anuran cerebellum. *Journal of Neurophysiology, 38,* 356–368.

Novak, G. P., Kurtzberg, D., Kreuzer, J. A., & Vaughan, H. G., Jr. (1989). Cortical responses to speech sounds and their formants in normal infants: Maturational sequence and spatiotemporal analysis. *Electroencephalography and Clinical Neurophysiology, 73,* 295–305.

Novak, G. P., Ritter, W., Vaughan, H. G., Jr., & Wiznitzer, M. L. (1990). Differentiation of negative event-related potentials in an auditory discrimination task. *Electroencephalography & Clinical Neurophysiology, 75,* 255–275.

Novick, B., Lovrich, D., & Vaughan, Jr., H. G. (1985). Event-related potentials associated with the discrimination of acoustic and semantic aspects of speech. *Neuropsychologia, 23,* 87–101.

Pandya, D. N., & Yeterian, E. H. (1985). Architecture and conditions of cortical association areas. In A. Peters & E. G. Jones (Eds.), *Cerebral cortex. Vol. 4. Association and auditory cortices* (pp. 3–61). New York: Plenum Press.

Parnavelas, J. G., Papadopoulos, G. C., & Cavanagh, M. E. (1988). Changes in neurotransmitters during development. *Cerebral cortex, Vol. 7, Development and maturation of cerebral cortex* (pp. 177–209). New York: Plenum Press.

Peters, A., & Jones, E. G. (Eds.). (1984–1988). *Cerebral cortex.* Vols 1–7, New York: Plenum Press.

Picton, T. W. (Ed.). (1988). *Handbook of electroencephalography and clinical neurophysiology, Vol. 3, Human event-related potentials.* Amsterdam: Elsevier Science Publishers.

Picton, T. W., & Hillyard, S. A. (1988). Endogenous event-related potentials. In T. W. Picton (Ed.), *Human event-related potentials, EEG handbook, Vol. 3* (pp. 361–426). Amsterdam: Elsevier Science Publishers.

Purpura, D. P. (1961). Analysis of axodendritic synaptic organizations in immature cerebral cortex. *Annals of New York Academy of Sciences, 94,* 604–654.

Purpura, D. P. (1975a). Normal and aberrant neuroanatomical development in the cerebral cortex of human fetus and young infant. In M. A. B. Brazier (Ed.), *Brain mechanisms in mental retardation* (pp. 141–169). New York: Academic Press.

Purpura, D. P. (1975b). Morphogenesis of visual cortex in the preterm infant. In M. A. B. Brazier (Ed.), *Growth and development of the brain* (pp. 33–49). New York: Raven Press.

Rabinowicz, T. (1984). The cerebral cortex of the premature infant of the 8th month. *Prog. Brain Research, 4,* 39–86.

Rakic, P., Bourgeois, J. P., Eckenhoff, M. F., Zecevic, N., & Goldman-Rakic, P. S. (1986). Concurrent overproduction of synapses in diverse regions of the primate cerebral cortex. *Science, 232,* 232–235.

Ritter, W., Simson, R., & Vaughan, H. G., Jr. (1983). Event-related potential correlates of two stages of information processing in physical and semantic discrimination tasks. *Psychophysiology, 20,* 168–179.

Ritter, W., Simson, R., Vaughan, H. G., Jr., & Friedman, D. (1979). A brain event related to the making of a sensory discrimination. *Science, 203,* 1358–1361.

Ritter, W., Simson, R., Vaughan, H. G., Jr., & Macht, M. (1982). Manipulation of event-related potential manifestations of information processing stages. *Science, 218,* 909–911.

Ritter, W., Vaughan, H. R.; Jr., & Costa, L. D. (1968). Orienting and habituation to auditory stimuli: A study of short term changes in average evoked responses. *Electroencephalography and Clinical Neurophysiology, 25,* 550–556.

Ritter, W., Vaughan, H. G., Jr., & Simson, R. (1983). On relating event-related potential components to stages of information processing. In A. W. K. Gaillard & W. Ritter (Eds.), *Tutorials in event related potential research: Endogenous components* (pp. 143–158). Amsterdam: North Holland.

Rosenblatt, F. (1958). The perceptron: a probabilistic model for information storage and organization in the brain. *Psychological Review, 65,* 386–408.

Rumelhart, R. E., McClelland, J. L., & the PDP Research Group (1986). *Parallel distributed processing: Explorations in the microstructure of cognition, Vol. 1: Foundations,* Cambridge, MA: MIT Press.

Sams, M., Hamalainen, M., Antervo, A., Kaukoranta, E., Reinikainen, K., & Hari, R. (1985). Cerebral neuromagnetic responses evoked by short auditory stimuli. *Electroencephalography and Clinical Neurophysiology, 61,* 254–266.

Scherg, M. (1989). Fundamentals of dipole source potential analysis. In G. Grandori, G. L. Romani, & M. Hoke (Eds.), *Auditory evoked potentials and fields. Advances in audiology* (Vol. 6). Basel: Karger.

Scherg, M., Vajsar, J., & Picton, T. W. (1989). A source analysis of the late human auditory evoked potentials. *Journal of Cognitive Neuroscience, 4,* 336–355.

Scherg, M., & Von Cramon, D. (1986). Evoked dipole source components of the human auditory cortex. *Electroencephalography and Clinical Neurophysiology, 65,* 344–360.

Schroeder, C. E., Tenke, C. E., Givre, S. J., Arezzo, J. C., & Vaughan, H. G., Jr. (in press). Striate cortical contribution to the surface-recorded pattern-reversal VEP in the alert monkey. *Vision Research.*

Simson, R., Vaughan, H. G., Jr., & Ritter, W. (1976). The scalp topography of potentials associated with missing visual or auditory stimuli. *Electroencephalography and Clinical Neurophysiology, 40,* 33–42.

Simson, R., Vaughan, H. G., Jr., & Ritter, W. (1977a). The scalp topography of potentials in auditory and visual discrimination tasks. *Electroencephalography & Clinical Neurophysiology, 42,* 528–535.

Simson, R., Vaughan, H. G., Jr., & Ritter, W. (1977b). The scalp topography of potentials in auditory and visual go/nogo tasks. *Electroencephalography & Clinical Neurophysiology, 43,* 864–875.

Squires, N. K., Squires, K. C. & Hillyard, S. A. (1975). Two varieties of long-latency positive waves evoked by unpredictable auditory stimuli in man. *Electroencephalography and Clinical Neurophysiology, 38,* 387–401.

Sternberg, S. (1969). The discovery of processing stages: Extensions of Donders' method. In W. G. Koster (Ed.), *Attention and performance II.* Amsterdam: North Holland. (*Acta Psychologica,* 1969, *30,* 276–315).

Vaughan, H. G., Jr. (1969). The relationship of brain activity to scalp recordings of event-related potentials. In E. Donchin & D. B. Lindsley (Eds.), *Averaged evoked potentials: Methods, results, evaluations.* Washington, D.C., National Aeronautics and Space Administration (NASA # SP-191). pp. 45–94.

Vaughan, Jr., H. G. (1975). Electrophysiologic analysis of regional cortical maturation. *Biological Psychiatry, 10,* 513–526.

Vaughan, Jr., H. G., & Arezzo, J. C. (1988). The neural basis of event-related potentials. In T. W. Picton (Ed.), *Human event-related potentials: EEG handbook, Vol. 3* (pp. 45–96). Amsterdam: Elsevier Science Publishers.

Vaughan, Jr., H. G., Costa, L. D., Gilden, L., & Schimmel, H. (1965). Identification of sensory and motor components of cerebral activity in simple reaction-time tasks. *Proceedings of the 73rd Conference of the American Psychological Association, 1,* 179–180.

Vaughan, H. G., Jr., & Kurtzberg, D. (1989). Electrophysiological indices of normal and aberrant cortical maturation. In P. Kellaway & J. L. Noebels (Eds.), *Problems and concepts in developmental neurophysiology* (pp. 263–287). Baltimore: Johns Hopkins University Press.

Vaughan, H. G., Jr., Ritter, W., & Simson, R. (1983). Neurophysiological considerations in event-related potential research. In A. W. K. Gaillard & W. Ritter (Eds.), *Tutorials in event related potential research: Endogenous components* (pp. 1–7). Amsterdam: North Holland.

Vogt, O. (1906). Der Wert der myelogenetischen Felder der Grosshirnrinde (Cortex pallii). *Anat. Anz., 29,* 273.

Vogt, C., & Vogt, O. (1919). Allgemeinere Ergebnisse unserer Hirnforschung. *Journal of Psychol. Neurology, 25,* 279–462.

Von Neumann, J. (1958). *The computer and the brain* (pp. 66–82). New Haven: Yale University Press.

Weitzman, E. D., & Graziani, L. J. (1968). Maturation and topography of the auditory evoked response of the prematurely born infant. *Developmental Psychology, 1,* 79–89.

Yakovlev, P. I., & Lecours, A. R. (1967). The myelogenetic cycles of regional maturation of the brain. In A. Minkowski (Ed.), *Regional development of brain in early life* (pp. 3–70). Oxford: Blackwell Science Publications.

2 Basic Mechanisms of Human Locomotor Development

Hans Forssberg
Virgil Stokes
Helga Hirschfeld
Karolinska Institute, Stockholm

NOMENCLATURE

CNS .... Central nervous system
GM .... Gluteus maximus muscle
RF .... Rectus femoris muscle
ST .... Semitendinosus muscle
SD .... Standard deviation
SM .... Semimembranosus muscle
TA .... Tibialis anterior muscle
HAM .... Hamstring muscles (ST-SM)
VL .... Vastus lateralis muscle
LG .... Lateral gastrocnemius muscle
EMG .... Electromyogram
SG .... Spinal generator
MLR .... Mesencephalic locomotor region
SLR .... Subthalamic locomotor region
NRG .... Nucleus reticularis gigantocellularis
PPN .... Pedunculopontine nucleus

INTRODUCTION

The purpose of locomotion is to transport the body through space. It requires the control of both propulsive and antigravitational forces with the capability to adapt to the changing surroundings. During locomotion, mechanisms within the body must simultaneously: control feet placement, speed and direction, maintain equilibrium and negotiate obstacles. Gait is the precise sequence of leg and body movements that enables a legged system to move from one place to another. A general mathematical description of gait from a robotics perspective has been given by Sun (1974).

The human body constitutes an active articulated system of extraordinary complexity with over 240 degrees of freedom. Joints are spanned by groups of muscles, which implies that a specific movement of the limbs does not necessarily have a unique pattern of muscle activity. Bernstein (1967) was one of the first to consider this problem of limb movement from a dynamics-neural control viewpoint. He proposed that the central nervous system (CNS) solved this problem by organizing its output (control signals) for muscle synergies rather than individual muscles. He argued that this grouping or lumping of muscles into synergies could greatly reduce the degrees of freedom (dimension) of the system and thus considerably simplify the control task for the CNS. In addition, Bernstein suggested that the motor control system was organized in an hierarchical structure with the muscle synergies at the lower level. Centers at the highest levels, informed by an evaluator system (decision maker), planned the motor commands according to the task to be executed. Meanwhile, at a lower level, other centers were coordinating the execution of the appropriate muscle synergies. The term "muscle synergy" has been used extensively by researchers in motor control and in several different contexts (Gelfand, Gurfinkel, Tsetlin, & Shik, 1971; Kelso, 1986; Lee & Mansour, 1984; Nashner, 1977; Saltzman, 1979; Turvey, Shaw, & Mace, 1978). In this chapter the term muscle synergy is defined as a group of muscles constrained by some coordinative central structure (control center) to act together.

This hierarchical or multilevel organization also follows from the application of system control theory to the control of bipedal locomotion. That is, the control system must be capable of dealing with different walking speeds, loads and environmental conditions while simultaneously maintaining the basic periodic movement patterns. This leads one to a natural decomposition of the control mechanisms into an invariant (fixed) part which deals with the fundamental repetitive movement patterns and an adaptive part which deals with the dynamics of the movement (decision implementation). The invariant part is concerned with turning on/off and proper temporal sequencing (phasing) of the actuators, while the adaptive part has feedback loops to maintain the outputs at the required levels of activity. In addition, the decision making process (selection of course of actions) is separated from the decision implementation process. Mathematically, this significantly reduces the dimensionality of the system, and from a biological viewpoint, this reduction in dimensionality of the control task greatly enhances the capability of the organism to survive. This has been referred to as the principle of maximum autonomy (Tomovic & Bellman, 1970).

We address primarily the development and underlying mechanisms of human locomotion. The first sections describe the biomechanics of human locomotion and the development of the mature plantigrade locomotion pattern. In order to understand the neural organization of human locomotion we examine later some of the more significant animal (namely the cat) experiments on locomotion.

BIOMECHANICS

Biomechanics is the application of mechanics to the structures of living animals, e.g., to the forces on the skeleton caused by the muscles and gravity and resulting movements (inertia). It is a blend of mechanical engineering and biology whose origin comes from the recognition that the components of a living organism may be viewed as mechanical systems to which engineering concepts can be applied.

A basic problem in studying human locomotion is to separate its mechanical demands from the behavior of the CNS. Also, the identification and understanding of those mechanical aspects which are relevant to the control strategies used by the CNS requires quantitative descriptors of locomotion (e.g., kinematic parameters). Biomechanical models that are neurophysiologically relevant can be useful in understanding how the CNS simplifies the organization and control of locomotion into a manageable task (Zajac, 1984). Bernstein (1967) argued that a complete understanding of locomotion must encompass both the underlying neural mechanisms and the dynamics of the body. Thus, the interactions between the CNS and movement must play a key role in the development of meaningful models for locomotion. Of course, models can offer little to the understanding of locomotion unless they are validated; i.e., they must provide experimentally testable hypotheses.

Wilhem and Eduard Weber (1836) were probably the first to apply biomechanics to humans and clearly demonstrated its importance in understanding human locomotion. They measured: inclination and vertical oscillations of the trunk, the periodicity of the free swinging leg, gait velocities, the relationship between the length, and duration of the stride cycle for adult males. This work helped to lay a foundation on which many of our current biomechanical models of locomotion have been developed. The contemporary biomechanical measurements usually made during human locomotion are: (1) temporal phases/events of the gait, (2) kinematics of the body segments, (3) forces acting on the feet, and (4) muscle activity.

Bipedal locomotion has several states (or phases) which impose quite different constraints on the dynamics of walking. These states can be represented by the temporal phases or events of the stride cycle (Fig. 2.1) and play an important role in the description, analysis and synthesis of locomotion. It is interesting to note that one of the major obstacles to the construction of a bipedal robot with human-like movement patterns is the processing of these changing dynamic constraints.

Kinematics is concerned only with the trajectory or movement patterns. One of the major goals in the analysis of locomotion is the description of its ki-

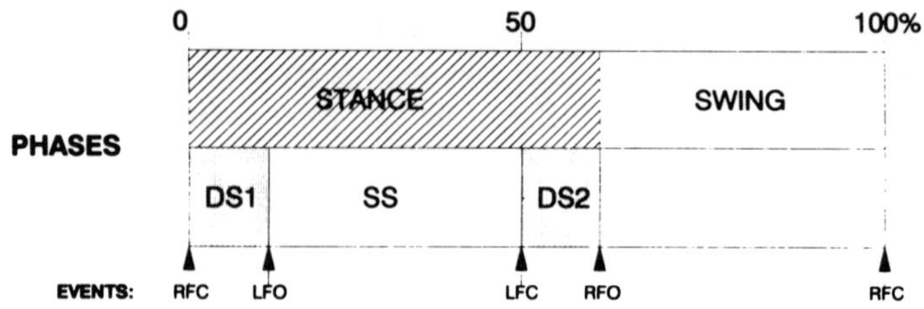

FIG. 2.1. Phases and events of a stride cycle (human walking). Phases: **DS**–double support, **SS**–single support. Events: **RFC (LFC)** Right (Left) foot contact, **RFO (LFO)** Right (Left) foot off. Note, we have assumed the stride cycle starts/stops with **RFC.**

nematics. Kinematics of the body segments are usually obtained by: (1) goniometers, or (2) spatial image systems. Our laboratory has used a spatial image system (SELSPOT) to obtain both two-dimensional (2D) and three-dimensional (3D) kinematics of the legs and trunk of animals and humans. Some of our more recent work (Stokes, Andersson, & Forssberg, 1989) includes the 3D kinematics of the pelvis and thorax during treadmill walking (Fig. 2.2).

Kinetics is concerned with the masses, moments of inertia and forces that act on the body and is an important part of human locomotion, especially gait pathologies. Force plates can be used to measure vertical (F_z), forward-backward (F_y) and lateral forces (F_x), which are applied to the foot while in contact with the force plate. From these surface reaction force components one can obtain: center-of-pressure, forces and torques about the various joints, forward speed of the center-of-mass, etc. Interestingly, force plates were already being used in Russia during the early 1900s, yet there was no mention of their use by Bernstein (Woltring, 1984).

Surface electromyogram (EMG) is particularly useful for recording the activity of superficial muscles during locomotion. Each muscle has a number of motor units and surface EMG electrodes record the sum of all motor unit potentials reaching the electrode site. EMG measurements can be used to estimate the relative magnitude and temporal relationships between various muscles during locomotion. Although EMG is an important tool for understanding muscle function, we should not forget that a muscle acts not only on the body segments and joints which its spans, but its contraction can also cause movement of other segments (Fischer, 1895).

In summary, a detailed study of human locomotion includes the simultaneous measurement of: temporal phases/events of the gait (foot switches), marked positions on the body (kinematics), reaction forces on the feet (kinetics), and muscle activity (EMG). The equipment necessary for such measurements has been available for some time. However, only recently, have data-acquisition systems been developed that are able to process the enormous amount of data simultaneously obtained from these different measurement systems. All of these data are contaminated with noise (often nonstationary)—an important characteristic of human locomotion data that is all to often overlooked. The processing, presentation, and interpretation of human locomotion data is a nontrivial problem that requires considerable computer power and can often benefit from a multidisciplinary approach.

BIPEDAL PLANTIGRADE GAIT

One of the distinguishing characteristics of the human species is its upright, bipedal form of locomotion. This is only found in humans, although other animals may walk on two legs occasionally. All other primates are basically quadrupedal as judged from the structure of their musculoskeletal system and their locomotor pattern (Lovejoy, 1988; Lovejoy, Heiple & Burstein, 1973). The anatomy of the pelvis and femur as well as preserved foot prints in volcanic ashes (White, 1980) indicates that hominids living about 3 million years ago were the first to use bipedal gait. The need to continuously stabilize the upright trunk and the forward tilted pelvis increased the demands of the hip extensor muscles. This is reflected by the enlargement of the gluteus maximus (GM) muscle in humans compared to the much smaller muscle in the chimpanzee. Similarly, the bipedal mode of locomotion increased the load on the hip abductors during stance, preventing a lateral tilt of the pelvis. Elftman and Manter (1935) found that the major propulsive force required for human locomotion was supplied by the calf muscles which is reflected by their comparatively large mass in humans.

The adaptation of the musculoskeletal system to the upright position has resulted in an unique gait pattern (Bresler & Frankel, 1950; Cavagna & Margaria, 1966; Morrison, 1970; Pedotti, 1977). Although the human gait is unique there is no unique way to describe the kinematics of the limbs during locomotion. However, for reasons of consistency and clarity, especially when comparing mature and immature gait, we will use five plantigrade determinants (Table 2.1). These were defined earlier by Forssberg (1985b) and are an extension of those given by Saunders, Inman, & Eberhart (1953).

Active dorsiflexion of the foot near the end of swing results in a prominent heel strike which is a significant feature of human foot-ankle control. The tibialis

TABLE 2.1

Foot movement—heel strike
Knee movement—stance leg flexion
Intralimb coordination—unique phasing
Pelvic movement—rotation, tilt and translation
Muscle activity—unique temporal sequencing

anterior muscle (TA) has its major burst around heel strike (Fig. 2.3), which induces an extending torque around the ankle, and plantarflexes the foot against a lengthening contraction of the TA. Activity in the quadriceps group at heel strike guarantees extension at the knee joint and controls flexion of the knee during the shifting of body weight onto the support leg near midstance. The plantarflexion of the stance ankle (foot movement just before push off), helps to establish the initial velocities of the shank and thigh for the following swing and smooth the transition from double support to swing. A forward thrust of the body is initiated by a push off movement in the ankle joint through a forceful contraction of the calf muscles (triceps surae) in the second half of support. This is followed by a knee flexion (largely passive) and active flexion of the hip by hip flexors including the rectus femoris muscle (RF). Knee flexion of the stance leg further smooths out the trajectory of the pelvis. The temporal sequence of extension-flexion: ankle extension, followed by knee flexion and then hip flexion, reflects the active forward propulsion of the body at the beginning of swing. The knee is passively extended during the later part of swing when the forward movement of the leg is decelerated by activity in hip extensors such as the GM and hamstrings. The purpose of these ankle-knee interactions is to effectively shorten the leg during midstance and lengthen it at heel strike and foot off and thus reduce the vertical oscillations of the body. 3D kinematic studies of the pelvis and trunk (Stokes et al., 1989) demonstrated a phase dependent pelvis-thorax interaction with respect to direction, amplitude and temporal sequence (Fig. 2.2). At heel strike, the pelvis and thorax rotate in opposite directions with respect to each other. Between heel strike and midstance the pelvis is tilted medially and quickly followed by a lateral tilt (anterior-posterior axis) with backward rotation over the support leg. The thorax is laterally flexed over the swing leg during this phase and rotates forward around the vertical axis. At midstance the rotation between thorax and pelvis are in alignment. In the following phase from midstance until toe off, the pelvis and thorax rotate again in opposite directions until contralateral heel strike. Pelvic rotation allows a rotary movement of the trunk about the vertical axis which effectively increases step length. Race walkers push this determinant to its limit with greatly exaggerated pelvic rotation that delays the transition from walking to running at high speeds (Stokes, 1989). The medial tilt of the pelvis (lowering of swing side of the hip) smooths out the trajectory of the pelvis and also forces knee flexion of the swing leg. The lateral translation of the pelvis is associated with the alternating transfer of support from one leg to the other. In general, all of the plantigrade determinants contribute to a reduced range of vertical oscillations of the center of gravity which can decrease the energy costs.

We have mainly described the extensor and flexor muscles acting on the leg joints, which counteract resistive forces and provide forward propulsion. Force plate measurements of reaction forces show a vertical force (F_z) peak with horizontal force peaks in the backward (F_y) and lateral (F_x) direction at the

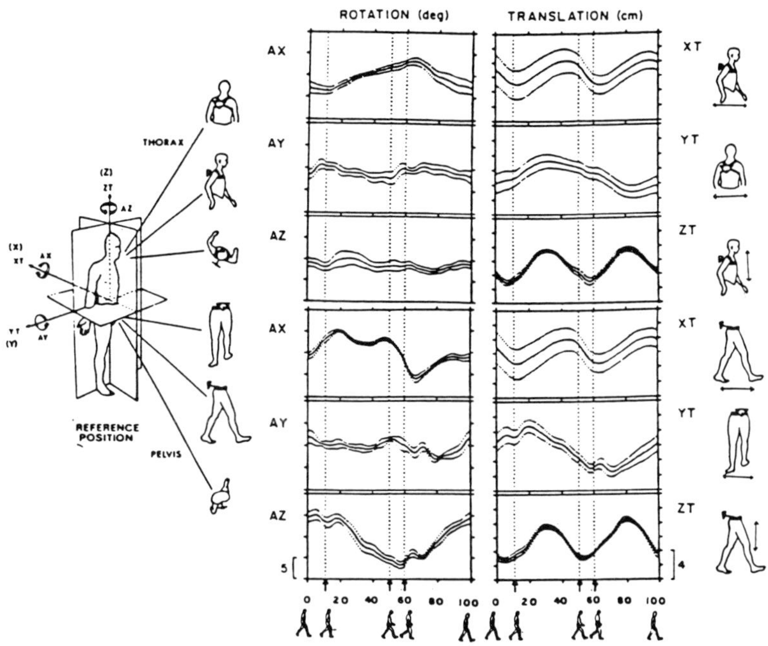

FIG. 2.2. To the left the reference planes and axes are shown. The movements are described with respect to rotations (AX,AY,AZ) about and translations (XT,YT,ZT) along the three orthogonal axes: bilateral (X), anterior-posterior (Y) and vertical axis (Z). These axes are perpendicular to the frontal, sagittal and transversal anatomical planes respectively. The arrows on the axes represent positive translations. To the right, the rotations and translations of a male subject over six normalized stride cycles at free walking speed (preferred by subject). Clockwise rotations correspond to increases in the slope of the rotational curves. From Stokes, Andersson, and Forssberg (1989).

beginning of support. Near the end of support there is a second vertical force (F_z) peak with horizontal force peaks in the forward ($-F_y$) and medial (F_x) direction. The patterns of these reaction forces suggest a complex interaction of internal–external forces during foot contact.

Changes in Walking Speed

Nilsson, Thorstensson, and Halbertsma (1985) and Grillner, Halbertsma, Nilsson, and Thorstensson (1979) found that as the speed of walking increased, the durations of the stride cycle and support phase both decreased. The increased speed also caused an increase in the range of hip, knee, and ankle rotations (Fig. 2.3).

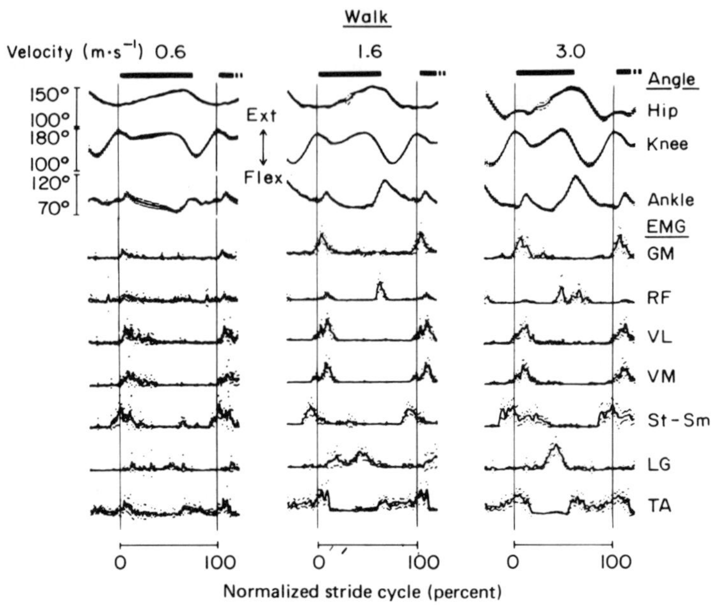

FIG. 2.3. Angular displacements in the hip, knee and ankle joints and activity of leg muscles in one subject (JH) during walking at different speeds. The curves are means (±SD) of several (5–10) normalized stride cycles. Vertical lines indicate touch down of the left foot. The amplitudes of the joint angles are comparable (see scale at upper left), but not the EMG amplitudes. Stance duration for the left leg is indicated with black bars at the top of the figure. Adapted from Nilsson, Thorstensson, and Halbertsma (1985).

The single joint muscles: GM, TA, and vastus lateralis muscle (VL) all showed increased activity with increasing walking speed with no significant changes in activation patterns. However, the biarticulate muscles: RF, ST-SM (hamstring) and LG (lateral gastrocnemius) showed changes in both burst patterns and envelope amplitudes as the speed changed. The changes in the burst patterns were most dramatic for the RF and LG. As walking speed increased, the RF shifted its main function from knee extension to hip flexion and the LG was turned on later in support.

These data support the idea that relative timing among muscles and kinematic components, is an invariant property of synergies used for walking. This is further illustrated by some earlier cat studies of Goslow, Reinhing, and Stuart (1973) where they noted that as the speed of locomotion increased, the duration of the stride cycle decreased with a corresponding decrease in stance duration and increase in extensor activity. This increase in muscle activity (and force increase) did not alter the relative timing among functionally linked extensor muscles, although individual activity durations changed markedly.

Backward Walking

Backward walking is interesting from a control viewpoint, since there are extensive changes in muscle activation patterns. If the same neural networks are being used (Grillner, 1985; Stein, Camp, Robertson, and Mortin, 1986) then these networks must be capable of being changed quickly and easily to allow rapid switches between forward and backward synergies.

Thorstensson (1986) found that the forward and backward trajectories of the legs were very similar. The durations of the stride cycle and support decreased with backward walking. The kinematic patterns of angular displacements in the hip, knee, and ankle joints were reversed (e.g., the hip flexed during support and extended during swing). One noticeable difference was the absence of knee flexion during support in backward walking. Forward propulsion is mainly due to the ankle extensors while backward propulsion is probably accomplished by ankle flexors.

From a clinical perspective, locomotion adaptations are extremely important, since the fundamental movement patterns often remain despite gross pathological disturbances of the limbs. Thus, the locomotor control system is capable of effectively compensating for a wide range of internal/external constraints. This compensation is partially accounted for by the interactions between the determinants of the human gait; i.e. increases in the range of one determinant may be offset by a corresponding decrease in another.

In summary, during human locomotion, the temporal sequencing pattern of muscle activity is unique and the onset, duration and shape of the EMG envelopes vary considerably between flexor and extensor muscles—even at the same joint. This is in contrast to the locomotor patterns of quadrupeds and non-human primates, in which hip, knee and ankle flexors (extensors) tend to be active during swing (stance) as described by Engberg and Lundberg (1969), Forssberg et al (1980a, 1980b), and Vangor and Wells (1983). In addition the unique pattern of muscle activity can be modified for adaptation to speed changes (e.g., slow walking), mode changes (e.g., running) and direction changes (e.g., backward walking).

ONTOGENY OF HUMAN LOCOMOTION

Locomotor movement sequences can be elicited within a few minutes of birth (Peiper, 1963) and locomotor like movements have been recorded in the human fetus as early as 10 weeks after gestation (de Vries, Visser, & Prechtl, 1984). An important feature of these kinematic sequences (infant stepping) is their lack of segment-specific movement; i.e., the leg tends to flex-extend as a unit (Forssberg, 1985b). Infant stepping can be elicited during the first neonatal period; but, deteriorates in most infants after a couple of months, although it may remain, especially if they are trained daily (Zelazo, 1983). Locomotor movements are normally absent until 7–9 months-of-age when voluntarily initiated locomotion begins to develop. During this initial period of locomotion the child requires external support to maintain equilibrium (supported locomotion). It is not until approximately 1 year of age that the child is able to walk without support (independent locomotion).

The locomotor pattern of an infant differs markedly from the plantigrade pattern of adults (Forssberg, 1985b). The leg is relatively flexed during the whole stride cycle, rotated forward by a hip flexion during swing and the foot kicked well above the surface (Fig. 2.4). This is followed by placement of the forefoot on the surface and a backward rotation of the leg by a hip extension during support. Force plate measurements of infants (8-weeks old) showed a vertical component (weight support) but the absence of a forward reaction force at the end of stance which indicated an inefficiency in propulsive force. The forward swing, was initiated by a flexion of the hip instead of a propulsive ankle extension as in adults. The hip, knee, and ankle joints tend to flex-extend together during the larger part of the stride cycle without mature ankle-knee coordination (Fig. 2.5). Flexor-extensor muscles tend to fire simultaneously with their larger bursts during stance (peaks at foot contact and foot off). The activity of the ankle extensors, concomitant to the other extensor muscles prior to touch down, plantarflex the foot and contribute to forefoot contact. The flexors show weak tonic activity during swing and the antagonists are coactivated during a large part of the stride cycle.

It is clear that infant locomotor patterns differ from the adult plantigrade gait, although the basic alternating movements are similar. These differences may be due in part to the mechanical constraints. That is, the infant was leaned forward, and partially supported under it's arms for the data in Fig. 2.5. However, the

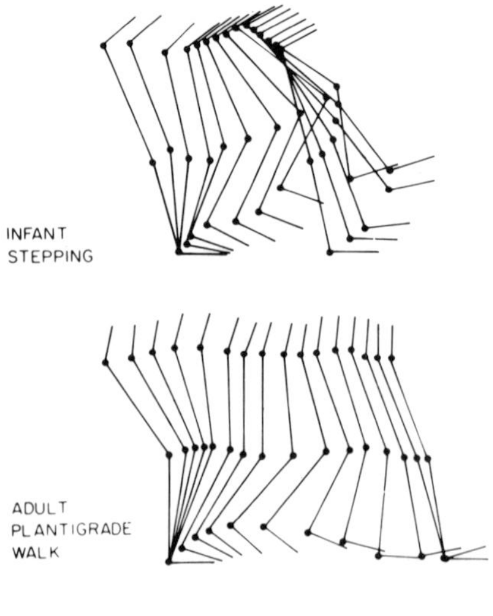

FIG. 2.4. Stick diagrams of infant stepping from a 6-week-old infant (top) and from an adult with plantigrade walk. From Forssberg (1985b).

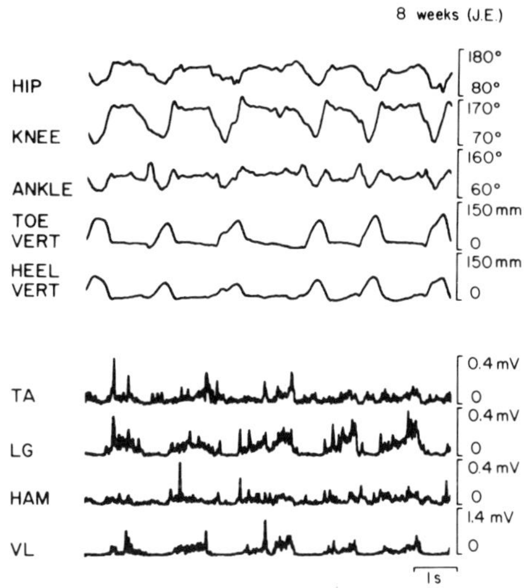

FIG. 2.5. Kinematic and EMG patterns of an eight-week old infant. The angular rotations in the sagittal plane around the hip, knee and ankle joints are plotted with extension upwards and flexion downwards for five consecutive stride cycles. Surface EMGs (recorded simultaneously with the movements) are shown after rectification and filtering. From Forssberg (1985b).

EMG patterns suggest that a simpler neuronal organization is used for the infant stepping movements.

The infantile pattern reappears when a child begins to walk (supported) near the end of the first year (Fig. 2.6). The leg is hyper-flexed and the joints are rotated more or less together (as in infant walking), although the foot now shows a tendency to move independently from the other segments. Foot contact is with the forefoot, which is followed by a dorsiflexion of the foot. Flexor-extensors are simultaneously activated with brisk reflex peaks of activity directly after foot contact and coactivation of antagonists remains. One important difference between infant stepping and supported locomotion is that the latter is voluntarily initiated, while the former is largely initiated in response to hip extension.

During the early stages of independent walking some characteristics of the infantile pattern will often reappear; i.e., antagonistic coactivation, simultaneous bursting of flexor-extensors with a lack of ankle-knee coordination (Okamato & Goto, 1982). A seemingly effortless quality of stepping develops rapidly after the establishment of an independent gait. Sutherland et al (1980, 1988) has given a detailed description (kinematics, temporal events, force-plate measurements and EMG measurements) on 369 normal children from ages 1–7. From this and other studies it is shown that the step length and duration of single-limb support increase almost linearly up to three years of age (Sutherland et al., 1980). The initial period of independent walking is followed by a long period over which the gait pattern is gradually transformed into the plantigrade pattern. Several plantigrade determinants develop before the child is 2 years old, while others such as the pelvis movements may take several years. The segments begin to show independent movements (decoupled) and the ankle a reciprocal type of rotation which is also present in mature locomotion. The leg is no longer rotated back-

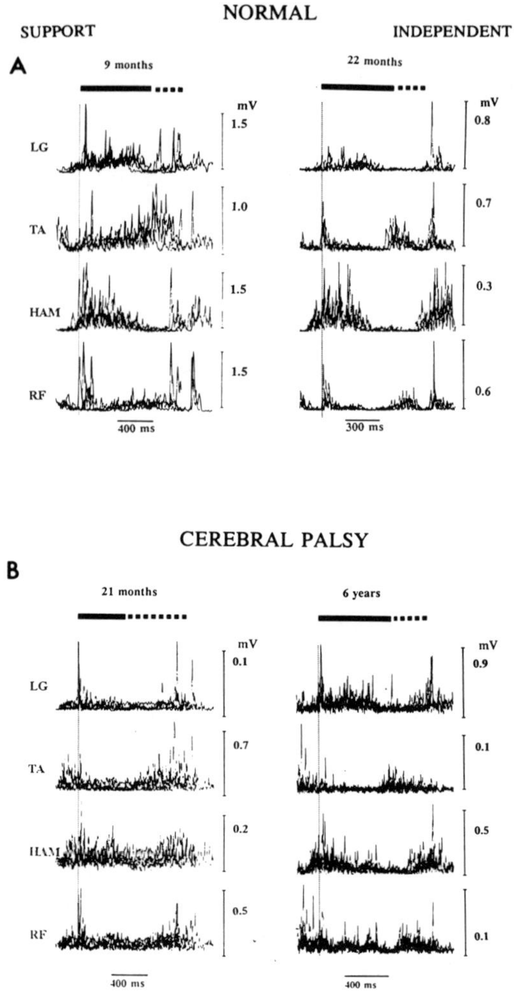

FIG. 2.6. Full-wave rectified surface EMGs for leg muscles during supported and independent treadmill walking (**A**–normal child, **B**–cerebral palsy child). Recordings show the muscle activity during five consecutive stride cycles, starting just prior to foot contact and ending shortly after the next foot contact. The initial foot contact is marked with a dotted vertical line. The solid bar, above, indicates stance and the dotted swing.

wards (from hip extension) during the end of swing and the ankle joint is maintained in flexion (Fig. 2.7) resulting in a clear heel strike at foot contact (Burnett & Johnson, 1971; Sutherland et al., 1980). The flexion directly after foot contact seen in infants is now reversed to a brisk plantarflexion (Fig. 2.7). The extension-flexion pattern of the knee is quite different, especially during midstance. The EMG synchronization across muscles is replaced by distinctive bursts at specific phases of the stride cycle (Fig. 2.6). Also, antagonistic coactivation is decreased and the reflex spikes following foot contact disappear.

An important consideration in the study of gait, especially during development, is the complexity of the movement. Intuitively, it would seem that a complex movement should require longer to mature; i.e. we tend to associate complexity with growth and development of the neural control mechanisms. However, this may not always be true, since robots with rather simple control systems, developed by Raibert (1986), can generate rather complex locomotion patterns. This underscores the importance of understanding the underlying neural mechanisms when studying locomotion.

Another principle that is often invoked in the field of motor development is that movement complexity increases proximal-to-distal. This is largely based on the observation that the effective number of degrees of freedom increases prox-

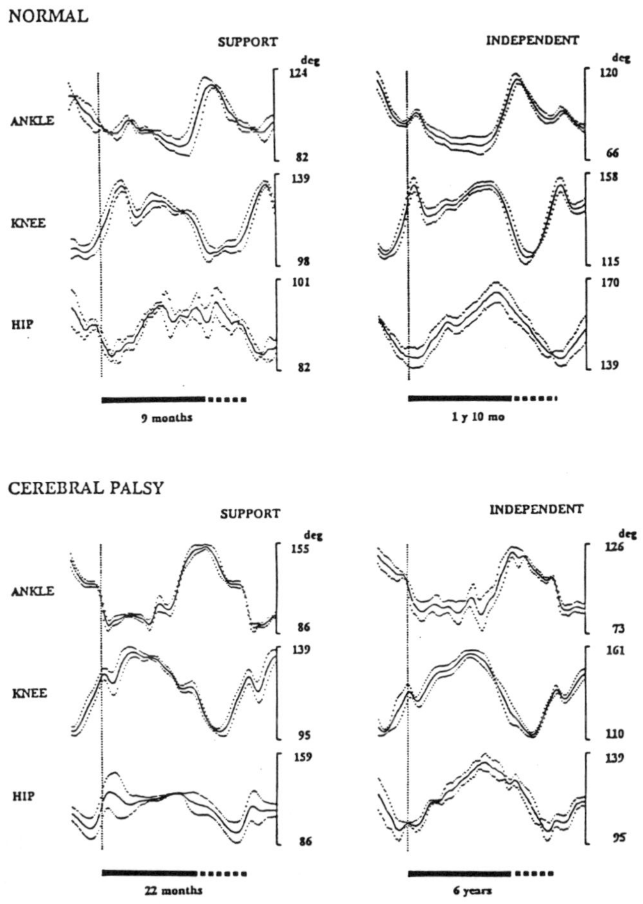

FIG. 2.7. Angular joint movements of the ankle, knee and hip in the sagittal lane during a stride cycle. Supported and independent treadmill walking for the same children as used for Fig. 2.6. The solid line represents the ensemble average (5 normalized stride cycles) and dotted lines ±SD. The solid bar, below, indicates stance and the dotted swing.

imal-to-distal. But, this is not a necessary condition for increased pattern complexity since the pattern complexity depends on what is actually measured. This is demonstrated by the spatial kinematic patterns of the pelvis (Fig. 2.2) and hip joint (Fig. 2.3). Of course, this begs another question—what makes one pattern more complex than another pattern? In general, this is a deep and still unanswered question in the field of image processing (Ramirez, 1989). However, in the interim, Sutherland's measure of complexity (the larger the number of Fourier coefficients needed to represent a pattern the greater its complexity) seems adequate for our purposes. Of course, this implies that patterns with high-frequency components are more complex. The point of discussing complexity is that we must remember that locomotion is intrinsically three-dimensional. That is, we should use measurement methodologies (e.g., 3D precision photogrammetry) which are matched to the level of detail in the movement pattern in order to obtain objective representations of its true complexity.

In summary, children are born with an immature locomotor pattern of low complexity. Flexor (extensor) muscles are contracted together with simultaneous flexion (extension) of hip, knee, and ankle joints. After the first year there is a slow and gradual transformation to a more complex pattern intrinsic to mature plantigrade locomotion.

SPINAL PATTERN GENERATORS

Bickel (1897) and Hering (1897) were the first to demonstrate in frogs, dogs, and monkeys that movements could be produced after dorsal root transection. Brown (1911) demonstrated in cats that the deafferented spinal cord could generate alternation between a pair of antagonist muscles, which partly resembled the locomotor rhythm. Von Holst (1935, 1939) proposed a central generation of the locomotor movements after elegant deafferentation studies in fishes and amphibians. Lundberg and Jankowska and collaborators (Jankowska et al, 1967a, 1967b; Lundberg, 1969) further demonstrated the existence of an intricate neuronal network within the cat spinal cord that could elicit reciprocally organized long lasting discharges in flexor-extensor nerves after injection of dopamine. They suggested that this network could generate a primitive locomotor pattern with alternation between extensor-flexor muscles and that the fine tuning and details of the locomotor pattern were shaped by interaction of peripheral reflexes. This was partly challenged by Grillner, when he suggested that the central network could generate a much more detailed output without any reflex interaction. He referred to the work of Székely, Czeh, and Voros (1969) on the newt forelimb in which a complex EMG pattern remained after dorsal root transection. Grillner and Zangger (1975, 1979) showed that, although the locomotor pattern was impaired after deafferentation in mesencephalic cats, it was not reduced to an alternation between flexor-extensor muscles. In search of the nature of the spinal pattern generator, Grillner developed a fictive locomotion preparation. In this preparation the cat's spinal cord was isolated from supraspinal influence by a spinal cord transection and from phasic sensory information by an immobilization of leg muscles via curare injections. He showed that the locomotor network could be activated by DOPA and many important characteristics of locomotion were retained (e.g., temporal sequencing of muscles). However, these descriptive measurements are insufficient to understand how a SG operates. To discover the basic neural mechanisms of the SG requires knowledge of: the connectivity matrix for the neurons in the SG network, the synaptic transmission and membrane properties of its neurons, and their behavior during locomotion. The extreme complexity of the mammalian CNS makes it unlikely that we will obtain this knowledge from mammalian preparations. However, since the general neuronal organization seems to be preserved during evolution one might gain considerable insight into the mammalian SG via studies on lower vertebrates. Grillner and coworkers have developed an in vitro preparation of the lamprey's brain stem—spinal cord, which can be induced to generate rhythmic locomotor activity. The lamprey is a rather primitive vertebrate with a comparatively small number of neurons embedded in a relatively simple structure. In this preparation it has actually been possible to reveal some of the neuronal organization underlying locomotion, in particular, the role of different spinal interneurons, their transmitters, and mode of interaction (Grillner et al., 1987).

To date, it has been impossible to induce spinal locomotion in humans with a spinal cord transection. On the other hand, there are several studies which give indirect evidence of spinal pattern generators in humans. The early locomotor-like movements in human fetuses (10–12 weeks gestational age) occur at a stage when then descending fibers are unmyelinated. Some descending reticulospinal, and cathecholaminergic and serotoninergic fibers exist (Okado & Kojima, 1984), and therefore, locomotion could (theoretically) be elicited from supraspinal structures. Prechtl (personal communication) has reported vivid locomotor movements in a fetus with severe malformation of the cervical cord completely lesioning supraspinal tracts (fetus later spontaneously aborted). Infant stepping has also been reported in anencephalic infants (Peiper, 1963). Some recent observations of myoclonus in adult patients with complete cervical cord lesions (Bussel et al., 1988) also suggest the existence of SGs in the human spinal cord.

In summary, we now have direct evidence for SGs in a lower vertebrate. This comes from data on identified spinal neural networks that are used during locomotion (swimming). We also have indirect evidence for SGs in mammals, including man.

ADAPTIVE MECHANISMS WITHIN THE SPINAL CORD

Although a SG is capable of acting autonomously, this is seldom realized in actual locomotion. Indeed, synchronization and proper phasing of leg movement patterns are obtained through nonautonomous SG interaction (interchange of internal states). It is important to note that a SG can operate in two distinctly different modes: open-loop and closed-loop (Rossignol, Lund, & Drew, 1988). In the open-loop mode, the SG is self-calibrated from information stored in its neural network as a result of learning and evolution (innate patterns). While in the closed-loop mode, the SG is continuously adapted (online calibration) by afferent feedback. Open-loop operation can be sufficient in some simple situations, however, closed-loop operation is necessary when changes in step length, speed, etc. are required. Open-loop control has the advantage of fast action but lacks the ability to compensate for disturbances. It is also important to realize that knowing the output of the SG in open-loop mode does not predict the output in closed-loop mode.

Close-loop control mechanisms have been observed at the spinal level during locomotor activity. After a chronic transection of the spinal cord at a low thoracic level, kittens as well as adult cats were able to walk with their hindlimbs (when supported) over a moving treadmill belt. The locomotor patterns closely resembled those of intact cats (Forssberg et al., 1980a; Smith et al., 1982, Rossignol & Drew 1986). The angular movements at the joints displayed the same trajectories and the muscles were consistently activated regarding timing and amplitude of the locomotor bursts (Fig. 2.8). A detailed and almost complete basic locomotor pattern can thus be produced in the spinal cord by the spinal generators interacting with peripheral feedback mechanisms without any contribution from supraspinal centers.

The walking hindlimbs of the spinal cats closely followed the speed of the treadmill belt. At lower velocities the limbs alternated as during walking or trotting. At higher speeds the limbs showed a faster walking gait and sometimes switched to a gallop (Forssberg et al., 1980a, 1980b). The temporal features of the stride cycle were adjusted in a similar way as in humans, e.g. stance duration decreased while swing duration remained unchanged as speed increased. Concurrently, extensor bursts were enhanced in amplitude and reduced in duration. This indicated the existence of an active peripheral feedback on the SGs which influenced the rhythm. The switch from an alternating to a more simultaneous coordination between the limbs (gallop) showed that the interlimb coordination was also controlled by spinal circuits. The latter mechanisms were further explored by allowing chronic spinal cats to walk on split belts moving at different speeds (Forssberg, 1980b). Each limb followed its own belt with respect to stance duration. However, the same rhythm was maintained by prolonging swing duration of the fast walking leg and different frequencies of the two legs could be achieved at extreme speed differences (integer multiples of the fundamental frequency). This behavior could be explained by two different groups of SGs, one for each side, mutually interacting with each other (same rhythm) and driven by afferent input from its own side. A similar organization of mutually interacting generators for coordination of fin movements during swimming in the gold fish has been suggested earlier by von Holst (1939).

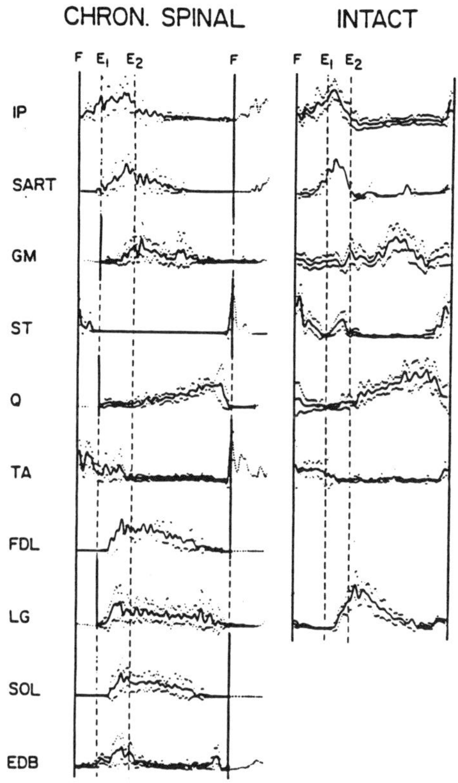

FIG. 2.8. Averaged EMGs from spinal and intact cats. Rectified and filtered EMGs from muscles indicated are ensemble averaged for normalized stride cycles (8–12 cycles). The mean is indicated as a continuous line and ±SD by a dotted line. Recordings are from different cats (chronic spinal, n = 2; intact, n = 2) and different experimental sessions. The cycle durations are chosen to be about 800 ms (20 ms) and the onset of the stride cycle is triggered by movement in the ankle where flexion (**F**) and first extension phases (**E1,E2**) have been used as trigger points. Different phases are marked with vertical lines. **IP**–iliopsoas; **SART**–sartorius; **Q**–quadriceps femoris, **FDL**–flexor digitorum longus, **SOL**–soleus, **EDB**–extensor digitorum brevis. From Forssberg, Grillner, and Halbertsma (1980a).

These experiments indicated that a highly detailed prescription from higher neural centers is unnecessary for the production of fixed (stable) locomotor rhythm or an abrupt change in ordering among the legs (e.g., backward walking). An early indication comes from von Holst's (1935) remarkable experiments on the centipede. Through amputation of leg pairs (until only three pairs remained) he transformed the centipede's gait into that of a six-legged insect. Further, when all but two pairs of legs were left, the asymmetric gaits of a quadruped were exhibited. It is unlikely that the CNS of the centipede possessed stored programs or SGs for these gaits in anticipation of its legs being amputated! Rather, given a novel configuration, the organism appears to adopt spontaneously those modes of locomotion that are dynamically stable.

Possible sources of this active feedback have been described for the cat. If a hindlimb in a walking spinal cat was not allowed to extend during stance the activity in the extensor muscles continued until the limb was extended (Grillner & Rossignol, 1978). By slowly moving the limb backwards it was found that the flexor activity was released at a certain position of the hip joint. This focused interest on the hip joint and from fictive locomotion experiments it was found that movements of the hip could entrain the rhythm of the SGs, i.e., the rhythm was increased and the burst amplitude of the neurogram was directly related to the velocity of hip rotation (Andersson, 1981; Andersson, Forssberg, Grillner, & Lindquist, 1978). In other studies it was shown that the onset of flexor muscle activity at the end of stance was prevented by loading of the ankle extensors (Duysen & Pearson, 1980; Pearson & Duysen, 1976). During normal cat locomotion the maximal load of these muscles occurs in the beginning of stance while it is decreasing during the later part (Manter, 1938). Thus the feedback systems associated with the hip joint and ankle muscles are position dependent and could explain the adaptation of the duration of stance. In addition, the feedback system of the hip is speed sensitive and could contribute to the increased muscle activity at higher speeds.

The spinal cord also has the capacity to compensate for unexpected perturbations of the limbs during walking. If the forward swinging limb met an unpredicted obstacle, a brisk flexion lifting the foot above the obstacle was elicited. This corrective movement was due mainly to flexor muscle activation superimposed on the ongoing locomotor activity. However, the same tactile stimulus during stance evoked an extensor reaction. This was a clear reversal of the flexor-extensor muscle activity patterns but the organization of the action patterns were actually modified during swing and stance, as well. The corrective movements were adapted so that functionally meaningful movements were evoked in each phase of the stride cycle. The same dynamic organization of the reaction was present in intact (Duysens & Loeb, 1980; Forssberg, 1979; Prochazka et al., 1978) as well as in spinal animals (Forssberg et al., 1977).

Intracellular recordings from motoneurons during fictive locomotion, showed that the transmission in the reflex pathways from the dorsum of the paw to extensor and flexor motoneurons, respectively, was phasically controlled by the spinal generators (Andersson, Forssberg, Grillner, & Lindquist, 1978), since there was no phasic sensory inflow from the periphery.

In summary, several reflex mechanisms exist in the spinal cord that can influence the SGs and allow for adaptation of the gait to the environment. Feedback mechanisms from hip joint and ankle muscles may influence the SG rhythm. Corrective reactions are centrally gated by the SG to produce meaningful responses at different phases of the stride cycle.

SUPRASPINAL CONTROL

Although spinal control mechanisms have neural machinery capable of processing many aspects of locomotion, several important functions are either lacking or greatly reduced in the spinalized animal. Often, the muscle tone and propulsive forces are reduced. The equilibrium control is very poor with impairment of lateral stability. Of course, the spinally transected animal has no capability to predict and avoid obstacles or to control foot (paw) placement. Supraspinal control is used to: drive and energize the SGs, maintain equilibrium, and adapt the stereotyped stepping patterns.

Descending Control of the Spinal Generators

Lesion experiments are the classical way to determine the contributions of different parts of the supraspinal structures for locomotion. Chronic decerebrate animals may walk with a well coordinated gait pattern partly adapted to the environment (Bard & Macht, 1958). After a bilateral removal of nucleus caudatus, cats exhibit compulsory locomotor movement and tend to keep following any moving object without avoiding obstacles (Villablanca, Marcus, & Olmstead, 1976). Acutely decerebrate cats, lower brain stem transection just above superior colliculi and the mammillary bodies (premammillary preparation), are capable of producing coordinated spontaneous locomotor movements (Hinsey, Ranson, & McNattin, 1930). However, a transection a few millimeters more caudally (postmammillary preparation) will abolish all spontaneous locomotor activity.

The Moscow group under the leadership of Shik and Orlovsky has contributed considerably to the understanding of the supraspinal control by using electrophysiological techniques. Shik, Severin, and Orlovsky (1966; Orlovsky, 1969) found that locomotion could be switched on in the decerebrated cat (postmammillary) by the delivery of trains of brief electrical pulses to different areas within the brain stem. One area was close to the subthalamic nucleus, and was termed subthalamic locomotor region (SLR). Another, was just ventral to the inferior colliculis in the mesencephalon, and was termed the mesencephalic locomotor region (MLR). A weak stimulation produced slow walk while stronger intensity increased the speed and could also change the interlimb coordination into a gallop. When these findings were made the actual mechanisms by which the locomotor movements were produced were not clear, as the organization of SGs and their reflex interaction were not explored. Today, it is clear that the locomotor regions in the brain stem plays a role at the middle of this multilevel locomotor control system. These locomotor regions receive and integrate information from several levels and they can initiate and control the speed and force generated by the SGs.

This experiment also gives direct evidence that a detailed prescription for the control of locomotion from supraspinal centers is not a requirement for stable gait. That is, rather diffuse inputs (midbrain electrical stimulation) can lead to a highly ordered behavior. The steady increase in level of stimulation induced changes in walking speeds and at a critical stimulation level even caused an abrupt change in gait mode (gallop). Another interesting aspect of this experiment (often overlooked) was that unstable regions were found in which the cat vacillated between trotting and galloping.

Initially, the MLR was defined functionally. That is, the MLR was that area from which controlled locomotion could be induced by electrical stimulation. From the work of Garcia-Rill (1986) it appears that the MLR is coexistent with a population of cholinergic neurons within the PPN. Microinjections of orthograde and retrograde tracer materials into the MLR have shown that it receives afferent projections from a number of sources including the basal ganglia, sensorimotor cortex, and the limbic system (Fig. 2.9). The MLR is under GABA-ergic influence since microinjections of GABA antagonists induce locomotion while GABA agonists as well as benzodiazepines block locomotion (Garcia-Rill et al., 1983a, 1983b). One source of the GABA-ergic influence is the substantia nigra, which probably is under GABA-ergic control of the subthalamic nucleus itself

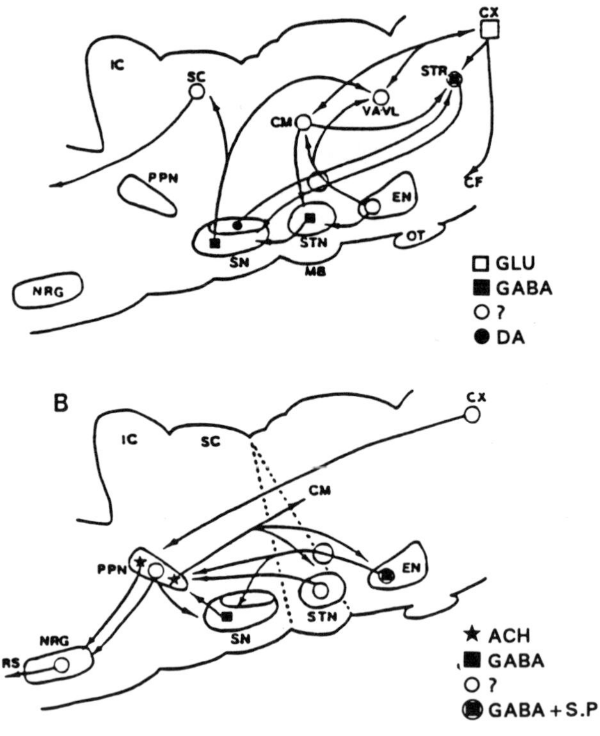

FIG. 2.9. Sagittal outlines of the upper brainstem of the cat. **A:** basal ganglia connections including striatal, pallidal, nigral and subthalamic systems. Corticosubthalamic, striatopallidal and accumbens projections not shown. **B:** pedunculopontine connections. Open circle dorsal to STN-subthalamic locomotor region; unknown transmitter systems; filled circle, dopamine system; open square, glutamic acid system; filled squares, GABA systems; open circle with filled squares, GABA and Substance P system; stars, cholinergic systems. From Garcia-Rill (1986).

since microinjections of antagonists into the substantia nigra block locomotion while agonists restore it (Garcia-Rill, 1986). Nucleus accumbens in the ventral part of striatum also project to the PNN with presumably inhibitory GABA-ergic control (Jones & Mogenson, 1980; Nauta, Smith, Faull, & Domesick, 1978). Lesions of the nucleus accumbens, release the GABA-ergic inhibition on the MLR, and result in hyperactive locomotor behavior (Pijnenburgh Honig & Vanrossum, 1973; Pijnenburg & Vanrossum, 1975). Mesolimbic DOPA-ergic afferents to the accumbens exert an inhibitory effect thus disinhibiting the MLR and other downstream motor centers.

There seems to be at least two different routes from the MLR down to the SGs. A major part of the pedunculopontine nucleus (PPN) cells project on neurones in the nucleus reticularis gigantocellulans (NRG) (Garcia-Rill et al., 1983b, Steeves & Jordan 1980). They are probably cholinergic as microinjections of acetylcholinesterase in NRG induce locomotion as does the cholinergic agonist carbachol while locomotion is blocked by atropine injections. There could be coexisting transmitters since microinjections of excitatory amino acids into NRG can evoke locomotion in decerebrate cats as well (Noga, Kettler, & Jordan, 1984). The NRG connects to the medial reticular formation and may convey information down to the spinal cord via the reticulospinal tract in the ventrolateral funicle. This is supported by the fact that stimulation of the MLR excites reticulospinal neurones and provokes an increase in their firing rate (Orlovsky, 1970). Experiments with hemi- and semi-transection of the spinal cord have also demonstrated that the integrity of the ventral funiculi is required for the preservation of locomotor activity in cats and monkeys (Eidelberg, Walden, & Nguyen, 1981; Steeves & Jordan, 1980).

An alternate route for initiation of locomotion from the MLR has been worked out by Shik and colleagues. In the lateral brainstem there is a sequence of locations, beginning at the MLR, through the pons and medulla, down to the level of the upper cervical cord which could be important for the initiation of locomotion (Shik & Yagodnitzyn, 1977, Mori, Shik, & Yagodnitsyn, 1977). This structure has been called the ponto medullary locomotor strip. Shik regards this strip as a system of fibers oriented longitudinally, with the signal for initiation propagating polysynaptically along it. This system continues down into the spinal cord in a similar chain of propriospinal neurones (Kazenikov, Shik, & Yakloveka, 1980, 1985).

Mori et al. (1982) have investigated another system originating from medial medullary structures that are involved in the control of posture and force during locomotion. Stimulation of dorsal and ventral areas in the pontine tegmentum set the postural tone of the extensor muscles in reflex standing cats. The same stimulation in mesencephalic cats altered the MLR stimulation threshold required for the initiation of locomotion. In a walking cat it increased the magnitude of the locomotor bursts in the extensor muscles. The stimulation was also accompanied by a set of appropriate postural adjustments.

There is some indirect evidence the humans and primates have a similar descending control of spinal locomotor circuits and that the same brain stem structures and descending neuronal tracts are involved. Lesions of medial reticular systems produced serious locomotor deficits in monkeys (Lawrence & Kuypers, 1986). Also, Eidelberg et al. (1981) induced locomotion in thalamic monkeys by electrical stimulation of brain stem structures which were analogs to the SLR and MLR. The locomotor drive effect was conveyed down into the ventral quadrant of the spinal cord, as it disappeared after selective lesions.

Of special interest are the gait disturbances found in patients with Parkinson's disease. In addition to bradykinesia, rigidity, tremor and a festinating gait they have great difficulty in initiating locomotion (Martin, 1967). The disease is secondary to degeneration of DOPA-ergic neurons projecting from pars compacta in substantia nigra to striatum (Hornykiewicz, 1963). The ventral striatum has a GABA-ergic inhibition on dorsal pallidum and zona reticulata in substantia nigra (Fuxe et al., 1979). All these structures project into the MLR. Thus, the net effect of the DOPA-ergic degeneration is an increased inhibition of MLR from the circuits within the basal ganglia. This increases the MLR threshold which makes it difficult to initiate locomotion. Another finding from Parkinsonian gait is that all plantigrade features have deteriorated (Forssberg et al., 1983). After treatment with DOPA the motor deficits are normalized including initiation of locomotion and a plantigrade pattern. The latter might indicate that the basal ganglia is also involved in the transformation of the immature walking pattern.

Descending Adaptive System

A second task of the supraspinal cord is to adapt the stereotyped output from the SGs and its segmental feedback mechanisms in order to achieve purposeful movements adapted to the external environment. Reticulospinal neurons (including MLR) and rubrospinal neurons discharge rhythmically in stepping preparations phase locked to the flexor phase of the stride cycle while neurons in the vestibulospinal tract are active during the extensor phase (Orlovsky, 1970, 1972a, 1972b; Rossignol & Drew, 1986).

The lateral vestibulospinal system projects to extensor motoneurons of the knee and ankle joint of the cat's hindlimb (Grillner & Udo 1970, Hongo, Lundberg, Phillips, & Thompson, 1984). Consistent with this, stimulation of Deiters' nucleus, enhanced activity in the extensor muscles in walking mesencephalic cats during MLR stimulation (Orlovsky, 1972a). However, the response was only present during stance. Stimulation during swing elicited no response at all. In analogy, stimulation of the rubrospinal tract evoked flexor responses only during the flexor period. The vestibulospinal and the rubrospinal tract might therefore provide the mechanisms by which the brain stem has separate, but parallel, control of the muscle force developed during stance and swing. In each case the descending excitement on the motoneurons is synergic with the influence from the SGs on the same motoneurons. While the SGs are responsible for determining the step frequency, the muscle force can partly be determined by rubrospinal and vestibulospinal tracts. In line with this Mori et al. (1988) found that the firing rate of Deiter's neurons varied with walking speed. He proposed that the vestibulospinal neurons might be important in controlling the rhythm and the phasing of the activity in addition to the power control. This is supported by findings of Russell and Zajac (1979) who showed that the rhythm could be reset by stimulation within the Deiters' nucleus (fictive preparation). This implies that the vestibulospinal tract may be able to both influence the activity of the SGs and "tune" the motor output at the motoneuronal level.

The cerebellum seems to have a central role in the adaptation of the locomotor movements. The rhythmic discharge of the descending tracts disappears following cerebellectomy (Orlovsky, 1972a, 1972b) and the movements become less coordinated (Orlovsky, Severin, & Shik, 1966). The cerebellum is constantly fed with information from the motor activities in the spinal cord. The dorsal spinocerebellar tract conveys messages related to peripheral locomotor events, since the cyclic modulation of the activity ceases after deafferentation of the hindlimbs. Neurons of the ventral spinocerebellar tract reflect mainly the activity in spinal interneurons as they continue to be active after deafferentation (Arshavsky & Orlovsky, 1985), which means that the cerebellum receives an efferent copy from the SGs. The cerebellum could act as a comparator between the programmed movement and the actual movement and then transmit corrective (adaptive) signals to the appropriate descending systems which fit nicely within Bernstein's framework (1967).

The finding that decorticated or pyramidotomized animals quickly regain the ability to walk on flat ground with little or no gait impairments but are unable to walk along a horizontal ladder or along a curved surface (Lidell & Phillips 1944) indicates that the motor cortex is active during "skilled" locomotion. A large proportion of motor cortical cells, including pyramidal tract neurons, discharge phasically during treadmill locomotion (Armstrong & Drew 1984; Durelli, Schmidt, McIntosh, & Bak, 1978). Stimulation of the motor cortex or the pyramidal tract during locomotion evokes short latency responses in muscle of the forelimbs and may even cause resetting of the rhythm (Armstrong & Drew, 1985; Orlovsky, 1972a). By recordings from identified pyramidal tract neurons during treadmill walking Drew (1988) has reported an increase in the firing rate when the cats adjusted their steps to overcome obstacles fixed to the moving treadmill belt. The increase was correlated to the enhancement of muscle activity required for obstacle avoidance. Thus, in these visuomotor adaptations, it is likely that the motor cortex has direct access to muscles which can be used to avoid collisions.

In our laboratory we have been trying to investigate the principles for adaptive mechanisms during human locomotion. Two different paradigms have been used, one involving visual and the other postural adaptations Forssberg, H. (1985a). Gelfand et al. (1971) suggested that a central program was involved in not only muscles which were related to the actual movement but also in the control of postural muscles which were used to counteract the disturbance of balance. Evidence for postural activity prior to and during voluntary movement was documented in humans by Belenkii, Gurfinkel, and Paltsev (1967) and Paltsev and Elner (1967). Postural adjustments are produced by consistent patterns of muscular contractions specific to the forthcoming voluntary movement in order to compensate for the equilibrium disturbance (Bouisset & Zattara 1981; Cordo & Nashner, 1982). These were the same as the adjustments elicited by external perturbations causing a similar type of equilibrium disturbance. In the spirit of Bernstein, the limited repertoire of postural activation patterns have been described as stereotyped synergies. The same synergy could thus be initiated either by higher levels in the motor hierarchy in advance of a voluntary movement or evoked reflexively by somatosensory inputs. The execution of voluntary arm movements during walking requires an interaction between locomotion, postural control and voluntary movement control.

Subjects were instructed to pull a handle during walking. The pull was cued by an audio signal that could be triggered to occur at different phases of the stride cycle. The same strategy as during standing was found, namely postural activity preceded arm muscle activity. Directional specific patterns of postural contractions were superimposed on the ordinary locomotor activity. The temporal and spatial organization of these patterns during midstance was strikingly similar to those during standing (Nashner & Forssberg 1986). A forward pull on the handle caused a wave of contractions along the dorsal aspect of the leg distal-to-proximal. A similar pull during swing, elicited activity in hip and ankle flexor muscles. A closer analysis of the postural activity during stance showed that the postural activation was constantly modulated in phase with the stride cycle (Forssberg & Hirschfeld, 1988). The temporal pattern between proximal and distal muscles changed as did the spatial distribution of the relative magnitudes of EMG (Fig. 2.10). During early support with the trunk behind the support leg, large bursts of muscle activity (postural) were recorded in the HAM and LG (prior to biceps brachii activity) which decelerated the forward rotation about the ankle and opposed the forward sway of the body caused by the arm pull. Near the end of support there was a complete switch to TA and quadriceps activity (again prior to recorded arm muscle activity). The TA reduced the propelling force produced by the calf muscle activity during the forward thrust around the ankle. The temporal ordering of activity was proximal-to-distal in the beginning of support (HAM activity in advance to calf muscle activity) and distal-to-proximal during midstance and the end of support (LG, TA activity prior to HAM, quadriceps). This study show two important principles. The first is that the motor pattern is gated in a similar mode as the stumbling corrective reaction in spinal and intact cats. This could be due to a control of the transmission at a spinal level by the SGs as in the case with the stumbling corrective reaction. From previous

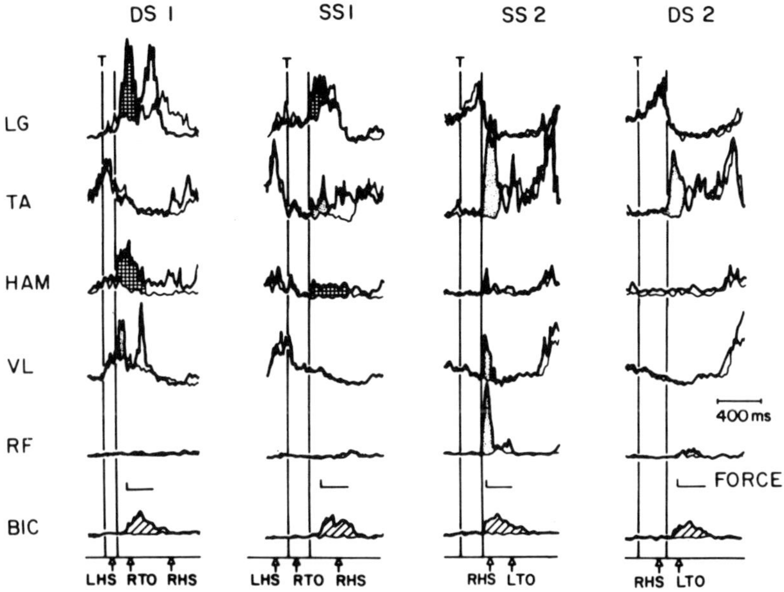

FIG. 2.10. Ensemble average (over 8 stride cycles) of filtered and rectified surface EMGs for both normal or unperturbed (fine lines) and pull-associated or perturbed (heavy lines) for one subject during support. The vertical line (labeled **T**) indicates when the tone signal was given and the other vertical line (unlabeled) indicates the absolute latency to the first activated muscle in the postural response. **LTO**–Left toe off, **LHS**– Left heel strike, **RHS**–Right heel strike. Postural responses are highlighted with checkered lines for dorsal muscles and dotted lines for ventral muscles. From Leonard, Hirschfeld, and Forssberg (1988).

descriptions of the cerebellar loop the gating could also take place at a higher level in the motor hierarchy. Secondly, a rigid synergy can not be used to describe the dynamic change of both temporal and spatial characteristics. A synergy should instead be regarded as a more flexible organization of synergistic muscles with the final output depending on the peripheral feedback at a lower level (i.e., the motoneurons) as well as on other simultaneously operating synergies, which could interact on several levels in the hierarchy.

In summary, electrical stimulation experiments have revealed areas in the brain stem which can initiate and control the speed of the SGs via several parallel descending systems. The brain stem centers receive information from the basal ganglia and the motor cortex. Movement patterns can be adapted to the demands of the environment via supraspinal descending systems which are capable modifying the stereotyped locomotor patterns.

LOCOMOTOR DEVELOPMENT AFTER EARLY BRAIN DAMAGE

In the earlier section it was mentioned that a destruction of sensorimotor cortex in adult animals did not interfere with the regular locomotor pattern and still allowed the cat to change direction and adapt the movements properly to the environment (Lidell & Phillips 1944). Leonard and Goldberger, 1987a, 1987b) studied the sparing and recovery of postural and locomotor mechanisms after unilateral sensorimotor cortex ablation in neonatal kittens and adult cats. They found some deficits in the neonatally operated cats after recovery, but their function was clearly superior to that of cats lesioned at an older stage. At the same time the early operated cats had retained crossed corticothalamic and corticorubral projections from the undamaged side. These were absent in adult normal and operated animals.

Cerebral palsy is a syndrome with movement disorders including muscular paresis, spasticity and in some children retained neonatal reflexes. The neural mechanisms subserving these deficits remain unknown. The limited autopsy data of children with cerebral palsy have revealed lesions localized to motor cortex (Lademann, 1978; Malamud, 1959). Some children with cerebral palsy achieve it secondary to brain damage during the perinatal period. Brain imaging with ultrasonography and CT scan in these children has revealed infarctions of the pyramidal tract and the sensorimotor cortex (Dubowitz et al., 1988).

We have studied, in a series of experiments, the development of locomotor mechanisms in children with cerebral palsy (Leonard, 1990c; Leonard, Hirschfeld, & Forssberg, 1988). During supported locomotion they had a similar locomotor pattern as normal children, i.e. a pattern resembling the infant stepping pattern features and lacking the plantigrade features (Figs. 2.6, 2.7). There was a synchronization of joint movements and muscle activity with extensive antagonist coactivation and reflex spikes following foot placement. The foot was placed without a clear heel strike. Normally these parameters change during development, but in children with cerebral palsy the infant locomotor pattern was retained. After several years of independent walking children with cerebral palsy had still not developed a clear heel strike, instead they maintained an onset of calf muscle activity (even during swing) initiating plantar flexion before foot placement. Also, a forceful activation of the calf muscles at the end of stance (forward propulsion force) was not achieved. Instead the limb was moved forward mainly by hip flexion. The dorsiflexion of the ankle to clear the foot from the ground was poorly developed. Children with cerebral palsy instead established their own locomotor patterns reflecting the size and nature of the brain damage and secondary changes of the musculoskeletal system. Antagonistic co-activation and short latency reflex spikes directly after foot contact remained as well. A similar lack of plantigrade features in older children with cerebral palsy has also been described by Berger, Altenmueller, and Dietz (1984).

In another experimental set up the mechanisms behind the failed development of reduced antagonist coactivation was investigated (Leonard et al., 1988). Reciprocal inhibition prevents normally antagonist coactivation during voluntary movements. It is mediated via Ia inhibitory interneurons, presynaptic inhibition and Renshaw cell inhibition (Granit, Genatsch, & Steg, 1956). H-reflex testing in normal adults has shown inhibition of antagonist muscles occurring before any activity in the agonist muscle. This inhibition is of supraspinal origin (Pierrot-Deseilligny, Lacert, & Cathala, 1971; Tanaka, 1974; Hultborn, 1976; Crone, Hultborn, Jespersen, & Nielsen, 1987). Studies with the H-reflex technique in children with cerebral palsy (Fig. 2.11) revealed that the supraspinal component to reciprocal inhibition did not develop properly (Leonard, Hirschfeld, & Forssberg, 1988). It is possible the cerebral damage interferes with the circuits that are responsible for the reciprocal inhibition and that a similar dysfunction underlies the high level of antagonist coactivation which remains.

The existence of short latency reflex spikes directly after foot placement is presumably due to an immature distribution and control of the segmental reflex effects. Myklebust, Gottlieb, and Agarwal (1986) showed that normal neonates had reflex responses in antagonist muscles after tendon taps in addition to agonist responses. A similar reflex distribution was maintained in children with cerebral

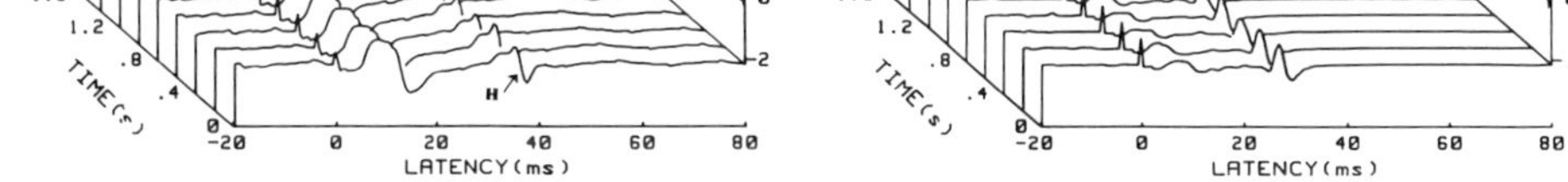

FIG. 2.11. Gastrocnemius-Soleus H-Reflex of a normal 13-year-old and a 14-year-old cerebral palsy subject during dorsiflexion. On the left a single 2-second dorsiflexion trial (13-year-old normal). Stimulus to the posterior tibial nerve (A) is immediately followed by an M- wave (M) and then by an H-wave (H). The EMG recording along the right side of each figure indicates the TA activity following the instruction to the subject to dorsiflex the foot. In this particular trial, inhibition of the H occurred 48 ms before the onset of TA activity. On the right a single 2-second dorsiflexion trial (14-year-old spastic diplegic). Note that in contrast to the normal response: a) there is no pre-inhibition of the H prior to TA activity and, b) rather than decreasing with the onset of TA activity, the H response becomes facilitated. From "Gait acquisition and reflex abnormalities in normal children and children with cerebral palsy." In Ambland, Berthoz, and Clarac (Eds.), *Posture and Gait: Development Adaptation and Modulation.*

palsy. This finding has been extended to a wider distribution of stretch reflexes and also to more proximal muscles (Leonard et al., 1988). The immature reflex pattern which remained after early brain damage can be explained by at least two different mechanisms. This could also be relevant in the discussion of the retained immature walking pattern in children with cerebral palsy. The first explanation would imply a neuronal reorganization within the spinal cord when supraspinal neurons grow down into the spinal cord. There are considerable competitive interactions for synaptic sites between segmental projections and descending supraspinal systems during development (Stanfield, O'Leary, & Fricks, 1982). Normal neural activity at this stage of development is important in establishing or maintaining neural circuits (Le Vay, Wiesel, & Hubel, 1980) and in the normal process of synapse elimination. It is probable that these mechanisms are effected by neonatal brain damage (cf. Leonard & Goldberger 1987b). In the absence of the right descending neurons making contact, exuberant segmental and supraspinal projections will be preserved, which could keep the immature reflex or locomotor pattern that otherwise would be lost in the acquisition of motor skills necessary for human bipedal locomotion. A second, alternative explanation would not involve any neuronal rearrangements in the spinal cord. The transmission in segmental reflex pathways are controlled by supraspinal centers (Lundberg, 1975). Early brain damage could disturb the development of descending systems that normally tonically inhibit the reflex pathways which are active during the neonatal period.

In summary, children do not develop a plantigrade gait after a perinatal brain damage including the motor cortex or corticospinal tracts. These children also exhibit an impaired reciprocal inhibition and an immature segmental reflex pattern.

SUMMARY AND CONCLUSIONS

In this chapter we have supported the idea that human locomotion is controlled by a multilevel organization which utilizes similar neuronal circuits as in lower mammals. However, there are two factors that dramatically differ between the control of human locomotion and the control of animal locomotion. One factor is the inability of the spinal cord, including SGs and adaptive feedback mechanisms, to generate locomotion after spinal cord transection; the second is the transformation to a plantigrade gait.

The inability to produce spinal locomotion is true also for other primates (Eidelberg et al., 1981). However, the early locomotor like movements in fetuses (de Vries et al., 1984), including those with cervical cord damage, and the early infant stepping as well as myoclonus in adult patients after complete spinal cord transection strongly support the existence of SGs in primates. This is further supported by the finding that stimulation of areas in the brain stem (analogs to

MLR and SLR) of thalamic monkeys, evoked locomotion (Eidelberg et al., 1981)—these structures are known to initiate SG activity in the cat. Thus, it seems that autonomous spinal locomotion in humans can be released early during ontogeny, but not later. This might reflect an increased dependency on supraspinal structures in primates. It has been suggested that spinal chock, which is more severe in primates (esp. humans), is correlated to the poor recovery of locomotor functions.

One possible mechanism would be that inhibitory circuits, depressing the SGs, develop in the human spinal cord during ontogeny. Normally these are under supraspinal inhibition but are released after spinal cord transection. It is worth noting that spinal locomotion in the cat and rat, in the first instance, could be evoked only after early neonatal lesions (Forssberg et al., 1980a, Stelzner et al., 1975) and that the locomotion after spinal cord transections in adult cats was documented as defective by Smith et al. (1982). Later, Barbeau, and Julien (1984) demonstrated that adult transected cats could also walk after several weeks of proper training. An active inhibition of the SG in some stages after spinal transection is also documented in the acutely spinalized adult cat, which cannot walk even if suspended over a treadmill. The same cat did directly start to walk after injection of DOPA or noradrenergic agonists (Budakova, 1973; Forssberg & Grillner, 1973). This indicated that the SGs were still intact and could be activated by proper stimulation. Locomotion of the chronic spinal cat could also be influenced by noradrenergic agonists and antagonists as well as by serotonergic and DOPA-ergic agonists (Rossignol et al., 1984).

The transformation to a plantigrade gait is unique for the human species. Not even modern bipedal apes have any of the plantigrade determinants (Table 2.1). These facts also imply that mechanisms responsible for the transformation can not be experimentally investigated in any other preparation. The development of an independent gait is not initially accompanied by any clear change of the locomotor pattern. This suggests that the original circuits for infant stepping, i.e., the SGs and reflex interaction, are still used. The slow and gradual maturation of the plantigrade locomotor pattern implies that these circuits are not new but only modifications of existing networks. Probably several different mechanisms are involved in this slow maturation process.

A changed input from the peripheral feedback might modify the output pattern using the same type of adaptive mechanisms as described previously for the spinal cat. The position of the body leaning forwards or backwards is known to modify the EMG pattern during supported locomotion (Okamoto & Goto, 1982). Unspecific changes, which do not involve the actual phasing of muscle activity could be the first to appear. An increased drive on the SGs and extensor muscle tone in parallel with a more efficient equilibrium system could contribute to the reduction of the general hyperflexion and to an increase in single limb support duration. This could change the movement and the inflow of peripheral sensory information.

The locomotor development of children with early brain damage involving the sensory motor cortex or the corticospinal tract indicates that the maturation to a plantigrade gait might be a genetically determined process. Children with cerebral palsy did not develop any of the plantigrade determinants. This is not to say that these systems are directly involved in the transformation process. It was found that children with cerebral palsy had not developed reciprocal inhibition of antagonists during voluntary movements and that they retained an immature distribution of segmental stretch reflexes (Leonard et al., 1988, 1990a, 1990b). This implies disturbances, in the normal rewiring of the circuits in the spinal cord, or a lack of tonic or phasic influence from supraspinal structures.

The maturation of human locomotion can indeed be regarded as a process whereby spinal circuits become progressively more influenced by higher brain centers. Descending systems from locomotor driving systems in the brain stem develop during the second half of the first year and can turn on and off the SGs, which earlier were driven and controlled from spinal feedback loops. Simultaneously supraspinal adaptive mechanisms, including equilibrium control, develop and allow the child to release its support and walk freely. Finally, higher brain circuits seem to be involved in a transformation of the locomotor output from a more primitive pattern with synchronized muscle activity and joint movements to a highly specific plantigrade gait pattern.

ACKNOWLEDGMENTS

Thanks to Anita Ljung for proof reading. Financial support for this work from MRC 4X-59250, Norrbacka Eugenia Stiftelsen, First of May Flower Annual Campaign for Children's Health, is greatly appreciated.

REFERENCES

Andersson, O. (1981). Peripheral control of the cat's step cycle. *Acta Physiologica Scandinavica, 113,* 80–101.

Andersson, O., Forssberg, H., Grillner, S., & Lindquist, M. (1978). Phasic gain control of the transmission in cutaneous reflex pathways to motoneurones during "fictive" locomotion. *Brain Research, 149,* 503–507.

Armstrong, D. M., & Drew, T. (1984). Discharges of pyramidal tract and other motor cortical neurones during locomotion in the cat. *Journal of Physiology,* (London) *346,* 471–495.

Armstrong, D. M., & Drew, T. (1985). Forelimb electromyographic responses to motor cortex stimulation during locomotion in the cat. *Journal of Physiology* (London), *367,* 327–351.

Arshavsky, Y. I., & Orlovsky, G. N. (1985). Role of the cerebellum in the control of rhythmic movements. In S. Grillner, G. S. Stein, G. Douglas, H. Forssberg, & R. M. Herman, *Neurobiology of vertebrate locomotion* (Vol. 45, pp. 677–689). Stockholm: Wenner-Gren International Symposium Series.

Bard, P., & Macht, M. B. (1958). The behaviour of chronically decerebrate cats. In G. E. W.

Wolstenholme & C. M. O'Connor (Eds.), *Neurological basis of behaviour* (pp. 55–75). London: Churchill.

Belenkii, V. Y., Gurfinkel, V. S., & Paltsev, Y. EI. (1967). Elements of control of voluntary movements. *Biofizika, 12,* 135–141.

Berger, W., Altenmueller, E., & Dietz, V. (1984). Normal and impaired development of children's gait. *Human Neurobiology, 3* 163–170.

Bernstein, N. (1967). *The coordination and regulation of movements.* Oxford, UK: Pergamon.

Bickel, A. (1897). Ueber den einfluss der sensiblen nerven und der labyrinthe auf die bewegungen der tiere. *PfluGgers Archiv fur die Gesamte Physiologie des Menschenundertiere, 67,* 299–344.

Bouisset, S., & Zattara, M. (1981). A sequence of postural movements precedes voluntary movement. *Neuroscience Letters, 22,* 263–270.

Bresler, B., & Frankel, J. P. (1950). The forces and movements in the leg during level walking. *Transactions of the Society of Mechanical Engineers, 72,* 27–36.

Brown, T. G. (1911). The intrinsic factors in the act of progression in the mammal. *Proceedings of the Royal Society of London Ser., B 84,* 308–319.

Budakova, N. N. (1973). Stepping movements in the spinal cat due to DOPA administration. *Fiziologicheskii Zhurnal USSR, 59,* 1190–1198.

Burnett, C. N., & Johnson, E. W. (1971). Development of gait in childhood: Part II. *Developmental Medicine and Child Neurology, 13* 207–215.

Bussel, B., Roby-Brami, A., Azouvi, P. H., Biraben, A., Yakovleff, A., & Held, J. P. (1988). Myoclonus in a patient with spinal cord transection. Possible involvement of the spinal stepping generator. *Brain, 111,* 1235–1245.

Cavagna, G. A., & Margaria, R. (1966). Mechanics of walking. *Applied Physiology, 21,* 271–278.

Cordo, P. J., & Nashner, L. M. (1982). Properties of postural adjustments associated with rapid arm movements. *Journal of Neurophysiology, 47,* 287–302.

Crone, C., Hultborn, H., Jespersen, B., & Nielsen, J. (1987). Reciprocal Ia inhibition between ankle flexors and extensors in man. *Journal of Physiology, 389,* 163–185.

Delcomyn, F. (1980). Neural basis of rhythmic behavior in animals. *Science, 210,* 492–498.

De Vries, J. I. P., Visser, G. H. A., & Prechtl, H. F. R. (1984). Fetal motility in the first half of pregnancy. In H. F. R. Prechtl (Ed.), *Continuity of neural function from prenatal to postnatal life clinics in developmental medicine* (No. 94, pp. 46–64). Oxford, Spastics International Medical Publications.

Drew, T. (1988). Motor cortical cell discharge during voluntary gait modification. *Brain Research, 457,* 181–187.

Dubowitz, L., Finnie, N., Hyde, S. A., Scott, O. M., & Vrbova, G. (1988). Improvement of muscle performance by chronic electrical stimulation in children with cerebral palsy. *Lancet, 1,* 587–588.

Durelli, L., Schmidt, E. M., McIntosh, J. S., & Bak, M. J. (1978). Single unit chronic recordings from the sensorimotor cortex of unrestrained cats during locomotion. *Experimental Neurology, 62,* 580–594.

Duysens, J., & Loeb, G. E. (1980). Modulation of ipsi- and contralateral reflex responses in unrestrained walking cats. *Journal of Neurophysiology, 44,* 1024–1037.

Duysens, J., & Pearson, K. G. (1980). Inhibition of flexor burst generation by loading ankle extensor muscles in walking cats. *Brain Research, 187,* 321–332.

Eidelberg, E., Walden, J. G., & Nguyen, L. H. (1981). Locomotor control in macaque monkeys. *Brain, 104,* 647–663.

Elftman, H., & Manter, J. (1935). Chimpanzee and human feet in bipedal walking. *American Journal of Physiological Anthropology, 20,* 69–79.

Engberg, I., & Lundberg, A. (1969). An electromyographic analysis of muscular activity in the hindlimb of the cat during unrestrained locomotion. *Acta Physiologica Scandinavica, 75,* 614–630.

Fischer, O. (1895). Contributions to muscular dynamics. *Abhandlungen der Koniglichen Sachsischen Gesellschaft der Wissenschaften, mathematisch-pyssische Klasse, 22*(2).
Forssberg, H. (1979). Stumbling corrective reaction: A phase-dependent compensatory reaction during locomotion. *Journal of Neurophysiology, 42,* 936–953.
Forssberg, H. (1985a). Phase dependent step adaptations during human locomotion. In W. J. P. Barnes & M. H. Gladden (Eds.), *Feedback and motor control in invertebrates and vertebrates* (pp. 451–464). London: Croom Helm.
Forssberg, H. (1985b). Ontogeny of human locomotor control I. Infant stepping, supported locomotion and transition to independent locomotion. *Experimental Brain Research, 57,* 480–493.
Forssberg, H. & Grillner, S. (1973). The locomotion of the acute spinal cat injected with Clonidine. *Brain Research, 50,* 184–186.
Forssberg, H., & Grillner, S. (1983). The locomotion of the acute spinal cat injected with clonidine. *Brain Research, 50,* 184–186.
Forssberg, H., Grillner, S., & Halbertsma, J. (1980a). The locomotion of the spinal cat. I. Coordination within a hindlimb. *Acta Physiologica Scandinavica, 108,* 269–281.
Forssberg, H., Grillner, S., Halbertsma, J., & Rossignol, S. (1980b). The locomotion of the spinal cat. II. Interlimb coordination. *Acta Physiological Scand, 108,* 283–295.
Forssberg, H., Grillner, S., & Rossignol, S. (1977). Phasic gain control of reflexes from the dorsum of the paw during spinal locomotion. *Brain Research, 132,* 121–139.
Forssberg, H., & Hirschfield, H. (1988). Phasic modulation of postural activation patterns during human walking. *Progress in Brain Research, 76,* 221–227.
Fuxe, K., Andersson, K., Ogren, S-O., Perez de la Mora, M., Schwarch, R., Hokfelt, T., Eneroth, P. Gustafsson, J-A., & Skett, P. (1979). GABA neurons and their interaction with monoamine neurons: An anatomical pharmacological and functional analysis. In P. Krogsgaard-Larsen, J. Scheel-Krueger, & H. Kofod (Eds.), *GABA-neurotransmitters: Pharmacochemical, biochemical, and pharmacological aspects* (p. 74). Copenhagen: Munksgaard.
Garcia-Rill, E. (1986). The basal ganglia and the locomotor regions. *Brain Research Reviews, 11,* 47–63.
Garcia-Rill, E., Skinner, R. D., & Fitzgerald, J. A. (1983a). Control of locomotion using localized injections of GABA agonists and antagonists into the mesencephalic locomotor region (MLR). *Neuroscience Abstracts, 9,* 357–357.
Garcia-Rill, E., Skinner, R. D., Gilmore, S. A., & Owings, R. (1983b). Connections of the mesencephalic locomotor region (MLR). II. Afferents and efferents. *Brain Research Bulletin, 10,* 63–71.
Gelfand, I. M., Gurfinkel, V. S., Tsetlin, M. L., & Shik, M. L. (1971). Some problems in the analysis of movements. In I. M. Gelfand, V. S. Gurfinkel, S. Fomin, & M. L. Tsetlin (Eds.), *Models of the structural functional organization of certain biological systems* (pp. 329–345). Cambridge, MA: MIT Press.
Goslow, G. E., Reinhing, R. M., & Stuart, D. G. (1973). The cat step cycle: Hindlimb joint angles and muscle lengths during unrestrained locomotion. *Journal of Morphology, 141,* 1–42.
Granit, R., Genatsch, H. D., & Steg, G. (1956). Tonic and phasic ventral horn cells differentiated by posttetanic potentiation in cat extensors. *Acta Physiologica Scandinavica, 37,* 115–126.
Grillner, S. (1985). Neurobiological bases of rhythmic motor acts in vertebrates. *Science, 228,* 143–149.
Grillner, S., Halbertsma, H., Nilsson, J., & Thorstensson, A. (1979). The adaptation to speed in human locomotion. *Brain Research, 165,* 177–182.
Grillner, S., & Rossignol, S. (1978). On the initiation of the swing phase of locomotion in chronic spinal cats. *Brain Research, 146,* 269–277.
Grillner, S., & Udo, M. (1970). Is the tonic stretch reflex dependent on suppression of autogenetic inhibitory reflexes. *Acta Physiologica Scandinavica, 79,* 13A–14A.
Grillner, S., Wallen, P., Dale, N., Brodin, L., Buchanan, J., & Hill, R. (1987). Transmitters,

membrane properties and network circuitry in the control of locomotion in lamprey. *Trends in NeuroSciences, 10,* 34–41.

Grillner, S., & Zangger, P. (1975). How detailed is the central pattern generation for locomotion? *Brain Research, 88,* 367–371.

Grillner, S., & Zangger, P. (1979). On the central generation of locomotion in the low spinal cat. *Experimental Brain Research, 34,* 241–262.

Hering, H. E. (1897). Ueber bewegungsstorungen nach centripetaler lahmung. *Arch. Experimental Pathol. Pharmakol, 38,* 266–283.

Hinsey, J. C., Ranson, S. W., & McNattin, R. F. (1930). The role of the hypothalamus and mesencephalon in locomotion. *Archives of Neurological Psychiatry, 23,* 1–43.

Hongo, T., Lundberg, A., Phillips, C. G., & Thompson, F. R. S. (1984). The pattern of monosynaptic Ia- connections to hindlimb motor nuclei in the baboon: A comparison with the cat. *Proceedings of the Royal Society of London, 22,* 261–289.

Hornykiewicz, O. (1963). Die topische lokalisation und das verhalten von nor-adrenalin und dopamin (3 hydroxytyramin) in der substantia nigra des normalen und parkinsonkranken menschen. *Wiener Klinische Wochenschrift, 75,* 309.

Hultborn, H. (1976). Transmission in the pathway of reciprocal Ia inhibition to motoneurons and its control during the tonic stretch reflex. In S. Homma (Ed.), *Understanding the stretch reflex* (pp. 649–660). New York: Elsevier.

Jankowska, E., Jukes, M. G. M., Lund, S., & Lundberg, A. (1967a). The effect of DOPA on the spinal cord, 5. Reciprocal organization of pathways transmitting excitatory action to alpha motoneurones of flexor and extensors. *Acta Physiologica Scandinavica, 70,* 369–388.

Jankowska, E., Jukes, M. G. M., Lund, S., & Lundberg, A. (1967b). The effect of DOPA on the spinal cord, 6. Half-centre organization of interneurones transmitting effects from the flexor reflex afferents. *Acta Physiologica Scandinavica, 70,* 389–402.

Jones, D. L., & Mogenson, G. J. (1980). Nucleus accumbens to globus pallidus GABA projections: Electrophysiological and iontophoretic investigations. *Brain Research, 188,* 93–105.

Kazennikov, O. V., Shik, M. L., & Yakovleva, G. V. (1980). Two pathways for the brainstem "locomotor influence" on the spinal cord. *Sechenov Physiological Journal of the USSR, 66,* 1260–1263.

Kazennikov, O. V., Shik, M. L., & Yakovleva, G. V. (1985). Synaptic responses of propriospinal neurons to stimulation of the stepping strip in the at dorsolateral funiculus. *Neurophysiology (Kiev), 17,* 270–278.

Kelso, J. A. S. (1986). Pattern formation in speech and limb movements involving many degrees of freedom. In H. Heuer & C. Fromm (Eds.), *Generation and modulation of action patterns, 15* (pp. 105–128). Berlin: Springer-Verlag.

Lademann, A. (1978). Postneonatally acquired cerebral palsy. *Acta Neurologica Scandinavica, Supplementum, 65,* 3–148.

Lawrence, D. G., & Kuypers, H. G. J. M. (1968). The functional organization of the motor system in the monkey. I. The effects of bilateral pyramidal lesions. *Brain 91,* 1–14.

Le Vay, S., Wiesel, T. N., & Hubel, D. H. (1980). The development of ocular dominance columns in normal and visually deprived monkeys, *Journal of Comparative Neurology, 191,* 1–51.

Lee, W. H., & Mansour, J. M. (1984). Linear approximations for swing leg motion during gait. *Biomechanical Engineering, 106,* 137–143.

Leonard, C. T., & Goldberger, M. E. (1987a). Consequences of damage to the sensorimotor cortex in neonatal and adult cats. I. Sparing and recovery of function. *Developmental Brain Research, 32,* 1–14.

Leonard, C. T., & Goldberger, M. E. (1987b). Consequences of damage to the sensorimotor cortex in neonatal and adult cats. II. Maintenance of exuberant projections. *Developmental Brain Research, 32,* 15–30.

Leonard, C. T., Hirschfeld, H., & Forssberg, H. (1988). Gait acquisition and reflex abnormalities in normal children and children with cerebral palsy. In B. Amblard, A. Berthoz, & F. Clarac (Eds.), *Posture and gait: Development adaptation and modulation* (pp. 33–45). Amsterdam: Elsevier.

Leonard, C. T., Hirschfeld, H., & Forssberg, H. (1990b). Myotatic reflex development in normal children and children with cerebral palsy. *Experimental Neurology.*

Leonard, C. T., Hirschfeld, H., & Forssberg, H. (1991). The development of independent walking in children with cerebral palsy. *Developmental Medicine and Child Neurology.*

Leonard, C. T., Moritani, T., Hirschfeld, H., & Forssberg, H. (1990a). Deficits in reziprocal inhibition in children with cerebral palsy as revealed by H reflex testing. *Developmental Medicine and Child Neurology 32*(11), 974–984.

Lidell, E. G. T., & Phillips, C. G. (1944). Pyramidal section in the cat. *Brain, 67,* 1–9.

Lovejoy, C. O. (1988, November). Evolution of human walking. *Scientific American,* pp. 82–89.

Lovejoy, C. O., Heiple, K. G., & Burstein, A. H. (1973). The gait of australopithecus. *American Journal of Physiological Anthropology, 38,* 757–779.

Lundberg, A. (1969). Convergence of excitatory and inhibitory action on interneurones in the spinal cord No. 11. In M. Brazier (Ed.), *The interneurone, UCLA forum medical science* (pp. 231–265). Los Angeles: University of California.

Lundberg, A. (1975). Control of spinal mechanics from the brain. In D. B. Tower (Ed.), *The nervous system* (pp. 253–265). New York: Raven Press.

Malamud, N. (1959). Sequelae of perinatal trauma. *Journal of Neuropathology and Experimental Neurology, 18,* 141–155.

Manter, J. T. (1938). The dynamics of quadrupedal walking. *Journal of Experimental Biology, 15,* 522–540.

Martin, J. P. (1967). *The basal ganglia and posture.* London: Pitman Medical.

Mori, S., Kawahara, K., Sakamoto, T., Aoki, M., & Tomiyama, T. (1982). Setting and resetting of postural muscle tone in the decerebrate cat by stimulation of the brainstem. *Journal of Neurophysiology, 48,* 737–748.

Mori, S., Matsuyama, K., Takakusaki, K., & Kanaya, T. (1988). The behaviour of lateral vestibular neurons during walk, trot and gallop in acute precollicular decerebrate cats. In O. Pompeiano & J. H. J. Allum (Eds.), *Vestibulospinal control of posture and locomotion progress in brain research* (Vol. 76, pp. 211–220). New York: Elsevier.

Mori, S., Shik, M. L., & Yagodnitsyn, A. S. (1977). Role of pontine tegmentum for locomotor control in mesencephalic cat. *Journal of neurophysiology, 40,* 284–295.

Morrison, J. B. (1970). The mechanics of the knee joint in relation to normal walking. *Journal of Biomechanics, 3,* 51–61.

Myklebust, M. B., Gottlieb, L. G., & Agarwal, C. G. (1986). Stretch reflexes of the normal infant. *Developmental Medicine and Child Neurology, 28,* 440–449.

Nashner, L. M. (1977). Fixed patterns of rapid postural responses among leg muscles during stance. *Experimental Brain Research, 30,* 13–24.

Nashner, L. M., & Forssberg, H. (1986). Phase-dependent organization of postural adjustments associated with arm movements while walking. *Journal of Neurophysiology, 55,* 1382–1394.

Nauta, W. J. H., Smith, G. P., Faull, R. L. M., & Domesick, V. B. (1978). Efferent connections and nigral efferents of the nucleus accumbens septi in the rat. *Neuroscience, 3,* 385–401.

Nilsson, J., Thorstensson, A., & Halbertsma, J. (1985). Changes in leg movements and muscle activity with speed of locomotion and mode of progression in humans. *Acta Physiologica Scandinavica, 123,* 457–475.

Noga, B. R., Kettler, J., & Jordan, L. M. (1984). Chemical excitation of cells in the pons and medulla produces locomotion in decerebrate cats. *Neuroscience, 10,* 632. (Abstract)

Okado, N., & Kojima, T. (1984). Ontogeny of the Central Nervous System: Neurogenesis, Fibre connection, Synaptogenesis and Myelination in the Spinal Cord. In H. F. R. Prechtl (Ed.),

Continuity of neural functions from prenatal to postnatal life clinics in developmental medicine no. 94 (pp. 31–45). Oxford: Spastics International Medical Publications.

Okamoto, T., & Goto, Y. (1982). Electromyographic study of normal infant and child gait. *Journal of Liberal Arts Department of Kansas Medical University, 9,* 72–100.

Orlovsky, G. N. (1969). Electrical activity in brainstem and descending paths in guided locomotion. *Sechenov Physiological Journal of the USSR, 55,* 437–444.

Orlovsky, G. N. (1970). Connections between reticulospinal neurons and locomotor regions of the brainstem. *Biofizika, 15,* 171–177.

Orlovsky, G. N. (1972a). Activity of vestibulospinal neuron during locomotion. *Brain Research, 46,* 85–98.

Orlovsky, G. N. (1972b). The effect of different descending systems on flexor and extensor activity during locomotion. *Brain Research, 40,* 359–372.

Orlovsky, G. N., Severin, F. V., & Shik, M. L. (1966). Effect of damage to the cerebellum on the coordination of movement in the dog on running. *Biophysics, 11,* 578–588.

Paltsev, Y. I., & Elner, A. M. (1967). Preparatory and compensatory period during voluntary movement in patients with involvement of the brain of different localization. *Biophysics, 12,* 161–168.

Pearson, K. G., & Duysens, I. (1976). Function of segmental reflexes in the control of stepping in cockroaches and cats. In R. M. Herman, S. Grillner, P. Stein, & D. G. Stuart (Eds.), *Neural control of locomotion* (pp. 519–538). New York: Plenum.

Pedotti, A. (1977). A study of motor coordination and neuromuscular activities in human locomotion. *Biological Cybernetics, 26,* 53–62.

Peiper, A. (1963). *Cerebral function in infancy and childhood.* New York: Consultants Bureau.

Pierrot-Deseilligny, E., Lacert, P., & Cathala, H. (1971). Amplitude et variabilite des reflexes monosynaptiques auant un mouvement volontair. *Physiological Behavior, 7,* 495–508.

Pijnenburg, A. J. J., Honig, W. M. M., & Vanrossum, J. M. (1975). Inhibition of D-amphetamine-induced locomotor activity by injection of haloperidol into the nucleus accumbens of the rat. *Psychopharmacology, 41,* 87–95.

Pijnenburg, A. J. J., & Vanrossum, J. M. (1973). Stimulation of locomotor activity following injection of dopamine into the nucleus accumbens. *Journal of Pharmacy, 25,* 1003–1004.

Prochazka, A., Sontag, K-H., & Wand, P. (1978). Motor reactions to perturbations of gait: Proprioceptive and somesthetic involvement. *Neuroscience Letters, 7,* 35–39.

Raibert, M. H. (1986). *Legged robots that balance.* Cambridge, MA: MIT Press.

Ramirez, D. E. (1989). On two nonequivalent measures of complexity. *IEEE Transactions on Systems, Man, and Cybernetics, 19,* 1073–1077.

Rossignol, S., Barbeau, H., & Julien, C. (1984). Locomotion of the adult chronic spinal cat and its modification by monoaminergic agonists and antogonists. In M. E. Goldberger, A. Gorio, & M. Murray (Eds.), *Development and plasticity of the mammalian spinal cord* (pp. 323–345). New York: Fidia Research Series.

Rossignol, S., & Drew, T. (1986). Phasic modulation of reflexes during rhythmic activity. In S. Grillner, H. Forssberg, P. S. G. Stein, D. Stuart, & R. M. Herman, *Neurobiology of vertebrate locomotion* (pp. 517–534). London: Macmillan.

Rossignol, S., Lund, J. P., & Drew, T. (1988). The role of sensory inputs in regulating patterns of rhythmical movements in higher vertebrates. A comparison between locomotion, respiration and mastication. In A. H. Cohen, S. Rossignol, & S. Grillner, *Neural control of rhythmic Movements in Vetebrates* (pp. 201–284). New York: Wiley.

Russell, D. F., & Zajac, F. E. (1979). Effects of stimulating Deiters' nucleus and medial longitudinal fasciculus on the timing of the fictive locomotor rhythm induced in cats by DOPA. *Brain Research, 177,* 588–592.

Saltzman, E. (1979). Levels of sensorimotor representation. *Journal of Mathematical Psychology, 20,* 91–163.

Saunders, M., Inman, V., & Eberhart, H. (1953). The major determinants in normal and pathological gait. *Journal of Bone Joint Surgery, 35,* 543–558.

Shik, M. L., Severin, F. V., & Orlovsky, G. N. (1966). Control of walking and running by means of electrical stimulation of the mid brain. *Biofizika, 11,* 659–666.

Shik, M. L., & Yagodnitsyn, A. S. (1977). The pontobulbar "locomotion strip." *Neurophysiology USSR, 9,* 72–74.

Smith, J. L., Smith, L. A., Zernicke, R. F., & Hoy, M. (1982). Locomotion in exercised and nonexercised cats cordotomized at two or twelve weeks of age. *Experimental Neurology, 76,* 393–413.

Stanfield, B., O'Leary, D., & Fricks, C. (1982). Selective collateral elimination in early postnatal development restricts cortical distribution of rat pyramidal tract neurons. *Nature 298,* 371–373.

Steeves, J. D., & Jordan, L. M. (1980). Localization of a descending pathway in the spinal cord which is necessary for controlled treadmill locomotion. *Neuroscience Letters, 20,* 283–288.

Stein, P. G. S., Camp, A. W., Robertson, G. A., & Mortin, L. I. (1986). Blends of rostral and caudal scratch reflex motor patterns elicited by simultaneous stimulation of two sites in the spinal turtle. *Journal of Neuroscience, 6,* 2259–2266.

Stelzner, D. J., Ershler, W. B., & Weber, E. D. (1975). Effects of spinal transaction in neonatal and weanling rats: Survival of function. *Experimental Neurology, 46,* 156–177.

Stokes, V. P., Andersson, C., & Forssberg, H. (1989). Rotational and translational movement features of the pelvis and thorax during adult human locomotion. *Journal of Biomechanics, 22,* 43–50.

Stokes, V. P. (1989). Walking vs. racewalking: 3D kinematic patterns for the trunk. In R. J. Gregor, R. F. Zernicke, & W. C. Whiting (Eds.), *Proceedings of the XII International Congress of Biomechanics.* Los Angeles: University of California.

Sun, S. S. (1974). *Theoretical study of gaits for legged locomotion systems.* Unpublished doctoral thesis, Ohio State University, Columbus.

Sutherland, D. H., Olshen, R. A., Cooper, L., & Woo, S. Y. (1980). The development of mature gait. *Journal of Bone Joint Surgery, 62,* 336–353.

Sutherland, D. H., Olshen, R. A., Biden, E. N., & Wyatt, M. P. (1988). *The development of mature walking.* Philadelphia: MacKeith Press.

Székely, G., Czeh, G., & Voros, G. (1969). The activity pattern of limb muscles in freely moving normal and deafferented newts. *Experimental Brain Research, 9,* 53–62.

Tanaka, R. (1974). Reciprocal inhibition during voluntary movements in man. *Experimental Brain Research, 21,* 529–540.

Thorstensson, A. (1986). Adaptation in trunk and leg movements and motor patterns to speed, mode and direction of progression in man. In S. Grillner, P. S. G. Stein, D. G. Stuart, H. Forssberg, & R. M. Herman (Eds.), *Neurobiology of vertebrate locomotion* (Vol. 45, pp. 609–621) Stockholm: Wenner-Gren International Symposium Series. London: MacMillan.

Tomovic, R., & Bellman, R. (1970). A systems approach to muscle control. *Mathematical Biosciences, 8,* 265–277.

Turvey, M. T., Shaw, R. E., & Mace, W. (1978). Issues in the theory of action: Degrees of freedom, coordinative structures and coalitions. In J. Requin (Ed.), *Attention and performance VII* (pp. 557–595). Hillsdale, NJ: Lawrence Erlbaum Associates.

Vangor, A. K., & Wells, J. P. (1983). Muscle recruitment and the evolution of bipedality: Evidence from telemetered electromyography of spider, woolly and patas monkeys. *Annales des Sciences Naturelles Z., 5,* 125–135.

Villablanca, J. R., Marcus, R. J., & Olmstead, C. E. (1976). Effects of caudate nuclei or frontal cortical ablations in cats. I. Neurology and gross behavior. *Experimental Neurology, 52,* 389–420.

Von Holst, E. (1935). Ueber den prozess der zentralnervosen koordination. *PfluGgers Archiv fur die Gesamte Physiologie des Menschenundertiere, 236,* 149–158.

Von Holst, E. (1939). Die relative koordination. *Ergebnisse der Physiologie, 42,* 228–306.

Weber, W., & Weber, E. (1836). *Mechanik der Menschlichen Gehwerkzeuge.* Goettingen, West Germany: Goettingen University.

White, T. D. (1980). Evolutionary implications of pliocene hominid footprints. *Science, 208,* 175–176.

Woltring, H. J. (1984). On methodology in the study of human movement. In H. T. A. Whiting (Ed.), *Human motor actions Bernstein reassessed* (pp. 35–76). Amsterdam: North-Holland.

Zajac, F. E. (1984). Are natural movements optimum with special reference to posture, locomotion and jumping? *Neuroscience 1984 Satellite Symposia: Organization of Movment, Society for Neuroscience.*

Zelazo, P. R. (1983). The development of walking: New findings and old assumptions. *Journal of Motor Behavior, 15,* 99–137.

3 Developing Emotions and Cortical Networks

Don M. Tucker
University of Oregon

In studying child development, the traditional assumption has been that a line can be drawn between the influences of nature and those of nurture. Nature contributes the structure of the brain and its schedule of maturation. Nurture provides for the psychological growth of the child and the flexible processes of learning. For those interested in cognitive and emotional development, nurture has seemed to be the relevant domain. Given that a child has an intact brain, a knowledge of neural mechanisms has not seemed necessary for a theory of human psychological development. Similarly, for studying brain development, it has not seemed important to consider whether psychological experience can alter the course of neuroanatomical differentiation.

Yet in the current literature in cognitive science and neuroscience, the line between brain and mind is getting harder to find. The differentiated anatomy of cortical networks is turning out to be achieved first by overabundant production of synaptic connections, then by a process of competitive interaction to select those connections that are effectively entrained to environmental information (Singer, 1987). The ineffective synapses and neural processes are eliminated, apparently through phagocytosis (Innocenti, 1983). The process that provides the raw material for network interconnections, synaptogenesis, is not only exuberant in the first years of life, it is responsive to novel experience, and may in fact index the information complexity encountered by the developing organism (Greenough, 1984; this volume). The dynamic process of selecting functional patterns in cortical networks has been likened to a kind of Neural Darwinism, in which the survival of patterns in neural tissue is dependent on their effective competition for information (Changeux & Dehaene, 1989). The causal agents in this kind of competitive interaction are not just physiological, but functional: The cognitive processes of the network, themselves shaped through commerce with the environment, may have the inherent capacity to instantiate their representation within neural tissue.

Although accepted principles of development in neural networks are only beginning to emerge, the evidence from this research is providing interesting new ways of thinking about how brains might achieve their functions. At the same time, research in cognitive science is producing formal models of computation that are built upon brain-like networks of dense interconnections among simple processing units. These parallel distributed processing (PDP) or connectionist models include a number of properties that are more reminiscent of human cognition than the traditional computer models of mental processes (Rumelhart & McClelland, 1986). For example, a common property of a connectionist model is pattern completion: Once the network is trained to produce a given output from an input pattern, it can yield this output from a fragmentary input pattern. Another example is graceful degradation. Like brains and unlike computers, when a connectionist network suffers damage to one part, its overall representation may be impaired but it still works.

It is sometimes argued that connectionist models are too simple to account for human cognition, or that their idealized architectures are too far removed from the structure of real brain networks. Yet there are increasing examples of applications of formal models to brain networks in which the precision of explanation offered by the formal model is clear (Ambros-Ingerson, Granger, & Lynch, 1990). Furthermore, if connectionism produces a paradigm shift in psychology and neuroscience, it may come not from specific modelling algorithms, but from the discovery of a more appropriate metaphor for understanding cognitive processes in the cortex. Just as earlier attempts to understand the brain were heavily influenced by implicit metaphors such as the telephone switchboard or the digital instruction-processing computer, current efforts in theoretical neuropsychology may draw from the properties of information representation in connectionist networks to suggest the form to be taken by theories of brain networks (e.g., Damasio, 1989). Although most approaches to neural networks deal with circumscribed model systems, it may not be too early to begin theorizing about broader implications of neural network models for understanding psychological development.

Perhaps the most remarkable aspect of the current work on neural plasticity is the inability to find a fundamental distinction between the synaptic plasticity that determines the anatomical differentiation of the cortex during ontogeny, and the synaptic plasticity that determines the storage of each memory trace in the adult brain (Malsburg & Singer, 1988; Squire, 1987). Although exuberant synaptogenesis in the young brain creates an uncommitted representational potential that will not be matched later in life, the basic mechanism of instantiating active synapses seems to remain the medium of information storage in the adult brain.

The neuropsychological evidence on the brain circuits required for memory may provide important clues to the puzzle of how neural plasticity of the cortex is regulated adaptively. To be retained in cortex, information must receive some sort of processing by the limbic system (Squire, 1987). Considering the limbic system's importance to motivational and emotional processes, its role in memory may be to evaluate the adaptive significance of information and then tune the representational plasticity of the cortex accordingly. Recent evidence on the anatomy of the cortex shows a multi-level network architecture, fanning out from the primitive cortex that first evolved from the limbic system (Pandya, Seltzer, & Barbas, 1988). Several features of cortico-limbic network architecture may suggest new ways of thinking about how adaptive influences from limbic regions could condition the operation, and indeed the structure, of developing neocortical networks.

This chapter considers the network architecture of the cortex and its interconnections with limbic cortex. The goal is to gain insights into the emotional and motivational influences that may regulate synaptic plasticity in the left and right hemispheres during the course of development. Although we have little knowledge about how information is actually represented in neocortical networks, there are intriguing suggestions that the psychological functions of the left and right hemispheres may be achieved through differing patterns of network organization. By considering hemispheric specialization in the context of the architecture of cortical networks, it may be possible to develop new hypotheses about the adaptive control of important domains of psychological function.

MORPHOGENESIS AND ACTIVITY-DEPENDENT NETWORK PLASTICITY

Brain development occurs through an intricate intercellular communication system that leads neurons to differentiate on schedule, migrate to their appropriate locations, then send out projections to the neural regions to which they are to be functionally linked. As it forms at the end of the neural tube, the brain's embryological differentiation proceeds through the progressive evolutionary layers of the hindbrain, midbrain, and forebrain, each differentiating from the neural proliferation zone adjoining its ventricle of cerebrospinal fluid. From the telencephalon of the forebrain, the cortical layer expands caudally and laterally, wrinkling in the process to form the characteristic convolutions of the cortex.

In the formation of the cortex, the neuroblasts or neuron precursors form in the periventricular cell proliferation zone, then migrate in a radial pattern outward to create the multiple layers of the cortex (Rakic, 1988). The first cortical layer to be established is the deepest, layer VI, and each successive wave of migration passes through the previous ones to form a more external layer.

After the sense organs differentiate from the embryologic tissue, they send axonal projections out to reach their target brain regions. By 40 days postconception, the human embryo has formed hands, eyes, outer ears, and feet. By 60 days the inner ear has formed, and each receptor surface is sending projections to find the brain structures that will implement its function (Trevarthen, 1985).

Connecting the sense receptors with their target brain regions presents a complex problem of mapping. For example, the fibers from the retina must find the appropriate locations in the midbrain tectum to form a retinotopic map of visual space. This process seems to be achieved in two stages: (1) a crude general point-to-point mapping in which chemical gradients allow projections from the eye to get to the midbrain and align themselves in the general framework of retinal topography, and (2) a fine specification of the topography which is activity-dependent (Malsburg & Singer, 1988). This second stage is termed "activity-dependent" because activity in the sensory pathway between eye and tectum is required to articulate the fine structure of the map.

The establishment of visual projections illustrates the general sequence of neural development. There an initial exuberant growth of connections and projections that substantially exceed what will be useful for the functioning network. Then there is a subtractive phase, in which inappropriate or ectopic connections are eliminated through competitive interaction within the matrix of exuberant projections (Singer, 1987). As the projections to a given area compete with each other for the terminal space in that area, the result may be a form of population-matching, where the number of inputs is pruned to match the appropriate number of targets (Janowsky & Finlay, 1983). Because only the most active synapses are retained, subtractive mechanisms may perform a kind of functional sculpting of brain tissue (Janowsky & Finlay, 1983). Although there is substantial evidence that the formation of new connections through synaptogenesis is an active process, thus preparing networks to respond to new environmental challenges throughout the life span (Greenough, 1984; this volume), the subtractive process of eliminating the less popular connections appears to be the primary mechanism for activity-dependent specification of patterns during network ontogenesis. An initial stage of overabundant synaptogenesis prepares the developing brain with a nascent representational potential which is then differentiated and specified through information-dependent competitive elimination.

THE INFORMATION ECOLOGY OF EARLY LIFE

Although theories of psychological development typically begin at birth or sometime thereafter, an important perspective may be gained by considering the trajectory of development that has completed its most remarkable transformations long before birth. Studies of animal embryogenesis show that within the spinal cord the ventral pathway of motor neurons matures earlier than the dorsal sensory pathway (Hamburger, 1977). This sequence may be a device for establishing patterned motor operations before they become entrained to sensory control. The behavior of the chick embryo is initially comprised of apparently random, convulsive muscle jerks, uncoupled from afferent influence. For most species, motor function will be brought under interoceptive and exteroceptive sensory control before birth. The exception may be humans, whose motor function seems to remain rather spasmodic into early infancy (Hamburger, 1977).

Having completed a morphological recapitulation of evolutionary anatomy, and not quite ready to act on cue, the young brain is launched with little ceremony into a highly complex culture. Much of the information now coming to the senses reflects physical qualities of the environment around which the mammalian brain is prepared to organize its representational abilities: colors, contours, affordances. A key task is connecting motor loops with interoceptive and exteroceptive sensations that are intrinsically correlated with them. Yet for the human brain, the most important information for successful development is conveyed by the social rather than physical environment. The baby brain must begin participating effectively in the process of social information transmission that offers entry into the culture.

In the morphogenesis of the embryo, specific anatomical features differentiate from each other, constrained within a matrix of relationships that defines a coherent whole. Bernstein (1967) proposes a similar process in the formation of integrated patterns in motor development. For example, as the baby learns to pick up an object, the control of this movement must anticipate how the weight of the object will change the mechanics of limb movement. The progressive differentiation of actions begins with proximal and axial movements, which become well integrated with sensory information by 3 to 6 months. It continues through the following months with the specification of distal grasp and manipulation (Trevarthan, 1984).

From his observation of infants and mothers interacting, Trevarthen has concluded that the development of patterns of emotional behavior may follow a similar course of differentiation as general motor behavior. It may also be constrained within an embedding context, formed by the flow of communication between infant and mother. Initially, the infant's attention and actions are highly synchronized with those of the mother, and mother's ability to modulate emotional expression may be an important training device for the infant's self-regulation. By 2 months of age infants can engage in face-to-face interaction in which they show intense interest in the mother's face and movements, and they respond with periodic, intense, but poorly organized expressions themselves. Later, the infant's increasing sensorimotor integration allows greater autonomy in directing attention to features of the environment. Around 6 to 9 months infants show signs of increasing self-awareness and a strong interest in other babies. Around 9 to 10 months, they attend to mother's cooperation in tasks such as playing with toys in which earlier they had interacted with the objects with no concomitant social awareness. At the end of infancy, most babies have gained substantial social competence, and are prepared to participate in the conventions of the local society (Trevarthen, 1984).

The major vehicle for cultural transmission is language, and the human brain shows an early propensity for specialized processing of speech information, in the left hemisphere. It has long been clear to neuropsychologists that a central question in human brain development is the neural mechanisms of language acquisition. Yet even in the first weeks and months of life, before skill in language is required, the infant must become competent in emotional communication. The ability to participate in processes of play and affectional interaction may be a key determinant of both information flow and the brain arousal that help to shape developing neural networks. Furthermore, the experiences with self-regulation of arousal state and attentional mechanisms gained through early play and affective exchanges may form the foundation for continued development of attentional and cognitive skills (Rothbart & Derryberry 1981). Through adult guidance of experiences with emotional arousal and behavioral inhibition, the child develops patterns of emotional reactivity and self-regulation that form the basis of approach and avoidance strategies in later development (Rothbart, 1989).

In traditional accounts of psychological development, emotional communication often seems taken for granted, as if it were reflexive or automatic. Although there are probably innate capacities for producing and reacting to primitive emotional displays, it is becoming clear that successful social development requires a high degree of skill in negotiating emotional communication, much of which is nonverbal (Denckla, 1986). Just as verbal communication appears to require specialized regions of the cortex, emotional information may also engage specialized neural networks in humans, within the right hemisphere. In right-handed adults, right hemisphere lesions impair both the expression and comprehension of nonverbal emotional communications, for both tone of voice and facial display (Borod, Koff, & Buck, 1986; Ross & Rush, 1981). Research with normals, using lateralized stimulus presentation, has shown a similar right hemisphere superiority for dealing with emotional materials (reviewed by Buck, 1984; Tucker & Frederick, 1989). The greater intensity of emotional facial expressions observed on the left side of the face in adults (Dopson, Beckwith, Tucker, & Bullard-Bates, 1985; Sackeim, Gur, & Saucy 1978) may also reflect right hemisphere specialization for emotional processes.

However, in infants emotional expressions may be more intense on the right side of the face (Best 1986; Rothbart, Taylor, & Tucker, 1989). In attempting to interpret this unexpected finding, Rothbart et al. pointed out that an important trend in early brain maturation is cortical inhibition of primitive subcortical reflexes (Brodal, 1969). With facial expressions specifically, cortical damage may disinhibit emotional expressions on the contralateral side of the face (Monrad-Krohn, 1924). Furthermore, there have been several suggestions that the right hemisphere matures more rapidly in infancy than the left (reviewed by Tucker, 1986). Therefore, one possibility is that the early maturing cortex of the right hemisphere may gain more inhibitory cortical control over subcortical facial displays than the relatively immature cortex of the left hemisphere.

Early maturation of the right hemisphere would be consistent with the importance of emotional communication in early life. In the second year, the child's increasing motor competence and rapid development of language skills suggests a major transition in brain maturation, with a shift toward left hemisphere dominance (Tucker, 1989). There may be a neuropsychological basis for the emotional characteristics of these developmental transitions. The negativism and autonomy strivings of the 2-year old seem to appear at about the same time as the signs of rapid left hemisphere cognitive and motor development. This may reflect a shift from a close attentional as well as emotional dependence on the social environment, mediated by the right hemisphere, toward increasing articulation of cognitive and motor control, and increasing emotional and attentional autonomy, as the functional role of the left hemisphere is established (Tucker, 1989).

Thus what appears to be maturational shift in hemispheric dominance may be superimposed on a gradient of increasing cortical control over subcortical processes. At this point in our knowledge, a neuropsychological theory of early emotional development needs to explain how the neocortex in each hemisphere interacts with more primitive subcortical mechanisms. The evidence from adults seems to show that, although the analytic cognition of the left hemisphere may play an important role in dealing with emotional experience (Buck & Duffy, 1980; Tucker & Newman, 1981), the cognitive processes that relate most closely with elementary emotional processes are those of the right hemisphere. This raises a key theoretical question. Does the right hemisphere somehow incorporate a greater degree of subcortical activity in its processing of emotional information?

Human neuropsychology often seems to suffer from "cortical chauvinism," the tendency to localize psychological faculties to cortical areas without understanding the functional dependence of neocortex on subcortical structures (Wood, 1986). The increasing evidence that the two hemispheres may be influenced differentially by emotional processes suggests that clearer concepts of cortical-subcortical relations may be important not just to understanding emotion, but to understanding both the psychological and physiological mechanisms of hemispheric specialization.

CONCEPTS OF HEMISPHERIC SPECIALIZATION

Because the language functions of the left hemisphere were the first sign of the psychological specialization of the hemispheres, the initial concepts of brain lateralization attempted to account for the phenomena of right handedness and left hemisphere dominance. Although it has often seemed to be assumed that language is an irreducible higher function, Kimura (1977) proposed that left hemisphere specialization for speech was due to a more basic left hemisphere specialization for complex motor functions. This view contrasted with the traditional interpretation that greater apraxia after left hemisphere lesions reflects a loss of the verbal control of movement. Much of the research on hemispheric specialization has taken a descriptive approach, attempting to characterize the psychological differences between the hemispheres. Yet there have also been attempts, such as Kimura's, to speculate on the neural mechanisms that might underly the observed differences.

Cognitive Models

Although most studies of hemispheric specialization have emphasized cognitive rather than emotional processes, the theoretical explanations from the cognitive studies may help address the issue of whether the basic differences between the hemispheres in representing information may figure in their differential involvement in emotional processes. It is particularly relevant that the right hemisphere's unique cognitive processes are receiving increasing attention.

Communication and Representation. In theorizing on hemispheric contributions to verbal and nonverbal communication (Tucker, 1986), I considered different hemispheric contributions to the form of the mental representation in the communication process. In its handling of language information, the left hemisphere manipulates words, discrete codes that substitute for culturally shared meaning, and that can be structured according to the regularized rules of syntax. The structured and sequential processing that may be possible with a "descriptive system" (Goldberg & Costa, 1981) like language may not be possible with nonverbal mental representations. These representations, for which the right hemisphere appears to be specialized, may be described as analogical. The representation is an analog of the perceptual experience, rather than an arbitrary code for it. It may be that as a child processes nonverbal communications, such as the father's tone of voice, the continuous, analogical representation will have an affective immediacy that does not accompany verbal representations.

In many findings on hemispheric cognitive and perceptual differences, the nature of the information does not seem as important as how it will be organized. The left hemisphere may excel with nonverbal information if it is to be analyzed, whereas the right hemisphere's perceptual skills are most strong when synthetic or holistic organization is required (Levy, 1969; Nebes, 1978). Similarly, in processing information over time, the left hemisphere has been found to deal in a sequential fashion, whereas the right hemisphere may be better able to represent multiple information channels in parallel (Bradshaw & Nettleton, 1981). Emotional experience has often been seen as requiring the ability to synthesize various forms of information, interoceptive as well as exteroceptive, into a unified percept (Safer & Leventhal, 1977). In the young child's perception of nonverbal communication, the right hemisphere's holistic representation may provide a syncretic fusion of sensory experience with the current affective state (Tucker, 1986).

Metric Representations. Although recent models of hemispheric processing in cognitive psychology have not dealt explicitly with emotion or social interactions, they may provide additional ways of thinking about the component operations which the young child's brain is acquiring in dealing with the tasks of early life. Consistent with the idea that hemispheric differences are concerned less with the specific information than with how it will be organized, recent models have emphasized both the left hemisphere's role in certain kinds of imagery, and the right hemisphere's role in certain aspects of language comprehension.

The superior spatial skills of the right hemisphere have led to the assumption that the right hemisphere is specialized for visual imagery. Yet certain imagery tasks may be performed better by the left hemisphere (Farah, Gazzaniga, Holtzman, & Kosslyn, 1985). In reviewing evidence from both normals and commisurotomy patients, Kosslyn proposes that the right hemisphere's special role in processing visual imagery is limited to operations dealing with the spatial coordinates of the parts of the image (Kosslyn, 1987, 1988). These operations are performed on what Kosslyn describes as metric representations, which seem to retain physical relations among the parts of the original perception. This form of mental content would appear similar to the analogical representation described above. In contrast, the left hemisphere has been found to make the greater contribution when the information used in forming images is categorical rather than metric.

Lateral Inhibition. Although severe language impairment is consistently associated with left hemisphere lesions in right handers, there may be subtle language deficits in right hemisphere lesioned patients as well, particularly when understanding the general meaning of a story or passage is required (Cicone, 1980; Ostrove, Simpson, & Garder, 1990). In experiments with normals that present a word that primes or facilitates responses to related words, left visual field (right) hemisphere presentation may result in more unusual associations showing priming effects, whereas right field (left hemisphere) presentation seems to prime the dominant association only (Burgess & Simpson, 1988).

These findings suggest not only that the right hemisphere may contribute to language comprehension, but that the two hemispheres may have differently organized semantic memories. In reviewing this evidence, Beeman (in preparation) proposes a theoretical model that could explain the differences. The left hemisphere may apply a greater degree of lateral inhibition at the word level. This would cause the word that is most strongly activated to suppress or inhibit access to related words. In contrast, the right hemisphere, without such strong lateral inhibition, would spread semantic activation over a broader range of related items.

Orienting and Routinizing. The cognitive models of hemispheric specialization are largely descriptive of the functions of the adult brain, and do not address developmental processes that may be involved in creating these functions. The theoretical approach of Goldberg and Costa (1981), however, is explicitly developmental in the sense that it specifies a sequence of hemispheric contributions in the process of learning. Initial orienting to novel information is facilitated by the right hemisphere's holistic cognition. As the information becomes integrated, the relevant mental operations become more systematized and routinized. Goldberg and Costa propose that language is the prime example of a set of regularized mental operations, a descriptive system. Yet they propose that the left hemisphere's contribution to cognition can be understood to be more general than just language; it is responsible for actualizing any problem-solving task into a well-ordered set of routinized cognitive operations. Because most experiences are novel for a young child, the course of ontogeny could be seen as a progression from mostly right hemisphere orienting in childhood to mostly left hemisphere routinizing in adulthood.

Neural Mechanisms

Some basis for hemispheric specialization appears to be innate. Yet the process of lateralization of function occurs during the course of the brain's psychological development. The task of explaining hemispheric specialization in ontogeny is thus complex, since the explanation must begin with mechanisms producing an asymmetry in embryologic differentiation, and proceed to account for the functional interaction between the two hemispheres in integrated cognitive activity. Roger Sperry's theory of chemoaffinity, developed from his studies of retinotectal mapping in the goldfish embryo, became the accepted view of neuron migration in brain differentiation (Purves & Lichtman, 1985). Sperry's Nobel prize, however, was for his more recent experimental studies of commisurotomy patients, providing dramatic demonstrations of each hemisphere's specialized cognitive functions (Sperry, Gazzaniga & Bogfen, 1969; Sperry, 1977).

Core Brain Vectors of Adaptive Differentiation. In considering hemispheric development from a perspective suitable to the scope of Sperry's work, Trevarthen proposed that inherent asymmetries of core brain activating systems may guide the functional differentiation of the left and right hemispheres (Trevarthen, in press). As the spontaneous activity in fetal motor circuits begins to be regulated by sensory feedback and control, an important form of regulation is exerted by the neuromodulator-specific reticular activating systems of the brainstem (Trevarthen, in press). Thus as functional circuits are forming in the embryonic brain, the integration of sensation and action depends on an appropriately controlled state of arousal.

Trevarthen points out that activation control mechanisms are also crucial to regulating the plasticity of synapses in the process of competitive elimination. It is this process that will differentiate neocortical networks and give the young brain its great information-representation ability. In the development of ocular dominance columns, for example, the capacity for plasticity is lost if the noradrenergic and cholinergic neuromodulator projection systems do not maintain an appropriate degree of excitability in the cortex (Singer, 1987). The Hebbian correlation between synapse function and activity of the postsynaptic neuron appears to determine the process of competitive elimination of synapses. Several findings suggest that the neuromodulator systems gate this process of synapse formation as a function of the organism's current adaptive state (Gold & Zornetzer, 1983).

The embryological mechanisms of chemoaffinity appear to impart only a general sketch of the brain's anatomical structure. Trevarthen argues that there must be a way of regulating the highly flexible mechanisms of synaptic plasticity if the eventual anatomy of the neocortex is to be achieved from the rudimentary genetic plan. As they guide the differentiation of cortical synapses, the core brain projection systems may act as adaptive control vectors, insuring that the process of differentiation remains coherent with the more primitive, genetically-specified sensorimotor circuitry. Given the evidence that the major neuromodulator projection systems in the human brain may differentially innervate the left and right hemispheres (Tucker & Williamson, 1984), Trevarthen speculates that processes determining emotional activation and arousal, such as parental communication and play, could be essential to the growth and education of the cerebral hemispheres.

Self-Regulation Through Activation and Arousal. Williamson and I (Tucker & Williamson, 1984) reviewed the evidence that the neurochemically-specific projection pathways of the reticular activating system are asymmetric in humans. Although the functional significance of this evidence is still a matter of speculation, this evidence seems relevant to the asymmetric hemisphere function observed in psychiatric conditions such as schizophrenia and depression which are thought to be associated with abnormal neurotransmitter function (Flor-Henry, & Gruzelier 1983). This evidence may also be relevant to suggestions that each hemisphere of normal persons may be sensitive to a particular affect dimension, the left hemisphere becoming engaged in anxiety states (Tyler & Tucker, 1982) and the right hemisphere becoming more engaged in elation and impaired in depression (Tucker, 1981; Tucker, Stenslie, Roth, & Shearer, 1981).

In developing a theoretical model that might account for these phenomena,

Williamson and I pointed out that lateralization is not entirely orthogonal to the anterior/posterior dimension of brain organization. Consistent with the work of Kimura (Kimura, 1977) and others, we emphasized the left hemisphere's specialization for motor control, and hypothesized that this would entail a close relation with the adaptive mechanisms of motor readiness such as the fight/flight reaction. This link to motor readiness could account for the augmenting of left hemisphere cognitive operations in anxiety.

The neural mechanisms of motor readiness were described by Pribram and McGuinness (1975) as supported by a tonic activation system, a system that supports brain preparedness by maintaining a steady activating influence. Williamson and I argued that this system may have dopamine pathways as a major control device, and that it may be particular important to the attentional mechanisms of the left hemisphere. Other aspects of alerting, such as in the orienting response, may be supported by a more phasic arousal mechanism that has the locus coeruleus noradrenergic pathways as its primary neuromodulator. We suggested that the phasic arousal system may be integral to the right hemisphere's skills in spatial orienting. Each of these systems thus has unique attentional effects, but each has emotional and motivational qualities as well. Tonic activation may be a neural substrate of anxiety and hostility. Phasic arousal may be strongly engaged in elation and relatively weak in a depressed emotional state.

There are several theoretical deductions about tonic and phasic controls on attention and working memory that might be consistent with the idea of their differential support of the two hemisphere's cognitive processes. The effect of tonic activation would be enhanced redundancy in the processing of information. In the time domain this would serve as a bias against change. Changes that did occur would then require substantial determination, facilitating a sequential ordering of thought and behavior such as may be found for the left hemisphere. In contrast, the reactivity to novelty produced by the habituation bias of the phasic arousal system would facilitate the right hemisphere's orienting to multiple parallel sensory channels, but at the expense of internal consistency in attention.

In the spatial domain, the redundancy bias of tonic activation would cause a few elements in working memory to receive extended and thus thorough representation. This could support the left hemisphere's focal attention (Kinsbourne, 1970), and perhaps its capacity for routinized cognitive operations as well (Goldberg & Costa, 1981). When it becomes exaggerated as in states of chronic anxiety, the redundancy bias may result in cognitive and behavioral stereotypies such as obsessions and compulsions (Rapoport, 1989). As the habituation bias acts as a negative feedback on the processing of each element in working memory, many more elements of information may be selected for attention. The result is an expansive model of attention and memory access, which may be observed in states of manic elation (Shaw, Mann, Stokes, & Manevitz, 1986). This mode may facilitate the right hemisphere's holistic concepts in verbal semantics as well as spatial visualization.

In our efforts to understand hemispheric differences in elementary attentional controls, Williamson and I found that our theoretical model included features of emotion and cognition within the same constructs. At the elementary level of tonic activation, for example, a focusing of attention may occur automatically when a state of vigilance is engaged by threat or hostility. Conversely, if the cognitive task at hand requires focused attention, this may not be possible unless a certain degree of anxiety can be recruited. In considering how the child's cerebral hemispheres are responding to the information processing demands imposed by emotional communication and language, concepts of asymmetric activation and arousal mechanisms could suggest how each hemisphere's engagement, and activity-dependent differentiation, might be facilitated by its characteristic state of emotional and motivational self-regulation (Trevarthen, in press; Tucker, 1989).

Asymmetries of Cortico-Limbic Connections. Although the constructs of tonic activation and phasic arousal are framed in terms of primitive cybernetics—habituation to input information, redundancy in output circuits—the important effects of these control systems are seen in working memory. There are intriguing indications that neuromodulator pathways alter the process of memory consolidation, and some suggestions that this might be responsive to specific features of the animal's current adaptive strivings (Gold & Zornetzer, 1983). Yet the control of memory is unlikely to be explained solely by diffuse modulatory projection systems. The evidence from animal studies and human lesion cases shows that the neocortex is dependent on commerce with limbic structures in the formation of memory traces (Squire, 1987). Could this cortico-limbic interaction be asymmetric?

Evidence that this may be the case has come from research on temporal lobe epilepsy (Bear & Fedio, 1977). Because limbic structures and the adjacent limbic cortex are particularly excitable electrophysiologically, seizure activity in the neocortex tends to develop a focus in the limbic system. Patients with a seizure focus in the right hemisphere are observed to be emotionally labile, although on self-report measures these patients deny problems and present themselves in a favorable light (Bear & Fedio, 1977). Patients with a left seizure focus show an emphasis on ideational rather than affective concerns, yet they are not entirely unemotional. They may show exaggerated intellectualization and hyperreligiousity. Furthermore, the left temporal epileptics show an opposite self-description bias from the right focus patients, tending to emphasize their shortcomings in relation to the evaluation of objective raters.

Bear and Fedio (1977) theorize that these psychological characteristics may reflect a functional hyperconnection between neocortical and limbic structures that occurs over time with the seizure disorder. Not only is the right hemisphere's contribution to emotional functioning exaggerated with a right seizure focus; the more abstract, verbally-mediated cognitive processes of the left hemisphere also seem to become strongly infused with personal, affective significance due to an exaggerated limbic involvement in the neocortex's mental operations.

Developing these questions of cortico-limbic interaction further, Bear (1983) included not only the left/right division of the neocortex, but the dorsal and ventral pathways that appear to provide differing routes for elaborating sensory information on its way to the limbic system. Studies of monkeys have shown that a dorsal pathway, from visual cortex through parietal regions and into hippocampus, supports peripheral vision and memory for spatial location (Ungerleider & Mishkin, 1982). In contrast, a ventral pathway, from occipital lobe through inferior temporal regions to the amygdala, seems to support the elaboration of foveal vision. The higher capacities emergent from this pathway seem to include the ability to conjoin features of objects independent of their physical location, and the ability to retain specific objects in memory (Ungerleider & Mishkin, 1982).

Although most accounts of limbic control of emotion emphasize the amygdala (LeDoux, 1987), and thus would seem to implicate the ventral pathway, Bear proposes that an important feature of human emotion has been the specialization of the right hemisphere for the functions of the dorsal pathway. Citing evidence of the right hemisphere's role in orienting attention, Bear suggests that the dorsal pathway may support the right hemisphere's "emotional surveillance." In its role of orienting attention to the emotional significance of events, Bear suggests that the right hemisphere may be particularly integrated with the limbic system. In contrast, the left hemisphere may have become specialized for nonlimbic cortico-cortical connections that integrate information across sensory modalities. Although in the left temporal lobe epileptics the seizure disorder may produce an exaggerated limbic infusion of the left hemisphere's cognition, in normal persons the decreased limbic involvement in the left hemisphere's representations may allow its verbal ideation to be less constrained by emotions.

A counterpart to Bear's ideas about lateralization and neocortical pathways has been offered by Derryberry and I in an account of motivational influences on attention (Tucker & Derryberry, in press). We proposed that in addition to a right hemisphere specialization for the spatial location information of the dorsal pathway, the left hemisphere may have a corresponding specialization for the object-formation functions of the ventral corticolimbic pathway. Many of the findings on left hemisphere cognitive specialization, including the parsing of speech objects in language comprehension, would be consistent with a strong reliance on object-formation skills. Furthermore, the affective and motivational characteristics of the ventral neocortical pathways are consistent with the notion that the left hemisphere is preferentially activated in states of anxiety or hostility. The limbic target of the ventral pathways is the amygdala, which seems to exert the primary limbic control over fear and hostility. The paleocortical extensions from the amygdala, in the temporal pole and orbital frontal lobe, have been found to be important to motivational processes in animal single unit studies

(Rolls, 1987), and to anxiety states in human neuroimaging studies (Johanson, Risberg, Silfverskiold, & Smith, 1986; Reiman, Fusselman, Fox, & Raichle, 1989). Particularly through the elaboration of ventral limbic processes in the orbital frontal cortex, the left hemisphere may be particularly important to integrating motivational dispositions within the frontal executive functions of planning and self-regulation (Tucker & Derryberry, in press).

More or Less Distributed Representations. Because it was thought that the hemispheres were anatomically symmetrical, early concepts of lateralization assumed that hemispheric specialization occurred without a tangible physical substrate. Yet as improved anatomical imaging became available with computer tomography in the 1970s (Galaburda, LeMay, Kemper, & Geschwind, 1978), it became clear that anatomical asymmetries must be explained by any comprehensive theory of lateral specialization.

An early effort to speculate on the anatomical basis for hemispheric specialization was made by Semmes (1968). She reasoned from evidence on lateralized patterns of somatosensory and motor deficits to propose different patterns of receptotopic distribution of information within the two hemispheres. For both the ipsilateral and contralateral hands, Semmes's studies showed that focal left hemisphere lesions tended to produce focal sensory and motor deficits. In contrast, equally focal right hemisphere lesions did not, and instead produced less specific functional impairments. Semmes deduced the implication of these differential locus-function specificities for the distribution of information across the cortex. Because of its greater locus-function specificity, a given parcel of cortical tissue in the left hemisphere would tend to contain *like* informational elements—things that are related to the same function. In the right hemisphere, on the other hand, elements at a given location would tend to contain *unlike* informational elements—things that are related to diverse functions. Although in the language of cognitive science both cortices would involve parallel distributed information representation, Semmes's data suggests that representations may be distributed more broadly across the right hemisphere's networks than across those of the left.

In their formulation of hemispheric development, Goldberg and Costa (1981) reviewed evidence that several areas of primary and secondary sensory cortex are more extensive in the left hemisphere than the right. One example is the posterior portion of the superior temporal gyrus that supports speech functions. Another is the occipital pole supporting vision (Galaburda et al., 1978). Goldberg and Costa suggested that these features of left hemisphere anatomy imply a more general anatomical pattern than specialization for language functions. The left hemisphere appears to have highly developed areas for processing each sensory modality.

If this is true, then because the total area of posterior cortical tissue is about the same on the left and the right, the right hemisphere must have a greater development of tissue specialized for cross-modal processing. In the frontal regions, the greater width for the right frontal lobe (Galaburda et al., 1978) could be accounted for by multimodal associative areas. These several asymmetries suggested to Goldberg and Costa that the left hemisphere's specialization entails complex processing of single sensory modalities, such as may be required in language comprehension, or complex control of discrete motor acts, as in speech articulation. In contrast, the right hemisphere's greater cross-modal integration would support its holistic representations in complex cognitive functions as well as in spatial orientation. This view would be consistent with Semmes's proposal that the right hemisphere's diffuse receptotopic architecture allows it to combine sensory information to achieve a "single supramodal space."

Research with anatomical and physiological measurements of the two hemispheres in intact brains has also been consistent with Semmes's views. Gur and associates (Gur et al., 1980) examined the differential clearance of inhaled Xenon that is due to differential blood flow clearance from gray and white matter in normal humans. They observed a greater ratio of white to gray matter in the right hemisphere than the left. A greater proportion of white matter implies that right neocortical tissue has a more dense pattern of axonal interconnections among its regions. Such a pattern could support the integration of *unlike* elements proposed for the right hemisphere by Semmes. Using measures of spectral coherence from a multichannel electroencephalogram, my associates and I hypothesized that Semmes's model would predict greater coherence among right hemisphere channels (Tucker, Roth, & Bair, 1986). Analysis of multiple coherence measures (between each channel and all others) supported this hypothesis for a sample of normal male subjects.

Examining children ages 5 to 16, Thatcher, Krause, and Rhybyk (1986) confirmed the presence of higher EEG coherence among channels from the right hemisphere than among those from the left. By partitioning coherence into long distance and local compartments, Thatcher et al showed that posterior brain areas appear to be dominated by local connections, whereas the variance in frontal EEG channels seems more constrained by long distance connections. In studying developmental changes in EEG coherence and phase, a hemispheric asymmetry was observed in frontal lobe connection patterns, with greater local coherence for right frontal regions than the left (Thatcher, Walker, & Guidice, 1987).

Thus on functional as well as anatomical grounds, there appear to be basic differences between the left and right hemisphere neocortices in the representation of sensory, motor, and cognitive processes. On both sides, the neocortical networks show parallel distributed representation of psychological processes. But in the rapid expansion of neocortex in hominid evolution, the left hemisphere seems to have become somewhat less distributed and perhaps less parallel than the right. As neuropsychology adopts the connectionist metaphor, the cortex is being reinterpreted as comprised of distributed networks, rather than localized centers (Damasio, 1989). If one hemisphere has its representations more distributed than the other, it may be important to develop a clearer understanding of this asymmetry of connectional architecture.

Psychological Embryology. The study of hemispheric specialization has provided the clearest evidence yet that specific neural systems can be identified with complex psychological domains. Trevarthen's (in press) speculations on the development of lateralization suggest a way of spanning the gap between the mechanisms of developmental neuroscience and the processes of communication and acculturation in psychological development. Innate lateral gradients in the brain may be formed by asymmetric activation and arousal systems. As these control systems facilitate the interconnection of sensory and motor patterns, they may do so differentially in each hemisphere, such that the process of synaptogenesis and connectional pruning takes on different forms on the two sides of the brain. To understand how this might occur requires an appreciation of hemispheric differences in several aspects of neuropsychological development, including regulation by elementary emotional activation and arousal systems, the formation of asymmetric cortico-limbic interactions, and the articulation of different strategies of network architecture in the two hemispheres. To consider the implications of these network strategies, and how they might be achieved in ontogenesis, it is necessary to examine the architecture of the neocortex in more detail. Recent anatomical studies with monkeys and humans have provided new insight into the patterns of connections among neocortical regions, and into the patterns of connections between neocortical regions and the limbic structures from which they evolved.

NETWORK ARCHITECTURE OF THE CORTEX

Early studies of the cortex showed that certain areas would, when stimulated, produce a muscular action, and other areas, when lesioned, would impair a specific sensory modality. Still other areas of the cortex were "silent." Later studies showed that some areas of silent cortex responded to several sensory modalities, leading to the concept of "association" cortex. Areas of the parietal lobe were seen to associate the perceptual modalities into more complex representations, and areas of the frontal lobe were seen to associate external perceptions with internal motivational states to regulate motor behavior. This traditional view of information processing in the brain (Pandya et al., 1988) is essentially a hierarchic model, in which control is exerted from the top of the hierarchy. It has been consistent with the view in psychology that mental processes operate on representational nodes constructed from combinations of more elementary sensory data.

In addition to the subcortical connections for sensory input and motor output, executive cognitive processes at the top of the cortical hierarchy must be informed of internal need states by connections from subcortical regions, and they must oversee the activating influences from brainstem centers. Furthermore, because of the extensive connections between frontal cortex and paralimbic cortex, anatomists since Papez (1937) have appreciated that corticolimbic routes must be important to interactions between cognition and emotion. A proposal for how such interactions might occur was offered by Nauta (1971), who suggested that the frontal lobes may preset limbic structures according to the expected emotional outcome of a behavioral plan, thus initializing affective monitoring mechanisms that can guide behavior.

Even when subcortical relations are included, the traditional model of the brain is a top-down model, with control exerted by the higher regions. Kinsbourne (1982) has argued that this architecture would eventually result in a "pontifical neuron" at the top of the hierarchy, directing all others. Particularly for understanding brain development, an adequate model must include bottom-up as well as top-down control. The question is how the growing brain can self-organize its executive functions when it begins life guided only by elementary adaptive controls. Recent anatomical studies have provided new perspectives on this issue, by showing that limbic circuits and their paralimbic cortices form the organizing base for developing cortical networks.

The Mammalian Primordia

In reptiles, the general cortex grows as a sheet connecting the hippocampal cortex (archicortex) and the olfactory piriform cortex (paleocortex) (Fuster, 1980). In the evolution of the mammalian brain, this general cortex became successively differentiated from these two primordial points of origin—the archicortex as the dorsal source and the paleocortex as the ventral source. Sanides (1970) discovered that tracing the evolutionary progression of the cortex from these two sources provided a simple and coherent explanation for the variety of cytoarchitectonic features of the primate neocortex. Students of the brain have believed for many years that cortical architectonics, the characterization of microanatomical features of cortex and its layers, could be used to define functionally distinct areas of cortex. Yet before Sanides's realization, architectonic studies such as Brodman's (Fig. 3.1) had been conducted in piecemeal fashion, with little appreciation for the general plan of an evolved neocortex (Pandya, et al., 1988).

Within each of the archicortical and paleocortical trends, a more differentiated cortical region first appeared as a specialized region in the center of existing cortex. Then with further evolution and neocortical expansion, the next wave of differentiation appeared within that. This pattern suggested to Sanides (1970) that the cortex has evolved through a series of "growth rings." Unlike the rings of a tree, which grow at the perimeter, the neocortical rings were formed as

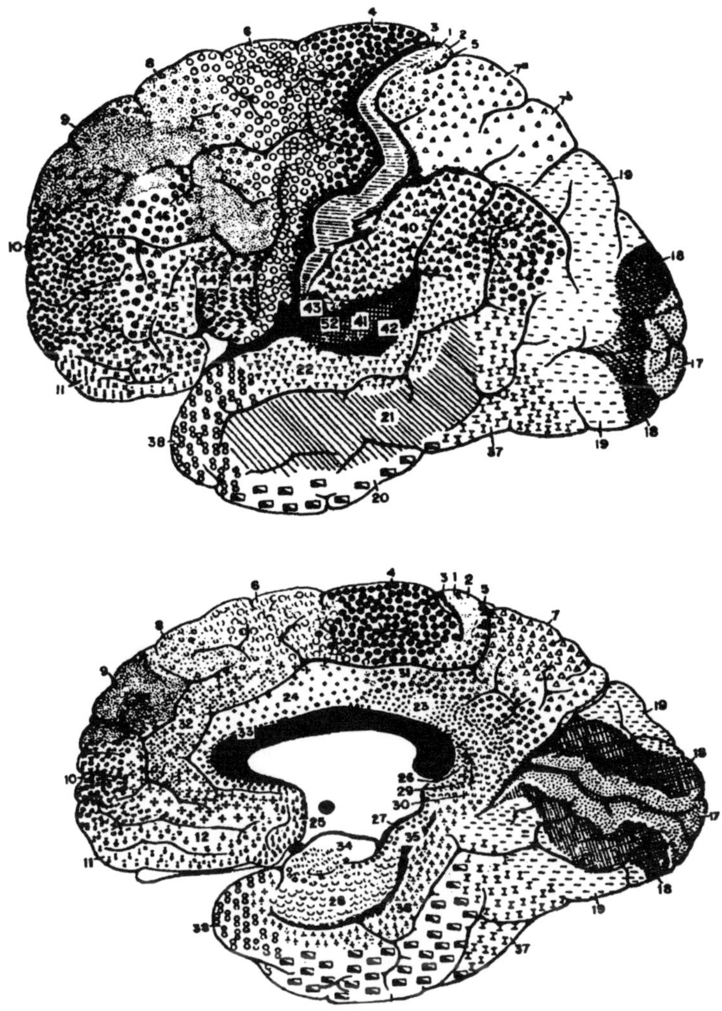

FIG. 3.1. Cytoarchitectonic areas of human brain described by Brodman (1909).

successive new foci of network differentiation evolved at the center of the previous focus, thus expanding the neocortex like a bubble, with successively more primitive cortical versions stretched out between the most recent, articulated layer and the archicortical or paleocortical limbic origin. Figure 3.2 shows how specialized network foci for sensory modalities and motor function may have appeared within the primitive general cortex. Figure 3.3 shows the paleocortical architectonic trend for the auditory modality in monkey, with increasingly differentiated cortex proceeding from the temporal pole caudally along the superior

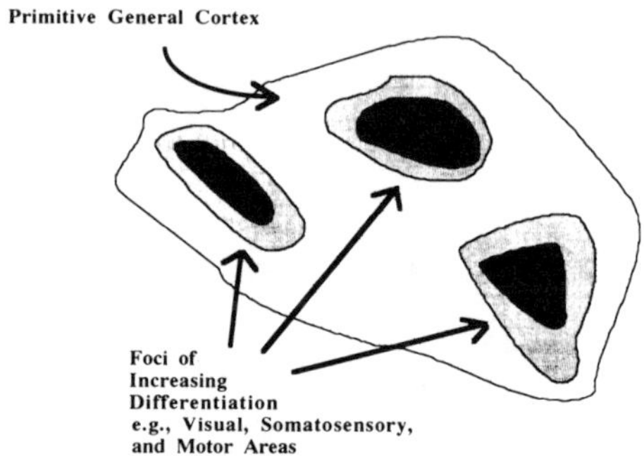

FIG. 3.2. Schematic of progressive differentiation of cortical growth rings within the primitive general cortex.

temporal sulcus. Schematic examples of possible shapes taken by successive growth rings in a given modality are suggested in Fig. 3.4.

Two Moieties of Architectonic Differentiation

Within each of the archicortical and paleocortical moieties of the cortex, evolution has produced increasing articulation of the cell layers in each new ring of the cortex (Sanides, 1970). Within the archicortical trend, the pyramidal cells of layer III became prominent. Within the paleocortical trend, there is greater development of the granular cells of layer IV (Eidelberg & Galaburda, 1984). Within both moieties, more recently evolved cortex shows a decrease in the

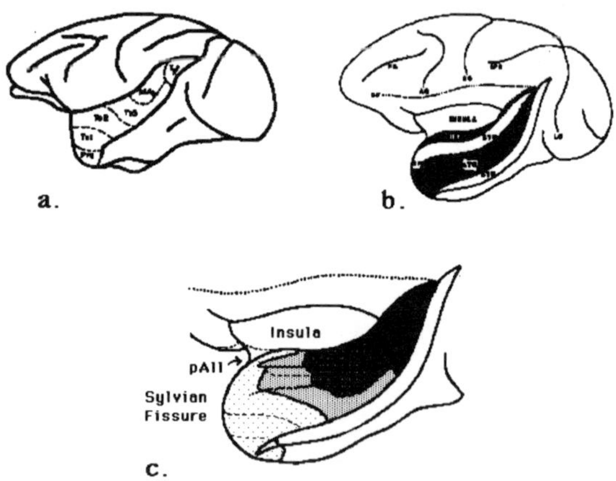

FIG. 3.3. Schematic of architectonic areas of auditory cortex. (a) cytoarchitectonic areas in superior temporal lobe. (b) temporal lobe opened out and down to reveal inner bank of superior temporal sulcus. (c) progression of increasing differentiation from paleocortex to temporal pole (light shading) to posterior superior temporal sulcus (darker shading). After Pandya and Yeterian (1985).

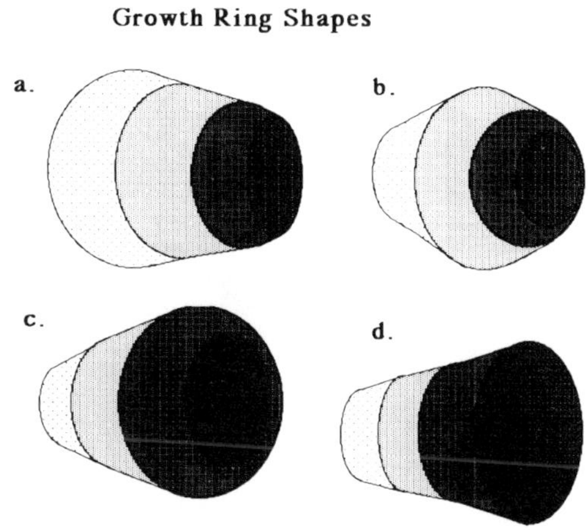

FIG. 3.4. Possible shapes taken by growth rings in a given modality due to relative sizes of various layers.

lower, infragranular layers V and VI, and an increase in the supragranular layers I, II, III, and IV.

Archicortical Phylogenesis. In premammalian evolution, the archicortex formed the primitive cortical anlage associated with the hippocampus. It gave rise in its center to more differentiated cortical tissue, termed the periarchicortex. This became the first growth ring of the cortex when a more differentiated network evolved within its center, which became the proisocortex. In more complex brains, the proisocortex became the second growth ring of the dorsal trend as it produced in its center the isocortex, which in primates corresponds to the supplementary motor area and the "true," medial, supplementary visual area (Sanides, 1970). In the higher mammals, a fourth center focus of differentiation appeared, producing the finely differentiated lamina of the koniocortex, making up the primary sensory and motor cortices. Within this dorsal, archicortical trend, primary sensory cortices evolved for the visual and the somatosensory modalities.

The large pyramidal cells of layer III are found throughout the dorsal trend, such as from the primary visual cortex through the parietal lobe as connections traverse each growth ring to reach the hippocampus (Fig. 3.5). A similar progression of connections proceeds from the dorsal moiety of somatosensory cortex to hippocampus. From the anterior cingulate on the medial surface of the hemispheres, through the supplementary motor area and over the dorsal surface of the frontal lobe to the primary motor cortex, the increasing articulation of the pyramidal layer results in the familiar pyramidal motor cortex (Fig. 3.6).

Paleocortical Phylogenesis. Evolving from the olfactory paleocortex, this ventral division of the neocortex eventually contributed to primary sensory cortices in visual, somatosensory, and auditory modalities, as well as to orbital and

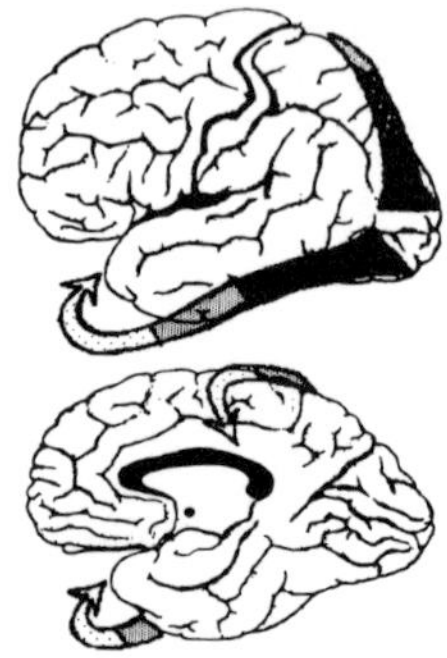

FIG. 3.5. Model of distribution of distribution of cytoarchitectonic levels in human visual system. Most differentiated cortex in primary visual area projects in dorsal trend toward cingulate cortex and hippocampus, and in ventral trend toward paleocortex and amygdala.

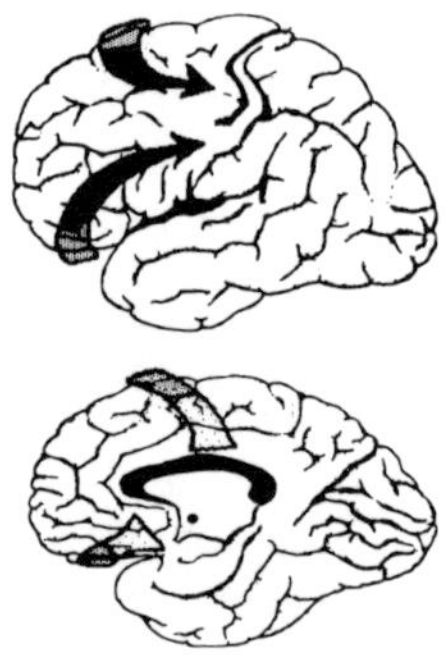

FIG. 3.6. Model of distribution of cytoarchitectonic levels in human motor system. Projections to most differentiated cortex in primary motor area originate in dorsal trend from cingulate cortex and in ventral trend from orbital cortex.

lateral frontal cortex. The visual pathway in the ventral trend proceeds from primary visual cortex in the occipital lobe through the inferior temporal lobe to reach the paleocortex (Pandya & Yeterian, 1985; Fig. 3.5). The portion of the primary somatosensory cortex derived from the paleocortical trend represents the neck, head, and face regions, while that from the archicortical trend represents the lower body. Unlike the other cortical modalities, primary auditory cortex appears to arise solely from the paleocortical trend.

In the frontal lobe, the orbital cortex extends the ventral trend from the anterior temporal pole and the insula, providing the neocortical representation of visceral and autonomic processes (Mesulam & Mufson, 1982). This trend extends from the orbital surface laterally around the frontal lobe to terminate in the koniocortex of the more ventral areas of the primary motor cortex, controlling the neck, head, and face (Barbas & Pandya, 1989; Fig. 3.6).

Given the importance of facial displays to emotional communication, it is interesting to note that the facial muscles derive embryologically from the gill arches, which in fish are solely concerned with respiration. Thus facial motor control is often considered to arise from the "visceral nervous system" (Rinn, 1984), which in the evolutionary view is seen to arise from paleocortical origins.

Connectional Structure

The evolutionary perspective has clarified not only the pattern of differentiation in neocortial cytoarchitectonics, but the patterns of connections among regions of the neocortex. These patterns may reveal the neocortex's functional systems. Drawing from the studies of Pandya and his associates with rhesus monkeys (Barbas & Pandya, 1989; Pandya et al., 1988; Pandya & Yeterian, 1984; Pandya et al., 1985; Yeterian & Pandya, 1988), several principles of neocortical connections can be summarized.

Intrinsic Connections. Connections within the pathway from a primary sensory cortex to limbic cortex are mostly local, between a ring and its adjacent neighbors. Thus a processing progression is implied, as sensory information reaches the limbic targets only through transformation through the network representational pattern of each more primitive ring of cortex.

Furthermore, this processing progression goes both ways. The assumption is often made that the information flow is one-directional, from primary sensory cortex to the limbic system. Yet the fact that there are equally extensive cortico-cortical connections in the opposite direction, from primitive to recent rings, must be included in any theory of cortical function (Pandya et al., 1988). There is a regular pattern to the inter-laminar projections between adjacent rings. The "forward" projections, from sensory to limbic, originate in supragranular layers of the more differentiated cortex and project to layer IV of the more primitive cortex. The "back" projections originate in the infragranular layers V and VI of the more primitive cortex and terminate in the superficial layers I and II of the more differentiated cortex (Pandya et al., 1988; Figure 3.7). Thus, if the general flow of information in the posterior brain is from sensory cortices to limbic regions, such extensive back projections must cause this flow to be quite turbulent.

Extrinsic Connections. The extrinsic or long-distance connections of the cortex, those that extend beyond the ring-to-ring boundaries, show a patterning that is also defined by the evolutionary trends. First, these connections are more

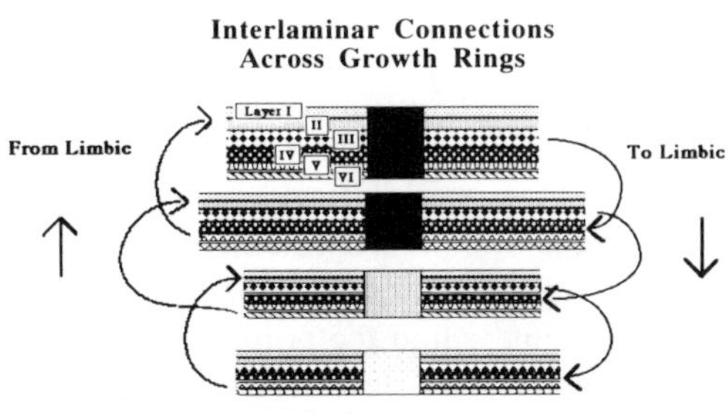

FIG. 3.7. Pattern of projections between adjacent cytoarchitectonic areas. In the direction from sensory cortex to paralimbic cortex, projections arise in supragranular layers, particularly layer III, and project to the granular layer IV. In the "backgoing" direction, projections arise in infragranular layers V and VI and project to the superficial layers I and II.

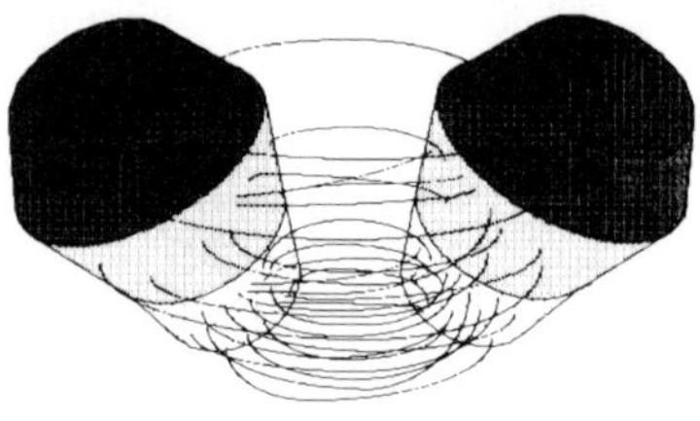

FIG. 3.8. Schematic of extrinsic connections, such as from one modality to another, or from a frontal to a sensory area. Connections keep to cytoarchitectonic levels, and connection density is greatest for more paralimbic cortex.

dense within than across moieties. Although there are connections between the archicortical and paleocortical trends, the greater density within trends suggests that evolution has maintained each trend as a distinct processing system.

Second, connections across modalities and across trends tend to keep within ring boundaries (Fig. 3.8). Therefore projections arising from the proisocortical ring in one region will likely target proisocortex of another region. This is particularly apparent for the extensive extrinsic connections between frontal cortex and posterior sensory regions (Pandya et al., 1985), such that whatever executive function is achieved by the frontal lobe is done so through influences across similarly differentiated networks. Although the traditional functional division of the cortex has viewed the lobes and sensory modalities as the major units of analysis, the strong interconnection within each evolutionary ring suggests that each ring must be an important functional system that integrates across sensory and motor processes.

Finally, extrinsic connection density is high for primitive cortex and low or absent for the finely differentiated koniocortex (Fig. 3.8). The primary sensory cortices of vision, audition, and somasthesis have few if any extrinsic connections, and each is connected with other areas of the brain only through connections with its adjacent ring of supplementary sensory cortex. Thus the general coordination of the brain must be achieved by the densely interconnected within-ring functional systems of the more primitive, rather than on the more highly differentiated, cortical networks.

TRENDS IN NETWORK DIFFERENTIATION

A coherent model of the network architecture of the neocortex is emerging not only from improved anatomical methods, but from the evolutionary analysis of the relations among cortical regions by researchers such as Sanides, Pandya, and Galaburda. This is a developmental analysis, tracing the successive waves of network differentiation that have occurred in each focus of sensory and motor specialization within the primitive general cortex. It may seem as if a developmental analysis on the evolutionary time scale is not relevant to the study of the neuropsychological development of the individual. From this viewpoint, what is important for the individual is the processing architecture of the brain, however it has been formed, not its past history. Yet, just as the recognition of the order within the connections of the cortex has been achieved only through tracing their evolutionary course, an appreciation of the functional operations of the cortex may require some understanding of how the evolution of each new network level extended the overall capacities of the brain. A phylogenetic theory may be particularly important for the key question of how processing and representations interact between the most articulated neocortex and the more primitive paralimbic levels.

Evolution of the Network Architecture

To begin speculating on the functional relations among the phylogenetic levels of the cortical networks, it may be useful to consider the pattern of the intralaminar connections between one network growth ring and the more differentiated network that appeared within it. The connections from the more articulated to the more primitive level arise in cortical layer III and terminate in layer IV (Fig. 3.7). In the general plan for sensory cortex, layer IV receives the input connections from the sensory relay nuclei of the thalamus. Thus, from the point of view of the more primitive network, the newly differentiated network level appears to be "standing in" for, and partially replacing, the thalamic stream of sensory data.

Progressive Modelling of the Environment Interface. Each newly evolved cortical level may have provided a more articulated representation of the information coming from the receptors of that sensory modality. As it took over the primary sensory connections, the new network level interposed itself between the existing cortex and the sensory input channels. Because each new level emphasized the articulation of the more superficial cortical lamina, and deemphasized the deeper layers, it would have provided greater intracortical processing of the sensory information before the information was passed to the existing cortical level. Instead of receiving the sensory data processed only at the thalamic level, the older cortical network now received information into its layer IV that was shaped by network representation at a cortical level.

The traditional view has been that the primary sensory cortices are the most elementary or primitive level of perceptual analysis, with primary visual cortex neurons, for example, responding to such properties of the environment as lines oriented in certain directions. "Later" levels of processing, such as along the ventral path to temporal lobe, combine stimulus features, such that neurons respond to complex objects such as faces (Perrett, Rolls, & Caan, 1982). The evolutionary analysis of cortical cytoarchitectonics may suggest a reinterpretation of this view. The response to multiple features may be the more primitive mode of cortical representation. The result of mammalian cortical evolution may have been initial sensory processing networks with increasingly distributed modes of information representation in each newly differentiated network level. This would have caused the information associated with a given environmental object to be spread over many neuronal units, any one of which would then respond in abstract fashion to features of the sensory array.

At the paralimbic core of the brain, the primitive cortical networks are closely connected with the animal's current emotional state. Connections with the hypothalamus and autonomic representational areas provide paralimbic cortex with continuous information on internal bodily states (Mesulam & Mufson, 1982). Connections with striatal areas may link the paralimbic networks with information on postural and motor tone (Nauta, 1986). Thus in several respects the paralimbic areas of cortex may have become specialized for representation of the animal's internal states, related to emotional and motivational processes. As successive waves of neocortical differentiation provided increasingly articulated, highly distributed, representations of the external context, the paralimbic core of the brain retained the highly integrated information on the organismic state. Cortical evolution thus seems to have produced a succession of network levels, like the layers of an onion, each outer shell yielding a more differentiated representation of the external interface, yet with all the outer layers under the adaptive control of the primitive, postural-affective corebrain networks (Derryberry & Tucker, in press).

The specialization for representing external, rather than internal, information seems to have occurred in the more recently differentiated neocortical networks of the motor regions as well. At the paralimbic core, both the dorsal (cingulate) and ventral (orbital) architectonic trends leading to motor cortex are closely fused with affective, visceral, and postural information (Brown, 1989; Goldberg, 1985). But the most differentiated level of the trends, the primary motor cortex, is unique in having the pyramidal tracts connect directly to brainstem motor nuclei. Although it receives substantial modulation from circuits through striatum and thalamus, the primary motor cortex has evolved a separate set of connections for motor control, bipassing the more primitive circuits of the extrapyramidal system of the basal ganglia. In this way, brain evolution has specialized the outer shell of the cortical networks for a finely articulated modeling of the output, as well as the input, connections with the environmental interface.

Integration at the Core. As the outer networks of the cortex were evolving, entrained by environmental information, it seems likely that the more paralimbic networks would adopt new functions commensurate with their positions at the core of an increasingly differentiated network hierarchy. Given their interconnections with postural and affective states, the paralimbic networks may have retained the more general function of adaptive evaluation, linking the increasingly sophisticated representations of the external context to an internal representation of the bodily state (Derryberry & Tucker, in press).

Although the qualities of the representations at the paralimbic core may remain primitive even in the human brain, reflecting visceral needs and postural attitudes, their adaptive functions may have evolved in parallel with the new representational capacities of the exterior networks. As the articulated sensory networks become tuned to the continuous flux of environmental events, the changing representations would need to be evaluated to determine which are significant enough to become instantiated through the network's mechanisms of synaptic plasticity. By recruiting the brainstem neuromodulator systems, the paralimbic networks could provide regulation of the more differentiated network not only in response to gross adaptive challenges such as hunger or predator threat, but in response to the more subtle demands for the self-regulation of the cognition of the network hierarchy. Thus the control influences that evolved initially to support novelty orientation and hedonic response may be recruited, in a more subtle form, in the corebrain resonance that maintains the representation of an interesting idea. This neurophysiological substrate of interest or curiosity remains primitive in that it has qualities of a feeling or an intuition rather than an articulated percept or action. Yet through such subtle adaptive influences the corebrain networks may form the evaluative basis for the representations forming within a complex, multilevel, hierarchy of cortical networks.

The connectional structure of this hierarchy is clear. The most differentiated networks handling the environmental interface are dedicated to that interface, and are relatively isolated from other brain regions. The primary cortices of both sensory and motor areas are connected to other brain regions only through their adjacent, more paralimbic, cortical growth rings. The closer the growth rings are to the limbic core, the more dense are their interconnections. Because of the dense interconnections, the processing at the corebrain level may be syncretic or undifferentiated. A sensory representation, for example, may be inherently fused with both visceral reactions and motor initiatives. Although it is primitive, the processing architecture of the cortex may cause the paralimbic level of systems integration to be the most important level, linking up the inherently isolated sensory modalities and motor control networks of the recently evolved neocortex.

In such a model, information processing could be described as going into the onion and coming out again. A stimulus is represented initially in the differentiated outer neocortex, then as representations cascade down toward the limbic core they become increasingly evaluated for adaptive significance, conjoined with visceral states and motor impulses. Through progressive organization back toward the outer surface, the adaptive urges and dispositions of the paralimbic cortex are increasingly articulated into a motor plan that becomes integrated within the differentiated environmental interface (Brown, 1989).

Although psychologists and neuroscientists typically assume that the brain is passive, and thus can only engage in information processing after a stimulus has been presented (Trevarthen, 1985), the integrated function of the cortical hierarchy can also be described as beginning with an action tendency that is recruited by a motivational state. From the limbic core, the action tendency becomes convolved with suitable autonomic states, with motor plans, and with anticipated sensory consequences. As behavior unfolds, processing must cross the multiple levels of the onion, negotiating between the environmental interface and the adaptive core.

Processing and Representation in the Corticolimbic Hierarchy

In addition to developing a general model for understanding the evolution of multiple layers of cortical networks, it will be important to formulate specific hypotheses about the nature of the representations at each level, and about the processing that allows information to cross the cytoarchitectonic levels. Each network level of a sensory-limbic pathway appears to form a receptotopic map of the sensory data, using some sort of distributed form of information representation. The representation at the primary sensory cortex may be the most highly distributed, with each neuron responding to fragmentary sensory features such as an oriented line. Representations closer to paralimbic cortex may be less widely distributed, with individual neurons showing more organismic integration of complex sensory and motor qualities with adaptive significance.

Within such an architecture, the question becomes how multiple maps and hierarchically distributed representations can be functionally integrated. In computational models this is sometimes termed the "binding problem." Damasio (1989) has proposed a model to account for the binding of distributed cortical representations. He begins by taking issue with the conventional assumption that, after initial sensory processing, an integrated mental representation is formed in association cortex. Damasio argues that the sensory features of a complex representation are still encoded at the primary sensory cortices, linked by binding mechanisms in the association cortices. The binding mechanisms are formed in "convergence zones" of connections downstream from sensory areas, and they operate through "retroactivations" to engage the sensory features at primary sensory cortices, thereby creating mental representations that are distributed widely throughout the brain.

Broad Modulation of Network States. Within the framework of evolutionary cortical anatomy, it becomes clear that the convergence zones—the cortical areas with the greatest fan-in from sensory and other areas—must be in paralimbic cortex. The recently differentiated multimodal cortical areas, such as in superior temporal sulcus (Pandya et al., 1985) or in inferior parietal lobule (Eidelberg &

Galaburda, 1984), share the connection isolation of other recently evolved networks, the primary sensory and motor cortices. Although multimodal networks must be important to widely distributed representations, the binding function itself must be provided by the most densely interconnected regions, the primitive paralimbic networks.

A general principle of brain connections could be described as "top-down fan-in" (Derryberry & Tucker, in press). The widespread neocortical connections funnel toward integrating regions of the paralimbic networks, which in turn are connected to their associated limbic structures and other circuits of the subcortex. In this architectural framework, the limbic system is situated midway between the cortex and the control systems of the brainstem. In terms of breadth of network control, the brain's most general self-regulation may be achieved as limbic mechanisms alter the functioning of the brainstem neuromodulator systems, which project to wide areas of cortex through a connection pattern of bottom-up fan-out.

Derryberry and I (Derryberry & Tucker, in press) proposed that the representations formed at the paralimbic level may characterize the emotional significance of events. Although these representations may be essential to complex cognition, they seem to emerge most fundamentally from bodily states and postural orientations. As they tune the activity in brainstem neuromodulator systems, the paralimbic networks may engage even more primitive modes of self-control, such as the noradrenergic phasic arousal or dopaminergic tonic activation systems formulated by Tucker and Williamson (1984). For example, when confronted with a threatening stimulus, the temporal and orbital frontal paleocortical areas recruit activity in the amygdala. Through its connections to hypothalamus, the amygdala elicits autonomic preparations; through its connections to basal ganglia it elicits motor readiness. This set of organizing processes in the ventral limbic and striatal circuits is encompassed by an envelope of tonic activation, mediated by the mesolimbic dopaminergic pathways. The primitive control of increased redundancy of information processing provided by the tonic activation system may be important not only to maintaining autonomic and motor preparedness, but to the tenacity of vigilance and the focusing of cognitive operations that occur under threatening circumstances (Tucker & Derryberry, in press).

In the research on plasticity in neural development, adequate cholinergic and noradrenergic modulation appears essential to the synaptic mechanisms of network differentiation (Singer, 1987). If the network plasticity of memory operates through similar mechanisms as the network plasticity of cortical ontogenesis, then neuromodulator control of the state of the postsynaptic neuron may be a key process in network self-regulation. An extensive literature shows that the brainstem neuromodulators, particularly noradrenaline and acetylcholine, play important roles in memory (reviewed by Gold & Zornetzer, 1983). Memory formation appears to be a temporally extended, perhaps developmental, process. During the period of consolidation there are a number of factors, particularly those that alter neuromodulator function, that can influence the storage of the memory trace (Gold & Zornetzer, 1983; Squire, 1986). If the extensive networks of the cortex are to self-regulate effectively they may need to call up the modulatory influences of the brainstem projection systems, through communication channels gated by paralimbic network representations.

Limbic Kindling and Adaptive Resonance. The paralimbic cortices and limbic structures are especially responsive electrophysiologically, such that in animal experiments electrical stimulation anywhere in the cortex may recruit electrical reactivity in limbic areas (Doane & Livingston, 1986). In the phenomenon of kindling, repeated low level electrical stimulation may result in exaggerated reactivity in limbic structures, to the point of seizures. The tendency of induced seizures to follow the paths of the limbic circuits was a major clue to the anatomical identification of the limbic system by Papez (1937). That the exaggerated limbic reactivity may be related to normal memory function is suggested by the finding that seizures induced by kindling may be classically conditioned by pairing them with an auditory stimulus (Janowsky, Laxer, & Rushmer, 1980).

A phenomenon related to kindling may be long-term potentiation (LTP), in which tetanic stimulation of the neuron's afferent connections increases the neuron's response to subsequent impulses across those connections (Teyler, 1986). Although it can be produced in neocortex, LTP is most often studied in the hippocampus, where it appears particularly strong (Gustafsson & Wigstrom, 1988). Synaptogenesis follows hippocampal LTP within a few minutes, possibly reflecting changes in network architecture supporting long-term memory (Black & Greenough, 1986).

As with the synaptic plasticity of ontogenetic differentiation, the electrophysiological response and synaptogenesis of LTP may be under brainstem control. During the consolidation phase after stimulation, LTP may be enhanced by facilitating the activation state of the postsynaptic neuron. Such influences have been produced both by stimulation of brainstem reticular formation and by application of norepinephrine (Gustafsson & Wigstrom, 1988).

Other evidence of neuromodulator control over limbic excitability has provided clues that the archicortical and paleocortical trends may be connected with different neurochemical systems. The influence of norepinephrine on hippocampal LTP may be consistent with the tendency for noradrenergic pathways to project to dorsal regions of cortex (Lewis & Morrison, 1989). However, other neuromodulator systems may have preferential connections with the ventral limbic structures and cortex. Mesulam and Mufson (1982) suggested that one reason for the electrophysiological excitability of amygdala and hippocampus may be the extensive cholinergic projections to these structures. Yet in tracing the connections from other brain regions to the origins of the cholinergic pathways in nucleus basalis, Mesulam and Mufson (1984) found these inputs came from ventral limbic structures and the associated cortex of the temporal pole, insula, and orbital frontal region. The inputs to nucleus basalis did not include the hippocampus. In earlier comparative studies, MacLean (1958) argued that the high density of acetylcholine found in ventral limbic regions and striatum reflects the more primitive nature of these regions, compared with the more recently evolved dorsal limbic structures.

The dopamine pathways also appear to have a largely ventral distribution, with the nigrostriatal projections influencing motor control, and mesolimbic projections influencing motivational and emotional processes. Recent anatomical studies have emphasized the interconnections between ventral limbic circuits and the motor control loops between striatum and motor cortex (Nauta, 1986). Dopaminergic control over limbic excitablity has been observed in animal models of seizures. Unless dopaminergic modulation is present, kindling of seizures may not develop (Dichter & Ayala, 1987).

Within the formulation of a dopaminergic tonic activation system, Williamson and I proposed that primitive mechanisms of motor readiness are important to motivational states of anxiety and hostility (Tucker & Williamson, 1984). A relation between anxiety and limbic irritability has long been suggested by the fact that anxiolytic drugs such as benzodiazepines are also anticonvulsants (Gray, 1982). Similarly, the anxiogenic beta-carbolines potentiate seizures, apparently through impairing benzodiazepine receptors (Ableitner & Herz, 1987). Kuhar (1986) suggested that dopaminergic increases in neural irritability in anxiety may normally be balanced by GABAergic and benzodiazepine modulation.

The counterpart in humans to the limbic kindling in animal studies may be temporal lobe epilepsy, in which seizure activity in the cortex tends to develop a focus in the temporal-limbic area. Bear's studies of temporal lobe epilepsy have suggested that there may be a psychological parallel to the electrophysiological irritability of the limbic regions. With the apparent "hyperconnection" of cortical with limbic processes in this disorder, the psychological processes of the involved hemisphere appear to become overly constrained motivationally, and thereby degraded cognitively (Bear, 1983; Bear & Fedio, 1977).

The role of the limbic circuits and paralimbic cortex in psychological functioning is a crucial one for neuropsychological theory because these structures seem to combine the control of motivation with the control of memory. Yet it may be difficult to characterize the psychological qualities of the representations formed in paralimbic networks. Cognitive psychology seems to deal most effectively with representations that can be specified, such as propositions or images, rather than the more syncretic or primitive representations, such as the sense of hedonic attractiveness. In speculating on the cognitive control exerted by limbic mechanisms, Tucker, Vannatta, & Rothlind (1990) suggested that these mechanisms may apply a kind of adaptive priming of semantic information, coding each representation on two dimensions, hedonic value and threat potential. The hedonic dimension arises as the representation elicits activity in the phasic arousal system, producing an affective quality varying from depression to elation. The threat dimension arises as the representation elicits the tonic activation system, engendering affect varying from relaxed to hostile or anxious.

When subjects describe their physiological arousal with questionnaire items, factor analysis of the item correlations separates a dimension of energetic vigor from a dimension of aversive tension (Thayer, 1989). These dimensions appear similar to those of Positive Affect and Negative Affect found as the underlying psychometric dimensions of emotion descriptions (Tellegen, 1985). If the limbic circuits are simultaneously regulating motivational dispositions and the memory processes of cortical networks, then a similar set of dimensions would be expected to form the basis of cognitive evaluation generally. In their classic factor analytic studies, Osgood, Suci, & Tannenbaum (1957) found Evaluation (good-bad), Activation (quick-slow), and Potency (strong-weak) to form the reference dimensions for semantic evaluation. In the emotion psychometric work, a 45-degree rotation was used to replace the good-bad and calm-intense factors with the Positive and Negative Affect factors, which are seen as a more accurate characterization of movement in emotion space (Tellegen, 1985). It seems quite possible that at the most elementary or primitive level, the reference frame for cognitive evaluation is the same as that for emotional response. Cognitive evaluation may occur as paralimbic networks resonate to emerging neocortical representations, thereby entraining activity in the brainstem mechanisms of elation and anxiety. Operating through neuromodulator control of synaptic plasticity, these mechanisms may condition not only the person's immediate subjective state, but the endurance of the network states encoding current experience.

Vertical Recursion Negotiating Internal and External Constraints. In addition to their possible roles in tuning the activity of neuromodulator projection systems, the limbic circuits and paralimbic networks have dense interconnections projecting back up the cortical hierarchy, such that adaptive resonance in the excitable paralimbic networks may have implications for the patterns of connections throughout the cortical hierarchy. Each evolutionary level of the network appears to have its own representation of the sensory data. Primary sensory cortex has the most dense thalamic input and the most articulated sensory map. The next level is the supplementary sensory cortex, with a less differentiated cytoarchitectonic structure and a less articulated representational map. Although the nature of interlevel relations and the form of paralimbic representations is still unclear, there may be a continued progression of increasingly undifferentiated representations down to the corebrain level.

In terms of network structure, the progression would be from general and holistic at the core to articulated and specified at the outer level. This pattern may be consistent with the extrinsic network connections, such that the more holistic representations in paralimbic areas are highly integrated across brain regions through dense horizontal interconnections, whereas the more differentiated representations at the outer levels are supported by highly discrete and local interconnections. In terms of the content of the information, the representations at the outer level are constrained by the sensory data at the receptor surface (or the feedback from articulated motor processes). The representations at the inner core are constrained by the internal state of the organism, including qualities of arousal, pain, posture, and visceral needs.

The different constraints operating at the outer and inner levels of the network may cause the processing across network levels to be a form of arbitration. Assuming a tendency toward maintaining coherence of the representations across network boundaries, the patterning of the representations may pass up and down the hierarchy, transformed in each transition by the constraints of that network level. Processing cascading up and down the hierarchy might be thought of as recursive, in that the output of each level continually returns to that level to transform itself within the developing hierarchic network pattern.

It has been assumed that the major direction of processing is from sensory cortex to limbic cortex, such that sensory representations are increasingly analyzed for adaptive significance as processing courses toward the primitive networks. However, recent evidence shows that features of the sensory data may reach paralimbic targets before reaching primary sensory cortices. (LeDoux, 1987) has identified connections from thalamus to amygdala that provide sensory information to limbic circuits in parallel to cortical routes. Furthermore, constraints on network processing arise from ongoing motivational and emotional states, such that the paralimbic networks may be prepared beforehand to organize the representations cascading through the hierarchy.

The process of concept formation, therefore, may occur through recursive interactions moving up as well as down the hierarchy. A concept would not be achieved by representation at any one level, but only when a linked cluster of representations stabilizes across the hierarchy. At the external networks, the concept may have the greatest data constraints, but the internal networks, with their greater excitability, may determine the duration of recursion, i.e., the extent of consolidation. With enough adaptive resonance, such as when noticing an attractive opportunity or when hearing an insult, the adaptive resonance and extended processing allows the stabilization of concepts that are well-constrained at all levels. Through a process such as vertical recursion, concept formation may involve more than an abstract representation of information. It may be a kind of reality-testing. The concept forms as a relation between one's adaptive needs and the information of the environmental context.

Three Frames of Embedded Network Structure

The structure of the adult brain may be achieved in ontogenesis by differentiation within three frames, each one nested or embedded within the previous ones. The first frame is the phylogenetic plan, the architecture of evolutionary differentiation that has created the multileveled cortex. As emphasized in the above speculations, it may be necessary to understand the structure of this evolutionary frame to interpret information processing in the cortex. The second frame is created through ontogenetic sculpting, as information-dependent competitive elimination provides an epigenetic articulation of the genetic plan. Within the outlines formed by ontogenetic plasticity, the daily processes of adaptive synaptic modification detail the third frame. This is the fine structure of cortical networks that instantiates memory for ongoing experience. As a nested matrix, the developing brain may form through increasingly constrained mechanisms of network differentiation.

Evolution of the Ontogenetic Plan. When the topic is child development, it may seem to be complicating things somewhat to worry about the history of mammalian brain evolution. But the processes of ontogenesis are the end products of evolutionary development. Natural selection works on variations in the ontogenetic plan, favoring those that increase morphology or behavioral fitness in the current environment (Gould, 1977a). The ontogenetic sequence of a species can be seen as a compilation of the phylogenetic history of successive refinements of the developmental process. In the human brain, as with that of other mammals, the evolutionary progression seems highly relevant, given that the cortical architecture incorporates multiple waves of network differentiation, each of which first appeared at a different phylogenetic juncture.

Selection may favor not only specific features, but general trends in the developmental course, such as the rate of maturation. The early embryologic stages can be seen as a storehouse of shapes and processes that can be brought to the fore in the mature organism by alterations in developmental timing (Gould, 1977a). The process of human evolution seems to have involved a fairly radical strategy of altered ontogenetic timing, neoteny. The ontogenetic course has been retarded. Features of the adult human form, such as the shape of the head and face, are similar to those of an infant chimpanzee but not to those of an adult chimpanzee (Gould, 1977a). Other features of fetal stages are retained in the adult human skull. One is the location of the foramen magnum, the opening at the base of the skull for the spinal cord, which in other mammals rotates caudally during development to support their quadrupedal posture. Another is produced by the delayed calcification of the skeleton, such that the ends of the long bones and fingers of human infants are still cartilaginous at birth (Gould, 1977b). Delays in skull calcification and in the closing of the skull sutures may avoid physical constraints on brain development.

By extending the juvenile period, the human ontogenetic plan has created a longer period of developmental plasticity, within which cortical networks may become finely differentiated. Extending plasticity has been a general characteristic in mammalian evolution, allowing increasingly flexible cortical networks to form customized brains for local environments. But it seems to have reached a radical form in humans, who may not be prepared for adult roles for two decades or longer, depending on the length of postgraduate training.

Genetic control of ontogenesis does not end at birth, but regulates the timing of the developmental process throughout life. Particularly with neoteny and extended cortical plasticity as adaptive strategies, important forms of genetic control may be exerted through processes that decrease the scope of network plasticity. For example, the period when callosal fibers may become rearranged, reflecting a high degree of plasticity, ends about the time that cortical myelination begins, perhaps implying that myelination dampens certain aspects of plasticity (Innocenti, 1983). Myelination has long been considered to index neural maturation, where maturation has been thought to reflect readiness for psychological function. In the context of changing periods of neural plasticity, the notion of maturation may take on a different meaning, reflecting decreased information responsivity of the network as well as increased behavioral competence.

An important genetic process constraining ontogenetic plasticity is sexual maturity. This marks a transition from a juvenile period, during which higher mammals engage in flexible learning under parental control, to an adult period, in which they must stabilize and implement the survival and reproductive strategies they have learned. The decrease in behavioral malleability with sexual maturity suggests that the hormonal or other changes of the ontogenetic program may suppress or terminate aspects of neural plasticity. For example, learning to speak a second language without an accent becomes much more difficult after puberty, suggesting a decrease in network plasticity. As another example, when chimpanzees reach sexual maturity they become aggressive and inflexible and can no longer be kept as pets. Many human parents report that puberty produces the same effect on their offspring.

Ontogenetic Constraints on Concept-Formation. Within the outlines of the multiple network levels formed in phylogenesis, from paralimbic to koniocortex, the functional networks of the cortex are formed through ontogenetic plasticity, i.e., through a natural selection of those connections that match the data in the environment. This process operates at a rapid pace early in development, carving out the general pattern of the individual brain, then slows to reflect the experience-dependent synaptic record of daily events.

The second frame of differentiation may be the enduring pattern taken by the individual's cortical networks as a result of ontogenetic plasticity. The third frame would then be the connections reflecting synaptic modifications, and thus changes in network connection strength, during event memory. This distinction may be similar to that between experience-expectant and experience-dependent plasticity (Greenough, 1984). It is an interesting question when the second and the third frames of differentiation can be separated. Certainly in early development the plasticity is great enough that it does not seem to make sense to separate memory differentiation from ontogenetic anatomical differentiation. At some point toward adulthood, it may be that the basic network architecture has been achieved, and the synaptic changes reflect the cortical network's function of representing experience, rather than organizing its connectional architecture anatomically.

But the most interesting theoretical position may be that there is no real transition between ontogenetic sculpting and the mechanisms of information representation (Malsburg & Singer, 1988). In the brain, physical growth may be psychological growth. Clearly the plasticity of early development must be limited to allow stable behavioral patterns to be attained in adulthood. But there may not be one form of synapse modification for anatomical differentiation and another one for memory, just periods of varying degrees of neural plasticity in response to the informational context. Thus although we suffer from infantile amnesia, the second frame of cortical structure could be said to be the memory of early childhood.

Whether the third frame of differentiation, event memory, can be separated from the second, ontogenetic plasticity, or whether it is a specialized form of it, there may be increasing constraints on concept-formation as ontogenesis proceeds. Initially, the cortex is a blank slate, a thick felt of connections with unused representational potential. But with increasing differentiation, that potential becomes constrained. A 4-year-old listens to a new language and begins to speak it with massively parallel networks only moderately differentiated, and thereby only moderately committed, by the first language. A 14-year-old listens to the new language through networks that are highly articulated, and constrained. The sounds that are heard, the proximal stimulus, may be different in these two brains because of decreasing degrees of freedom for ontogenetic differentiation.

In connectionist networks, the connection weights that represent previous experiences of the network may interfere with the representation of new input patterns (Rumelhart & McClelland, 1986). Conversely, finding weights to represent a new input pattern may disrupt the representations established previously. This has been termed the "stability-plasticity dilemma" (Grossberg, 1984). The mammalian brain seems to be biased toward plasticity early on, then toward stability. As children or adolescents encounter a novel event, they can represent the event within a limited context of past experience, and they can allocate a major portion of their uncommitted connections to that event. A summer vacation becomes the phenomenological universe, and it lasts a long time. Adults, on the other hand, have a rich set of contexts that are applied in the process of understanding each new event. And these contexts—reflected in the synaptic connection weights of a highly differentiated network—constrain the understanding. Perhaps this is why new tricks are so hard for old dogs, and why only graduate students can participate in paradigm shifts. The changes in memory with development may reflect not only the degeneration of age, but the increasingly constrained operation of an increasingly differentiated neural architecture.

Progressive Underspecification. Although it may be important to recognize the constraints imposed by one frame of network differentiation on another, the general effect of neoteny has been to loosen these constraints. Mammals have behavioral flexibility because their plan for brain ontogenesis is open-ended, allowing information-dependent plasticity. Humans have exaggerated this trend, stretched out the fetal period of brain development, such that what the genetic plan provides is a massive embryonic connection matrix, which becomes reasonably functional only after many years of training.

By underspecifying the form to be taken by the network architecture, and by extending the period during which competitive elimination may occur, human evolution may have produced highly idiosyncratic forms of ontogenetic outcome. Each brain is so reflective of its local environment, and so much a product of its own self-organizing process, that it becomes unlike any other brain. For simpler organisms whose end structure is specified by the genetic plan, individuals in the species are highly similar. For organisms whose features are formed by epigenetic mechanisms, each individual is different. Because of the radical extension of ontogenetic plasticity, each human brain may become a highly unique experiment of nature.

The trend toward underspecification may continue from the second to the third frame. Ontogenetic plasticity may be attenuated only gradually, such that human adults, in comparison to those of other species, retain a juvenile quality, an extended capacity for differentiating cortical networks to incorporate new experience. Given the demands for both consistent adjustment and response to a rapidly evolving culture, human adulthood could be seen as a continuing struggle with the stability-plasticity dilemma.

NEOTENY AND THE GRADIENTS OF CORTICAL MATURATION

Because our ancestors formed social groups that tolerated neotenic, incompetent juveniles, and because they still proved successful in gaining food and warding off predators, our line evolved an extended period of neural plasticity, and the resultant flexible intelligence. Human brain ontogenesis became a slow and increasingly epigenetic process. Within the general mode of neoteny, the temporal unfolding of brain structure must coordinate several dimensions of cortical organization. The major dimension may be the "vertical" dimension, the evolutionary levels of successively differentiated cortical networks. The functional implementation of hierarchic networks must be coordinated with other dimensions of neocortical organization, including anterior motor versus posterior sensory function, ventral object versus dorsal spatial memory systems, and the cognitive specialization of the left and right hemispheres.

It is unlikely that neoteny would have been effective if it produced an indiscriminate extension of neural plasticity. Rather, certain systems would need to stabilize to provide some continuity in the interaction with the environment, while other systems could be left unconstrained and therefore maximally reactive to local conditions. The stability-plasticity dilemma would need to be worked out within each of the major dimensions of cortical organization, resulting in several distinct gradients of network maturation.

Embryological Recapitulation of Network Differentiation

Perhaps the simplest plan for ontogenetic organization of the vertical dimension would be phylogenetic recapitulation: Establish the primitive paralimbic networks first, then "grow" the more articulated networks out from this base in the same order as the evolutionary progression. As discussed below, the evidence on myelination suggests that, at least for that aspect of maturation, this is not what happens. The first cortical areas to myelinate are the primary sensory and motor cortices (Yakovlev & Lecours, 1967), i.e., the most recently evolved networks.

Yet there are interesting parallels between the ontogenetic differentiation of cortical lamina and the evolutionary articulation of increasingly laminated cortical networks. In ontogenesis, the first wave of radial migration of cells from the ventricular proliferation layer produces the deepest cortical layer, VI. The next wave migrates past this layer to form layer V, and so on until the most superficial of the cortical layers has been formed (Rakic, 1988). In the evolutionary frame, the primordial paralimbic networks are not only less laminated, they show a prominence of the deeper layers, V and VI (Pandya et al., 1985). Each successive network level to evolve, eventually producing neocortex, shows greater laminar differentiation, greater articulation of the superficial cortical layers, and a decreased prominence of the deep layers (Pandya et al., 1985). Therefore an interesting possibility is that natural selection tended to emphasize the later ontogenetic processes, i.e., the formation of the more superficial layers, as each new network was added to the hierarchy.

It would almost seem as if the routine for cell migrations to the successive cortical lamina would be repeated, with increasing elaboration of the final movements, for each more articulated network. This notion of variations on a basic theme of cell migrations might suggest that there should be a phylogenetic recapitulation of the evolutionary order during embryological cortical differentiation, with the primitive paralimbic networks formed first, then the cycle repeated with increasing variations for each more articulated network.

Although we can still only speculate on the functional advantages actually conferred by the more differentiated networks, it would seem likely that these would involve the elaboration of cortico-cortical interactions in the increasingly prominent superficial lamina. Yet in the scheme of inter-ring connections, the superficial layers receive projections from the deep layers of the more primitive adjacent cortex (Pandya et al., 1988), as if the evolutionary strategy were to evolve more articulated cortical processing, but to keep it under control of the more venerable paralimbic network algorithms.

Caudal to Rostral Progression: Slow Maturation of the Core and Its Frontal Extent

The importance of effective control of an increasingly complex network hierarchy may have been an important issue in the selective pressures leading to the human ontogenetic plan. Whatever the embryologic progression in the differentiation of cortical networks, the appearance of myelination suggests there is an early maturation of the sensory and motor cortices, prior to the maturation of "association" cortex (Yakovlev & Lecours, 1967). These classic myelination observations are consistent with more recent positron emission tomographic studies of glucose metabolism (Chugani & Phelps, 1986). Infants show enhanced metabolic activity in sensory and motor cortices; 3-month-olds show increases in several posterior areas, and by 8 months the frontal areas begin to show increased activity. In the myelination studies, the frontal lobes and the reticular areas of the brainstem continue to show changes in myelination throughout childhood (Yakovlev & Lecours, 1967), as if the self-regulatory systems of the frontal lobes and their associated activation control mechanisms undergo a protracted developmental process.

If myelination signals the end of a period of unconstrained plasticity (Innocenti, 1983), then an important ontogenetic progression in the cortex may be early maturation, and decreased plasticity, in the caudal sensory areas, and a slower maturation of the frontal functions of self-regulation and complex motor control. This caudal-to-rostral trend is the reverse of the embryological trend, in which motor systems become differentiated earlier than sensory systems (Hamburger, 1977). It seems reasonable that motor systems would differentiate and organize themselves to achieve internal coherence prior to birth, whereas sensory systems would assume the dominant role in leading the organization of cortical networks after birth, linking up sensory and motor routines into integrated behavioral assemblies when the full streams of sensory data become available.

If the most recently evolved sensory and motor cortices mature first, there may be a maturation progression in the vertical or radial dimension. The differentiated networks may become functional to provide the exterior interface, and then the more primitive core brain networks organize slowly, allowing a complex and extended differentiation of the evaluative, adaptive mechanisms. If so, this would be the opposite of phylogenetic recapitulation. Ontogenesis would be configured to implement the recent networks first, then to allow greater experience-dependent plasticity to refine the adaptive control exerted by the architectonically more primitive networks.

It may be important in this context to reconsider what is meant by "recent" in the evolutionary frame. The koniocortex of the sensory modalities is the most recently evolved of the major cortical networks (Pandya et al., 1988), and species differences across cats, rats, and humans suggest that humans have extensive development of these cortical regions. But other areas that have become particularly large in humans, such as the prefrontal cortex, also include large areas of cortex of intermediate evolutionary differentiation. It may be that recent human evolution has selected for expansion of primitive as well as articulated cortical areas, such that slow maturation and extended developmental plasticity of the frontal regions would be consistent with their recent evolution.

Frontal cortex has traditionally been described as the neocortical extension of the limbic system (Nauta, 1971). Although the recent anatomical evidence shows the hierarchic relation of all neocortex to paralimbic cortex, it seems clear that the frontal executive functions of planning and self-control must rely heavily on frontolimbic interactions, integrating plans with their emotional significance (Nauta, 1971; Tucker & Derryberry, in press). The anatomical connections of frontal regions with posterior regions provide channels for self-regulation of sensory representation; the links with limbic structures may provide memory for the sensory data that are significant (Goldman-Rakic, 1987). Distributed networks throughout frontal and posterior regions may be coalesced through thalamic circuits to provide large systems of network integration (Goldman-Rakic, 1988). Blood flow studies have suggested that activity in any posterior cortical region is coupled with activity in a corresponding frontal area, suggesting a functional tuning of posterior activity by frontal areas (Roland, 1985).

During early cortical development, frontal tuning of activity in posterior areas could result in the connections of the active networks being selected for synaptic instantiation (Thatcher, 1990). A mechanism like this would cause the enduring structure of cortical networks to be achieved not only through passive response to information, but through active organization of the cumulative effects of the organism's self-regulation of cognitive processing. As they provide an extension of limbic interactions with brainstem neuromodulators, frontal regions may be crucial to vertical integration of the network hierarchy, linking complex motivational processes to elementary adaptive mechanisms (Derryberry & Tucker, in press).

Because the extrinsic connections of cortex follow the horizontal pattern, with interconnections keeping to areas of similar architectonic differentiation (Pandya et al., 1985), frontal control of other cortical areas must be exerted in network-specific fashion, with the greatest density of connections and therefore of control influences at the more paralimbic levels. The functions of the paralimbic frontal networks thus become particularly important. In studies of cerebral blood flow during cognitive tasks, increasing the demands for attentional control of cognition has been found to increase activity of dorsomedial frontal cortex particularly (Posner, Petersen, Fox, & Raichle, 1988). This attentional effect includes the supplementary motor area within the dorsal trend from the paralimbic cingulate area to motor cortex. Lesion studies and clinical observations have suggested that, within this limbic-cortical trend, the intention to act on the environment becomes progressively articulated (Goldberg, 1985). During the slow maturation of the human frontolimbic circuitry, motivational influences may become organized within increasingly complex systems of self-control.

An outer-to-inner gradient of maturation may permit continued integration of the multiple levels of the cortical network hierarchy throughout the extended juvenile period. The exterior interface networks achieve stability early, providing a reliable sensorimotor foundation. The slow organization of the corebrain evaluative processes may be necessary to allow general and flexible control modes to maintain a long period of cortical growth and development. During the juvenile period, higher animals are behaviorally flexible, responsive to the unique characteristics of the local environment. They exercise sensory and motor capacities through play. Although the sexual and aggressive content of juvenile play shows the early influence of adaptive control themes, the emotional and motivational control mechanisms of the juvenile may need to remain generic and unspecified to support the growth and differentiation of the cortex's representational capacity. With sexual maturity, animals become motivationally rigid, seeking out their needs to dominance, reproduction, and territory without distraction. To organize an extensive cortical hierarchy, humans may need to stave off this rigidity longer than usual, through slow maturation of motivational systems, so they can nurture and refine flexible modes of self-control such as curiosity and mastery.

Asymmetric Limbic Roots

Through an extended period of developmental flexibility, core brain regulatory systems may continue to exert an organizing influence on cortical differentiation. Mediated at the brainstem level by neuromodulator projection pathways, these regulatory systems may guide network differentiation not only in the embryological process of coordinating spontaneous motor activity with sensory feedback (Trevarthen, 1985), but in the activity-dependent specification of network structure in the early months and years of life (Singer, 1987). These systems could continue to shape the selection of synaptic patterns in the mature cortex through their adaptive control of memory (Gold & Zornetzer, 1983). If there are intrinsic asymmetries of these regulatory systems in the human brain, then, consistent with Trevarthen's (in press) hypothesis, their control influences may shape each frame of network differentiation. To understand the operation of these lateralizing influences, it may be necessary to appreciate how they interact with the maturational course of the other major dimensions of cortical organization, including the caudal-rostral dimension, the dorsal-ventral dimension, and the vertical dimension.

In the Tucker and Williamson (1984) model, hemispheric specialization was seen as a way of elaborating more complex forms of attention and cognition from the differing neural control algorithms of motor readiness (anterior or rostral) versus perceptual orienting (posterior or caudal). The left-lateralization of the dopaminergic tonic activation system was proposed to arise because the left hemisphere's cognitive functions have evolved in close relation to the motor control mechanisms of the anterior brain. The adaptive control of motor readiness, as in the fight-flight response, gives the tonic activation system its affective quality of anxiety or hostility. The noradrenergic phasic arousal system, on the other hand, is theorized to be right-lateralized because the right hemisphere's cognitive functions are specialized most fundamentally to elaborate on the perceptual orienting of the posterior brain, providing a holistic integration of sensory modalities. The affective quality of the phasic arousal system, varying from depression to elation, is proposed as a hedonic basis for mechanisms of perceptual orienting.

Lateral Specialization for Limbic Trends. Although the identification of the left hemisphere with expressive, motor, functions and the right hemisphere with receptive, perceptual, functions has a long tradition in neuropsychology (Jackson, 1879), another way to understand the more elementary basis for the asymmetry of neuromodulator systems has been suggested by the indications of their differential distributions within the dorsal and ventral cortical moieties. A more ventral distribution of dopamine pathways (Kuhar, 1986) would be consistent with the importance of the amygdala and the associated paralimbic cortex of the temporal pole and orbital frontal region in anxiety (Baxter, Phelps, Mazziotta, & Guze, 1987; Johanson et al., 1986; Tucker & Liotti, 1990). The more dorsal distribution of the cortical targets of norepinephrine pathways (Lewis & Morrison, 1989) may fit with the notion of a hedonic dimension underlying the phasic arousal system, and with the idea of a cingulate (archicortical paralimbic) map coding the hedonic significance of stimuli whose spatial localization is represented in parietal lobe (Mesulam, 1981).

The fact that certain neuromodulators preferentially target certain cortical regions may be an important clue to specific modes of self-regulation by cortical networks. It now seems clear that the dorsal/ventral asymmetry of the major brainstem projection systems must be considered as well as the lateral asymmetry. A coherent theoretical model of neuromodulator control of development may help explain what appear to be intrinsic relations between hemispheric specialization and the functional roles of the archicortical and paleocortical divisions of the human cortex. Since the discovery was made of the spatial processing role of dorsal cortical pathways and the object identification role of the ventral trend

(Kaas, 1988; Ungerleider & Mishkin, 1982), an important theoretical question has been whether an alignment of lateralization with this dorsal-ventral dimension of cortical organization may be necessary to explain the right hemisphere's spatial cognitive skills (Bear, 1983) and the left hemisphere's analytic cognitive skills (Tucker & Derryberry, in press).

Asymmetric Embryological Gradients. Evidence that human cortical maturation may involve asymmetric development of the dorsal and ventral trends has come from observations of fetal cortical growth patterns. Galaburda (1984) reviewed Fontes's collection of fetal brain photographs and found that cortical features in the perisylvian areas, including frontal and parietal opercula and the planum temporale, first appear in the right hemisphere. These are areas of the ventral, paleocortical trend. Galaburda suggests that these areas develop earlier in the right hemisphere because their development in the left hemisphere is slower, eventually resulting in a more extensive and highly organized ventral trend in the left hemisphere. More extensive organization with a protracted developmental course would be consistent with the principle of neoteny (Gould, 1977a).

A greater elaboration of the ventral trend in the left hemisphere of the adult brain was found in cytoarchitectonic studies of human brains by Eidelberg & Galaburda (1984). The angular gyrus shows the prominant granular layer IV that is characteristic of the paleocortical derivation. This area was larger in the left hemisphere of most brains examined, particularly those with a large left hemisphere planum temporale. This region of the temporal lobe is thought to reflect the left-lateralization of language functions (Eidelberg & Galaburda, 1984).

The cytoarchitectonic feature distinguishing the dorsal, archicortical trend is the appearance of large pyramidal cells in layers III and V. Eidelberg and Galaburda (1984) examined the inferior parietal lobule in human brains. The dorsal lip of this area, which has enlarged pyramidal layers reflecting archicortical origins, was consistently larger in the right hemisphere (Eidelberg & Galaburda, 1984). In the fetal brains in Fontes's photographs, the features of dorsomedial cortex of the archicortical trend were found to become differentiated earlier in the left hemisphere than the right, suggesting to Galaburda (1984) that there is a more sustained and extensive development of the archicortical trend in the right hemisphere.

Hemispheric Modes of Corticolimbic Self-Regulation. If there are intrinsic asymmetries of neuromodulator systems that guide brain differentiation, their influences on cortical differentiation may need to be understood in terms of how they are controlled by, and how they interact with, limbic mechanisms. These mechanisms appear to respond to the adaptive significance of the representations in cortical networks, and to call up brainstem projection systems to tune cortical synaptic plasticity accordingly. Given the critical role that corticolimbic connections play in adult memory (Squire, 1986), it seems likely that these connections play a similar role in the regulation of synaptic plasticity in the early stages of cortical network differentiation.

Given the susceptibility of the limbic structures to seizure recruitment (Doane & Livingston, 1986), it may be relevant that the human brain becomes increasingly less vulnerable to seizures as development occurs in the first years of life (Taylor, 1969). Could the early seizure sensitivity reflect a particularly active role of limbic recruitment in shaping cortical networks during the period of massive synaptogenesis and pruning? Consistent with other indications of early maturation of the right hemisphere (Tucker, 1986), the right hemisphere is less sensitive than the left to seizures in the first year of life. When the period of language acquisition begins, the incidence of seizure laterality reverses (Taylor, 1969).

If seizure incidence is a pathological reflection of normal developmental trends in limbic excitability, this evidence may suggest that in early development the factors influencing the child's emotional state will also influence the state of cortical plasticity. Furthermore, the two hemispheres may have different critical periods, during which the control of neural plasticity may have permanent effects on the network structure that will constrain experience throughout life.

One model for how limbic regulation of hemispheric activity could influence broad psychological domains is the seen in the degraded hemispheric function in certain patients with temporal lobe epilepsy (Bear, 1979; Bear & Fedio, 1977). As described above, many left temporal lobe epileptics seem to become highly intellectualized, chronically excited by moral or religious contemplation. At the same time, they become self-critical. In contrast, patients with a seizure focus in the right hemisphere often show exaggerated emotionality, they tend to deny their problems and limitations (Bear & Fedio, 1977). These syndromes, apparently resulting from asymmetric forms of exaggerated limbic control, seem to parallel the differences between internalizing and externalizing disorders shown in child psychopathology (Achenbach, 1982). The lateralization of the exaggerated personality styles in the epileptic patients is consistent with the theory that exaggerated function of the left hemisphere occurs in introverted, anxious persons, whereas a major reliance on right hemisphere operations occurs in extraverted, psychopathic, or hysteric personalities (Tucker, 1981; Tucker & Williamson, 1984).

Further research on neuropsychological mechanisms in psychopathology may shed light not only on the nature of hemispheric roles, but on the question of the optimal levels of control from brainstem and limbic mechanisms in the neural organization of personality and intelligence. In the integrative processing of the cortical hierarchy, it seems to be the resonance within corebrain networks that generates excitement, the activity of vertical recursion transferring constraints across multiple levels of representation. Without this activity, the multiple networks are poorly integrated. Yet when processing in the hierarchy is highly constrained by the primitive networks, constrained by concerns of threat or hedonic gratification, the representational function of the hierarchy degrades. The corebrain activity required for optimal network function must be vigorous and active, but it must be responsive to the quality of the representations being formed as well as to elementary motivational states. Adaptive resonance reflecting such psychological processes as interest in an unexpected implication, or the sense of order in a line of reasoning, may allow cortical networks to organize themselves into complex structures of intelligence.

Laterality and Network Neoteny

In addition to different processes for network control, hemisphere specialization may have drawn on the advantages of different levels of the network hierarchy. The recognition of the evolutionary structure of the cortex may suggest new ways of understanding asymmetries in cortical anatomy. The clearer anatomical picture may in turn suggest how the two hemispheres' differing forms of cognitive representation are linked to specific forms of network architecture.

Islands in the Cortex. Within the general envelope of retarded ontogenesis, the shift from genetic specification to information-dependent specification of cortical networks may have been particularly important for elaborating the most recently evolved and highly articulated networks of the primary sensory and motor areas. Several features of the gross anatomy of the left hemisphere suggest that there may be an extended development and enlargement of the primary sensory and motor areas on that side of the brain. In the initial computed tomography studies, it became apparent that certain regions, such as the occipital pole or the planum temporale, were typically larger in the left hemisphere, while other areas such as the frontal lobe were correspondingly larger in the right hemisphere (Galaburda et al., 1978). As noted earlier, Goldberg & Costa (1981) interpreted these data to suggest that the left hemisphere has become specialized for processing of single modality information. In contrast, the right hemisphere's specialization may entail greater cross-modal representation. A related anatomical argument was provided by Bear (1983), who proposed that the left hemisphere is specialized for cortico-cortical integration across sensory modalities, whereas the right hemisphere is specialized for corticolimbic integration.

Within the framework of cortical evolution, the primary sensory and motor areas have not only the greatest laminar articulation, but also have few if any extrinsic connections (Pandya et al., 1988). Thus any intermodal integration must involve at least the next ring down from primary sensory cortex, because the primary sensory areas are essentially isolated from all but local connections.

Within Bear's (1983) hypothesis, if there is an emphasis on cortico-cortical intermodal connections in the left hemisphere, these would not connect one primary sensory area to another. Yet if the left hemisphere has become specialized for the most articulated networks, its overall interconnection pattern might be expected to emphasize those horizontal connections that are farther from, rather than closer to, the paralimbic base of the hierarchy.

If there is greater development of the primary sensory and motor cortices in the left hemisphere than the right, these areas would become not only relatively isolated from other left hemisphere regions, but from the right hemisphere as well, since callosal connections like other extrinsic cortical connections do not include primary sensory areas. These architectural features would result in highly organized networks in the left hemisphere that are unmatched in the right hemisphere, and not directly accessible to it.

As future research clarifies the relation of limbic and brainstem controls to asymmetric cortical networks, it may become possible to understand how the left hemisphere's unique cognitive skills emerge from such factors as specialization for the object identification skills of the ventral cortical trend or specialization for the focal attention and analytic perception of the tonic activation system. It seems likely that asymmetric physiological mechanisms will be closely related to the asymmetries of network architecture. The left hemisphere's utilization of formal symbol systems (Goldberg & Costa, 1981), its arbitrary, substitutive representations (Tucker, 1986), and perhaps its all-or-none form of semantic activation (Beeman, in preparation; Burgess & Simpson, 1988) may reflect the operation of distributed networks that are relatively less constrained by the densely interconnected paralimbic base.

A full theoretical account of left hemisphere function may require an understanding of its mode of vertical integration, across specialized brainstem, limbic, and neocortical systems. Yet at the cortical level, the hypothesis of a particular elaboration of the most differentiated neocortical networks in the left hemisphere may be consistent with several findings on the anatomical asymmetry of the cortex. Because of the low density of extrinsic interconnections for the most articulated networks, the left hemisphere would be expected to have relatively less white matter than the right (Gur et al., 1980), and less electrophysiological coherence (Thatcher, et al., 1986; Tucker et al., 1986). The formation of representations within isolated, locally-organized networks would be consistent with Semmes's (1968) hypothesis of the representation of *like* elements in a given location in the left hemisphere.

The Primitive Right Hemisphere. Because the right hemisphere appears to have about the same overall cortical surface as the left hemisphere, its lesser expansion of primary sensory and motor areas may be balanced by a greater proportion of association areas (Goldberg & Costa, 1981). In the evolutionary network hierarchy, this would translate to an increased emphasis on more paralimbic, rather than highly differentiated, networks. Given that the paralimbic networks have the greater density of extrinsic interconnections (Pandya et al., 1988), a more primitive network organization of the right hemisphere would be consistent with the indications of more dense interconnections across regions of the right hemisphere than of the left (Gur et al., 1980; Thatcher, et al., 1986; Tucker et al., 1986).

In functional terms, the right hemisphere's importance to understanding and expressing emotional communications may occur because its representations are more integrated with paralimbic networks than those of the left hemisphere. In cognition as well as emotion, a densely interconnected processing architecture may be integral to the right hemisphere's holistic abilities. Yet there may be disadvantages to dense extrinsic interconnections as well. Representations of the environment that are formed with massive interconnections among the processing units may be highly accurate, but also highly context-dependent, and thus difficult to generalize to other situations. An analogy to this phenomenon is found in multivariate statistics, wherein characterization of a domain with a large number of measures may result in overspecification and poor generalization to related domains. This concreteness of the right hemisphere's holistic representations may be a fundamental limitation, and overcoming this limitation may have been an important feature in the left hemisphere's achievement of the arbitrary and flexible symbol systems of language and mathematics.

The differing connectional architectures of the two hemispheres may allow the human brain to optimize its psychological potential by fully elaborating one cortical hierarchy to support the most differentiated level, and another hierarchy to support the broad horizontal integration at the more primitive levels. Within the general mode of neoteny, the human brain has extended the phase of ontogenetic neural plasticity to remarkable lengths, allowing network differentiation to continue over many years of experience. Each level of the genetically-specified evolutionary hierarchy may offer important advantages as an organizing framework, within which competitive elimination and experiential specification may operate. The left hemisphere seems to have refined a set of locally-connected, highly articulated networks that operate at a relative distance from adaptive limbic constraints. This may have allowed not only increasingly articulated motor control, and discretely focused attentional mechanisms, but systems of regularized symbol manipulation that can operate objectively, minimally constrained by a concrete, stimulus-bound context.

Yet this form of network specialization has its costs. Through a complementary development of extensive primitive networks in the right hemisphere, human evolution may have provided a powerful contextual frame for the more articulated networks. The networks of the right hemisphere have the connection density, and the access to adaptive constraints, to integrate the operations of the whole brain within a matrix that defines the general significance of each event and action.

As fetal neural plasticity became drawn out into juvenile period, hominid children required a long period of nurturance. As with other social mammals, interaction with family group members allowed the life experiences of other individuals to serve as epigenetic determinants of brain differentiation and intelligence. Because their neural networks were so plastic for so long, human juveniles became powerful vessels for accumulating the epigenetic constraints on network differentiation, ready to offer them to the next generation.

The adaptive advantage of even rudimentary cultural knowledge in the hominids must have been considerable, such that a major criterion for selecting mechanisms of brain ontogenesis became the capacity these mechanisms conferred for both learning and teaching the epigenetic patterns of culture. Good learners and teachers created social groups with increasingly powerful forms of knowledge.

The rate of change in cultural evolution has been many orders of magnitude greater than that of genetic evolution. Each modern baby is born with a genetic program that was the product of the environmental demands of the stone age. It is a sign of the success of the underspecified, neotenic brain that humans are now coping, more or less, with the information age. Successful epigenetic network differentiation in these times requires not only a decade or two of organized instruction, but many subtle and implicit forms of knowledge. To survive effectively, children must come to understand the irritation in a parent's tone of voice, and what brands of sneakers will escape peer ridicule in elementary school.

The neural plasticity that gives each child a chance at socialization is extensive, but it is not unlimited. It is constrained by the course of development, as the ontogenetic plan brings forward the selected developmental menu from the evolutionary pantry. A neuropsychological approach to development may eventually uncover both the mechanisms of neural plasticity and the developmental processes that constrain these, thereby characterizing the processes of brain organization in terms that also describe psychological development. In this effort, the obviously important brain systems are those that we can relate to the communication processes, that mediate socialization. As it establishes unique representational systems for language and for nonverbal emotional communication, hemispheric specialization becomes a key organizing influence on the young vessels of culture.

Yet research and theory that focuses only on uniquely human brain features, such as hemispheric specialization or neocortical expansion, may not be able to explain what makes those features important. An adequate theory of cortical differentiation may need to be formed within an evolutionary framework, just as the brain's networks are. It may not be intuitive to find that the human brain's anatomy is comprised of nested structures, ranging from primitive to complex organizational forms. But in its anatomy, and perhaps in its intelligence as well, the human brain seems to integrate a cumulative strategy across residual mechanisms formed in many successive eras of neural evolution. The continuity across these mechanisms may have come from the need for continuous and effective self-control at each stage of evolution, such that certain themes of emotional arousal and self-regulation have been elaborated upon, from brainstem through limbic to cortical levels of organization. These themes of adaptive neural cybernetics, beginning with elementary neuromodulator mechanisms of sensitization and habituation, perhaps extended in time by the capacity for excited resonance in limbic circuits, may be continue to be important organizing vectors for ontogenetic differentiation, providing motivational and emotional controls to guide the self-organization of young neural networks.

REFERENCES

Ableitner, A., & Herz, A. (1987). Changes in local cerebral glucose utilization induced by the beta-carbolines FG 7142 and DMCM reveal brain structure is involved in the control of anxiety and seizure activity. *Journal of Neuroscience, 7,* 1047–1055.

Achenbach, T. M. (1982). *Developing psychopathology.* New York: Wiley.

Ambros-Ingerson, J., Granger, R., & Lynch, G. (1990). Similation of paleocortex performs hierarchical clustering. *Science, 247,* 1344–1348.

Barbas, H., & Pandya, D. N. (1989). Architecture and intrinsic connections of the prefrontal cortex in the rhesus monkey. *Journal of Comparative Neurology, 286,* 353–375.

Baxter, L. R., Phelps, M. E., Mazziotta, J. C., & Guze, B. H. (1987). Local cerebral glucose metabolic rates in obsessive-compulsive disorder: A comparison with rates in unipolar depression and in normal controls. *Archives of General Psychiatry, 44,* 211–218.

Bear, D. M., & Fedio, P. (1977). Quantitative analysis of interictal behavior in temporal lobe epilepsy. *Archives of Neurology, 34,* 454–467.

Bear, D. M. (1979). Temporal lobe epilepsy—a syndrome of temporal-limbic hyperconnection. *Cortex, 15,* 357–384.

Bear, D. M. (1983). Hemispheric specialization and the neurology of emotion. *Archives of Neurology, 40,* 195–202.

Beeman, M. (in preparation). *Right hemisphere contributions to language comprehension: Distributed processing in the right hemisphere.*

Bernstein, N. (1967). The coordination and regulation of movements. Oxford: Pergamon.

Best, C. T. (1986). *Hemispheric asymmetries of the perception and expression of infant facial emotions.* Paper presented at the meeting of the International Neuropsychological Society, Denver, CO, February.

Black, J. E., & Greenough, W. T. (1986). Developmental approaches to the memory processes. In J. L. Martinez, Jr., & R. P. Kesner (Eds.), Learning and memory: A biological view (pp. 55–81). Orlando, FL: Academic Press.

Borod, J. C., Koff, E., & Buck, R. (1986). The neuropsychology of facial expression: Data from normal and brain-damaged adults. In P. Blanck, R. Buck, & R. Rosenthal (Eds.), *Nonverbal communication in the clinical context.* University Park, PA: Penn State Press.

Bradshaw, J. L., & Nettleton, N. C. (1981). The nature of hemispheric specialization in man. *The Behavioral and Brain Sciences, 4,* 51–91.

Brodal, A. (1969). Neurological anatomy in relation to clinical medicine. New York: Oxford University Press.

Brown, J. W. (1989). The nature of voluntary action. *Brain and Cognition, 10,* 105–120.

Buck, R. (1984). Communication of emotion. In R. Buck (Ed.), The communication of emotion. New York: Guilford.

Buck, R. (1985). Prime theory: An integrated view of motivation and emotion. *Psychological Review, 92,* 389–413.

Burgess, C., & Simpson, G. B. (1988). Cerebral hemispheric mechanisms in the retrieval of ambiguous word meanings. *Brain & Language, 33,* 86–103.

Changeux, J., & Dehaene, S. (1989). Neuronal models of cognitive functions. *Cognition, 33,* 63–109.

Chugani, H. T., & Phelps, M. E. (1986). Maturational changes in cerebral function in infants determined by 18 FDG positron emission tomography. *Science, 231,* 840–843.

Cicone, M., Wapner, W., & Gardner, H. (1980). Sensitivity to emotional expressions and situations in organic patients. *Cortex, 16,* 145–158.

Damasio, A. R. (1989). Time-locked multiregional retroactivation: A systems-level proposal for the neural substrates of recall and recognition. *Cognition, 33,* 25–62.

Denckla, M. B. (1986, March). The neuropsychology of social emotional learning disabilities. Symposium on brain and emotion: The neuropsychology of affect. New York Neuropsychology Group.

Derryberry, D., & Tucker, D. M. (in press). The adaptive base of the neural hierarchy: Elementary motivational controls on network function. In R. Dienstbier (Ed.), *Nebraska Symposium on Motivation.* Lincoln: University of Nebraska Press.

Dichter, M. A., & Ayala, G. F. (1987). Cellular mechanisms of epilepsy: A status report. *Science, 237,* 157–164.

Doane, B. K., & Livingston, K. E. (Eds.). (1986). *The limbic system: Functional organization and clinical disorders.* New York: Raven Press.

Dopson, W. G., Beckwith, B. E., Tucker, D. M., & Bullard-Bates, P. C. (1985). Asymmetry of facial expression in spontaneous emotion. *Cortex, 20,* 243–251.

Eidelberg, D., & Galaburda, A. M. (1984). Inferior parietal lobule: Divergent architectonic asymmetries in the human brain. *Archives of Neurology, 41,* 843–852.

Farah, M. J., Gazzaniga, M. S., Holtzman, J. D., & Kosslyn, S. M. (1985). A left hemisphere basis for visual mental imagery? *Neuropsychologia, 23,* 115–118.

Flor-Henry, P., & Gruzelier, J. (Eds.). (1983). *Laterality and psychopathology. Vol. II.* Amsterdam: Elsevier.

Fuster, J. M. (1980). *The prefrontal cortex: Anatomy, physiology, and neuropsychology of the frontal lobe.* New York: Raven Press.

Galaburda, A. M. (1984). The anatomy of language: Lessons from comparative anatomy. In D. Caplan, A. R. Lecours, & A. Smith (Eds.), Biological perspectives on language. Cambridge, MA: MIT Press.

Galaburda, A. M., LeMay, M., Kemper, T. L., & Geschwind, N. (1978). Right–left asymmetries in the brain. *Science, 199,* 852–856.

Gold, P. E., & Zornetzer, S. F. (1983). The mnemon and its juices: Neural modulation of memory processes. *Behavioral and Neural Biology, 38,* 151–189.

Goldberg, E., & Costa, L. D. (1981). Hemisphere differences in the acquisition and use of descriptive systems. *Brain and Language, 14,* 144–173.

Goldberg, G. (1985). Supplementary motor area structure and function: Review and hypotheses. *Behavioral and Brain Sciences, 8,* 567–616.

Goldman-Rakic, P. S. (1987). Circuitry of the primate prefrontal cortex and regulation of behavior by representational memory. In F. Plum (Ed.), *Handbook of physiology. Section 1: The nervous system. Volume V. Higher functions of the brain, Part 1.* Bethesda, MD: American Physiological Society.

Goldman-Rakic, P. S. (1988). Changing concepts of cortical connectivity: Parallel distributed cortical networks. In P. Rakic & W. Singer (Ed.), *Neurobiology of neocortex.* New York: Wiley.

Gould, S. J. (1977a). Ontogeny and phylogeny. Cambridge, MA: Harvard University Press.

Gould, S. J. (1977b). *Ever since Darwin: Reflections in natural history.* New York: Norton.

Gray, J. A. (1982). *The neuropsychology of anxiety.* London: Oxford.

Greenough, W. T. (1984). Structural correlates of information storage in the mammalian brain: A review and hypothesis. *Trends in Neuroscience, 7,* 229–233.

Grossberg, S. (1984). Some psychophysiological and pharmacological correlates of a developmental, cognitive and motivational theory. In R. Karrer, J. Cohen, & P. Tueting, (Eds.), Brain and information: Event-related potentials. *Annals of the New York Academy of Science, Vol. 425.*

Gur, R. C., Packer, I. K., Hungerbuhler, J. P., Reivich, M., Obrist, W. D., Amarnek, W. S., & Sackeim, H. A. (1980). Differences in the distribution of gray and white matter in human cerebral hemispheres. *Science, 207,* 1226–1228.

Gustafsson, B., & Wigstrom, H. (1988). Physiological mechanisms underlying long-term potentiation. *Trends in Neuroscience, 11.*

Hamburger, V. (1977). The developmental history of the motor neuron. *Neuroscience Research Progress Bulletin, 15,* 1–37.

Innocenti, G. M. (1983). Exuberant callosal projections between the developing hemispheres. In R. Villani, I. Papo, M. Giovanelli, S. M. Gaini, & G. Tomei (Eds.), *Advances in Neurotraumatology.* Amsterdam, Excerpta Medica.

Jackson, J. Hughlings (1879). On affections of speech from diseases of the brain. *Brain, 2,* 203–222.

Janowsky, J. S., & Finlay, B. L. (1983). Cell degeneration in early development of the forebrain and cerebellum. *Anatomy and Embryology, 167,* 439–447.

Janowsky, J. S., Laxer, K. D., & Rushmer, D. S. (1980). Classical conditioning of kindled seizures. *Epilepsia, 21,* 393–398.

Johanson, A. M., Risberg, J., Silfverskiold, P., & Smith, G. (1986). Regional changes of cerebral blood flow during increased anxiety in patients with anxiety neurosis. In U. Hentschel, G. Smith, & J. G. Draguns (Eds.), *The roots of perception.* Amsterdam: North-Holland, 1986.

Kaas, J. H. (1988). Development of cortical sensory maps. In P. Rakic & W. Singer (Eds.), *Neurobiology of neocortex.* New York: Wiley.

Kimura, D. (1977). Acquisition of a motor skill after left-hemisphere damage. *Brain, 100,* 527–542.

Kinsbourne, M. (1970). The cerebral basis of lateral asymmetries in attention. *Acta Psychologica, 33,* 193–201.

Kinsbourne, M. (1982). Hemispheric specialization and the growth of human understanding. *American Psychologist, 37,* 411–420.

Kosslyn, S. M. (1987). Seeing and imagining in the cerebral hemispheres: A computational approach. *Psychological Review, 94,* 148–175.

Kosslyn, S. M. (1988). Aspects of a cognitive neuroscience of mental imagery. *Science, 240,* 1621–1626.

Kuhar, M. J. (1986). Neuroanatomical substrates of anxiety: a brief survey. *Trends in Neuroscience, 7,* 307–311.

LeDoux, J. E. (1987). Emotion. In F. Plum (Ed.), *Handbook of physiology. Section 1: The nervous system. Volume V. Higher functions of the brain, Part 1.* Bethesda, MD: American Physiological Society.

Levy, J. (1969). Possible basis for the evolution of lateral specialization of the human brain. *Nature, 224,* 614–615.

Lewis, D. A., & Morrison, J. H. (1989). Noradrenergic innervation of monkey prefrontal cortex: A dopamine-b-hydroxylase immunohistochemical study. *Journal of Comparative Neurology, 282,* 317–330.

MacLean, P. D. (1958). Contrasting functions of limbic and neocortical systems of the brain and their relation to psychophysiological aspects of medicine. *American Journal of Medicine, 25,* 611–626.

Malsburg, C., Von de, & Singer, W. (1988). Principles of cortical network organization. In P. Rakic & W. Singer (Eds.), *Neurobiology of neocortex,* New York: John Wiley.

Mesulam, M. M. (1981). A cortical network for directed attention and unilateral neglect. *Annals of Neurology, 10,* 309–325.

Mesulam, M. M., & Mufson, E. J. (1982). Insula of the old world monkey. I: Architectonics in the insulo-orbito-temporal component of the paralimbic brain. *Journal of Comparative Neurology, 212,* 1–22.

Mesulam, M. M., & Mufson, E. J. (1984). Neural inputs into the nucleus basalis of the substantia innominata (Ch4) in the rhesus monkey. *Brain, 107,* 253–274.

Monrad-Krohn, G. H. (1924). On the dissociation of voluntary and emotional innervation in facial paresis of central origin. *Brain, 47,* 22–35.

Nauta, W. J. H. (1986). Circuitous connections linking cerebral cortex, limbic system, and corpus striatum. In B. K. Doane & K. E. Livingston, (Eds.), *The limbic system: Functional organization and clinical disorders.* New York: Raven Press.

Nauta, W. J. H. (1971). The problem of the frontal lobe: A reinterpretation. *Journal of Psychiatric Research, 8,* 167–187.

Nebes, R. D. (1978). Direct examination of cognitive function in the left and right hemispheres. In M. Kinsbourne (Ed.), *Asymmetrical function of the brain.* New York: Cambridge University Press.

Osgood, C. E., Suci, G. J., & Tannenbaum, P. H. (1957). *The measurement of meaning.* Urbana: University of Illinois Press.

Ostrove, J. M., Simpson, T., & Garder, H. (1990). Beyond scripts: A note on the capacity of right hemisphere-damaged patients to process social and emotional content. *Brain and Cognition, 12,* 144–154.

Pandya, D. N., Seltzer, B., & Barbas, H. (1988). Input-output organization of the primate cerebral cortex. In *Comparative primate biology, Vol IV: Neurosciences* (pp. 39–80). Allen Ardis, Inc.

Pandya, D. N., & Yeterian, E. H. (1984). Proposed neural circuitry for spatial memory in the primate brain. *Neuropsychologia, 22,* 109–122.

Pandya, D. N., & Yeterian, E. H. (1985). Architecture and connections of cortical association areas. In A. Peters & E. G. Jones (Ed.), *Cerebral cortex. Volume 4. Association and auditory cortices.* New York: Plenum Press.

Papez, J. W. (1937). A proposed mechanism of emotion. *Archives of Neurology and Psychiatry, 38,* 725–744.

Perrett, D. I., Rolls, E. T., & Caan, W. (1982). Visual neurones responsive to faces in the monkey temporal cortex. *Experimental Brain Research, 47,* 329–342.

Posner, M. I., Petersen, S. E., Fox, P. T., & Raichle, M. E. (1988). Localization of cognitive operations in the human brain. *Science, 240,* 1627–1631.

Pribram, K. H., & McGuinness, D. (1975). Arousal, activation, and effort in the control of attention. *Psychological Review, 82,* 116–149.

Purves, D., & Lichtman, J. W. (1985). *Principles of neural development.* Sunderland, MA: Sinauer.

Rakic, P. (1988). Specification of cerebral cortical areas. *Science, 1988, 241,* 170–176.

Rapoport, J. L. (1989). The biology of obsessions and compulsions. *Scientific American,* pp. 83–89.

Reiman, E. M., Fusselman, M. J., Fox, P. T., & Raichle, M. E. (1989). Neuroanatomical correlates of anticipatory anxiety. *Science, 243,* 1071–1074.

Rinn, W. E. (1984). The neuropsychology of facial expression: A review of the neurological and psychological mechanisms for producing facial expressions. *Psychological Bulletin, 95,* 52–77.

Roland, P. E. (1985). Cortical organization of voluntary behavior in man. *Human Neurobiology, 4,* 155–167.

Rolls, E. T. (1987). Information representation, processing, and storage in the brain: Analysis at the single neuron level. In J. P. Changeaux, & M. Konishi (Ed.), *The neural and molecular bases of learning*. New York: Wiley.

Ross, E. D., & Rush, A. J. (1981). Diagnosis and neuroanatomical correlates of depression in brain-damaged patients: Implications for a neurology of depression. *Archives of General Psychiatry, 38,* 1344–1354.

Rothbart, M. K. (1989). Temperament in childhood. In G. A. Kohnstamm, J. E. Bates, and M. K. Rothbart (Eds.), *Temperament in childhood.* New York: Wiley.

Rothbart, M. K., Taylor, S., & Tucker, D. M. (1989). Right-sided facial asymmetry in infant emotional expression. *Neuropsychologia, 27,* 675–687.

Rothbart, M. K., & Derryberry, D. (1981). Development of individual differences in temperament. In M. E. Lamb & A. L. Brown (Eds.), *Advances in developmental psychology: Volume 1.* Hillsdale, NJ: Lawrence Erlbaum Associates.

Rumelhart, D. E., & McClelland, J. L. (1986). *Parallel distributed processing: Explorations in the microstructure of cognition. Vol I: Foundations.* Cambridge, MA: MIT Press.

Sackeim, H. A., Gur, R. C., & Saucy, M. C. (1978). Emotions are expressed more intensely on the left side of the face. *Science, 202,* 434–436.

Safer, M. A., & Leventhal, H. (1977). Ear differences in evaluating emotional tone of voice and verbal content. *Journal of Experimental Psychology: Human Perception and Performance, 3,* 75–82.

Sanides, F. (1970). Functional architecture of motor and sensory cortices in primates in the light of a new concept of neocortex evolution. In C. R. Noback & W. Montagna (Eds.), *The primate brain: Advances in primatology* (Vol. 1). New York: Appleton-Century-Crofts.

Semmes, J. (1968). Hemispheric specialization: A possible clue to mechanism. *Neuropsychologia, 6,* 11–26.

Shaw, E. D., Mann, J. J., Stokes, P. E., & Manevitz, Z. (1986). Effects of lithium carbonate on associative productivity and idiosyncratic in bipolar outpatients. *American Journal of Psychiatry, 143,* 1166–1169.

Singer, W. (1987). Activity-dependent self-organization of synaptic connections as a substrate of learning. In J. P. Changeux & M. Konishi (Eds.), *The neural and molecular basis of learning.* New York: Wiley.

Sperry, R. W. (1977). Forebrain commisurotomy and conscious awareness. *Journal of Medicine and Philosophy, 2,* 101–126.

Sperry, R. W., Gazzaniga, M. S., & Bogen, J. E. (1969). Interhemispheric relationships: The neocortical commissures; syndromes of hemisphere disconnection. In P. Vinken & C. Bruyn (Eds.), *Handbook of clinical neurology.* Amsterdam: North Holland.

Squire, L. R. (1986). Mechanisms of memory. *Science, 232,* 1612–1619.

Squire, L. R. (1987). *Memory and brain.* New York: Oxford University Press.

Taylor, D. C. (1969). Differential rates of cerebral maturation between sexes and between hemispheres. *Lancet,* July 19, 140–142.

Tellegen, A. (1985). Structures of mood and personality and their relevance to assessing anxiety, with an emphasis on self-report. In A. H. Tuma & J. D. Maser (Eds.), *Anxiety and the anxiety disorders.* Hillsdale, NJ: Lawrence Erlbaum Associates.

Teyler, T. J. (1986). Memory: Electrophysiological analogs. In J. L. Martinez, Jr., & R. P. Kesner (Eds.), *Learning and memory: A biological view.* Orlando, FL: Academic Press.

Thatcher, R. W., Walker, R. A., & Guidice, S. (1987). Human cerebral hemispheres develop at different rates and ages. *Science, 236,* 1110–1113.

Thatcher, R. W. (1990). Nonlinear dynamics of human cerebral development. In E. John & L. Prichep (Eds.), *Machinery of the mind.* Berkhauser Publishing Co.

Thatcher, R. W., Krause, P. J., & Rhybyk, M. (1986). Cortico-cortical associations and EEG coherence: A two-compartmental model. *Electroencephalography and Clinical Neurophysiology, 64,* 123–143.

Thayer, R. E. (1989). *The biopsychology of mood and arousal.* New York: Oxford University Press.

Trevarthen, C. (1984). Emotions in infancy: Regulators of contacts and relationships with persons. In K. Scherer & P. Ekman (Eds.), *Approaches to emotion.* Hillsdale, NJ: Lawrence Erlbaum Associates.

Trevarthen, C. (1985). Neuroembryology and the development of perceptual mechanisms. In F. Falkner & J. M. Tanner (Eds.), *Human growth, a comprehensive treatise: Volume 2, Postnatal growth, neurobiology.* New York: Plenum.

Trevarthen, C. (in press). Growth and education of the hemispheres. In C. Trevarthen (Ed.), *Brain circuits and functions of the mind: Essays in honor of Roger W. Sperry.* New York: Cambridge University Press.

Tucker, D. M., & Newman, J. P. (1981). Verbal versus imaginal cognitive strategies in the inhibition of emotional arousal. *Cognitive Therapy and Research, 5,* 197–202.

Tucker, D. M. (1981). Lateral brain function, emotion, and conceptualization. *Psychological Bulletin, 89,* 19–46.

Tucker, D. M. (1986). Neural control of emotional communication. In P. Blanck, R. Buck, & R. Rosenthal, (Eds.), *Nonverbal communication in the clinical context.* Cambridge, England: Cambridge University Press.

Tucker, D. M. (1989). Neural and psychological maturation in a social context. In D. Cicchetti (Ed.), *The emergence of a discipline: Rochester symposium on developmental psychopathology.* Hillsdale, NJ: Lawrence Erlbaum Associates.

Tucker, D. M., & Derryberry, D. (in press). Motivated attention: Anxiety and the frontal executive functions. *Neuropsychiatry, Neuropsychology, & Behavioral Neurology.*

Tucker, D. M., & Frederick, S. L. (1989). Emotion and brain lateralization. In H. Wagner & T. Manstead (Eds.), *Handbook of psychophysiology: Emotion and social behaviour.* New York: Wiley.

Tucker, D. M., & Liotti, M. (1990). Neuropsychological mechanisms of anxiety and depression. In F. Boller & J. Grafman (Eds.), *Handbook of neuropsychology.* Amsterdam: Elsevier.

Tucker, D. M., Stenslie, C. E., Roth, R. S., & Shearer, S. L. (1981). Right frontal lobe activation and right hemisphere performance decrement during a depressed mood. *Archives of General Psychiatry, 38,* 169–174.

Tucker, D. M., Vannatta, K., & Rothlind, J. (1990). Activation and arousal systems and the adaptive control of cognitive priming. In N. Stein, B. Leventhal, & T. Trabasso (Eds.), *Psychological and biological approaches to emotion.* Hillsdale, NJ: Lawrence Erlbaum Associates.

Tucker, D. M., & Williamson, P. A. (1984). Asymmetric neural control systems in human self-regulation. *Psychological Review, 91,* 185–215.

Tucker, D. M., Roth, D. L., & Bair, T. B. (1986). Functional connections among cortical regions: Topography of EEG Coherence. *Electroencephalography and Clinical Neurophysiology, 63,* 242–250.

Tyler, S. K., & Tucker, D. M. (1982). Anxiety and perceptual structure: Individual differences in neuropsychological function. *Journal of Abnormal Psychology, 91,* 210–220.

Ungerleider, L. G., & Mishkin, M. (1982). Two cortical visual systems. In D. J. Ingle, R. J. W. Mansfield, & M. A. Goodale (Eds.), *The analysis of visual behavior.* Cambridge, MA: MIT Press.

Wood, F. (1986). personal communication.

Yakovlev, P. I., & Lecours, A.-R. (1967). The myelogenetic cycles of regional maturation of the brain. In A. Minkowski (Ed.), *Regional development of the brain in early life.* Oxford: Blackwell.

Yeterian, E. H., & Pandya, D. N. (1988). Corticothalamic connections of paralimbic regions in the rhesus monkey. *Journal of Comparative Neurology, 269,* 130–146.

4 Cortical Versus Limbic Immaturity: Relationship To Infantile Amnesia

Jocelyne Bachevalier
National Institute of Mental Health

Early childhood is a period rich in experience in which young children are capable of acquiring, registering, and recalling events and episodes, as well as recognizing places and people. They can also vividly react to impressions, manifest pain and pleasure, and express love, jealousy and other passions. It is thus astonishing that this period is usually lost to memory entirely except for a few fragments. It was Freud who first described this lack of recall as a kind of amnesia and referred to it as infantile amnesia. Infantile amnesia is a universal phenomenon. No one can remember his very early childhood, although the age at which a person forms what later will be his earliest memory, generally from three to four years, varies among individuals. Why are our earliest memories so rare, evasive, and random, and why can we not recollect them? For Freud, infantile amnesia was due to an internal force of repression. That is, having resolved the Oedipal crisis by rejecting our infantile sexual wishes, we cannot tolerate any associated memory that might bring them back to consciousness. Although very few other systematic attempts have been made to explain this phenomenon, psychological mechanisms (such as pro- and retroactive experience, stimulus generalization, changes in information processing) as well as neurological mechanisms (such as developmental changes in brain structure and function) have been advanced as explanatory factors of infantile amnesia (see for review Campbell & Coulter, 1976; Coulter, 1979; Spear, 1979). Renewed attempts to describe and explain infantile amnesia emerged from the recent discovery that memory involves different processes, one of which develops late during ontogeny. These new findings have led to the idea that infantile amnesia may be due to the absence of a functional memory system in early childhood (Bachevalier & Mishkin, 1984; Nadel & Zola-Morgan, 1984). The major aim of this chapter will be to review findings indicating that retention of experience can proceed by two different systems, subserved by separate neural circuits, that develop at different rates during ontogeny. In this survey we will see that although young infants have the ability to acquire habits and skills, their capacity to form memories matures slowly during the first years of life. A final section will present evidence that, in primates, delayed maturation of the cortical association areas of the brain appears to be responsible for the delayed maturation of the memory system and, by implication, might be responsible for the phenomenon of infantile amnesia.

MULTIPLE MEMORY PROCESSES

Evidence that retention of the effects of experience proceeds according to different principles, each served by a different neural system, has come mainly in the last decade from studies of brain-damaged amnesic subjects. Bilateral damage to the medial temporal lobe in humans results in a profound anterograde amnesia. The most striking characteristic of amnesic patients is their inability to remember recent events and to learn many types of new information, even though intelligence, perception, and language are either unaffected or only minimally impaired. The amnesia is also referred to as "global" in that it extends to many types of information derived from all sensory modalities (Corkin, 1965; Milner, 1972). Despite this severe impairment in memory functions, amnesic patients may still learn new habits and skills in an entirely normal manner. The first piece of evidence for the existence of preserved learning ability in profoundly amnesic subjects came from Milner's (1962) dramatic demonstration of a nearly normal rate of improvement of mirror-drawing skill in the severely amnesic patient, H.M., who underwent bilateral surgical removal of the medial temporal lobe to relieve his epilepsy. Since the report of H.M., there have been numerous studies showing the ability of amnesic patients to learn despite their inability to remember (Brooks & Baddeley, 1976; Cohen & Squire, 1980; Corkin, 1968; Warrington & Weiskrantz, 1968.) All these studies demonstrate that gradual learning of skills and habits can proceed independently of the ability to recollect specific events or episodes.

Experimental studies in nonhuman primates converge upon a similar conclusion (Mishkin, Malamut, & Bachevalier, 1984; Mishkin & Petri, 1984; Zola-Morgan & Squire, 1985a). In our laboratory, Mishkin and his colleagues had found corresponding losses and hidden learning capacities in monkeys with brain damage like H.M.'s. For example, when tested on a one-trial visual recognition task, such as delayed nonmatching-to-sample or object-reward association, both with trial unique objects, monkeys with combined ablation of the medial temporal lobe (including the amygdala, hippocampus, and entorhinal cortex) seem unable either to recognize an object they had seen just a minute or two earlier (Mishkin, 1978), or to remember for even a few seconds whether or not the object had been baited (Spiegler & Mishkin, 1979). Also their memory deficits appear to be global since monkeys with limbic lesions are also severely impaired on a nonmatching-to-sample test of tactile recognition (Murray & Mishkin, 1983). Paradoxically, the same monkeys are able to learn a long series of different object pairs, each containing one baited object, when the series is presented only once a day (Malamut, Saunders, & Mishkin, 1984). Thus, in this object-discrimination test, with time they learn to choose the object carrying the reward by forming an automatic connection between a stimulus and a response.

What are we to make of the fact that both patients and experimental animals can be amnesic in some situations and yet not in others? The conclusion to which most investigators have come is that there are at least two different forms of retention, only one of which is affected in amnesia. As a result, several dichotomous classifications of memory have been advanced, such as procedural versus declarative (Cohen, 1984; Squire, 1982), semantic versus episodic (Tulving, 1983), reference versus working (Olton, Becker, & Handelmann, 1979), habit versus memory (Hirsh, 1974; Mishkin et al., 1984; Mishkin & Petri, 1984), and taxon versus locale (O'Keefe & Nadel, 1978). However, all of these distinctions have in common the implication that one learning and retention system supports gradual or incremental learning and is involved in the acquisition of habits and skills (as object-discrimination), while the other supports rapid one-trial learning and is necessary for forming memories that represent specific situations and episodes (as object recognition). Furthermore, the fact that one of the system is dependent upon the integrity of the limbic structures whereas the other is not has led Mishkin and his collaborators (1984, 1987) to propose that these two retention systems are in fact subserved by two independent neural circuits.

THE NEURAL CIRCUITS FOR MEMORIES AND HABITS

The detailed knowledge now available concerning the neuroanatomy of the medial temporal lobe and its interconnections with diencephalic, prefrontal, and basal forebrain areas, as well as the memory loss described following lesion or neuropathology in these neural structures has guided the formulation of a functional neural system for the formation of cognitive or representational memory.

The neuroanatomical studies have shown that the amygdala directly and the hippocampus via the perirhinal and entorhinal cortex receive highly processed sensory information from sensory specific cortical areas (Amaral, 1987; Turner, Mishkin, & Knapp, 1980; Van Hoesen & Pandya, 1975). The amygdala and the hippocampus are connected in turn reciprocally, with various medial and midline thalamic nuclei and the mamillary bodies (Aggleton, Desimone, & Mishkin, 1986; Aggleton & Mishkin, 1984). In addition, these diencephalic regions are connected not only with medial temporal lobe structures, but also with the ventral and medial portions of the prefrontal cortex (Baleydier & Mauguiere, 1980; Nauta, 1962; Tobias, 1975). Finally, both the limbic, diencephalic, and prefrontal areas are interconnected with the basal forebrain which sends widespread projections back to the entire cortical mantle (Amaral & Cowan, 1980; Mesulam, Mufson, Levey, & Weiner, 1983). A diagrammatic summary of the anatomical circuit that has been implicated in visual recognition memory is shown in Fig. 4.1. Severe lesion-induced memory losses have been demonstrated in monkeys at different loci along this pathway:

1. area TE, the visual higher-order association area in the anterior portion of the inferior temporal cortex (Mishkin, 1982);
2. the connections between area TE and the amygdalo-hippocampal complex (Zola-Morgan, Squire, & Mishkin, 1982);
3. the amygdala, hippocampus, and rhinal cortex (Mishkin, 1978; Murray, Bachevalier, & Mishkin, 1989; Zola-Morgan, Squire, Amaral, & Suzuki, 1989);
4. the limbo-diencephalic pathway (Bachevalier, Parkinson, & Mishkin, 1985);
5. the limbic targets in the medial thalamus, including the medial parts of the medial dorsal nucleus, the anterior nuclei, and the mamillary bodies (Aggleton & Mishkin, 1983a, 1983b; Aggleton & Mishkin, 1985; Zola-Morgan & Squire, 1985b);
6. sub-, pre- and supracallosal, and orbital prefrontal cortex (Bachevalier & Mishkin; 1986a);
7. the basal forebrain (Aigner et al., in press).

As for the neurological evidence, these different regions comprising the proposed circuit are also the major sites of neuropathology associated with amnesia in humans (Fig. 4.1). These sites include the medial temporal area, in patients with temporal lobe resections or herpes encephalitis (Penfield & Milner, 1958; Scoville & Milner, 1957; Lilly, Cummings, Benson, & Frankel, 1983), the medial diencephalic area in patients with Korsakoff's disease (Butters & Cermak, 1980; Mair, Warrington, & Weiskrantz, 1979; Squire, 1987; Talland, 1965; Victor, Adams, & Collins, 1971), the ventromedial aspect of the prefrontal cortex in patients with aneurysms of the anterior communicating artery (Alexander & Freedman, 1984; Gade, 1982; Talland, Sweet, & Ballantine, 1967), frontal lobe neoplasms (Angelergues, Hecaen, & De Ajuriaguerra, 1955; Provansal, 1951) or prefrontal surgical removals (Whitty & Levin, 1960), and the basal forebrain in patients with Alzheimer's disease (Arendt, Bigl, Arendt, & Tennstedt, 1983; Candy, et al., 1983; Whitehouse, et al., 1982).

As shown for visual recognition memory in Fig. 4.1, the neural model proposed by Mishkin and his colleagues (e.g., Mishkin & Appenzeller, 1987) postu-

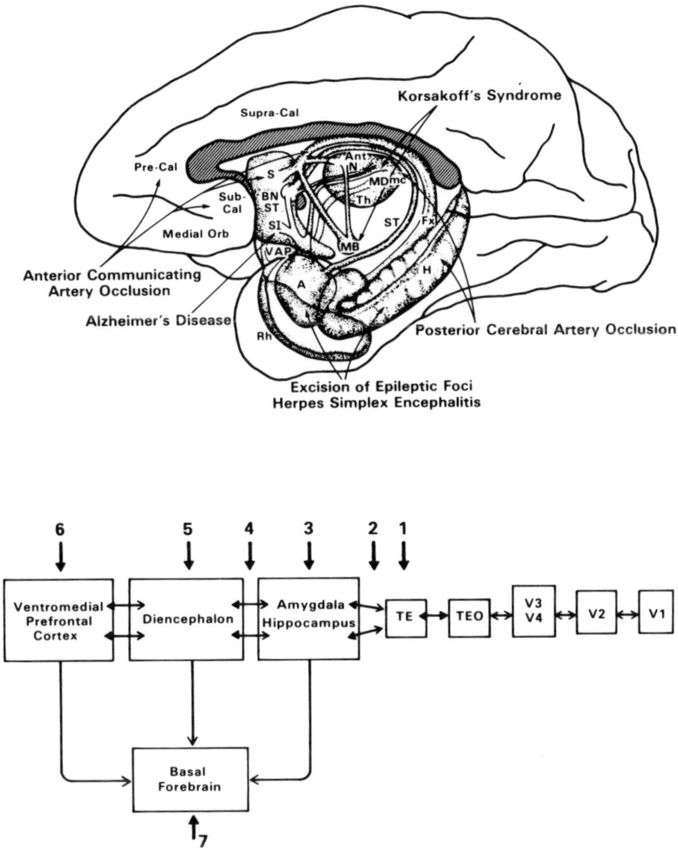

FIG. 4.1. The cognitive memory system: The diagram at the top indicates the brain structures crucial for memory functions and the sites of brain damage by diseases that can cause memory loss in human beings. The chart at the bottom indicates the flow of visual information from striate cortex (V1), to prestriate cortex (V2, V3, V4), to inferior temporal cortex (TEO and TE), to the limbic structures (amygdala, A; hippocampus, H; rhinal cortex, Rh), and via the limbo-diencephalic pathways (fornix, Fx; stria terminalis, ST; ventroamygdalofugal pathway, VAP) to the diencephalon (anterior, Ant. N., and medial dorsal, MD, nuclei of the thalamus; mamillary bodies, MB), to the ventromedial prefrontal cortex (supra-, pre- and subcallosal cortex, and orbital cortex), and to the basal forebrain (substantia innominata, SI; bed nucleus of the stria terminalis, BNST; septum, S). The numbers indicate lesion-induced visual recognition loss in monkeys.

lates that visual information is processed sequentially along an occipitotemporal pathway. This ventrally directed chain of cortical visual areas (V1, V2, V3, V4, and TEO) appears to extract stimulus-quality information, such as size, color, shape, and texture, from the retinal input reaching the striate cortex, until the final stations of the inferior temporal cortex (area TE) synthesize a complete representation of the object. Storage of the object's representation (and assignment of some meaning or association to it) is realized each time a perception formed in the final station of the visual cortical sensory system activates one or both of two parallel circuits. One circuit is anchored in the amygdala and the other in the hippocampus and includes their projection target areas in the diencephalon and the ventromedial prefrontal cortex. Each of these structures in turn sends signals to the basal forebrain which, through its widespread cortical projections, reaches back to the sensory cortical areas. It is postulated that the feedback action of these circuits on sensory and limbic areas strengthens synapses among active neurons and so perhaps stores the neural representation of the sensory event that had just taken place. Once established, this central representation can be reactivated whenever the same stimulus reappears in the field, yielding visual recognition. Furthermore, since all the sensory modalities appears to be represented centrally by a hierarchical arrangement from primary to higher processing areas, and since the highest cortical levels in each modality appears to project to both the amygdala and the hippocampus (Turner et al., 1980; Van Hoesen & Pandya, 1975) it is postulated that the same circuit that mediates recognition memory in vision does so in the other sensory modalities.

As for the neural circuit that underlies the formation of visual habits, here the evidence is still relatively sparse. Both neuroanatomical and lesion studies, however, indicate that the striatum is the most likely candidate. As shown in Fig. 4.2, the striatum receives projections from sensory processing areas of the cerebral cortex and sends projections to the globus pallidus, substantia nigra, and associated structures within the extrapyramidal system that control movements. Behavioral evidence also support the view that the corticostriatal system serves noncognitive habit formation. For example, impairments in visual discrimination have now been demonstrated following lesions of either (1) the inferior temporal cortex (Mishkin, 1954; Phillips, Malamut, Bachevalier, & Mishkin, 1988); (2) the projections from the visual areas to the neostriatum (Horel, 1978; Zola-Morgan et al., 1982); or (3) the striatal regions (Buerger, Gross, & Rocha-Miranda, 1974; Divac, Rosvold, & Szwarcbart, 1967; Wang, Aigner, & Mishkin, 1990). Thus, for visual habit formation (Fig. 4.2), the neural model proposed by Mishkin and his colleagues (Mishkin & Appenzeller, 1987; Phillips et al., 1988) postulates that information about objects is processed through a series of cortical visual areas, including striate and prestriate cortex and inferior temporal cortical areas TEO and TE. Through a series of connections from the striatum to the globus pallidus and substantia nigra, to the ventral thalamus, and, finally, to the premotor cortex, cortically processed visual inputs could become associated with

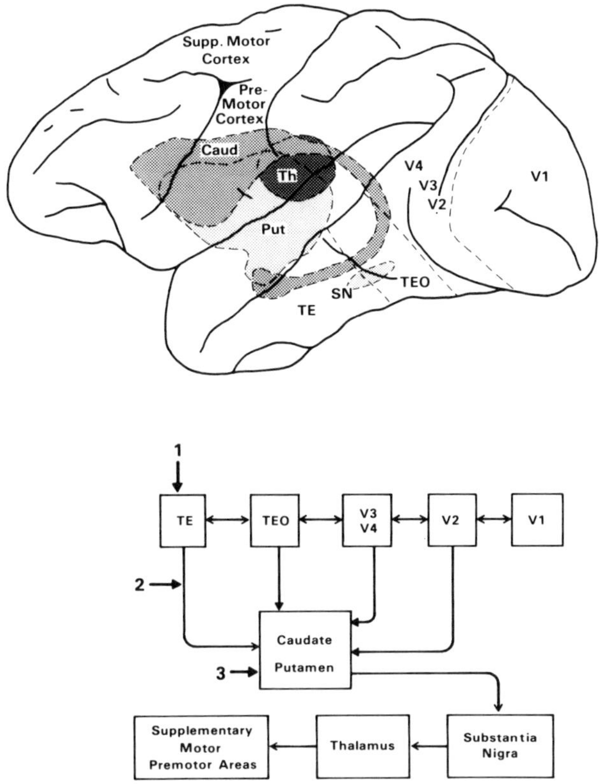

FIG. 4.2. The noncognitive habit system: The diagram at the top indicates the brain structures crucial for the formation of habits. The chart at the bottom indicates the flow of visual information in the postulated neural circuit for visual habit formation. The numbers indicate lesion-induced visual habit deficit. Abbreviations: Caud, caudate; Put, putamen; SN, subtantia nigra; Th, thalamus.

extrapyramidally generated motor outputs and so yield the stimulus-response bonds that constitute visual habits.

On the evidence that in adult monkeys there may be two relatively independent systems for retention of information, we sought to compare the functional development of the two systems ontogenetically (Bachevalier & Mishkin, 1984).

THE MATURATION OF HABIT FORMATION

The relatively early appearance in life of the noncognitive habit system was demonstrated by testing 3-month-old monkeys in a multiple-trial concurrent object discrimination task that was used to demonstrate the preserved ability in adult monkeys with limbic lesions (Malamut et al., 1984). In this task, a series of 20 pairs of objects was presented just once a day as follows (Fig. 4.3). A positive and a negative object (i.e., one baited and one not) were presented simultaneously over the lateral wells of the test tray. After the animal made a choice by displacing one of the objects, there was a 20-sec delay, following which the second pair of objects was presented for choice, and so on until all 20 pairs had been presented once each. The same series of objects was then repeated once every 24 hours (24-hr ITI task). The positive and negative objects within each pair, as well as the serial order of the pairs, remained constant across sessions, but the objects' left-right positions were randomized daily. Testing was continued in this way until the monkeys attained the criterion of 90 correct responses in 100 consecutive trials, first on the one set of 20 object-pairs (Set A), and then on a second set (B).

Three-month-old infant rhesus monkeys were clearly able to form visual discrimination habits as quickly as adults, averaging 16 sessions as compared to 9 sessions for the adults. As shown in the learning curves (Fig. 4.4), although the infant monkeys did take a few more sessions than the adults to learn Set A, they learned Set B even more quickly than the adults. Although we did not test infant

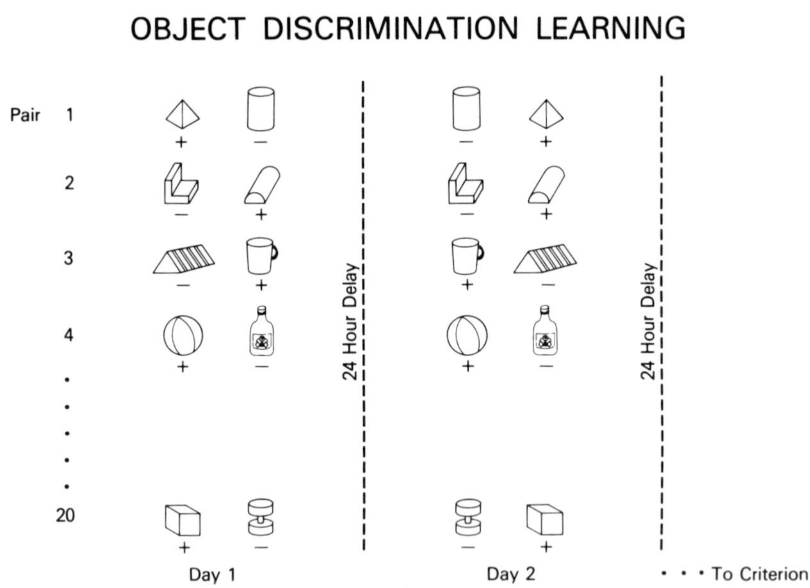

FIG. 4.3. Concurrent object discrimination task employs a sequence of 20 pairs of objects. One object (+) in each pair conceals a reward. A monkey is shown the same sequence repeatedly, at 24-hour intervals, until it learns to choose the baited object in each pair consistently. From Bachevalier (1990b).

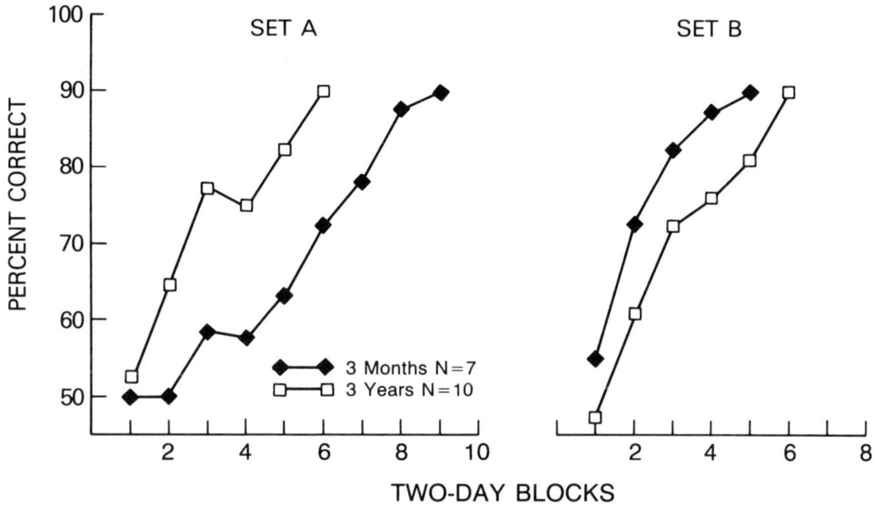

FIG. 4.4. Learning curves on two sets (A and B) of concurrent object discriminations for 3-month-old and 3-year-old monkeys. Scores for 2-day blocks were averaged until the learning criterion was met. From Bachevalier & Mishkin, (1984).

monkeys younger than 3 months of age, acquisition of visual discrimination habits is known to occur in infant monkeys even younger than 1 month of age (Harlow, 1959; Zimmerman & Torrey, 1965). Together, the data indicate that young monkeys readily acquire visual discrimination habits independently of whether the discriminations are presented one object-pair at a time with massed practice and short intertrial intervals (Zimmerman & Torrey, 1965), or in short lists of object-pairs with massed practice and short intertrial intervals (Mahut & Zola-Morgan, 1977), or even in long lists of object-pairs with distributed practice and extremely long intertrial intervals (Bachevalier & Mishkin, 1984).

In addition, although not expressly noted in our first report, the female infant monkeys tended to learn the 24-hr ITI task faster than the male infants, requiring an average of 12 sessions as compared to 20 sessions for the males. This sexual dimorphism in the development of visual discrimination habits was clearly evident in a more recent study (Bachevalier, Hagger, & Bercu, 1989), in which 3- and 6-month-old male and female monkeys were tested in the 24-hr ITI task and their performance compared to that of male and female adult monkeys. There it was shown that the 3-month-old male monkeys required significantly more sessions and made more errors to learn Set A than did the females (Fig. 4.5). This sex difference was absent in the 6-month-old group, in which both the male and female animals performed as efficiently as the male and female adults. Additional evidence of sexual dimorphism in visual discrimination learning by infant

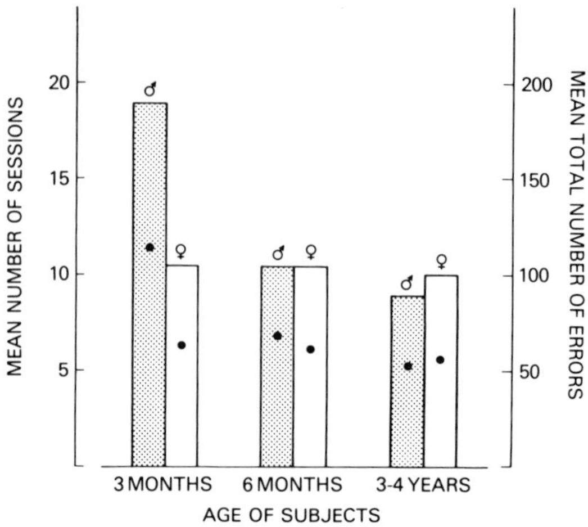

FIG. 4.5. Mean number of sessions (bars) and errors (circles) preceding criterion on Set A. Numbers of animals were 8 males and 5 females at the age of 3 months, 6 males and 3 females at the age of 6 months, and 7 males and 3 females at the age of 3-4 years. From Bachevalier (1990b).

macaques comes from a study showing that 4- to 5-month-old males learned both single and concurrent visual discriminations with short intertrial intervals at a slower rate than females (H. Mahut, personal communication).

In a neuroendocrinological study (Bachevalier et al., 1989), we have further demonstrated that the prenatal surge of androgens present in male infants until about 3–4 months of age (Bercu, et al., 1983; Bercu, Spiliotis, Reed, & Lee, 1987) is probably responsible for the sexual dimorphism in visual habit formation, since a significant correlation appeared in male infants between their circulating levels of testosterone and learning scores (the higher the level, the poorer the score). Furthermore, this sexual dimorphism can be reversed in the two sexes by perinatal manipulation of androgen levels. In this latter study (Hagger, Bachevalier, & Bercu, 1987), plasma testosterone levels were reduced in male monkeys by neonatal orchiectomy and increased in neonatally ovariectomized female monkeys treated with dihydrotestosterone. When trained in the 24-hr ITI task at three months of age, orchiectomized male monkeys mastered the task faster (average, 12 sessions) than intact males (average, 18 sessions) and at the same rate as intact females (average, 11 sessions). Conversely, neonatally androgenized female monkeys learned the task more slowly (average, 19 sessions) than intact females and at the same rate as intact males. It seems, therefore, that the presence of perinatal testosterone can affect performance on the 24-hr ITI task by some as yet unspecified action on the maturing neural circuit underlying visual discrimination learning. One hint of where in this circuit (Fig.

4.2) androgens might exert their influence has come from studies of the effects of neonatal ablations of the anterior portion of the inferior temporal cortex (area TE). As shown in Fig. 4.6, whereas female infants with area TE lesions performed worse than the female controls, the male infants did not differ from the normal male infants (compared to the severe impairment in both male and female adults with the same lesions). Thus, such neonatal lesions affect performance of 3-month-old female monkeys more than that of 3-month-old males presumably because at that age area TE is more fully developed in females than in males (Bachevalier, Brickson, Hagger, & Mishkin, 1990). Together with the finding of our neuroendocrinological study, these data suggest that the high levels of androgens found in infant male monkeys before and shortly after birth retard the development of visual habit formation, presumably by slowing the maturation of either cortical area TE, or its projection targets in the striatum, or both.

Although there are no comparable data about differential maturation rates of specific cortical loci in humans, there is accumulating evidence that steroid gonadal hormones in humans might influence brain and behavior in a manner similar to that documented in primates. First, it is well established that both physical and cognitive development is protracted postnatally in boys as compared to that of girls (Maccoby & Jacklin, 1974). Boys generally learn to sit, crawl, and walk later than girls. This precocious physical ability in girls is accompanied by precocious abilities in stimulus processing (Held, Sinshuke, & Gwiazda, 1984; Bauer, Shimojo, Gwiazda, & Held, 1986; Tighe & Powlison, 1978; Creighton, 1984; Clifton, Morrongiello, & Dowd, 1984) and in learning

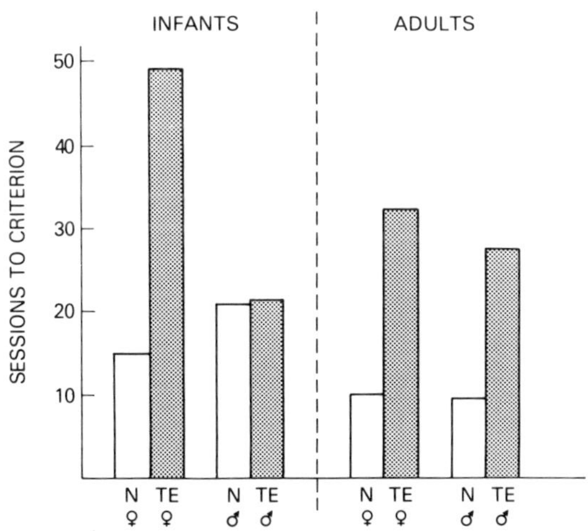

FIG. 4.6. Average number of sessions to attain criterion on Set A by 3-month-old monkeys (operated neonatally) and adult monkeys of both sexes. N, normal controls; TE animals with bilateral area TE lesions.

and memory functions (Diamond, 1985). Also, girls acquire language earlier than boys (McGuiness, 1976) and are superior in most forms of visual and verbal recall (Zahorsky, 1969; Mittler & Ward, 1970; Duggan, 1950), although in spatial-mechanical tasks, the superiority of boys is well documented (Guilford, 1967; Tyler, 1965; Garai & Scheinfeld, 1968; Hutt, 1972). In addition, indirect evidence points to a faster brain maturation in girls than in boys. For example, Taylor (1969, 1971) has reported that the onset of temporal-lobe seizure activity begins to decline markedly during the second year of life in girls, but does not show a comparable decline until the fourth year of life in boys. He argued that the earlier decline in girls reflects a more mature nervous system which is less vulnerable to seizures than that of boys at the same chronological age.

THE MATURATION OF MEMORY FORMATION

As reviewed above, the system for noncognitive learning, which Mishkin and others have referred to as habit formation (Hirsch, 1974; Mishkin et al., 1984; Mishkin & Petri, 1984; O'Keefe & Dostrovsky, 1971) and which is preserved in adult monkeys rendered amnesic by limbic lesions, seems to be present in very early infancy and to mature a few weeks earlier in female than in male monkeys. However, although infant monkeys can learn in as few trials as normal adults to pick the baited object of two, they appear to be unable to remember in a single trial an object that they have seen 10 sec earlier (Bachevalier & Mishkin, 1984). This was demonstrated by testing monkeys between 3 months and 4 years of age in a one-trial object recognition test that was used to demonstrate anterograde amnesia in adult monkeys with lesions of the amygdala and hippocampus (Mishkin, 1978).

In this task, called delayed nonmatching-to-sample (DNMS), the animal has to remember on the basis of a single trial whether or not an object had been seen before. Each trial consisted of two parts (Fig. 4.7A). First, an object was presented over the central well of the test tray. The animal displaced the object to uncover the well and to obtain a concealed food reward. Ten seconds later, the sample object and a new object were presented simultaneously over the test tray's lateral wells, and now the animal found the reward only if it chose the new object. Thirty seconds later, another set of trials was presented in the same way, but with a new pair of objects, and so on for 20 trials a day, each with a completely new pair of objects (Mishkin & Delacour, 1975). A pool of 320 objects was available and none was repeated until all were used; as a result, no item appeared more often than about once every two weeks. This procedure ensured that correct choice depended on memory for the sample object gained from its single presentation 10 sec earlier (hence the term one-trial object recognition).

Once the monkeys had learned the rule of avoiding the familiar item in favor

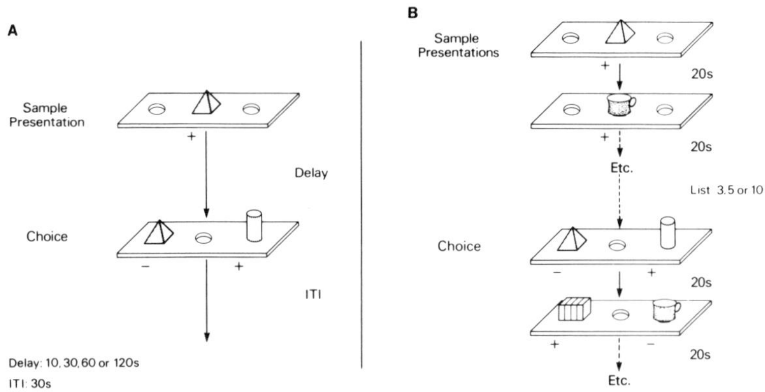

FIG. 4.7. In the delayed nonmatching-to-sample task (A), a monkey is confronted with an unfamiliar object, which it displaces to find a reward (+). After a delay of 10 sec, the animal sees the same object paired with a new one. The monkey must recognize the object it saw earlier and move the new one (+) instead in order to get a reward. The monkey memory can be assess further by first increasing the delay between sample presentation and test (A) and, then, increasing the list of objects to remember (B). From Bachevalier (1990b).

of the new one, and thereby shown that it could remember each sample for at least a few seconds, its recognition memory was then taxed further through progressive increase in the delay between sample presentation and choice test (from the initial 10-sec delay to 30 sec, 60 sec, and finally 120 sec), or progressive increase in the number of sample items to be remembered (from the initial 1 object to 3 objects, 5 objects, and finally 10 objects). In this last stage, for example, all 10 sample objects were presented one at a time for familiarization, after which each of the ten was paired with a different novel object for the test trials (Fig. 4.7B). Since there was a 20-sec interval between presentations throughout the performance test, the minimum retention interval for the list of 10 objects was more than 3 min. The entire performance test took 6 weeks, 1 week at each of the longer delays and lists. As indicated by the learning curves (Fig. 4.8A), speed of learning varied systematically with age. The 3- and 2-year-olds showed a sharp improvement in score from the first 2-day block to the second and continued to improve rapidly thereafter, whereas both the 1-year and the 6-month groups improved significantly only on the third block. The 4-month group showed significantly slower progress, their scores improving only on the sixth block. The most striking result, however, was found in the 3-month group, which failed to improve through the first 9 blocks of training. It was only on the 10th block (i.e., 20 days after the onset of training) that the mean scores of these animals differed significantly from their initial scores, after which they showed slow but steady improvement to criterion. In short, infant rhesus monkeys failed

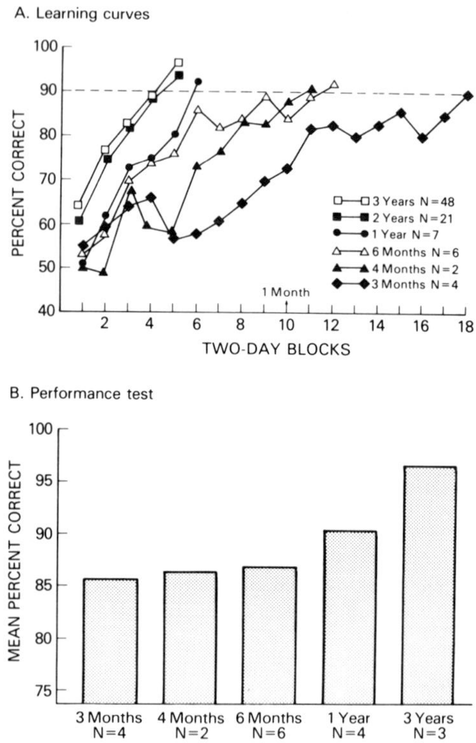

FIG. 4.8. Learning curves on the DNMS task (A) for six age groups and mean performance scores (B) in the six conditions of the performance test (three delays and three lists) for the five age groups tested in that part of the task. (For computation of the learning curves, criterion was set at 90% correct responses in a 2-day block, and scores were than averaged in 2-day blocks until criterion was met. Animals that met criterion prior to the last 2-day block for the group were given a score of 90% on all blocks following their attainment of criterion. The arrow on the abscissa indicates that approximately one month elapsed for 10 blocks of testing.) From Bachevalier (1990b).

to solve the DNMS task until they were approximately 4 months old. With further maturation, there was a gradual improvement in learning ability, yet their performance on DNMS did not reach the adult level of proficiency even at 1 year (Bachevalier & Mishkin, 1984). Only at about 2 years of age do monkeys master the recognition task as efficiently as adult animals.

This slow ontogenetic development of visual recognition memory was shown even more directly in the memory performance test. The overall performance across the 3 delays and the 3 lists conditions for the five age groups tested in this portion of the task is shown in Fig. 4.8B. The data demonstrate clearly that recognition memory improves systematically with age.

As argued in our earlier study (Bachevalier & Mishkin, 1984), the poor performance of young subjects in the DNMS task cannot be attributed to any inadequacy of perception, attention, motivation, or stimulus-response association, since these same factors are required for visual discrimination learning tasks, on which they perform excellently. Their difficulty must be in memory ability per se. These considerations strongly suggest that the two learning systems that were found to be separable in the adult monkeys are also dissociable developmentally.

In short, by contrast to the noncognitive habit system, the system for cognitive memory, which is severely impaired in adult monkeys with limbic lesions, develops late in infancy, presumably because the neural circuitry on which it depends undergoes a relatively slow maturation. The question, then, is what are the neural structures developing later in life that allow the formation of cognitive memories? A possible answer to this question emerges from a comparison between the effects on the recognition memory of early versus late lesions to higher-order association areas of the cortex.

IMMATURITY OF CORTICAL ASSOCIATION AREAS OF THE BRAIN

To examine the possibility that immaturity of one or more of the neural stations in the neural pathway underlying visual recognition memory (see Fig. 4.1) could be responsible for the late development of cognitive memory, we initiated a series of neurobehavioral experiments on the effects of early damage to the cortico-limbic memory circuit as well as some developmental neurobiological studies.

To start our behavioral investigation, we prepared sixteen newborn monkeys with removals of either the limbic structures (amygdala and hippocampus), or the inferior temporal cortical area TE. The bilateral lesions shown in Fig. 4.9 were performed in two unilateral stages at approximately one week and three weeks of age, respectively. These operated monkeys were age-matched with eleven normal animals.

The formation of visual discrimination habits in the three groups was measured with the 24-hr ITI task when the animals were 3 months of age (Bachevalier et al., 1990). Performance of infant monkeys was compared with that of monkeys that had been tested in the same way after receiving identical brain lesions when they were adults. As shown in Fig. 4.10, damage to the limbic system appeared to leave habit formation intact whether the lesions were early or late. By contrast, lesions of area TE yielded a severe and long lasting deficit in visual habit formation if the damage occurred late, but they produced only a mild and transitory deficit of this function if the damage occurred early. Indeed, by the second set of visual discriminations, infant monkeys with area TE damage required no more sessions to learn than normal adult monkeys (averaging 11 and 10 sessions, respectively). These data thus suggest a functional sparing of habit formation following early damage to the inferior temporal cortical area TE.

With regard to cognitive memory (as measured by the DNMS task), there is again evidence of a greater compensatory potential after neonatal cortical than after neonatal limbic damage (Bachevalier & Mishkin, 1986b). Thus, whereas infants with neonatal limbic lesions were severely impaired in visual recognition memory at 10 months of age, those with neonatal ablation of visual association cortex (area TE) showed significant functional sparing. As shown in Fig. 4.11,

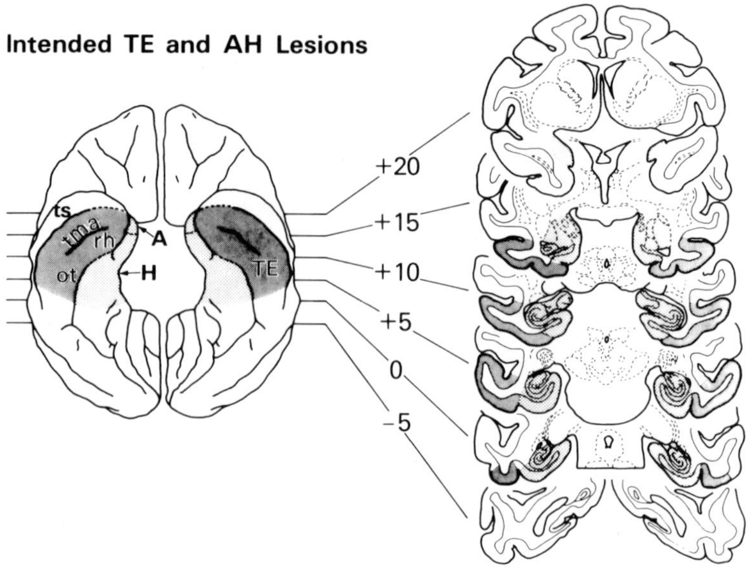

FIG. 4.9. Ventral surface view and coronal sections illustrating the intended neonatal area TE lesions (dark stippling) and amygdala-hippocampal lesions (light stippling). Abbreviations: A, amygdala complex; H, hippocampal formation; ot, occipitotemporal sulcus; rh, rhinel sulcus; Te, anterior two-third of inferior temporal cortex, tma, anterior middle temporal sulcus; ts, superior temporal sulcus. From Bachevalier (1990a).

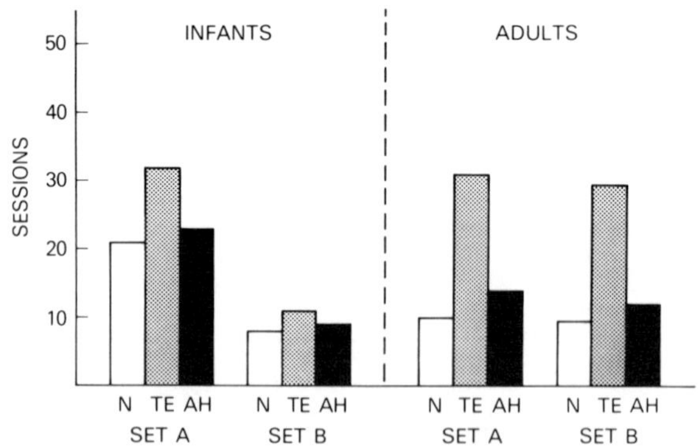

FIG. 4.10. Average number of sessions to attain criterion on two consecutive sets of discriminations (Sets A and B) by 3-month-old monkeys (operated neonatally) and adult monkeys. N, normal controls; TE, animals with bilateral area TE lesions; AH, animals with bilateral amygdalo-hippocampal lesions. From Bachevalier (1990a).

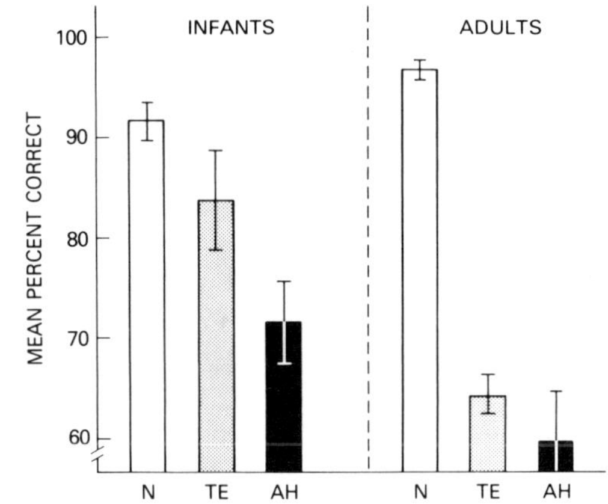

FIG. 4.11. Average scores on the recognition performance task by 10-month-old monkeys (operated neonatally) and adult monkeys. Abbreviations as in Fig. 4.10. From Bachevalier (1990a).

both early and late damage to the limbic structures yielded severe impairment in visual recognition, reflected in drops in performance of 22% for the infants and 32% for the adults (as compared with their normal controls). By contrast, although late damage to area TE resulted in a drop in performance of 29%, early lesions of this cortical area resulted in a drop of only 8%.

Some of the first infants to receive these specific neonatal lesions are now 4-year-olds and were recently retested to assess the long-term effects of these early lesions on the formation of noncognitive habits and cognitive memories (Bachevalier & Mishkin, 1988). Their performance on the 24-hr ITI and DNMS tasks was compared to that of 4-year-olds that had received the same lesions in adulthood. At this age, the monkeys with neonatal damage to area TE exhibited the same differential sparing of memory *vs* habit formation as that found earlier when they were between 3 and 10 months old. By contrast, the monkeys with neonatal limbic lesions resembled those with late limbic lesions in that they were unimpaired in habit formation but severely impaired in cognitive memory.

In summary, these behavioral data indicate that compensatory mechanisms appear to operate early to promote long lasting recovery from neonatal temporal cortical lesions but not from limbic lesions. They are thus consistent with the notion that association areas of the cortex possess considerable plasticity at birth, implying that they are still functionally immature.

In support of this proposal, we have recently obtained direct evidence of functional immaturity of the neocortex in the infant macaque. First, in collaboration with the Laboratory of Cerebral Metabolism at NIMH, we have applied the 2-deoxyglucose method (2-DG) postoperatively to a series of infant monkeys that had received unilateral optic tract section combined with forebrain commissurotomy at 1 day, 1 week and 3 weeks, and 1, 2, 3, and 5 months of age (Hagger, Bachevalier, Macko, Kennedy, Sokoloff, & Mishkin, 1988; Macko, Bachevalier, Kennedy, Suda, Sokoloff, & Mishkin, 1983). This surgical procedure allowed comparison of the metabolic activity in a visually intact and a visually deafferented hemisphere in each animal. The 2-DG experiment was performed about 2 days postoperatively in the two youngest animals and about 1 month postoperatively in the six others while each was awake and visually stimulated. Rates of glucose utilization in the visually intact hemispheres, and differences in rates between the visually intact and deafferented hemispheres indicated that although adult levels of glucose utilization are attained in all striate and prestriate areas as early as 3 months of age, they are not attained in inferior temporal areas until the animals are about 4 months of age, just the age at which object vision reaches maturity according to the studies of visual discrimination learning.

We have obtained additional supporting evidence for this conclusion by mapping the distribution of opiate and muscarinic receptor binding sites in the brains of newborn and adult monkeys (Bachevalier, Ungerleider, O'Neill, & Friedman, 1986; O'Neill, Friedman, Bachevalier, & Ungerleider, 1986). The distribution of these receptors appeared to be adult-like in subcortical structures (both limbic and nonlimbic) and allocortical areas. By contrast, major differences between the infant and adult brains were seen in the neocortex. The first distinction is that, whereas in the adult brains the density of receptor bindings varied from field to field, in the newborn it was distributed uniformly throughout the neocortex. The second important difference is that, whereas the adult brain was characterized by area-specific laminar patterns across the 6 layers of cortex, the newborn brain was not. In the newborn, all neocortical areas, except primary visual cortex, had a unimodal laminar distribution.

Thus, in the context of the proposed neural memory circuit, the data from our developmental studies lead to the conclusion that the poor memory ability shown by infant monkeys in delayed nonmatching-to-sample is likely to be due to immaturity of inferior temporal cortical areas rather than to immaturity of the limbic structures.

RELATIONSHIP TO INFANTILE AMNESIA

To recapitulate, both clinical findings in brain-damaged patients and lesion studies in adult monkeys have suggested that an experience can enter into memory in two ways: as cognitive information stored in a cortico-limbic system and as a habit stored in a cortico-striatal system. Our studies of behavioral development in infant monkeys have provided complementary evidence by showing that these two systems are dissociable developmentally, in that the nonlimbic habit system appears to mature considerably earlier than the limbic memory system. Our investigation of the effects of early lesions on the development of cognitive behavior in primates has indicated that early damage to the limbic system (like damage in adulthood) leaves habit formation intact but severely impairs the formation of new memories. By contrast, neonatal damage to area TE yields relative sparing of both habit and memory formation (as compared to the severe deficit in both functions seen in adults with the same lesions). Thus, association areas of the cortex appear to possess considerable plasticity at birth, implying a degree of functional immaturity. These behavioral data are supported by direct neurobiological evidence of neonatal cortical immaturity, reflected in the homogeneous distribution of opiatergic and cholinergic receptors as well as in the low level of metabolic activity, resulting from visual stimulation. Together, the behavioral and neurobiological findings suggest that the relatively poor recognition ability of normal neonates is more likely due to slow maturation of the association areas of the cortex than to slow maturation of limbic structures.

As was noted at the outset, human neonates also possess poorly developed memory abilities, with substantial changes in mnemonic functions occurring only near the end of the first year (Sophian, 1980; Fox, Kagan, & Weiskopf, 1979; Kagan, Kearsley, & Zelazo, 1978; Rovee-Collier & Fagen, 1981). Interestingly, recent studies (Overman, 1990; Diamond, 1990) have indicated a developmental dissociation of retention processes in human infants similar to the dissociation described here for the monkeys. In Overman's study, recognition memory was tested in human subjects using the same visual recognition task with trial-unique objects (DNMS) as we have used to test infant monkeys. Human infants 12 months of age did very poorly in learning the task and learning scores improved only gradually with age. It was not until when they were 22 and 32 months of age that performance in the DNMS task reached the adult level of proficiency. Again, when recognition memory was taxed further with increasing delays and list of objects, performance was very poor in the youngest subjects. Also, just as for the infant monkeys, whereas 12-month-old human infants had difficulty recognizing an object they had seen a minute or so earlier in the DNMS task, they were clearly able to pick the baited object of two in a visual discrimination task. Thus, in both humans and monkeys, the ability to form noncognitive habits is present early in infancy, whereas the ability to form cognitive memories matures only slowly during the first years of life.

Before considering how this differential development of retention processes may explain the phenomenon of infantile amnesia, we must first consider some findings from studies in human and monkey infants indicating that visual recognition may in fact be a primitive process. Although visual recognition memory as measured by delayed nonmatching-to-sample develops late in ontogeny, this memory ability can be demonstrated in early infancy by use of paired-comparison task. In this task, recognition memory is inferred from the infant's tendency to look more at a novel than at a previously exposed target (Fantz, 1956; Fagan, 1970). Both 1-month-old monkeys and 4-month-old infants show a consistently reliable visual response to novelty when measured by a paired-comparison technique. Furthermore, we have demonstrated that although performance on paired-comparison tasks antedates performance on delayed nonmatching tasks, this primitive type of visual recognition is nevertheless markedly impaired by either early or late limbic-system damage (Brickson & Bachevalier, 1984). One possible explanation to this paradox is that visual cortical areas posterior to area TE, such as area TEO (see Fig. 4.1), which mature earlier than area TE (Hagger et al., 1987) could mediate novelty-preference early in life. In fact, the existence in newborn monkeys of transient projections from area TEO to the limbic structures, which then retract with maturation (Webster, Ungerleider, & Bachevalier, 1991), is consistent with this idea. Thus area TEO (or areas even earlier in the occipitotemporal pathway) may be sufficient to support novelty-preference early in life, even while it is insufficient to support learning and memory on the DNMS task.

In conclusion, these similarities in the development of cognitive memory functions in human and nonhuman primates may provide the clue to understanding the neurobiological basis of infantile amnesia. That is, in humans as in monkeys, immaturity of the higher-order association areas of the cortex (such as area TE) could underlie the absence of a fully functional memory system and, by implication, could help explain why memory for the events of infancy and earliest childhood are lost to memory: perhaps they were never stored in the cortex to begin with or they were stored in cortical areas other than higher-order cortical areas and cannot be retrieved.

ACKNOWLEDGMENTS

I thank Mortimer Mishkin for his support and encouragement, and for comments on the manuscript.

REFERENCES

Aggleton, J. P., Desimone, R., & Mishkin, M. (1986). The origin, course, and termination of the hippocampo-thalamic projections in the Macaque. *Journal of Comparative Neurology, 243,* 409–421.

Aggleton, J. P., & Mishkin, M. (1983a). Visual recognition impairment following medial thalamic lesions in monkeys. *Neuropsychologia, 21,* 189–197.

Aggleton, J. P., & Mishkin, M. (1983b). Memory impairments following restricted medial thalamic lesions in monkeys. *Experimental Brain Research, 52,* 199–209.

Aggleton, J. P., & Mishkin, M. (1984). Projections of the amygdala to the thalamus in the cynomolgus monkey. *Journal of Comparative Neurology, 222,* 56–68.

Aggleton, J. P., & Mishkin, M. (1985). Mammillary-body lesions and visual recognition in the monkey. *Experimental Brain Research, 58,* 190–197.

Aigner, T. G., Mitchell, S. J., Aggleton, J. P., DeLong, M. R., Struble, R. G., Price, D. L., Wenk, G. L., & Mishkin, M. (in press). Transient impairment of recognition memory following ibotenic-acid lesions of the basal forebrain in monkeys. *Experimental Brain Research.*

Alexander, M. P., & Freedman, M. (1984). Amnesia after anterior communicating artery aneurysm rupture. *Neurology, 34,* 752–757.

Amaral, D. J. (1987). Memory: The anatomical organization of candidate brain regions. In J. M.

Brookhart & V. B. Mountcastle (Eds.), *Handbook of physiology: The nervous system V,* Bethesda: American Physiological Society Press.

Amaral D. J., & Cowan, W. (1980). Subcortical afferents to the hippocampal formation in the monkey. *Journal of Comparative Neurology, 189,* 573–591.

Angelergues, R., Hecaen, H., & De Ajuriaguerra, J. (1955). Les troubles mentaux au cours des tumeurs du lobe frontal (Mental disorders following frontal lobe tumors). *Annales de Médecine Psychologique, 113,* 577–642.

Arendt, T., Bigl, V., Arendt, A., & Tennstedt, A. (1983). Loss of neurons in the nucleus basalis of Meynert in Alzheimer's disease, paralysis agitans, and Korsakoff's disease. *Acta Neuropathology Journal, 61,* 101–108.

Bachevalier, J. (1990a). Memory loss and socio-emotional disturbances following neonatal damage to the limbic system in monkeys: An animal model for childhood autism. In C. A. Tamminga & S. C. Schulz (Eds.), *Advances in psychiatry: Schizophrenia* (Vol. 1). New York: Raven Press.

Bachevalier, J. (1990b). Ontogenetic development of habit and memory formation in primates. In A. Diamond (Ed.), *Development and neural bases of higher cognitive functions.* New York: Academic Press.

Bachevalier, J., Brickson, M., Hagger, C. S., & Mishkin, M. (1990). Age and sex differences in the effects of selective temporal lobe lesion on the formation of visual discrimination habits in rhesus monkeys. *Behavioral Neuroscience, 104,* 885–899.

Bachevalier, J., Hagger, C. S., & Bercu, B. B. (1989). Gender differences in visual habit formation in 3-month-old rhesus monkeys. *Developmental Psychobiology, 22,* 585–599.

Bachevalier, J., & Mishkin, M. (1984). An early and a late developing system for learning and retention in infant monkeys. *Behavioral Neuroscience, 98,* 770–778.

Bachevalier, J., & Mishkin, M. (1986a). Visual recognition impairment follows ventromedial but not dorsolateral prefrontal lesions in monkeys. *Behavioral Brain Research, 20,* 249–261.

Bachevalier, J., & Mishkin, M. (1986b). Cortical *vs* limbic immaturity: Relationship to infantile global amnesia in monkeys. *Society for Neuroscience Abstracts, 12,* 22.

Bachevalier, J., & Mishkin, M. (1988). Long-term effects of neonatal temporal cortical and limbic lesions on habit and memory formation in rhesus monkeys. *Society for Neuroscience Abstracts, 14,* 1.

Bachevalier, J., Parkinson, J. K., & Mishkin, M. (1985). Visual recognition in monkeys: Effects of separate *vs* combined transection of the fornix and amygdalofugal pathways. *Experimental Brain Research, 57,* 554–561.

Bachevalier, J., Ungerleider, L. G., O'Neill, B., & Friedman, D. P. (1986). Regional distribution of [^{3}H] naloxone binding in the brain of a newborn rhesus monkey. *Developmental Brain Research, 25,* 302-308.

Baleydier, C, & Mauguiere, F. (1980). The duality of the cingulate gyrus in monkey: Neuroanatomical study and functional hypothesis. *Brain, 103,* 525–554.

Bauer, J. A., Shimojo, S, Gwiazda, J., & Held, R. (1986). Sex differences on the development of binocularity in human infants. *Investigative Ophthalmology and Visual Science, 27,* 265.

Bercu, B. B., Lee, B. C., Pineda, J. L., Spiliotis, B. E., Denman, D. W. III, Hoffman, H. J., Brown, T. J., & Sachs, H. C. (1983). Male sexual development in the monkey. I- Cross-sectional analysis of pulsatile hypothalamic-pituitary-testicular function. *Journal of Clinical Endocrinology and Metabolism, 56,* 1214–1226.

Bercu, B. B., Spiliotis, B. E., Reed, G. F., & Lee, B. C. (1987). Male sexual development in the monkey: IV- Further analysis of hypothalamic pituitary-testicular function and correlation with electron and light microscopy of the testis. *Journal of Pediatric Endocrinology, 2,* 7–22.

Brickson, M., & Bachevalier, J. (1984). Visual recognition in infant monkeys: Evidence for a primitive process. *Society for Neuroscience Abstracts, 10,* 137.

Brooks, D. N., & Baddeley, A. D. (1976). What can amnesic patients learn? *Neuropsychologia, 14,* 112–122.

Buerger, A. A., Gross, C. G., & Rocha-Miranda, C. E. (1974). Effects of ventral putamen lesions on discrimination learning by monkeys. *Journal of Comparative and Physiological Psychology, 86,* 440–446.

Butters, N., & Cermak, L. S. (1980). *Alcoholic Korsakoff's syndrome—an information-processing approach to amnesia.* New York: Academic Press.

Campbell, B. A., & Coulter, X. (1976). The ontogenesis of learning and memory. In M. R. Rosenzweig & E. L. Bennett (Eds.), *Neuromechanisms of learning and memory* (pp. 209–235). Cambridge, MA: MIT press.

Candy, J., Perry, R., Perry, E., Irving, D., Blessed, G., Fairbairn, A., & Tomlinson, B. (1983) Pathological changes in the nucleus of Meynert in Alzheimer's and Parkinson's diseases. *Journal of Neurological Science, 54,* 277–289.

Clifton, R. K., Morrongiello, B. A., & Dowd, J. (1984). A developmental look at an auditory illusion: the precedent effect. *Developmental Psychobiology, 17,* 519-536.

Cohen, N. J. (1984). Preserved learning capacity in amnesia: evidence for multiple memory systems. In L. R. Squire & N. Butters (Eds.), *The neuropsychology of memory* (pp. 83–103). New York: Guilford Press.

Cohen, N. J., & Squire, L. R. (1980). Preserved learning and retention of pattern-analyzing skill in amnesia: Dissociation of "knowing how" and "knowing that". *Science, 210,* 207–209.

Corkin, S. (1965). Tactually-guided maze learning in man: Effects of unilateral cortical excisions and bilateral hippocampal lesions. *Neuropsychologia, 3,* 339–351.

Corkin, S. (1968). Acquisition of motor skill after bilateral medial temporal-lobe excision. *Neuropsychologia, 6,* 225–266.

Coulter, X. (1979). The determinants of infantile amnesia. In N. E. Spear & B. A. Campbell (Eds.), *The ontogeny of learning and memory.* Hillsdale, N. J.: Lawrence Erlbaum Associates.

Creighton, D. E. (1984). Sex differences in the visual habituation of 4-, 6-, and 8-month-old infants. *Infant Behavior and Development, 7,* 237–249.

Diamond, A. (1985). Development of the ability to use recall to guide action, as indicated by infant's performance on AB. *Child Development, 56,* 868–883.

Diamond, A. (1990). Infants' and young children's performance on delayed non-match to sample (direct and indirect) and visual paired comparison. In A. Diamond (Ed.), *The development and neural bases of higher cognitive functions.* New York: New York Academy of Sciences Press.

Divac, I., Rosvold, H. E., & Szwarcbart, M. K. (1967). Behavioral effects of selective ablation of the caudate nucleus. *Journal of Comparative and Physiological Psychology, 63,* 184–190.

Duggan, L. (1950). An experiment on immediate recall in secondary school children. *British Journal of Psychology, 40,* 149–154.

Fagan, J. F. III. (1970). Memory in the infant. *Journal of Experimental Child Psychology, 9,* 217–226.

Fantz, R. L. (1956). A method for studying early visual development. *Perceptual and Motor Skills, 6,* 13–15.

Fox, N., Kagan, J., & Weiskopf, S. (1979). The growth of memory during infancy. *Genetic Psychology Monographs, 99,* 91–130.

Gade, A. (1982). Amnesia after operations on aneurysms of the anterior communicating artery. *Surgical Neurology, 18,* 46–49.

Garai, J.E., & Scheinfeld, A. (1968). Sex differences in mental and behavioral traits. *Genetic Psychology Monographs, 77,* 169–299.

Guilford, J. P. (1967). *The nature of human intelligence,* New York: McGraw-Hill.

Hagger, C. S., Bachevalier, J. & Bercu, B. B. (1987). Sexual dimorphism in the development of habit formation: Effects of perinatal gonadal hormones. *Neuroscience, 22,* (Suppl.), S520.

Hagger, C. S., Bachevalier, J., Macko, K. A., Kennedy, C., Sokoloff, L., & Mishkin, M. (1988). Functional maturation of inferior temporal cortex in infant rhesus monkeys. *Society for Neuroscience Abstracts, 14,* 2.

Harlow, H. F. (1959). The development of learning in rhesus monkeys. *American Scientist, 47,* 458–479.

Held, R., Shinsuke, S., & Gwiazda, J. (1984). Gender differences in the early development of human visual resolution. *Investigative Ophthalmology and Visual Science, 25,* 220.

Hirsh, R. (1974). The hippocampus and contextual retrieval of information from memory: A theory. *Behavioral Biology, 12,* 421–445.

Horel, J. A. (1978). The neuroanatomy of amnesia: A critique of the hippocampal memory hypothesis. *Brain, 101,* 403–445.

Hutt, C. (1972). Sex differences in human development. *Human Development, 15,* 153–170.

Kagan, J., Kearsley, R. B., & Zelazo, P. R. (1978). *Infancy: Its place in human development,* Cambridge, MA: Harvard University Press.

Lilly, R., Cummings, J. L., Benson, F., & Frankel, M. (1983). The human Kluver-Bucy syndrome. *Neurology, 33,* 1141–1145.

Maccoby, E. E., & Jacklin, C. N. (1974). *The Psychology of Sex Differences,* Stanford, CA: Stanford University Press.

Macko, K. A., Bachevalier, J., Kennedy, C., Suda, S., Sokoloff, L., & Mishkin, M. (1983). Functional development of the ventral cortical visual pathway measured by the 2-deoxyglucose method. *Society for Neuroscience Abstracts, 9,* 375.

Mahut, H., & Zola-Morgan, S. (1977). Ontogenetic time-table for the development of three functions in infant macaques and the effects of early hippocampal damage upon them. *Society for Neuroscience Abstracts, 3,* 428.

Mair, W. G. P., Warrington, E. K., & Weiskrantz, L. (1979). Memory disorder in Korsakoff's psychosis. A neuropathological and neuropsychological investigation of two cases. *Brain, 102,* 749-783.

Malamut, B. L., Saunders, R. C., & Mishkin, M. (1984). Monkeys with combined amygdalo-hippocampal lesions succeed in object discrimination learning despite 24-hour intertrial intervals. *Behavioral Neuroscience, 98,* 759–769.

McGuiness, D. (1976). Sex differences in the organization of perception and cognition. In B. Lloyd & J. Archer (Eds.), *Exploring sex differences* (pp. 123–156). New York: Academic Press.

Mesulam, M., Mufson, E., Levey, A., & Wainer, B. (1983). Cholinergic innervation of cortex by the basal forebrain: Cytochemistry and cortical connections of the septal area, diagonal band nuclei, nucleus basalis (substantia innominata), and hypothalamus in the rhesus monkey. *Journal of Comparative Neurology, 214,* 170–197.

Milner, B. (1962). Les troubles de la mémoire accompagnant des lésions hippocampiques bilatérales. In P. Passouant (Ed.), *Physiologie de l'hippocampe (pp. 257–272). Paris: Centre National de la Recherche Scientifique.*

Milner, B. (1972). Disorders of learning and memory after temporal lobe lesions in man. *Clinical Neurosurgery, 19,* 421–446.

Mishkin, M. (1954). Visual discrimination performance following partial ablations of the temporal lobe: II. Ventral surface *vs.* hippocampus. *Journal of Comparative and Physiological Psychology, 47,* 187–193.

Mishkin, M. (1978). Memory in monkeys severely impaired by combined but not by separate removal of amygdala and hippocampus. *Nature (Lond.), 273,* 297–298.

Mishkin, M. (1982). A memory system in the monkey. *Philosophic Transaction of the Royal Society of London,* B298, 85–95.

Mishkin, M., & Appenzeller, T. (1987). The anatomy of memory. *Scientific American, 256,* 80–89.

Mishkin, M., & Delacour J. (1975). An analysis of short-term visual memory in the monkey. *Journal of Experimental Psychology: Animal Behavior Processes, 1,* 326–334.

Mishkin, M., Malamut, B. L., & Bachevalier, J. (1984). Memories and Habits: Two neural systems. In G. Lynch, L. McGaugh, & N. M. Weinberger (Eds.), *Neurobiology of learning and memory* (pp. 65–77). New York: Guilford Press.

Mishkin, M., & Petri, H. L. (1984). Memories and Habits: Some implications for the analysis of learning and retention. In N. Butters & L. Squire (Eds.), *Neuropsychology of memory* (pp. 287–296). New York: Guilford Press.

Mittler, P., & Ward, J. (1970). The use of the Illinois test of psycho-linguistic abilities on British four-year-old children: A normative and factorial study. *British Journal of Educational Psychology, 40,* 43–54.

Murray, E. A., Bachevalier, J., & Mishkin, M. (1989). Effects of rhinal cortical lesions on visual recognition memory in rhesus monkeys. *Society for Neuroscience Abstracts, 15,* 342.

Murray, E. A., & Mishkin, M. (1983). Severe tactual memory deficits in monkeys after combined removal of the amygdala and hippocampus. *Brain Research, 270,* 340–344.

Nadel, L., & Zola-Morgan, S. (1984). Infantile amnesia: A neurobiological perspective. In M. Moscovitch (Ed.), *Infant Memory* (pp. 145–172). New York: Plenum Press.

Nauta, W. J. H. (1962). Neural associations of the amygdaloid complex in the monkey. *Brain, 85,* 505–520.

O'Keefe, J., & Dostrovsky, J. (1971). The hippocampus as a spatial map: Preliminary evidence from unit activity in the freely moving rat. *Brain Research, 34,* 171–175.

O'Keefe, J., & Nadel, L. (1978). *The hippocampus as a cognitive map.* New York: Oxford University Press.

Olton, D. S., Becker, J. T., & Handelmann, G. E. (1979). Hippocampus, space, and memory. *Behavioral and Brain Sciences, 2,* 313–317.

O'Neill, J. B., Friedman, D. P., Bachevalier, J., & Ungerleider, L. G. (1986). Distribution of muscarinic cholinergic receptors in the brain of a newborn monkey. *Society for Neuroscience Abstracts, 12,* 809.

Overman, W. H. (1990). Performance on traditional match-to-sample, nonmatch-to-sample, and object discrimination tasks by 12- to 32-month-old children: a developmental progression. In A. Diamond (Ed.), *The development and neural bases of higher cognitive functions.* New York: New York Academy of Sciences Press.

Penfield, W., & Milner, B. (1958). Memory deficit produced by bilateral lesions in the hippocampal zone. *Archives of Neurology and Psychiatry, 79,* 475–497.

Phillips, R. R., Malamut, B. L., Bachevalier, J., & Mishkin, M. (1988). Dissociation of the effects of inferior temporal and limbic lesions on object discrimination learning with 24-hr intertrial intervals. *Behavioral Brain Research, 27,* 99-107.

Provansal, J. C. (1951). *Les tumeurs frontales. Etudes Anatomo-cliniques de 82 observations* (Frontal lobe tumors. Anatomical studies in 82 cases). Thesis, Marseille.

Rovee-Collier, C. K., & Fagen, J. W. (1981). The retrieval of memory in early infancy. In L. P. Lipsitt (Ed.), *Advances in infancy research* (Vol. 1). Norwood, NJ: Ablex.

Scoville, W. B., & Milner, B. (1957). Loss of recent memory after bilateral hippocampal lesions. *Journal of Neurology, Neurosurgery and Psychiatry, 20,* 11–21.

Sophian, C. (1980). Habituation is not enough: Novelty preferences, search, and memory in infancy. *Merrill-Palmer Quarterly, 26,* 239–257.

Spear, N. E. (1979). Memory storage factors leading to infantile amnesia. In K. W. Spence et al. (Eds.), *Advances in Research and Theory: The Psychobiology of learning and motivation* (Vol. 13, pp. 91–155), New York: Academic Press.

Spiegler, B. J., & Mishkin, M. (1979). Associative memory severely impaired by combined amygdalo-hippocampal removals. *Society for Neuroscience Abstracts, 5,* 323.

Squire, L. R. (1982). The neuropsychology of human memory. *Annual Review of Neuroscience, 5,* 241–273.

Squire, L. R. (1987). *Memory and brain.* New York: Oxford University Press.

Talland, G. A. (1965). *Deranged memory.* New York: Academic Press.

Tobias, T. J. (1975). Afferents to prefrontal cortex from the thalamic mediodorsal nucleus in the rhesus monkey. *Brain Research, 83,* 191–212.

Talland, G. A., Sweet, W. T., & Ballantine, H. T. (1967). Amnesic syndrome with anterior communicating artery aneurysm. *Journal of Nervous Mental Disease, 145,* 179–192.

Taylor, D. C. (1969). Differential rates of cerebral maturation between sexes and between hemispheres: Evidence from epilepsy. *Lancet, 2,* 140–142.

Taylor, D. C. (1971). Ontogenesis of chronic epileptic psychoses: A Reanalysis. *Psychological Medicine, 1,* 247–253.

Tighe, T. J., & Powlison, L. B. (1978). Sex differences in infant habituation research: A survey and some hypotheses. *Bulletin of Psychonomic Society, 12,* 337–340.

Tulving, E. (1983). *Elements of episodic memory.* Oxford: Oxford University Press.

Turner, B. H., Mishkin, M., & Knapp, M. (1980). Organization of the amygdalopetal projections from modality-specific cortical association areas in the monkey. *Journal of Comparative Neurology, 191,* 515–543.

Tyler, L. (1965). *The psychology of human differences.* New York: Appleton-Century-Crofts.

Van Hoesen, G. W., & Pandya, D. N. (1975). Some connections of the entorhinal (area 28) and perirhinal (area 35) cortices of the rhesus monkeys. III. Efferent connections. *Brain Research, 95,* 39–59.

Victor, M., Adams, R. D., & Collins, G. H. (1971). *The Wernicke-Korsakoff syndrome.* Oxford: Blackwell.

Wang, J., Aigner, T., & Mishkin, M. (1990). Effects of neostriatal lesions on visual habit formation in rhesus monkeys. *Society for Neuroscience Abstracts, 16,* 617.

Warrington, E., & Weiskrantz, L. (1968). New method of testing long-term retention with special reference to amnesic patients. *Nature (Lond.), 217,* 972–974.

Webster, M. J., Ungerleider, L. G., & Bachevalier, J. (1991). Connections of inferior temporal areas TE and TEO with medial temporal-lobe structures in infant and adult monkeys. *Journal of Neuroscience.*

Whitehouse, P., Price, D., Struble, R., Clark, A., Coyle, J., & DeLong, M. (1982). Alzheimer's disease and senile dementia: Loss of neurons in the basal forebrain. *Science, 215,* 1237–1239.

Whitty, C. W. M., & Levin, W. (1960). A Korsakoff syndrome in the postcingulectomy confusional state. *Brain, 83,* 648–653.

Zahorsky, T. (1969). Short-term memory in children as a specific function of different sensory modalities. *Psychologia a Patapsychologia Dietata, 4.*

Zimmerman, R. R., & Torrey, C. C. (1965). Ontogeny of learning. In A. M. Schrier, H. F. Harlow, & F. Stollnitz (Eds.), *Behavior of nonhuman primates: Modern research trends* (Vol. 2, pp. 405–447). New York: Academic Press.

Zola-Morgan, S., & Squire, L. R. (1985a). Complementary approaches to the study of memory: human amnesia and animal models. In N. W. Weinberger, J. L. McGaugh, & G. Lynch (Eds.), *Memory systems of the brain: Animal and human cognitive processes* (pp. 463–477). New York: Guilford Press.

Zola-Morgan, S., & Squire, L. R. (1985b). Amnesia in monkeys following lesions of the mediodorsal nucleus of the thalamus. *Annals of Neurology, 17,* 558–564.

Zola-Morgan, S., Squire, R. L., Amaral D. G., & Suzuki, W. A. (1989). Lesions of perirhinal and parahippocampal cortex that spare the amygdala and hippocampal formation produce severe memory impairment. *Journal of Neuroscience, 9,* 4355–4370.

Zola-Morgan, S., Squire, L.R., & Mishkin, M. (1982). The neuroanatomy of amnesia: Amygdalo-hippocampus versus temporal stem. *Science, 218,* 1337–1339.

5 Induction of Brain Structure by Experience: Substrates for Cognitive Development

William T. Greenough
James E. Black
University of Illinois at Urbana-Champaign

INTRODUCTION

The goal of this chapter is to present a view of the ways in which experience interacts with intrinsic forces in development to yield a functionally competent brain. The broad issue addressed is the manner in which the developing brain acquires its ability to guide the organism through the demands of a complex, changing environment and the manner in which the knowledge acquired through the evolutionary history of the species is combined with the knowledge acquired by the individual. We have attempted to write this chapter at a level that does not require extensive knowledge of the detailed workings of the nervous system to follow the basic logic. A warning is noted at the outset of some of the more daunting sections.

The essential points to be made are that (1) there are intrinsic forces that contribute substantially to brain development, probably providing more than just a scaffolding for cognitive development in the sense that they also shape the directions in which further development can occur; (2) one kind of intrinsic force, synapse overproduction, is actually designed to capture information from experience during development, and (3) a separate mechanism appears to be responsible for experience that will be unique to each individual, a mechanism that also involves synapse formation, but in response to experience rather than to intrinsic forces. This mechanism remains functional throughout most of life. The quality of the child's experience, whether expected or opportunistic, is also very important. The information must have sufficient contrast, e.g., the enriched lexicon a young child hears that allows formation of new concepts and relationships. Experience must also be *coherent,* i.e., the consequences of a baby's action must be reliable so that confused and overlapping relationships are not assimilated. We also consider some issues regarding the development of the metabolic support systems associated with synaptic change because we believe they, too, have implications for cognitive development.

A basic assumption of this work is that the brain and the mind really are *the same thing*. Few readers would probably challenge this point, but there is a difference between *believing* this and actually *thinking* it all of the time. When you really *think* this way, you recognize that studying what is going in the brain can actually help to tell you what is going on in the mind. The organization of this chapter reflects this belief in that we have tried to show how findings at the neural level lead to insights regarding functional development with clear implications for behavior. For example, we consider in some detail the concept of a "sensitive" or "critical" period when particular events have maximal impact upon the process of development. Traditional views of critical periods in developmental psychology have been similar to that of Bateson (1979), who compared them to the brief opening of a window that allowed experience to act upon development only until the window again closed. While this may be a useful descriptive analogy, it is not particularly useful from a heuristic perspective. In subsequent sections, we show how understanding the brain information storage substrates of critical (experience-expectant) and noncritical (experience-dependent) periods suggest evolutionary origins and consequent constraints. For example, the reliability of a critical period event must be absolute in nature. Such knowledge also suggests the adaptive values of each type of information storage for the individual, a *reason* that timing is critical, and the role of the organism's *behavior* in these processes.

To the vast majority of neuroscientists, the idea that the nervous system is functionally plastic and appears to incorporate information, at least in part, through changes in its structural organization is an accepted fact. Most neuroscientists have grown up, scientifically speaking, since the early 1960s, when Bennett, Diamond, Krech, and Rosenzweig (1964) began to demonstrate the gross morphological plasticity of the brain. Those with longer histories may have overlapped the early 1950s demonstrations of the sensitivity of the developing primate visual system to deprivation of visual input (Riesen, 1965). Through this long history, a coherent pattern has emerged that describes many of the influences of experience on early sensory system *development*. The extent to which this pattern extends to higher cognitive levels remains a subject of debate, as does the relationship of early developmental brain mechanisms that incorporate experience to later developmental mechanisms. We present our own views here. While most neuroscientists are comfortable with the fact of neural plasticity in adult animals that range in complexity from mollusks and crustaceans to primates, our specific view regarding experience-expectant and experience-dependent synapse formation has yet to be embraced by the whole field of neuroscience.

INTRINSIC AND INTERACTIVE FORCES IN DEVELOPMENT

The Hierarchy of "Environments"

It is natural to perceive a dichotomy between the organism and its surrounding environment and to consider this the only boundary that is relevant for assessing the influence of intrinsic, sometimes equated with genetic, and extrinsic, sometimes equated with nongenetic, forces in development. An interesting alternative is to consider that the organism consists of a hierarchy of environments, extending from the environment that the nucleus of each cell provides for its DNA, thus most directly influencing which genes are expressed, to the organism-environment boundary as indicated in Fig. 5.1. At each level, nucleus, cytoplasm of the cell, adjacent cells, organs, multiorgan interactive systems, and organism, forces act back towards the regulation of the expression of genes, and genetic specifications are manifest in structure. (Gottlieb [1991] has also expressed this concept very lucidly.) One can assess the relative impact of actions at each of these levels, but the ability to attribute an aspect of the organism strictly to genotype or to experience is rarely absolute.

Within the nucleus of every cell in the nervous system (or, for practical purposes, every cell in the entire organism) there exists a set of chromosomes that has identical DNA, the genetic material. Which of the tens of thousands of genes in the DNA gets expressed, such that it can affect cell characteristics, is most commonly a function of the environment that the nucleus provides for the DNA. Substances that are present in the nucleus can turn on some genes and turn off others. (Some genes, such as "housekeepers" needed for the function of all cells, may not be regulated in this manner.) The characteristics of a cell—from whether it is a brain cell or a liver cell to what specific neurotransmitter it uses and how its dendritic branches are arranged—are determined by which genes are turned on, thus governing the pattern of proteins produced by the cell.

The substances that govern the pattern of gene expression can arise from the nucleus itself, the cytoplasm of the cell it is in, or from other levels of the hierarchy of environments illustrated in Fig. 5.1. Classic examples of developmental *induction,* in which substances of one organ affect the development of another, are based upon the ability of these substances to affect gene expression, although many specific mechanisms remain unknown. The retina of vertebrates, for example, induces the overlying ectodermal tissue, from which the skin arises, to differentiate into the lens, cornea and other elements of the eye. Similarly, but throughout life, processes from the brainstem neurons that innervate the tongue to provide taste sensation induce the differentiation of cells in the tongue into the taste receptor cells. Information arriving from the extraorganismic environment can work through similar mechanisms: protein synthesis is induced in various components of the visual system when animals are first exposed to light (Rose & Sinha, 1974).

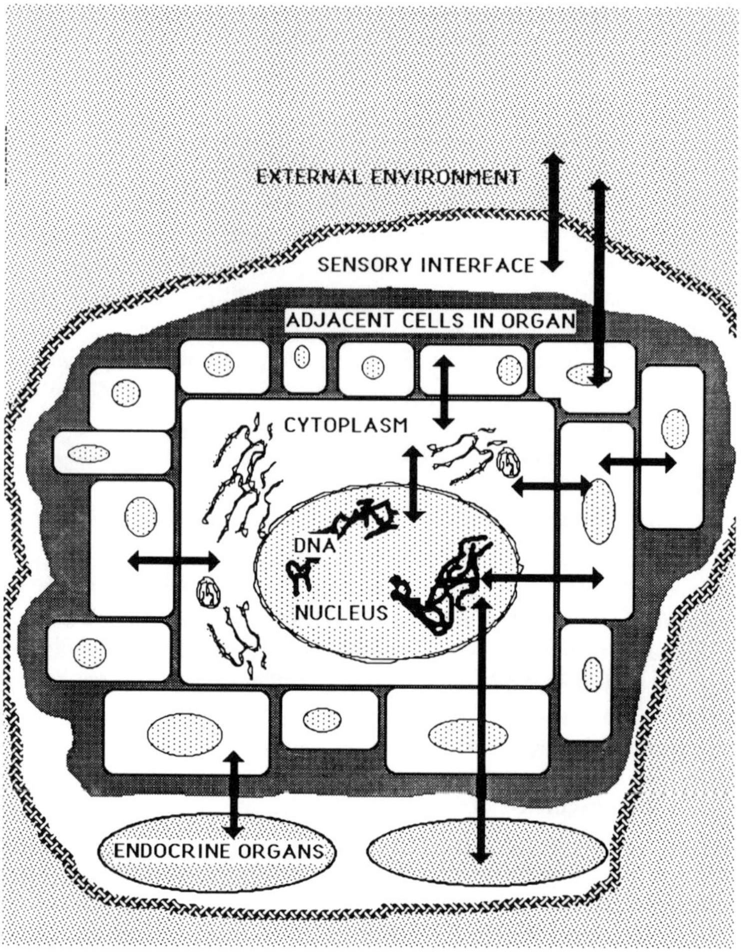

FIG. 5.1. A schematic depiction of the organism's hierarchy of environments, starting from the genes, to cell, to organs, to the animal as a whole, and finally to include its environment. Each of these levels has complex interactions during development and in maintaining homeostasis.

As development progresses, most cells become ever more committed to their ultimate *fates*. A cell that initially might have had the potential to become either a nerve cell or a glial cell becomes ever more neuronal and eventually becomes a specific type of brain or spinal cord neuron. Underlying this is a particular sequence of patterns of activation of genes that becomes increasingly difficult to reverse or change. Typically large groups, or batteries, of functionally-related genes are activated together or in sequence in the achievement of a particular developmental course, and single substances have been described that begin processes ultimately affecting many genes. Certain genes, or families of genes with common structural elements, are expressed in a coordinated fashion to direct the differential expression of other genes in tissues. Other substances, such as retinoic acid, have been discovered that can direct patterns of tissue maturation and gene expression in local regions (Ingham, 1988; Keeble & Maden, 1989; Robertson, 1987; Summerbell & Maden, 1990). Recently a family of genes (named "int1") coding for secreted proteins has been discovered in vertebrates that appears to label regions of the developing embryo (McMahon & Moon, 1989). (These genes are related to one that affects wing development in fruit fly embryogenesis.) For example, in the *neural tube,* or the embryonic nervous system, different regions secrete these proteins, which direct different patterns of gene expression both in the neural tube and in those portions of the surrounding tissue that take their instructions in part from the neural tube.

Thus substances given off in one set of cells can organize gene expression in other cells. As development proceeds, more and more of the characteristics of a cell become intrinsic to that cell, such that the cell will express these characteristics independently of the environment that surrounds it.

This view of development as involving large groups of interacting genes has contributed to a re-evaluation of the manner in which the evolution by selection of phenotypes occurs. Large scale changes in phenotype are thought to most commonly involve modification of developmental patterns, rather than single-point mutations in the genes that code for individual proteins, although changes in proteins also occur over time (Bonner, 1982; Raff & Kaufman, 1983). Thus it is the *regulatory process,* rather than the genes that are regulated, that is most commonly the source of phenotypic change. We assume that a similar process would apply to species-typical behavior patterns generated in part through the specification of complex arrays of nerve cell connections, although our knowledge of the details of the circuitry underlying species typical behaviors remains rudimentary. (For one of the more thoroughly studied examples, see Nottebohm, 1989).

Black and Greenough (1986) used the term "genotype driven" to refer to developmental processes that appeared to remain stable across a wide range of environmental variation. Their purpose was to indicate that there are both simple organisms and components of complex organisms to which the term "intrinsic maturation" might apply in general or at some point in development. This, in turn, implies a dominance of the developmental process by genetic factors, expressed in the characteristics and interactions of cells. There are many processes within the developing nervous system that fit this description. The overall organization of the brain and spinal cord and the gross features of sensory system organization are insensitive to broad variations in the sensory environment of the womb, for example, as is much of the general fine structure of most brain regions. (The emerging discipline of behavioral teratology, however, has found important examples of environmental influences such as drugs that influence early nervous system development and later behavior.) Interactions among neurons and glial cells allow successively migrating cells to organize into complex multilaminated structures such as the cerebellar and cerebral cortices. Defects in a single gene that affects these intercellular interactions can result in massive disorganization (e.g., Goldman-Rakic, Isserof, Schwartz & Bugbee, 1983; Rakic, 1973; Rakic & Sidman, 1973; Hatten & Edmondson, 1988).

At some point in development, aspects of neuronal form become intrinsic to the neuron, essentially independent of its surroundings (e.g., Montague & Friedlander, 1989). At this point, genotype-driven characteristics become evident: in simple organisms, patterns of the branching of dendrites often show more similarity among genetic twins than otherwise, although substantial variation exists (e.g. Levinthal, Macagno & Levinthal, 1975). Variation must arise from the effects of the surroundings of those identical genes. Connection patterns for neurons, for example, depend inherently upon the available choices and, in many cases, upon activity characteristics of those choices (e.g., Constantine-Paton, Cline & Debski, 1990). We note this in a subsequent section for visual cortex neurons. Nerve cell connections also depend upon prespecified preferences that are likely to involve particular molecules available upon the surfaces of cells.

Genotype → Environment Interactions

It is important to reiterate briefly another point made by Black and Greenough (1986) that is also evident in Fig. 5.1. Aspects of the genotype can act through the extraorganismic environment to affect the development of phenotypic characteristics. One example of this involves the organism's selection of particular aspects of the information provided by the environment. Some aspects of this are trivial—we do not see ultraviolet light or hear sounds at frequencies above 30 KHz, such that they have no significant developmental impact. The apparent existence of phonetic feature detectors (Eimas, 1975) similarly limits the range of acoustic features in language that can affect development. There is also evidence of preferences for specific sources of speech input, such as the mother's voice (Fernald, 1984; Lecanuet, Granier-Deferre, DeCasper, Maugeais, Andrieu, & Busnel, 1987). Many features of the perceptual environment are more salient or attractive than others, and these change as the infant matures (Cohen, 1979; Teller & Movshon, 1986). The fact that experience modifies many of these preferences and abilities (Cohen, 1979; Werker & Tees, 1984) should not overshadow the fact that the developing organism's genotype can have substantial effects on neural organization through both absolute limits on sensory sensitivity and constraints on behavioral choice. (For further elaboration of this point and its role with respect to experience-dependent information storage, see Black & Greenough, 1986).

EXPERIENCE—EXPECTANT BRAIN DEVELOPMENT: SCULPTURE YIELDS FUNCTIONING SYSTEMS

Synapse Overproduction Anticipates Experience

It came as a real surprise to many neuroscientists during the 1970s that many regions of the brain actually produced more synapses than they *retained* as development progressed. This phenomenon has been very widely reported in intervening years, but the original region in which the reason for this was first worked out—the development of stereoscopic visual systems—still remains the most illustrative.

Stereoscopic depth perception requires that some neurons in the visual cortex receive input from both eyes. Input from the two eyes follows parallel but separate pathways from the point at which the optic nerve enters the brain to the neurons of layer IV in the visual cortex. At this point the eyes are represented in *ocular dominance columns,* strips of neurons about a third of a millimeter wide, control of which alternates from left eye to right to left, representing corresponding areas of the visual field. These neurons connect to the binocular neurons in other cortical layers. The ocular dominance columns reflect the pattern of termination of axons carrying visual input, and the bands can be visualized by injecting a radioactive tracer into one eye. Transported to these axon terminals, the radioactivity appears in strips that alternate with nonradioactive strips.

Fairly early in the history of sensory development research, Wiesel and Hubel (1963) found that if one eye of a cat or monkey was closed or occluded during a sensitive period of development, that eye lost much of its visual ability and also lost control over visual cortex neurons to the other or open eye, which retained normal vision. Later it was found that merely deviating an eye inward or outward from the normal alignment position caused a similar but more gradual loss of vision and visual control (von Noorden & Dowling, 1970). This paralleled the clinical condition in human children termed *strabismic amblyopia*. (Poor focus in one eye can lead to this as well, a strong argument for early correction of visual impairment in children; Quick, Tigges, Gammon, & Boothe, 1989; Movshon, Eggers, Gizzi, Hendrickson, Kiorpes, & Boothe, 1987). LeVay, Wiesel, and Hubel (1980) described the sequence of events that leads to the loss of control by a deprived eye. Early in the developmental sequence axons make connections that are not restricted to the ocular dominance column pattern of the adult. These intertwined connections become pruned back in development, such that those which remain form the ocular dominance columns. The evidence that experience is involved in this shrinking back process is schematically depicted in Fig. 5.2. When one eye is closed, its axons shrink back to a greater degree than normal, while those of the open eye remain more expanded than normal. Thus the pattern that emerges is one of alternating wide (open eye) and narrow (closed eye) columns. Only those neurons in the visual cortex that received most of their input

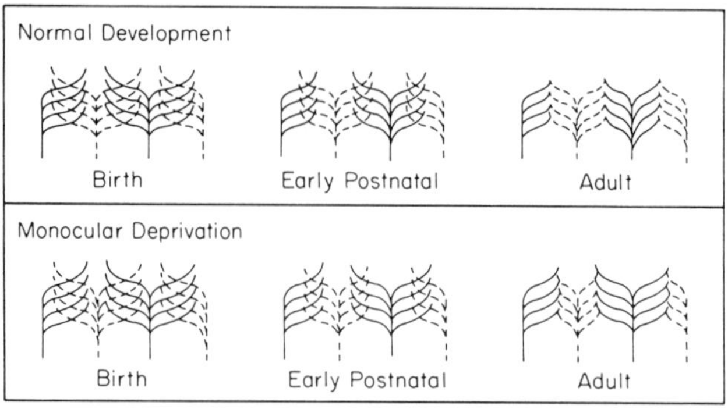

FIG. 5.2. Depiction of ocular dominance column development in kittens reared normally or monocularly deprived. The left panels represent the substantial overlap of axon terminals from the two eyes at birth. In normal development (top row), the competitive interactions result in a balanced pruning back of the branches from each eye in the adult (top right panel). After monocular deprivation (lower row), axons from the non-deprived eye (solid lines) retain more branches while the axons from the deprived eye (dashed lines) lose more branches in adulthood (lower right panel). Modified from Black and Greenough (1986). Reprinted with permission.

within the narrow column would be controlled by the closed eye. While this process remains reversible during the peak sensitive period (e.g., by closing the open eye), it becomes increasingly irreversible thereafter. It is thus analogous to a "sensitive period" in the developmental psychology sense of the term. Subsequent research has shown that optimal development requires synchronized input via both eyes and has also shown that the electrical activity of optic nerve and optic tract axons is a crucial aspect of the development process (Miller, Keller, & Stryker, 1989).

This process of *overproduction* of synaptic connections followed by their *selective elimination,* (or *selective preservation*) to yield a more specific pattern of connections has turned out to be a remarkably common mechanism of neural development, perhaps a universal one. It has been suggested by several theorists that a continuing synapse overproduction process may underlie learning and memory (Changeux & Danchin, 1977; Cotman, Nieto-Sampedro & Harris, 1981; Greenough, 1978). We now think otherwise and our reasoning is outlined in this and a subsequent section.

In development, overproduction of synapses tends to occur in situations in which some highly reliable source of information can guide the synapse elimination process. In the case of the visual system, patterned, simultaneous binocular input will be available in the natural environment, assuming no optical abnormalities. Thus the visual system can use this information to establish the connections in the ocular dominance columns and to establish the binocularly-connected neurons, representing slight degrees of disparity between the two retinas, that are appropriate to stereoscopic depth perception. When abnormal input is substituted, the visual cortex organization process appears to work in the same fundamental way, but the end result may be different. It has been shown, for example, that if both eyes are given equal experience, but in an alternating fashion that precludes the eyes' seeing the same thing at the same time, binocular depth perception does not develop (Singer, 1986). As might be expected, binocular visual cortex neurons rarely develop in this case, with about half of the neurons "captured" by each eye, instead of being shared by both eyes as in the normal animal (Singer, 1986). As the elaborate arrangements necessary to create alternating monocular experience indicate, this situation is unlikely to occur in nature. Hence, assuming normal eye alignment and focal length, stereoscopic vision is extremely likely to develop in the natural case.

This property of *reliability of the nature of a particular experience or event* is a fundamental characteristic of what we call *experience-expectant information* storage. This contrasts with the more flexible and idiosyncratic *experience-dependent* information storage, which is discussed in a subsequent section. These categories map reasonably well to categories of information stored by organisms, as described by Piaget (1980).

Our terminology for this synapse overproduction process reflects the apparent fact that the synapses are produced in the evolutionarily-based *expectation* that appropriate experience will provide the information that the nervous system needs in order to select the appropriate subset of synaptic connections. For example, kittens, rats, and children all undergo a predictable, species-typical sequence of eye opening, visuomotor interaction and reaching that provides reliable information for the nervous system to use. Implicit in the term experience expectant is the understanding that, if the experience, expected, based on the evolutionary history of the species, does not occur, development will occur based on whatever aberrant information experience does provide. Hence asymmetrical visual input yields asymmetrical visual system organization and independent binocular input yields independent binocular organization. The sensitive period is largely defined as a period during which excess connections exist, such that their selective survival depends on experience. Once the selection has been made, the fundamental organization of the system has been determined. While some capacity for adjustment (and for learning) may remain (LeVay et al., 1980), the period of potential for species-typical development has passed.

Experience-expectant processes, defined as an effect of experience mediated by the selective survival of a subset of a previously generated population of synapses, appear to be very widespread. This can be judged from (1) the general tendency for neurons in cerebral cortex (Cragg, 1975; Boothe, Greenough, Lund, & Wrege, 1979; Huttenlocher, 1979; Huttenlocher, de Courten, Garey, & Van der Loos, 1982), cerebellum (Weiss & Pysh, 1978; Mariani & Changeux, 1981), brainstem (Falls & Gobel, 1979; Feng & Rogowski, 1980), and the periphery (Purves & Lichtman, 1980) to overproduce synapses, dendrites, and axons during early development, and (2) the tendency for the development of those systems to be sensitive to experience and its associated neural activity.

At least some cases of synapse overproduction are not evident with traditional techniques, as in the somatosensory cortex of the mouse as illustrated in Fig. 5.3. The large facial whiskers (mystacial vibrissae), complicated sensory devices for the mouse, are represented by cell groupings called "barrels," in which the wall

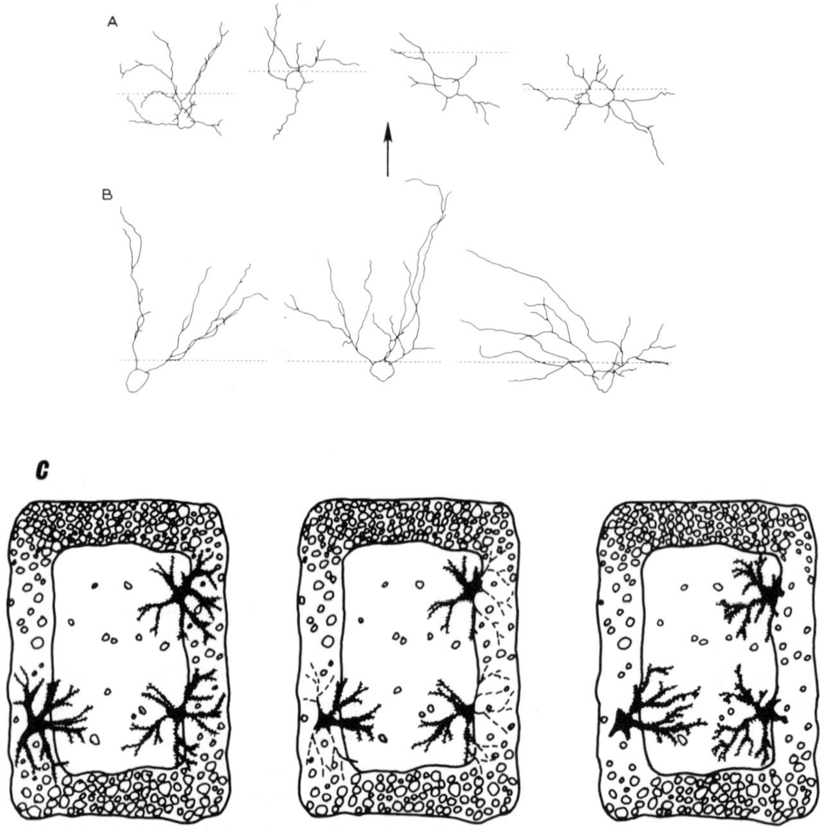

FIG. 5.3. In the newborn rat, neurons in somatosensory cortex facial whisker region send dendrites in all directions, as these stick figures indicate. B. In the adult rat, dendrites are highly oriented. C. The development process is shown in the context of the "barrels," groups of cell bodies arranged in rings around a cell-sparse center where the inputs from the whisker terminate. There is one barrel for each of the large facial whiskers. In the left drawing, the dendrites extend in all directions. As development proceeds, branches extending in the "wrong" direction (out of the barrel, away from the whisker inputs) degenerate, while those in the barrel center form additional connections with the whisker inputs. Thus the oriented form of the neuron in the adult (right figure) arises by loss of some connections and addition of others.

of the barrel is composed of a ring of cell bodies and the hollow of the barrel contains their dendrites and their synapses with whisker input axons. The dendrites of these neurons are thus highly oriented in adults, as illustrated in the lower row of drawings in Fig. 5.3. Greenough and Chang (1988) examined the development of this ordered pattern across ages and found that the dendrites progressed from a state in which they showed only a small degree of orientation, at 10 days of age, to the oriented adult form. The development of orientation involved the regression of dendrites that were oriented in the "wrong" direction, away from the barrel hollow, and the simultaneous extension of those dendrites that extended in the right direction, towards the hollow. Rarely does one know the position of the cell with regard to features that determine its ultimate developmental form. If these cells had been like most neurons, where we have no landmarks and can merely measure the average amount of dendrite per nerve cell, the results would have been interpreted as reflecting a slow pattern of growth with no regression evident. Likewise, counting of synapses per nerve cell would have revealed only averages. The case of the barrel neuron suggests that much more overproduction and loss of synapses may occur than is evident from the measures we are usually able to make. It is also of interest that much of the sensory input that shapes these dendrites probably arises from contact with the mother during nursing and other interactions—certainly a reliable source of information, since the young mouse would die without it.

It is interesting to consider why the process of evolution would select such a mechanism over seemingly more reliable cell-surface molecules that appear to specify connections in simpler invertebrates and in some vertebrate pathways (Harrelson, Bastiani, Snow, & Goodman 1988; Landmesser, 1988). A distinct possibility in some cases is that the quality of system performance that can be achieved through experiential "fine tuning" may be greater than that achievable with cell-surface molecular codes determined solely by the genome. This might be particularly true for something as complicated as a mammalian stereoscopic visual system and much less so for that of spinal connections to muscles or for an insect nervous system in which a smaller number of elements also requires vastly less information to specify its organizational pattern. It also appears that we initially underestimated the degree to which neural activity is involved in the specification of even the simple systems, as has become evident, for example, in the retina to brain connection of amphibians (e.g., Reh & Constantine-Paton, 1984). This connection was thought to be specified exclusively by molecular mechanisms when Sperry (1963) studied it and for a good period thereafter.

As Black and Greenough (1986) argued, experience-expectant developmental mechanisms appear to have evolved in cases in which a particular set of circumstances exists:

1. The information to be acquired is *common to all young members of a species*. Young members of a species that are deprived of this "expected" input

will thus be at a developmental disadvantage. This is clearly true for basic visual system development, as it is for the development of most basic qualities of other sensory and of motor systems. Imprinting, the process whereby newly hatched chicks, for example, rapidly learn to recognize their mothers visually, appears to involve both the generation of some new synapses and the elimination of some previously existing ones (Horn, Bradley, & McCabe, 1985; Patel, Rose, & Stewart, 1988). Thus it is interesting that imprinting appears to involve learning both of general species characteristics and of the characteristics of the chick's own mother (Bateson, 1979). (It should be noted, however, that acquisition of species characteristics may occur at a point beyond the periods examined in the above studies [Vidal, 1980].) "Language" learning in the Mynah bird, presumably utilizing the system that normally underlies development of species-typical calls, is associated with extensive synapse elimination of some types of neurons (Scheich, 1987; Wallhausser & Scheich, 1987). Song learning in canaries actually involves the addition of new neurons, a process that, thus far, appears to occur quite rarely in postnatal or posthatching development (Nottebohm, 1989). Whether synapse elimination (or neuron elimination) is involved at some point in song learning is not yet clear.

2. The event(s) that provide the information must be ones that a) will occur reliably for all species members and b) have occurred reliably throughout the evolution of this developmental system, as was noted previously. For example, the timing of eye opening in kittens must have evolved in synchrony with the sensitive period in visual cortex, even though they involve quite different systems. The events discussed, patterned visual (or other sensory system) experience and input associated with maternal contact, fall easily into this category.

3. The timing of the event(s) that provide the information is typically relatively critical. It is not clear how the overproduction and loss process is regulated; that is, what makes a sensory system stop being sensitive (see pp. 184-186). For many of the processes discussed, early acquisition would be essential as a basis for further development. Imprinting is necessary for survival. On the other hand, some processes may be rather protracted in humans. While the density of synapses in the human visual cortex peaks at 8–12 months of age and drops rapidly thereafter (Huttenlocher et al., 1982), synapse loss in the human frontal cortex appears to continue to at least 7 and possibly 14 years of age (Huttenlocher, 1979).

Figure 5.4. is an attempt to schematically illustrate the neural events that might underlie an experience-expectant process from the viewpoint of the recipient neuron.

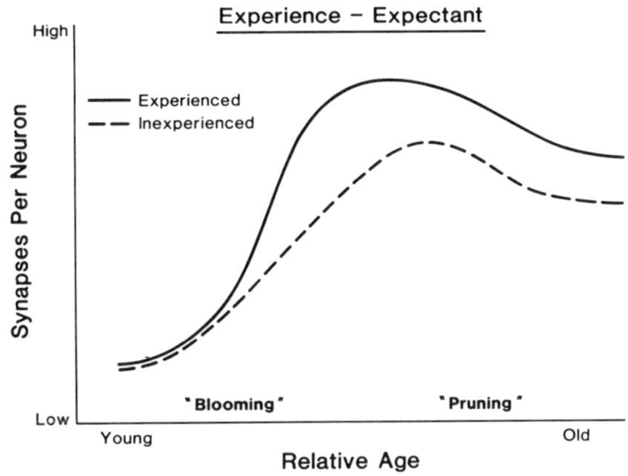

FIG. 5.4. Diagram of synapse overproduction ("blooming") and deletion ("pruning") during an experience-expectant process. From Black and Greenough (1986). Reprinted with permission.

Applications to Cognitive Development?

Because so much of the experience sensitive systems of a species are inextricably tied to its evolution, we can only speculate on the relevance of the information from animal research to our understanding of human cognitive development. Nonetheless, several research findings are of interest. First, while somewhat controversial, it seems clear that both phonemic boundary perception and, to a lesser extent, phoneme production involve initial sets of categories or boundaries that become more restricted as vocalization and later language develop (Eimas, 1975; Werker & Tees, 1984). This is an excellent parallel to the overproduction and loss of connections in the nervous system, although it may be only that.

A second speculation that is intriguing but quite controversial involves the question of whether these processes of synapse overproduction and refinement might occur at an early age in sensory systems and at a later age in structures such as the frontal cortex that are related to later-developing higher cognitive functions. In contract to this speculation, Rakic, Bourgeois, Eckenhoff, Zecevic, and Goldman-Rakic (1986) have proposed, on the basis of synapse density counts in monkeys, that the process of synapse overproduction and loss occurs nearly synchronously throughout the cerebral cortex. While this is an interesting report, we are reluctant to accept its conclusions at face value for a variety of reasons.

There are two basic arguments that we have with their data, the first technical, the second resting on data from others. The technical argument involves the specific measurement used—the density of synapses (number of synapses per unit of volume) in the cerebral cortex. Put very simply, the density of synapses does not necessarily accurately reflect the total number that are being formed or lost at any point in time. The reason for this is that, when synapses form, supportive tissue that seems to be required for synaptic function may expand to an equivalent degree, at least in development (Turner & Greenough, 1985; Sirevaag & Greenough, 1987). This tissue includes both glia, the ill-understood supportive "glue" cells of the nervous system, and the brain's capillary network as we detail in a later section (see pp. 186-189). Because of this, the density of synapses may not be a very good measure of the number of synapses per nerve cell or per functional system during development. In short, the synchronous peaks could represent some other process (e.g., glial or capillary development) that affects the density of synapses but not the number of synapses.

The second argument involves the fact that asynchronies have been reported among brain areas in equally relevant measures (including synapse density). One of the first attempts to quantify regional cortical development (Conel, 1939–1967) used the thickness of the human cerebral cortex as an index of its status. Those nearly forgotten data were presented in tabular form that obscured regional differences in the pattern of development. We have plotted data for some regions in Fig. 5.5. It seems clear that visual cortex reaches peak thickness early, after which it stabilizes or declines, whereas frontal cortex shows a more protracted pattern of peak and stabilization. (Of course, cortex has 3 dimensions, and the volume of functional subregions was not assessed in Conel's work.) A similar conclusion arises from the work of Huttenlocher and colleagues (1979; Huttenlocher et al., 1982) who quantified synaptic density, with all of its attendant problems, in the visual and frontal cortices of human autopsy samples from groups of different ages ranging from early childhood to elderly. Again, a pattern of delayed synapse loss in frontal, relative to visual, cortex was evident.

Multiple Interacting Systems in Cognitive Development

Thus far we have concentrated on studies within a single sensory modality. An important finding of these studies has been the role of competitive processes in establishing neural structure. This has been extended theoretically as a general organizing principle for brain development, where balanced and scheduled competition both between and within brain areas encourages one system to help prepare others to incorporate experience (Turkewitz & Kenny, 1982). Turkewitz and Kenny (1982) argue that the lengthy sequence of perceptual development (described by Gottlieb, 1971) helps reduce and organize the information with which the infant must cope. For example, they suggest that the initially low quality vision of infants ensures that only a small fraction of the visual environment must be attended to at any one time. The surplus information would only distract the infant and complicate experience if it were not filtered out. The slow and gradual development of humans can allow information from a more mature

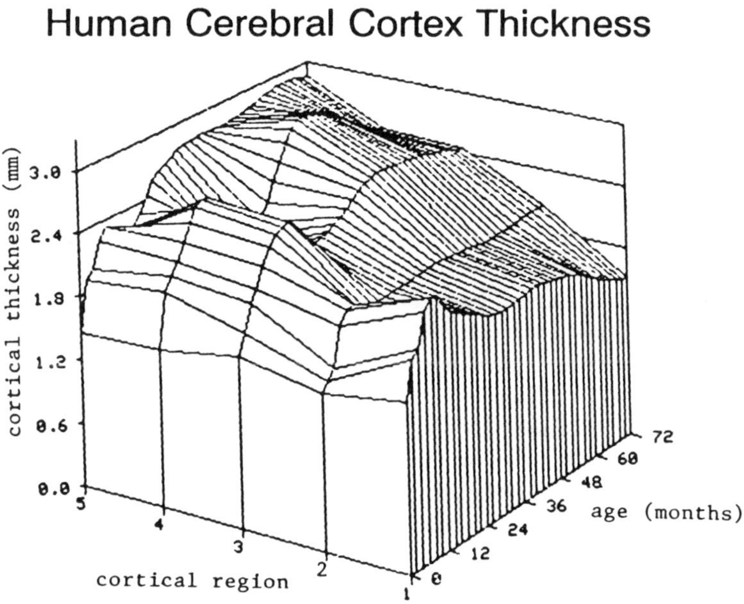

FIG. 5.5. Cortical thickness in humans is plotted as a function of age and cortical region of the cerebral cortex, using data from Conel (1939–1967). Postnatal changes in cortical thickness indirectly reflect the addition or delection of brain components, such as synapses, blood vessels, and glial cells. Note that the different regions each have unique patterns of developmental changes in cortical thickness.

modality (e.g., touch) to help integrate and organize input from a newly developing modality (e.g., vision). Their use of Piaget's term "disequilibration" seems appropriate: information from an established modality disrupts and challenges the premature processing of a new emerging modality, facilitating its reorganization into a more stable and advanced form.

Multiple sensitive periods can exist within the layers of a single structure, or they can be distributed across many components of a neural system. Experience deprivation may not reveal multiple sensitive periods within one neural system because their behavioral consequences may overlap. In addition, some experience-expectant processes could be so tightly linked that an experimental manipulation for dissociating them has not yet been found.

Visuomotor development provides an example of how experience-expectant processes can fit into a complex developmental sequence. Held and Hein (1963) had kittens ride in a gondola yoked to another freely-moving kitten. the kittens in the gondola received ample visual stimulation but, apparently because the gondola movement was not correlated with their body movements, the kittens failed to develop normal, visually guided behavior (such as traversing a maze or pawing an object). Movement by the yoked kitten caused the gondola to move, possibly providing noncoherent relationships between self-produced motion and the retinal image. Thus the developmental failure might be caused by: (1) a lack of experience needed to maintain a genetically-driven structure, or (2) neural induction of inappropriate information.

In a study demonstrating partial dissociation of visuomotor functions, Hein and Held (1967) raised freely moving cats with "Elizabethan" collars that prevented sight of their paws. Consequently, they had normal experience with retinal image changes produced by self-locomotion, but none relating a visual image of a paw to its self-initiated movement. These kittens extended their paws in response to an approaching object, but could not accurately guide them toward an object. Extension of the paw requires only knowledge of how objects move relative to the body, whereas visually guided behavior requires paw movement to be related to its visual image. This suggests that an induction process may help relate visual feedback about paw and object to the motor systems controlling paw position.

Kittens apparently first need to experience walking freely in order to encode the location of objects in a body-centered map and relate them to visual changes caused by locomotion (Hein & Diamond, 1971). Only after that map has been built up can the kittens integrate: (1) the visual image of their paw, (2) feedback about their paw position, and (3) the visual image of the target object. This chain of linked integrations is built on the developmental "expectation" that appropriate experience will be available when needed. Each step apparently prepares the foundation for the next by making more experience available (i.e., experiential contrast) or improving its quality (i.e., experiential coherence). Locomotor practice may prepare the kitten to understand and coordinate the relative visual positions of its paw and a target object. Without a body-centered map, the juxtaposed images would be shifty, uncoordinated and nonsensical.

Hein and Diamond (1983) suggest an important role for proprioceptive feedback from the course eye movements of early vision. By providing a rough check on the starting and stopping positions for eye movement, proprioceptive feedback can help relate the retinal image to the direction of gaze. However, this feedback is needed only to develop more refined control, since the kittens managed quite well without proprioceptive feedback if they had previous normal experience. The kittens that had lost visually guided behaviors still retained some integration of oculomotor control and changes in the retinal image from their earlier experience, and were thus able to reconstruct visually guided behavior without proprioceptive feedback. Fiorentini and Maffei (1977) found that normally reared adult cats without proprioceptive feedback could control their eye movements accurately in the light but had abnormal eye movements in the dark. Collectively, these results argue for a progressive integration in which proprioceptive feedback serves as a coarse system for eye control in early development, and then in later development serves to refine the emerging, better quality visuomotor systems.

Very young infants can effectively, if crudely, track an object swung from right and left by shifting the entire trunk from right to left (Bullinger, 1983). Bullinger suggests that visual tracking develops from crudely orienting the whole trunk and arms to precisely aiming only the head. This progression from coarse to refined systems seems analogous to that described in the kitten. Perhaps when the infant can use only basic reflexes, unable even to roll over reliably, aiming the eyes by twisting the trunk may serve to crudely stabilize and benchmark the relationship between retinal image and body position. As more sophisticated systems are built, the crude systems may be obscured or eliminated. Developing a complex spatial code is not a trivial task for the young infant because it requires coordinating the retinal image with feedback from gaze, head, and body orientation. It is generally suggested (e.g., Bertenthal, Campos, & Barrett, 1984; Bremner, 1982; Grusser, 1983; Piaget & Inhelder, 1956) that the infant first codes object location unreliably within a body-centered map, acquiring a spatial code with external landmarks at about the same time that crawling starts. The very young infant's relative immobility helps the general orientation of objects remain somewhat stable, but simple egocentric codes can be severely disrupted by simply turning over or twisting the head. The kitten studies suggested that crude proprioceptive processes were used to initiate visuomotor search patterns and facilitate acquisition of better spatial codes. Feedback from eye muscles was essential for acquisition of visually guided behaviors, but not necessary for performance once the behavior is acquired. In analogy, the infant's crude egocentric code may allow for experience with which a framework code can be induced. A wobbly baby would simply have to tolerate the frequent disappointments when first trying out a newly refined spatial code, but the older coarse orientation could assist (and even temporarily dominate) newer systems if the infant became frustrated.

This view suggests that spatial codes are built up from intermodal correlation, starting from learning about body parts to incorporating the proximal and then distal spatial regions. Infants may use repetitive actions to discover coherent and stable relationships, e.g., by mouthing fingers and toes, rocking or kicking, or grasping objects while mouthing and looking at them. Self-modulation of these interactions can be accomplished by actively seeking it out when bored, or by ignoring frustrating or complex stimulation (Thelen, 1980). Some developmental units (e.g., visually guided locomotion of kittens) improve the coherence and contrast needed for development of a later unit (e.g., visually guided reaching). In the process, the simpler and more automatic systems used to provide and stabilize experience for the juvenile may be transformed, suppressed, or erased in the adult. Their early assistance may be crude, but is seemingly vital to development of later, more refined and accurate systems.

EXPERIENCE-DEPENDENT PLASTICITY

A strong case can be made that the rules governing brain information storage in much of later development and later life are different from those associated with the experience-expectant information storage process as outlined above. First, the type of information that is stored throughout most of life is largely of the sort that is *unique to the individual,* as opposed to being common to all species members. Second, while there may be some sequential dependencies, there are *no specific age limitations* with regard to when particular items of information can be acquired. Location of food, warmth and shelter in the case of animals, or the myriad knowledge that humans acquire, constitute a lifelong learning process. Finally, as we will detail subsequently, the neural mechanisms underlying lifelong information storage appear to differ from those involved in experience-expectant information storage. We have adopted the term experience-dependent information storage for this process to reflect our view that the information storage process is initiated and driven by the organism's response to events in its environment (and/or in its brain) that generate information that the organism in some way deems important. Because it is somewhat difficult to delineate the character of this process other than by example, we now describe the core body of research that has led us to this formulation.

Manipulating The Complexity of the Rearing Environment: Behavioral Effects

Since the early demonstrations of Hebb (1949) there has been an array of research that has reinforced the view that animals reared in groups in complex, play-exploration object-filled environments (EC rats) are superior in learning many different behavior tasks to rats reared socially (SC) or individually (IC) in standard laboratory cages. The kinds of tasks for which this has generally been demonstrated include mazes (Brown, 1968; Greenough, Madden & Fleischmann, 1972b; Greenough, Wood & Madden, 1972a; Hymovitch, 1952; Juraska, Henderson & Muller, 1984), visual discriminations (Greenough, Yuwiler & Dollinger, 1973b) and other complex, appetitive tasks (e.g. Morgan, 1973; Nyman, 1967; Warren, Zerweck, & Anthony, 1982). Differences in performance on aversively-motivated tasks have also been described (Edwards, Barry, & Wyspianski, 1969; Freeman & Ray, 1972; Greenough, Fulcher, Yuwiler, & Geller, 1970).

The behavioral substrates of this superiority do not appear to be limited to any particular ability or characteristic such as reduced emotionality in the EC rats or differential exploratory tendencies among the groups, although these may play a role in some cases (Brown, 1968; Donovick, Burright, & Swidler, 1973; Forgays & Read, 1962; Forgus, 1954; Greenough et al., 1972b; Morgan, 1973; Rosenzweig, 1971). EC rats have been shown to be more dependent on extramaze cues when available (Brown, 1968; Hymovitch, 1952) but to remain superior in performance even when these cues are hidden (Ravizza & Herschberger, 1966). One component of the enhanced learning ability appears to be a general familiarity with the properties of a more complicated spatial environment (Bernstein, 1973; Forgus, 1954; Wilson, Warren, & Abbott, 1965). In addition, there may be a more general component of the effect, in the sense that direct transfer of specific information acquired in prior experience may not account for all effects that have been reported in any obvious, simple way. For example, Greenough et al. (1972a) found that EC mice learned a maze whether trials were massed one right after the other or spaced by hours, while SC and IC mice did very poorly in the massed trial situation. They suggested that something about the rate of information processing may have differentiated the groups. Thinus-Blanc (1981) reported what appears to be differential information processing capability for tasks resembling Piagetian volume conservation tasks. EC and SC hamsters were trained to choose between a large and a small cube target in a T-maze, a task the ECs learned faster. The animals were then tested on volumes that could differ from the target cube along 0, 1, 2, or 3 dimensions. The SC hamsters tended to use only width in their comparisons, whereas ECs used both width and depth in their choices.

Manipulating the Complexity of the Rearing Environment: Brain Effects

What the behavioral results do indicate is that the EC rats acquire information from their environment —information that alters behavioral function. Because of this, the comparison of the brains of EC, SC and IC rats appeared to be an excellent place to begin looking for the neural substrates of learning and memory. An incidental finding of a project initially directed largely at differences these environments induced in brain chemistry was the Rosenzweig, Krech, Bennett, and Diamond (1962) report that the visual cortex was heavier in EC than in IC rats. This was followed up by reports of a thicker visual cortex with larger nerve cell bodies (Diamond, 1967) and a higher ratio of RNA and protein to DNA (Rosenzweig & Bennett, 1978) in the EC rats, the latter result indicating either that more genes are expressed or that the same genes are expressed at higher levels in ECs. This issue has remained unclarified, although it seems clear that there are differences in synthetic activity at some points during the course of differential rearing (Levitan, Mushynski, & Ramirez, 1972; Uphouse, 1980).

The studies that have produced the most clearly interpretable results have had to do with measures of altered functional connectivity resulting from EC housing. A number of reports have presented enticing evidence that the *strength of preexisting synaptic connections between neurons* may be altered, based on measurement of various structural features (e.g., West & Greenough, 1972; Greenough, West & DeVoogd, 1978; Sirevaag & Greenough, 1985 [We exclude Mollgaard, Diamond, Bennett, Rosenzweig, and Lindner, 1971, from this list because this result was later explicitly deemed unreplicable by the junior authors: Diamond, Lindner, Johnson, Bennett, and Rosenzweig, 1975.]). These reports are especially interesting because they fit in well with the use of synaptic strength alterations in neural network modelling of cognitive and related functions (e.g., McClelland & Rumelhart, 1986). However, there is as yet no direct evidence that any of these structural modifications is associated with altered synaptic strength.

The studies that have made the greatest contribution to our understanding of the individual information storage process have focused upon measures of alterations in the *number of synapses*. Holloway (1966) first reported differences in dendritic fields between EC and IC rats, although technical difficulties prevented accurate measurement in many subjects. Volkmar and Greenough (1972; Greenough & Volkmar, 1973) provided detailed measurements of visual cortex neurons in animals reared from weaning in EC, SC or IC conditions: Across four different types of visual cortex neurons EC rats had about 20% more dendrite per neuron than IC rats. Turner and Greenough (1983, 1985) supported this finding, reporting a difference of 20–25% in the number of synapses per neuron, using electron microscopy (Fig. 5.6), and this basic finding has also been confirmed by others (e.g., Bhide & Bedi, 1984). This type of plasticity is not limited to visual cortex. Similar, though generally smaller, differences between EC- and IC-like conditions have been reported in other regions of the cerebral cortex (Greenough, Volkmar & Juraska, 1973a), the hippocampal formation (in female, and not male, rats; Juraska, Fitch, Henderson, & Rivers, 1985; Juraska, Fitch, & Washburne, 1989) and the cerebellar cortex (Pysh & Weiss, 1979). The results are not limited to rodents. Similar findings have been reported in, for example, cats and monkeys (Beaulieu & Colonnier, 1987; Floeter & Greenough, 1979). Thus synapse formation, possibly accompanied by overproduction and losses not evident in the aggregate measures (as in the somatosensory whisker studies mentioned above), is a widespread form of plastic response to increased experiential stimulation.

Synapse formation in response to a complex environment is not limited to the

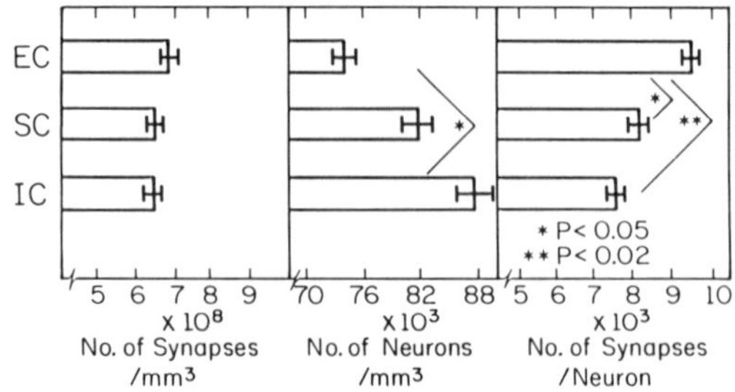

FIG. 5.6. Synaptic density, neuronal density, and synapses per neuron in upper visual cortex of rats reared for 30 days after weaning in complex environments (EC), social cages (SC), or in isolation (IC). The lower neuronal density of EC rats reflects increased amounts of glia, blood vessels, and other neuropil components that spread neurons apart. After Turner and Greenough (1985) with permission.

period of development, in contrast to the apparent rules for experience-expectant information storage discussed previously. Adult, and even middle-aged rats living in complex environments increased visual cortex dendritic branching, relative to individually or socially housed animals, when placed in EC housing (Juraska, Greenough, Elliott, Mack, & Berkowitz, 1980; Green, Greenough & Schlumpf, 1983; Uylings, Kuypers & Veltman, 1978). (Prior studies showed that cortical thickness changes occurred in adults as well; Bennett et al., 1964; Riege, 1971) The magnitude of these responses is nearly as great as that seen in weanling rats. It has also become clear that dendritic plasticity is a rapid response to complex environment exposure. Experience-induced changes in visual cortex dendritic field structure are evident after as little as 4 days of exposure to a complex environment (Kilman, Wallace, Withers, & Greenough, 1988). As a significant amount of dendritic change must occur before it can be detected in average dendritic field measures, this indicates that these changes must begin to occur almost as soon as the animals are placed in the complex environment. As these local changes accumulate over a month or more of exposure to the complex environment, the large aggregate differences evident in the right panel of Fig. 5.6 gradually arise.

Experience-expectant and experience-dependent neural plasticity are best distinguished by their control, rather than by fundamental differences in mechanisms. While experience-dependent processes may share many genetic mechanisms, they cannot anticipate the timing of the necessary experience and must therefore leave the window of the critical period wide open. Thus in contrast to experience-expectant processes, which have synapses created in anticipation of experiences, experience-dependent processes generate synapses on demand. Instead of a single wave of synapse production that is synchronously pruned back, experience-dependent processes have a quiltwork of small blooms that may further regress on individual schedules. Repeated exposures to new information may result in a gradual, smooth accumulation of synapses (Fig. 5.7). The individual blooms may indeed be very localized, but most training procedures (e.g., maze training) involve a complex set of learned behaviors and information, such that many different brain areas may be involved in synapse production.

EFFECTS OF TRAINING ON ADULT BRAIN: ARE THEY DUE TO LEARNING?

The findings that these structural changes continued into adulthood and that they could occur rapidly suggested that these mechanisms were involved in aspects of brain information storage. There now is a substantial body of evidence indicating that this information storage includes learning of traditional psychological tasks. Early evidence of this was the Greenough, Juraska, and Volkmar (1979) report

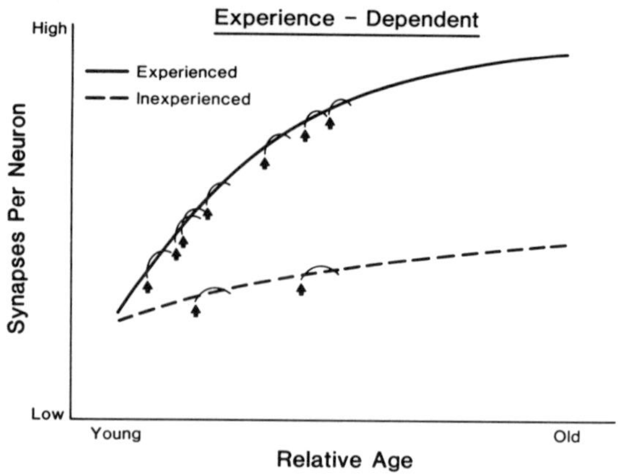

FIG. 5.7. Diagram of synapse formation and selective retention during an experience-dependent process. The arrowheads mark salient experiences that generate localized synaptic overproduction and deletion (small curves). The cumulative effects of such synaptic blooms is a smooth overall increase in synapses per neuron, which is greater for the animals with more experience. From Black and Greenough (1986). Reprinted with permission.

that dendritic fields of visual cortex neurons were altered as a consequence of extensive maze training. There have also been a number of contemporary and subsequent reports of apparent changes in synaptic organization resulting from various types of training or learning experiences, such as operant conditioning, song-learning in birds, and learning of flight path in bees, which will not be detailed here (e.g., Coss, Brandon & Globus, 1980; DeVoogd, Nixdorf & Nottebohm, 1985; Wenzel, Kammerer, Frotscher, Kirsche, Matthies, & Wenzel, 1980). Thus there appears to be reasonable consistency in reports of morphological change in association with learning and memory formation. The more difficult question has been that of determining whether these changes are (1) *brought about by learning*, and (2) *involved in memory*.

Are the Effects Upon Brain Structure Caused by Hormonal or Metabolic Consequences of Different Environments or Training?

The case that these structural effects arise from learning is made largely on the basis of the *exclusion of alternative causes of the brain changes*. A very serious problem in studies attempting to assess the relationship between some change in the nervous system and learning or memory formation is the fact that procedures that induce learning are likely to have other consequences for the subjects, such as stress, motor activity, sensory activity, non-learning neural activity, etc., that could in themselves be responsible for any changes seen in the brain. Two commonly proposed side effects in the EC–IC paradigm are stress responses, either to the individual cage condition or to the complex, group-living condition, and *differences in various aspects of general metabolism,* as suggested by the fact that IC rats eat more and weigh more than EC rats (Fiala, Snow, & Greenough, 1977).

Several results from the EC–IC paradigm argue against the general metabolism hypothesis, as well as against effects involving generally-acting hormones, such as thyroxin or growth hormone. First, different areas within the cerebral cortex, such as the visual cortex, auditory cortex and frontal cortex, show diverse sensitivity to the complex environment. There were no effects of complex environment rearing on two neuron types that were analyzed in the frontal cortex, and much smaller effects on the two types studied in the temporal cortex than on comparable cells in the visual cortex (Greenough & Volkmar, 1973; Greenough et al., 1973a). Similar variation from region to region was reported in the pattern of cortical thickness changes (Rosenzweig, Bennett, & Diamond, 1972a). These differences cannot be accounted for by regional differences in rate of brain development: The frontal, temporal, and visual cortexes are in comparatively close synchrony relative to the length of the 30-day postweaning period during which the animals were exposed to the various environments. Thus the fact that *these cortical (and other brain) regions are differentially affected by experience argues against any generally-acting hormonal or metabolic cause of the EC–IC differences.* Likewise, within brain regions, the extent of the effects of experience or training varies across different types of neurons, in contrast to expectations of a general hormonal or metabolic hypothesis.

Second, the effects of the EC and IC conditions on somatic measures are often in the opposite direction from those on brain measures. As Fig. 5.8 shows, IC-reared rats not only weigh more than their EC (and, typically, SC) counterparts but also exhibit more rapid growth of the long bones of the body, as well as of some internal organs such as the liver, kidney, spleen, and thymus (Black, Sirevaag, Wallace, Savin, & Greenough, 1989; Uphouse & Brown, 1981). (SC rats generally parallel IC rats on these measures.) *Any general metabolic stimulus* (except one that shifted resources from the periphery to the brain or vice versa) *would not have the opposite effect upon the body's periphery and select brain regions.*

Third, when input from a training experience is lateralized, the morphological effects of training tend to be correspondingly lateralized in the brain. Chang and Greenough (1982) used split-brain surgery and unilateral opaque contact lens insertion to direct visual input from a multipattern maze training experience to one hemisphere. Results indicated that pyramidal cell apical dendritic branching changes were largely restricted to the hemisphere receiving training input. In a

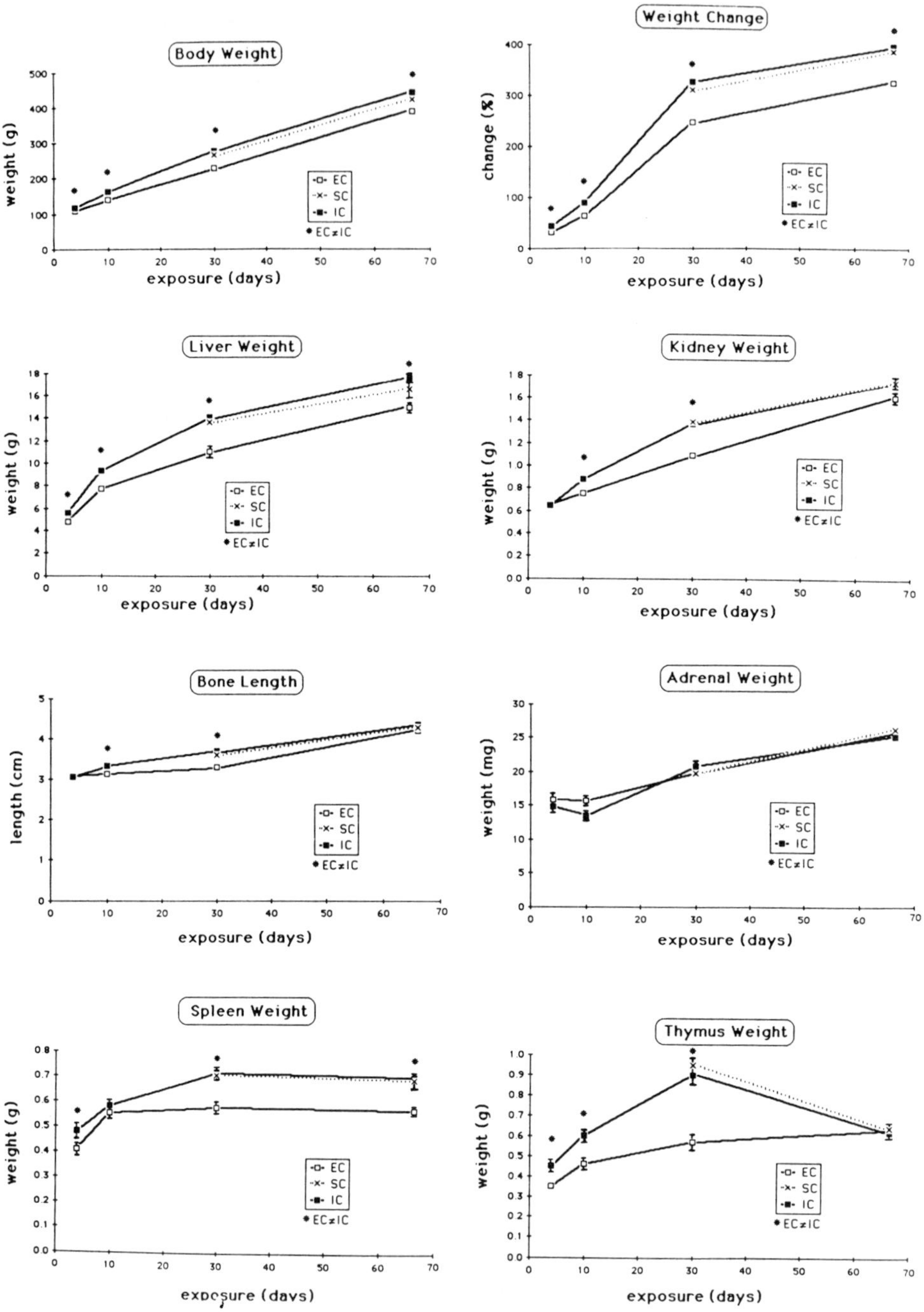

FIG. 5.8. Group means and standard errors for weanling rats exposed to EC, SC, or IC for different durations. Asterisks denote significant differences between EC and IC means. Standard error bars were not plotted if they were smaller than the group symbol. Reprinted from Black et al. (1989) with permission

group that was trained bilaterally by alternating the occluder position each day, dendritic branching increases occurred bilaterally, relative to nontrained controls. Similar lateralization of effects of training was seen in rats trained to reach for food with the same forelimb every day (Greenough, Larson, & Withers, 1985). General hormonal and metabolic effects certainly cannot account for these *shifts in laterality of morphological effect in accord with the input from behavioral experience*. This result argues strongly that training-related experience acts directly upon the brain regions involved in the learning.

As noted earlier, it has been proposed that *the hormonal consequences of stress* might underlie the brain differences arising from differential experience or training. This hypothesis has been strengthened by recent demonstrations (1) that removal of the stress-sensitive adrenal glands can increase cortex growth while administration of the adrenal hormone corticosterone can reduce brain growth (Meyer, 1987; Thomas & Devenport, 1988), (2) that chronic stress can damage the hippocampus (Landfield, Lindsey, & Lynch, 1978; Sapolsky, 1987), and (3) that acute stress can induce pathology in brainstem and visual cortex (Bogolepov, Verbitskaya, Belova, & Sudakov, 1985). Nonetheless the data from EC–IC studies argue strongly against stress hormones as a source of brain structure differences. First, brain morphology differences have been commonly reported in postweaning differential environmental complexity studies in which differences in adrenal weight, an indicator of a history of stress, could not be detected (e.g., Bennett et al., 1964; Black et al., 1989). Second, cortex measurements favor EC rats consistently across studies in which differences in adrenal weights favoring either EC or IC rats were reported (Black et al., 1989; Geller, Yuwiler, & Zolman, 1965; Uphouse & Brown, 1981). Third, typical EC-IC differences in brain morphology occurred in rats with the pituitary removed, effectively blocking differential activation of the adrenal stress response (Rosenzweig, Bennett, & Diamond, 1972b). Fourth, EC–IC differences in brain morphology occurred in rats that were also subjected to daily tumbling stress that increased adrenal weight and should have masked any effects of the milder environmental differences (Riege & Morimoto, 1970). What is interesting is that *individual* differences in stress history, as reflected in individual adrenal weight levels correlate with individual astrocyte process density in the hippocampal dentate gyrus in animals that did not show EC–SC–IC differences on this measure (Sirevaag, Black, & Greenough, 1991). Thus the brain was *sensitive* to stresses that the rats encountered, but these stresses were not tied to the environmental conditions that we imposed.

Thus, while hormonal or metabolic factors may play a permissive role with regard to experience effects upon the brain, the effects of complex versus social and individual housing upon the brain do not appear to be attributable to differential contributions of any general hormonal or metabolic system. (There may well be regulation via local actions within broadly distributed systems, such as the cholinergic or adrenergic innervation of the cerebral cortex [e.g., Bear & Singer,

1986].) Thus is seems most likely that *the morphological changes are a result of the activity of the neurons that are altered.*

Can Any Form of Neural Activity Alter Neuronal Structure, or is Information Storage Necessary?

One plausible explanation for morphological changes occurring in response to experience is that they arise as a consequence of mere neural activity, independent of any learning that might or might not occur. Synapse formation could occur in direct proportion to the amount of activity of a neuron or the amount of activation of its inputs, and no relationship to brain function would be required (or such a relationship could develop subsequently). While it does not seem intuitively likely that the brain would work in this manner, there is evidence that could be interpreted as indicating it. For example, Rutledge, Wright, and Duncan (1974) reported that electrical stimulation of the cerebral cortex evoked dendritic growth in the opposite hemisphere, while pairing a US forelimb shock with the electrical stimulation CS evoked additional changes such as increased dendritic spine density. (Spines are the postsynaptic component of one kind of synapse.) While the Rutledge work could indicate that mere neural activity is *sufficient* in some cases to alter neuronal morphology, other evidence indicates that morphological change need not be a necessary consequence of neural activity even when that activity is equivalent to or greater than that associated with learning.

We noted earlier that not all neuron types in a brain region change as a result of experience manipulation. In at least some cases, neurons may change while those that provide input to them, which, in the aggregate, must have received equivalent activation, do not. Floeter and Greenough (1979), for example, reported that the spiny branchlets of cerebellar Purkinje cells were larger in monkeys reared in a complex environment than in counterparts reared individually or in pairs. The granule cells, sources of the only excitatory input to the spiny branchlets, were not detectably altered.

An experiment using electrical stimulation also has shown a dissociation of neural activity per se from plastic change. Lee, Schottler, Oliver, and Lynch (1980) and Lee, Oliver, Schottler, and Lynch (1981) showed that new synapses formed in the hippocampus following the induction of long-term potentiation (LTP), a change in the response to electrical stimulation that has served as a model of the memory process. Chang and Greenough (1984) studied this process following the induction of LTP in the hippocampal slice *in vitro*. Synapse formation was robust in the slices given LTP-inducing stimulation, while there was no synapse formation detectable in either (1) slices that had received an equal number of electrical stimuli over the same time period but at lower frequency, or (2) slices that had received many more stimuli at a continuous high frequency level—a procedure that did not yield LTP. Thus the functional change, and not the amount of activity, was correlated with synapse formation.

Differentiation of Effects of Learning From Effects of Activity on Cerebellar Cortical Structure

Previous experiments have compared animals provided access to simple exercise devices such as running wheels with animals reared in complex environments and have, in general, found little effect of exercise on gross brain measures such as cortical weight (Krech, Rosenzweig & Bennett, 1960; Zolman & Morimoto, 1965). A study of motor learning in our laboratory has allowed behavior dissociation of brain consequences of learning from those of motor activity and associated neural activity. This study (Black, Isaacs, Anderson, Alcantara, & Greenough, 1990) makes a more direct comparison with learning. We placed adult rats in one of four conditions: (1) *Acrobatic Learning,* in which the rats were required to traverse a series of increasingly difficult elevated obstacles (e.g., narrow runways, often equipped with barriers such as a board on a fulcrum, rope ladders, chains) for food reward (and with gentle encouragement from the experimenters' hand), a learning condition with relatively mild physical activity demands, over a 30 day period; (2) *Forced Exercise* on a treadmill, a condition involving relatively little learning but considerably more motor activity, and, judging by its effects on vasculature, more cerebellar neuronal activity in regions related to the behavior; (3) *Voluntary Exercise* in a running wheel to which the animals had free access, another condition involving considerable motor and cerebellar activity (these animals exhibited a statistically elevated heart weight, an indication of aerobic exercise levels) and relatively little learning, and (4) an *Inactivity Condition,* in which the rats were kept in standard laboratory cages and handled daily in a manner similar to the handling of the other groups. As the reference structure, we chose the Purkinje neuron—the final output pathway of the cerebellar cortex. We calculated the density of synapses and of Purkinje neurons in the paramedian lobule of the cerebellar cortex, a region driven largely by anterior body (forelimb and head) afferents. Figure 5.9 shows that, as in the postweaning EC–IC cortex comparison (Fig. 5.6), synapse density remained fairly constant across groups. In the Acrobatic Learning animals the volume of the tissue increased and the number of synapses per Purkinje neuron increased, such that the aggregate number of synapses per Purkinje neuron was greater in the Acrobatic Learning group than in the other 3 groups. None of the other groups differed in the number of synapses, but the two exercise groups had a greater density of capillaries in the paramedian lobule than either the acrobatic learning group or the inactive controls. This indicates that the exercise was effective in increasing neural activity. Thus, results suggest that mere activity of the cerebellum, as is involved in simple locomotion, had no detectable effect upon morphology, whereas activity that accompanied learning had a substantial effect.

Taken together, these studies argue effectively that *neuronal activation alone is typically not sufficient to alter neuronal structure*. This appears to be the case

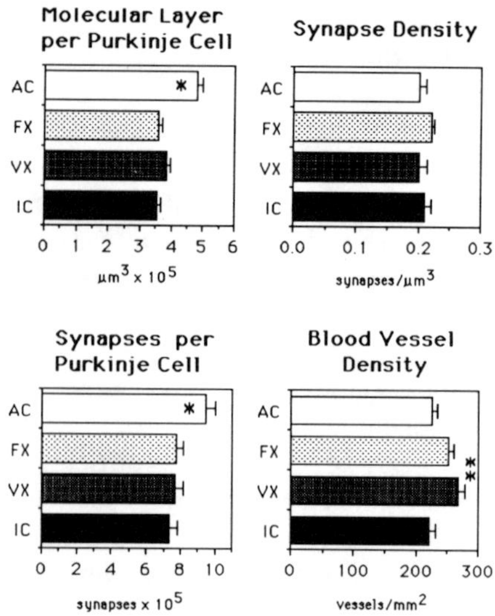

FIG. 5.9. Summary of neuronantomical measures from the motor learning study. (A) Volume of molecular layer per Purkinje cell. (B) Synapse density. (C) Synapses per Purkinje cell. (D) Blood vessel density. AC rats had more molecular layer per Purkinje cell, with similar synapse density, so they corresponsingly had greater numbers of synapses per Purkinje cell. Single asterisks denote that AC was different from other groups, $p < .05$. Double asterisks denote that VX was different from IC. Reprinted from Black et al. (1990), with permission

even when the neuronal activity is comparable to or greater than that accompanying learning that does alter synapse numbers or patterns. Thus, *the relevant feature of behavioral experience that brings about changes in synaptic organization is learning or the formation of a memory*. The implication is that *synapse formation underlies or is a component of at least some types of memory.*

ADDITIONAL QUESTIONS

Are Rats Reared in a Complex Environment "Enriched"?

It has been traditional to use terms like "Enriched condition" and "Impoverished condition," following the tradition established by the well known Berkeley research group (Bennett et al., 1964). We choose the terms "environmental complexity" and "individual cage" to emphasize the fact that we are probably studying varying degrees of *deprivation,* relative to the complexity provided by the typical environment of feral rats. We assume that the processes that take place in the EC rat brain are those typical of normal brain development, and that, barring malnutrition damage or infection, the values that we see for our various measurements of visual cortex in EC rats would approximate those of the same rat reared in natural conditions. It is interesting to speculate on what a truly "enriched" rat brain might look like, as a beginning would involve adding to our EC conditions an array of learning tasks such as those we have used in the experiments that we have described. Greater emphasis on information processing in nonvisual modalities might serve to bring the amount of deviation from the IC or SC level, in cortical areas related to those modalities, into closer alignment with what is seen in the visual cortex with our current procedures. One thing we really would not expect to see, however, is an equally dramatic further increase in the number of synapses per neuron in the visual cortex. There is little empirical evidence upon which to base this statement, although we did find that rearing rats in an environment similar to that termed "superenriched" by Kuenzle and Knusel (1974), which included two of our usual EC cages separated by a 5-level maze, produced little, if any, greater net change, relative to IC, than the conditions we have usually employed (Camel, Withers, & Greenough, 1986). We feel, however, that there will be limits to the degree that the brain can form new connections, the aggregate, and that the solution that instead must be employed is to reallocate neurons in ways that use them more efficiently—that is, that more information is stored per neuron or synapse. One way to think of this, which is highly speculative proposal, is in terms of "chunking" (Miller, 1956; Wickelgren, 1977), in which knowledge already in place can be used to more efficiently encode information.

Another way of conceptualizing this, at the neuronal level, arises from a far too uncritical comparison of three experiments that examined the activity of single neurons during the performance of learned tasks. (The activity of a single neuron does not necessarily indicate the neuron's "function," but provides a sample of the activity of the circuitry of which it is a part that can be correlated with behavior.) In the first experiment, Thompson (1983) and his colleagues (Weisz, Clark, Yang, Thompson, & Solomon, 1978) studied the activity of neurons in the hippocampus during the performance of an associatively conditioned eyeblink response in rabbits. They found that a very high proportion of these neurons, virtually all from which they recorded, "modeled" the conditional response, increasing their activity just prior to the peripheral response. On first impression it seems surprising that so many cells would be devoted to this comparatively simple response. However, it may simply be that the neurons have *nothing else* to devote themselves to, since this is the first unconventional event in the rabbit's entire life! In a similar vein, Fuster (1980) studied neurons in the frontal cortex of monkeys performing a delayed—response task. In this task, the monkey observes a reward placed in one of two identical wells which are then covered and hidden from the monkey's view. After a delay of a few seconds or longer, the monkey must remember which well contained the food to retrieve it successfully. Fuster (1980) also found that *most* neurons in the region from which he recorded (the principal sulcus) showed activity correlated with the features of this task. There were various types of responding: neurons that were more active during exposure and choice, for example, and neurons that remained active during the delay. (The latter type of neuron appeared in subsequent work to encode target position; see Nicki [1976] and Goldman-Rakic, et al. [1983]) While this is, no doubt, a more complicated task than the eyeblink, it is hard to imagine that it requires the involvement of most principal sulcus neurons, given the more complex repertoire of behaviors of which monkeys are capable.

A third experiment (or set thereof) provides some indication that, when animals are trained on *multiple tasks,* neurons appear to be *selectively* allocated. Rolls (in press) and his colleagues trained monkeys on a series of tasks designed to assess the role of cortical and hippocampal regions in choice behavior. Rolls reports that only a small percentage of neurons sampled exhibited activity correlated with elements of any particular task. What is suggested by this comparison of studies, which, of course, differed extensively in many other details, is that neurons, or particular parts of the neuronal circuitry, may come to be assigned to some tasks and remain relatively uninvolved in others when multiple tasks are used. If so, we would expect the *pattern of functional connectivity* to be continually altered with the addition of new tasks, even if the *absolute number* of connections were to remain stable (due to simultaneous gains and losses of connections). Unfortunately, our present techniques cannot detect changes in pattern, only those in number, and we would thus miss the effects of providing an "enriched" rat with more information about its environment. Whether this would involve the more-or-less simultaneous formation of new connections and loss of old ones remains a potentially testable hypothesis, as does the possibility that connection strengths may change. Once a stable number is achieved it may be that microelectrodes will be better tools than microscopes for assessing change in neuronal circuitry.

We should note that there should be some theoretical limit to the extent to which the circuitry could be divided across tasks and still function effectively. A simple neural analogy would be that there is interference between memories that one is trying to recall utilizing common components of the neural circuitry involved in multiple memories.

What Controls Experience —Expectant Information Storage?

This section is a bit more technical than most of the rest of the chapter. It can be scanned or skipped without significant loss of understanding of the general principles laid out in the chapter as a whole, but is included for purposes of completeness.

Controls over experience—expectant *neural* processes—probably occur at several levels. A very basic issue involves what *starts the process,* that is, *what triggers synapse formation?* It is by no means likely that a single mechanism would account for all cases of synapse initiation. We do know *some things* that, directly or indirectly, govern synapse formation in *some* places. We should note that anything that might initiate synaptogenesis or synaptic sensitivity to experience could also act to *terminate* those processes, which is an equally perplexing question, assuming that changes in the same substance do not do both. One category of developmental events that may be important is *hormones*. It has been proposed, for example, that thyroid hormone levels, which fluctuate in development (Samel, 1968), may trigger a shift from a cell division stage to a synapse formation stage in the cerebellar cortex (see, e.g., Lauder & Krebs, 1986). Gonadal (sex) steroid, hormones are involved at some level in governing the sex differences in organization, some synaptic, of the hypothalamus and spinal cord (e.g., Ayoub, Greenough, & Juraska, 1983; Breedlove, 1985; Gorski, Gordon, Shryne, & Southam, 1978; Greenough, Carter, Steerman, & DeVoogd, 1977; Raisman & Field, 1973). Another factor that could initiate or terminate synapse formation or sensitivity are *neurotransmitters,* either those released by the axons that are altered or those released by other inputs to the same region. For example, Lauder and Krebs (1986) report that the neurotransmitter serotonin, released by ingrowing axons, appears to initiate events leading to differentiation and synaptogenesis in the embryonic brain. *Neuromodulators* such as *norepinephrine* have been proposed to regulate the sensitivity of the visual cortex to monocular deprivation (Kasamatsu & Pettigrew, 1976, 1979). A more current view suggests that some combination of effects of norepinephrine and the neurotransmitter acetylcholine may regulate visual cortex sensitivity (Bear & Singer, 1986). Finally, there are a host of *neurotrophic* and otherwise neuroactive compounds released by cells in the brain. A classic example is nerve growth factor, which has been shown to promote the growth of peripheral sensory and sympathetic axons and which has recently been found to be present, along with receptors for it, in the brain (Lander, 1987; Snider & Johnson, 1989). This list is not meant to be exhaustive (or exhausting to the reader!), but rather is included to indicate the existence of a large number of plausible sources of controls that could selectively render a system, or one of its components, sensitive to incoming neural activity. Such chemical factors, and their genetic controls, can produce a staggering variety of influences on experience-sensitive mechanisms. For example, juvenile play is an important species-typical opportunity for extracting information from the environment (Fagen, 1981). Its expression is strongly influenced by the sex hormones that were present during the perinatal period (Beatty, 1979).

It should be noted that there is no necessary reason that a regulatory signal would have to be extrinsic to the neuron that was generating the synapses. As indicated in the preceding "Hierarchy of Environments" section, all cells contain *intrinsic developmental programs* that may run on for many sequential steps, independent of any input. Cells may even provide their own "clocks"; for example, changing their position in a developmental program according to the number of cell divisions they had undergone (Summerbell & Honig, 1986). Likewise, *termination* of sensitivity could be intrinsic to the neuron, either through an intrinsic program or through some predetermined limit upon the number of stabilized synapses, beyond which all others would be eliminated (e.g., in a competitive manner favoring the most active synapses).

A second-level question, *what preserves (or eliminates) synapses,* has produced some very interesting results recently. One phenomenon of some interest is the NMDA (n-methyl-D-aspartate) receptor, a receptor that is probably activated by the neurotransmitter glutamate at synapses. The NMDA receptor requires both activation by neurotransmitter and activation of the postsynaptic cell before it will become active, allowing calcium to enter the postsynaptic cell. This detection of conjoint pre- and postsynaptic activation is the property of "Hebb synapses" (after Hebb, 1949) which has made them useful to connectionist models of neural plasticity (McClelland & Rumelhart, 1986). Calcium entry typically serves to activate specific metabolic pathways within cells, such as a pathway that could lead to stabilization of a synapse. This allows for a synapse that is coherent in its firing with a large number of others that also terminate on the same cell to be very likely to be stabilized, while one not in synchrony with other inputs would rarely receive stabilizing postsynaptic activation. It is easy to see how a "winner take all" result, where cells are driven by one or the other eye but not both, could arise with alternating monocular deprivation. At the outset of the period of sensitivity to monocular deprivation, most cells are driven more strongly by one eye than the other, predisposing them to capture by the stronger input. It is not a terribly complicated extension to model the development of other features of the visual system, assuming some intrinsic bias in connectivity between the retina and the cortex at the outset and considering that patterned environmental stimuli will provide high coherence of local retinal activity and low coherence among sites on the retina that are distal to one another. In sum, the NMDA receptor's characteristics are quite plausible ones for organizing the brain through experience.

ADAPTIVE MODIFICATION OF NON-NEURONAL COMPONENTS OF THE BRAIN

Having discussed how the connections get into place, we now draw attention to an aspect of brain development that has received remarkably little attention to date—the issues of the metabolic and functional support of these synapses. This is a somewhat technical topic, but we feel that it is an important part of a comprehensive appreciation of neurobehavioral development (and what can go wrong with it). In discussing Fig. 5.6, we noted that synapses and neuronal cell bodies were being pushed apart by intervening material that includes glial cells and blood vessels. The implication of this is that synapses generate a "need" for glial and vascular support and that, at least in the case of the EC rat, that need requires about the same additional glial and vascular material for each new synapse. (The logic here is that, if *synapse density* in the tissue does not change when new synapses are formed, then an equivalent amount of *nonsynaptic* material must ultimately accompany each new synapse.)

Blood Vessel Plasticity

A great many of the essential contributions of vasculature to brain functioning have been worked out in detail. The most obvious include transport of oxygen, carbohydrate, lipid and protein components as well as the removal of carbon dioxide and unneeded byproducts of brain metabolism. In addition, the blood supply plays roles in ionic balance and, at least at some times in life, contributes phagocytic cells that can respond to brain damage. On a moment-to-moment basis, however, the most important functions relate to the oxygen supply. One very good measure of the vascular capacity to supply oxygen is the average distance to a blood vessel from a random point in the tissue, which can be easily calculated from straightforward measurements performed on tissue sections. Two other measures of value in interpreting blood vessel data are the average diameter (and distribution) of blood vessels and their volume fractions, or the proportion of the tissue occupied by blood vessels, also easily calculated.

We first used these techniques to examine blood vessels in visual cortex of rats reared in EC, SC and IC conditions for 30 days after weaning (Black, Sirevaag, & Greenough, 1987). To limit our sample to capillaries, the source of oxygen and metabolic transfer, we studied vessels under 10 micrometers in diameter. Results were dramatic, as illustrated in Fig. 5.10. EC rats had a nearly 50% greater

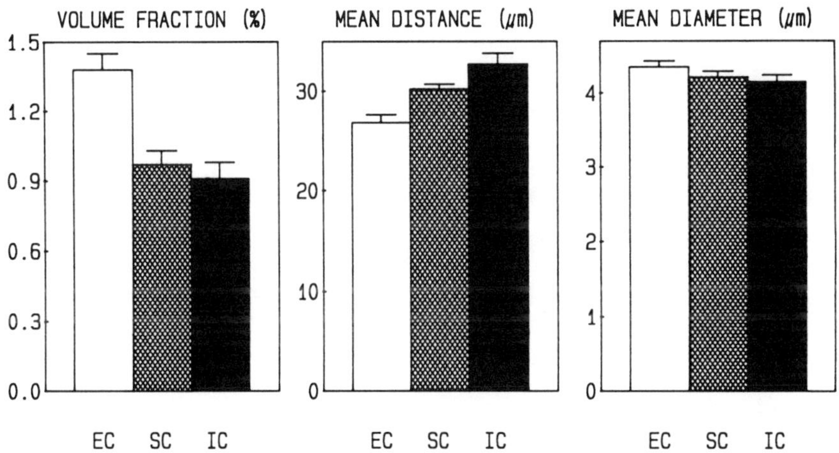

FIG. 5.10. The volume fraction blood in the tissue of EC rats was significantly greater after 30 days of exposure, and the vessels themselves were packed significantly closer together. A small, but significant increase in mean vessel size was also found in the EC rats. These results suggest angiognesis occurred in this tissue in response to increased metabolic demand. Reprinted from Black et al. (1987), with permission.

volume fraction of blood vessels in visual cortex than the IC rats and the average distance to a blood vessel was more than 20% less in the ECs. The increased density occurred on top of blood vessel increases necessitated just to "keep even" with the expanding brain tissue volume. Thus this response was much larger than the increase in the number of synapses, suggesting a demand exceeding that necessitated by new synapses with the same activity level. This suggests that the vascular system was adapting to a higher overall level of activity of neuronal and other elements. It is worth recalling here that the EC rats probably represent the closest case to the feral animal. Thus typical laboratory rats probably have an abnormally low vascular supply. It is interesting to speculate on whether regional variations in human brain vasculature might exist as a function of experiential history.

Subsequent studies revealed that, in young adults, the vascular response to a complex environment was still present, but that it just barely kept pace with the increase in tissue volume (Black, Zelazny, & Greenough, 1988). As the age of animals at the onset of exposure to the complex environment increased, the vascular response further diminished, such that in 2 year old rats vascular plasticity was essentially absent (Black, Polinsky, & Greenough, 1989). An interesting question is whether this declining vascular plasticity is one of the causes of declining neuronal plasticity that appears to occur in old age (Black, Parnisari, Eichbaum, & Greenough, 1986).

In the cerebellar acrobatic learning study described earlier, we saw that vascular support can vary independently of synaptic change. The animals that were using the neuronal circuitry of the paramedian lobule for treadmill and wheel activity added vasculature but not, to a significant degree, synapses. It is interesting to speculate that from the viewpoint of the brain as simply another organ that adapts to the organism's environmental demands, changes in synapses and changes in blood vessels are both forms of "memory." The organism's experience caused the brain to adapt to respond more appropriately, assuming that the past is the best predictor of future demands. The vascular response is appropriate to high levels of neural activity, the synaptic response is appropriate to the need for skilled movement.

Plasticity of Glial Cells

Similarly, glial cells, their name derived from the Greek for "glue," once thought merely to hold the all-important neurons together, exhibit adaptive change. Glial cells are now known to play important roles in regulating the "microenvironment" of neurons, a critical aspect of proper function. Glial cells do this by adjusting levels of the ions that neurons use in communication and integration and by regulating the effects of the neurotransmitters with which neurons communicate. Plasticity of glial cells was evident in some of the early work of Diamond and her collaborators (1967) on the effects of environmental complexity on the brain, although failure to examine the time course systematically left the appearance of conflict between reports of glial change and reports of its absence. Our work shows that glial cells respond to increases in synaptic number and/or activity in a two-phase manner that parallels, in a protracted way, the glial cell response to damage to the brain (Siervaag & Greenough, 1991). In this study we used an antibody to glial fibrillary acidic protein, an essential component of the insinuated tissue processes of astrocytes, to identify glial astrocytes in the tissue of the brain. The primary measure of astrocyte function that we used was *surface density,* the amount of cellular surface per unit volume of tissue, measured with a new technique that avoids artifacts that may be induced by group differences in the overall size or shape of the cells (Braendgaard & Gundersen, 1986). As most astrocyte functions involve movement of substances across the cell membrane, this measure is thought to provide an appropriate indicator of their functional capacity.

Figure 5.11 presents the time course of the response of the surface density of astrocytes to rearing in individual cage, social, and EC environments at 3 points ranging from 10 days after placement in the environments at weaning to 67 days of exposure to the environments. In Fig. 5.11a, we see that the amount of astrocyte tissue processes increases in the EC rats over the period of exposure to the different environments. Figure 5.11b shows that, if the size of an individual astrocyte is measured, it increases for the first 30 days that the animals are in the EC environment but then decreases to a level comparable to that at the outset of the experiment. Even though the amount of astrocytic surface continues to increase, the average astrocyte is shrinking during the second month of exposure to the complex environment in the EC rats. Figure 5.11c provides a resolution of this seeming conflict. The astrocytes increase in number during the second 30 days of environmental exposure. That is, the cells divide. It is not clear whether more astrocytes are born or perhaps fewer astrocytes die in the generation of this result. Astrocytes are known to divide and, apparently, to be removed in the developing and mature rat brain. What is clear is that this supportive component of the brain tissue adapts to the environmental demands placed on the organism, and that the response mirrors, in a very protracted way, the response of the brain to damage. Again, the brain is adapting in a way that adjusts to the demands placed upon it. There is a really very profound message for us in all of this. We put the substrates of memory on a sort of psychological altar. The brain, however, does not. It assesses what needs to be done to adapt to the conditions that currently and in recent history have prevailed, and it does the best it can to perform the adaptation.

SUMMARY

The goal of this essay was to relate developmental effects of experience evident in behavior to their underlying neural substrates. While this is very much a work in progress, some benefits of thinking about behavioral development in terms of

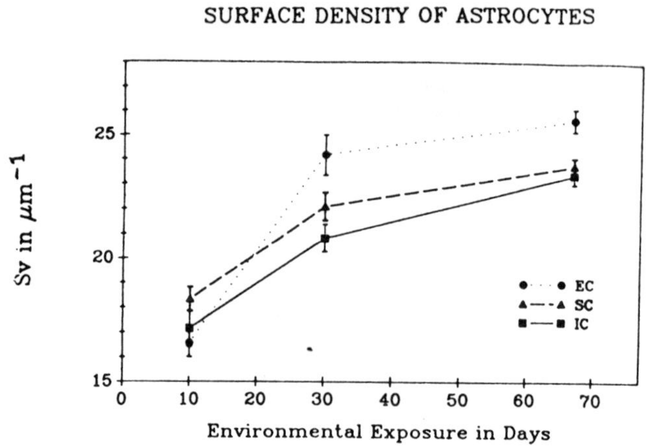
SURFACE DENSITY OF ASTROCYTES
Sv in μm⁻¹
15
20
25
0
10
20
30
40
50
60
70
EC
SC
IC
Environmental Exposure in Days

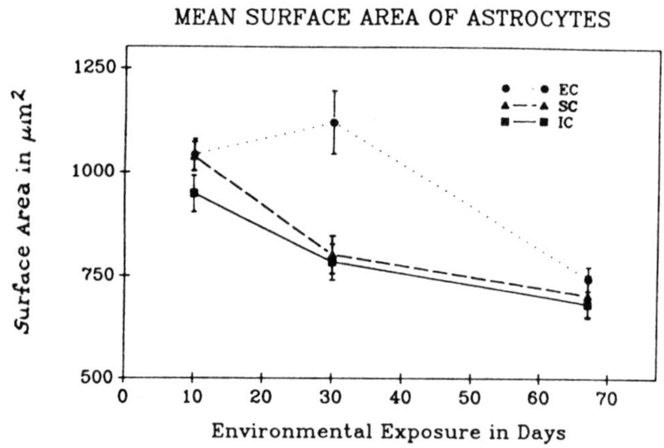
MEAN SURFACE AREA OF ASTROCYTES
Surface Area in μm²
500
750
1000
1250
0
10
20
30
40
50
60
70
EC
SC
IC
Environmental Exposure in Days

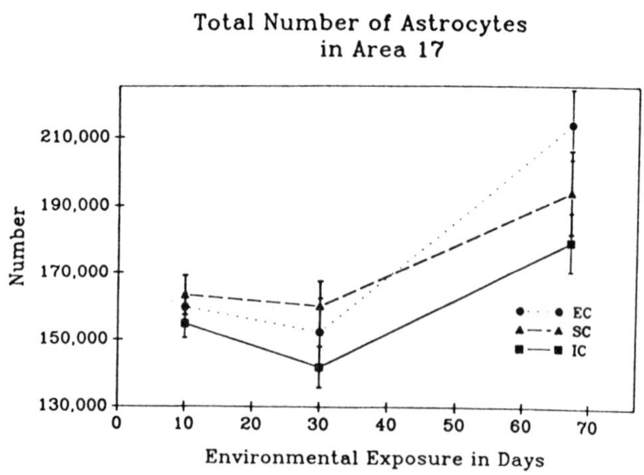
Total Number of Astrocytes
in Area 17
Number
130,000
150,000
170,000
190,000
210,000
0
10
20
30
40
50
60
70
EC
SC
IC
Environmental Exposure in Days

what may be going on in the nervous system may have become clearer. We have stressed three different sources of information used by the developing nervous system in achieving functional competence. The first source is the *intrinsic genotype,* which must be viewed as enclosed within a hierarchy of environments that govern its expression at the level of the individual cell. The second is the *expected experiential information,* that which is usually common to all species members. The third is the *unpredictable environment of each individual,* which requires formation of memories unique to the individual. We have noted some ways in which information from these sources is incorporated in the developing brain. Genomic information is always expressed as a pattern of proteins and their products within the cell that reflects the individual history of the cell. These cellular constituents play a major role in establishing the functional organization of the brain. Expected information appears to be stored, at least in part, by a process in which synapses are overproduced, such that experience determines which of the synapses are preserved and which are eliminated. Unpredictable information appears to be stored largely by a process in which synapses are produced in response to the demand for storage of information. These three general types of information determine the functional organization of the brain, both in terms of its discrete memories and in terms of the general semantic or procedural knowledge around which behavior is organized.

ACKNOWLEDGMENTS

The recent work reported here and the preparation of this chapter were supported by Office of Naval Research Grants N00014-85-K-0587 and N00014-89-J-1556; National Institute of Mental Health Grants MH43830, MH40631, MH35321; National Science Foundation BNS-82-16916, and the Retirement Research Foundation. We are especially indebted to Michael Weiss, who in the process of helping us with a chapter that remains unfinished, inspired much of the novel thinking in this chapter.

FIG. 5.11. (A) The surface density of astrocytic processes was significantly greater in the EC cortex after 30 and 67, but not 10 days, of environmental exposure. (B) After 30 days of exposure, the mean size of EC astrocytes was larger than those from the other groups. (C) The total number of astrocytes in Area 17 of occipital cortex was unaffected after 10 or 30 days, but EC rats had greater numbers of astrocytes in this region than the other groups after 67 days. Collectively, these results indicate a gradual response to experience that includes changes in glial cell size and number. Reprinted from Sirevaag and Greenough (1991).

REFERENCES

Ayoub, D. M., Greenough, W. T., & Juraska, J. M. (1983). Sex differences in dendritic structure in the preoptic area of the juvenile macaque monkey brain. *Science, 219,* 197–198.

Bateson, P. (1979). How do sensitive periods arise and what are they for? *Animal Behaviour, 27,* 470–486.

Bear, M. F., & Singer, W. (1986). Modulation of visual cortical plasticity by acetylcholine and noradrenalin. *Nature 320,* 172.

Beatty, W. W. (1979). Gonadal hormones and sex differences in nonreproductive behaviors in rodents: Organizational and activational influences. *Hormones & Behavior, 12,* 112–163.

Beaulieu, C., & Colonnier, M. (1987). Effects of the richness of the environment on the cat visual cortex. *Journal of Comparative Neurology, 266,* 478–494.

Bennett, E. L., Diamond, M. C., Krech, D., & Rosenzweig, M. R. (1964). Chemical and anatomical plasticity of brain. *Science, 146,* 610–619.

Bernstein, L. (1973). A study of some enriching variables in a free-environment for rats. *Journal of Psychosomatic Research, 17,* 85–88.

Bertenthal, B. I., Campos, J. J., & Barrett, K. C. (1984). Self-produced locomotion: an organizer of emotional, cognitive, and social development in infancy. In R. N. Emde & R. J. Harmon (Eds.), *Continuities and discontinuities in development* (pp. 175–210). New York: Plenum.

Bhide, P. G., & Bedi, K. S. (1984). The effects of a lengthy period of environmental diversity on well fed and previously undernourished rats. II. Synapse to neuron ratios. *Journal of Comparative Neurology, 227,* 305–310.

Black, J. E., & Greenough, W. T. (1986). Induction of pattern in neural structure by experience: Implications for cognitive development. In M. E. Lamb, A. L. Brown, & B. Rogoff (Eds.), *Advances in developmental psychology, Vol. 4,* (pp. 1–50). Hillsdale, NJ: Lawrence Erlbaum Associates.

Black, J. E., Isaacs, K. R., Anderson, B. J., Alcantara, A. A., & Greenough, W. T. (1990). Learning causes synaptogenesis, while motor activity causes angiogenesis, in cerebellar cortex of adult rats. *Proceedings of the National Academy of Science, 87,* 5568–5572.

Black, J. E., Parnisari, R., Eichbaum, E., & Greenough, W. T. (1986). Morphological effects of housing environment and voluntary exercise on cerebral cortex and cerebellum of old rats. *Society for Neuroscience Abstracts, 12,* 1579.

Black, J. E., Polinsky, M., & Greenough, W. T. (1989). Progressive failure of cerebral angiogenesis supporting neural plasticity in aging rats. *Neurobiology of Aging, 10,* 353–358.

Black, J. E., Sirevaag, A. M., & Greenough, W. T. (1987). Complex experience promotes capillary information in young rat visual cortex. *Neuroscience Letters, 83,* 351–355.

Black, J. E., Sirevaag, A. M., Wallace, C. S., Savin, M. H., & Greenough, W. T. (1989). Effects of complex experience on somatic growth and organ development in rats. *Developmental Psychobiology, 22,* 727–752.

Black, J. E., Zelazny, A. M., & Greenough, W. T. (1988). Complex experience induces capillaries in visual cortex of adult rats. *Society for Neuroscience Abstracts, 14,* 1135.

Bogolepov, N. N., Verbitskaya, L. B., Belova, T. I., & Sudakov, K. V. (1985). Ultrastructural changes in the brain of rats that have suffered acute emotional stress. *Neuroscience Behavioral Physiology, 15,* 284.

Bonner, J. T. (Ed.). (1982). Evolution and development. *Dahlem Workshop Reports, Vol. 22.*

Boothe, R. G., Greenough, W. T., Lund, J. S., & Wrege, K. (1979). A quantitative investigation of spine and dendritic development of neurons in visual cortex (Area 17) of Macaca nemistrina monkeys. *Journal of Comparative Neurology, 186,* 473–490.

Braendgaard, H., & Gundersen, H. J. G. (1986). The impact of recent stereological advances on quantitative studies of the nervous system. *Journal of Neuroscience Methods, 18,* 39–78.

Breedlove, S. M. (1985). Hormonal control of the anatomical specificity of motoneuron-to-muscle innervation in rats. *Science, 227,* 1357–1359.

Bremner, J. G. (1982). Object localization in infancy. In M. Potegal (Ed.), *Spatial abilities: development and physiological foundations* (pp. 79–106). New York: Academic Press.

Brown, R. T. (1968). Early experience and problem solving ability. *Journal of Comparative and Physiological Psychology, 65,* 433–440.

Bullinger, A. (1983). Space, the organism and objects, their cognitive elaboration in the infant. In A. Hein & M. Jeannerod (Eds.), *Spatially oriented behavior* (pp. 215–222). New York: Springer-Verlag.

Camel, J. E., Withers, G. S., & Greenough, W. T. (1986). Persistence of visual cortex dendritic alterations induced by postweaning exposure to a "superenriched" environment in rats. *Behavioral Neuroscience, 100,* 810–813.

Chang, F. -L., & Greenough, W. T. (1982). Lateralized effects of monocular training on dendritic branching in adult split-brain rats. *Brain Research, 232,* 283–292.

Chang, F. -L. F., & Greenough, W. T. (1984). Transient and enduring morphological correlates of synaptic activity and efficacy change in the rat hippocampal slice. *Brain Research, 309,* 35–46.

Changeux, J. -P., & Danchin, A. (1977). Biochemical models for the selective stabilization of developing synapses. In G. A. Cottrell & P. M. Usherwood (Eds.), *Synapses* (pp. 705–712). New York: Academic Press.

Cohen, L. B. (1979). Our developing knowledge of infant perception and cognition. *American Psychologist, 34,* 894–899.

Conel, J. L. (1939–1967). *The postnatal development of the human cerebral cortex* (Vols. 1–8). Cambridge, MA: Harvard University Press.

Constantine-Paton, M., Cline, H. T., & Debski, E. (1990). Patterned activity, synaptic convergence, and the NMDA receptor in developing visual pathways. *Annual Review of Neuroscience, 13,* 129–154.

Coss, R. G., Brandon, J. G., Globus, A., (1980). Changes in morphology of dendritic spines on honeybee calycal interneurons associated with cumulative nursing and foraging experience. *Brain Research, 192,* 49–56.

Cotman, C. W., Nieto-Sampedro, M., & Harris, E. W. (1981). Synapse replacement in the nervous system of adult vertebrates. *Physiological Reviews, 61,* 84–784.

Cragg, B. G. (1975a). The development of synapses in the visual system of the cat. *Journal of Comparative Neurology, 160,* 147–166.

DeVoogd, T. J., Nixdorf, B., & Nottebohm, F. (1985). Synaptogenesis and changes in synaptic morphology related to acquisition of a new behavior. *Brain Research, 329,* 304.

Diamond, M.C. (1967). Extensive cortical depth measurements and neuron size increases in the cortex of environmentally enriched rats. *Journal of Comparative Neurology, 131,* 357–364.

Diamond, M. C., Lindner, B., Johnson, R., Bennett, E. L., & Rosenzweig, M. R. (1975). Differences in occipital cortical synapses from environmentally enriched, impoverished, and standard colony rats. *Journal of Neuroscience Research, 1,* 109–119.

Donovick, P. J., Burright, R. G., & Swidler, M. A. (1973). Presurgical rearing environment alters exploration, fluid consumption, and learning of septal lesioned and control rats. *Physiology and Behavior, 11,* 543–553.

Edwards, H. P., Barry, W. F., & Wyspianski, J. O. (1969). Effect of differential rearing on photic evoked potentials and brightness discrimination in the albino rat. *Developmental Psychobiology, 2,* 133–138.

Eimas, P. D. (1975). Speech perception in early infancy. In L. B. Cohen & P. Salapatek (Eds.), *Infant perception* (pp. 193–231). New York: Academic Press.

Fagen, R. (1981). *Animal play behaviors.* New York: Oxford University Press.

Falls, W., & Gobel, S. (1979). Golgi and EM studies of the formation of dendritic and axonal arbors: The interneurons of the *substantia gelatinosa* of Rolando in newborn kittens. *Journal of Comparative Neurology, 187,* 1–18.

Feng, A. S., & Rogowski, B. A. (1980). Effects of monaural and binaural occlusion on the morphology of neurons in the medial superior olivary nucleus of the rat. *Brain Research, 189,* 530–534.

Fernald, A. (1984). The perceptual and affective salience of mothers' speech to infants. In L. Feagans, C. Garvey, & R. Golinkoff (Eds.), *The origins and growth of communication* (pp. 5–29). Norwood, NJ: Ablex.

Fiala, B. A., Snow, F. M., & Greenough, W. T. (1977). "Impoverished" rats weigh more than "enriched" rats because they eat more. *Developmental Psychobiology, 10,* 537–541.

Fiorentini, H., & Maffei, L. (1977). Instability of the eye in the dark and proprioception. *Nature, 269,* 330–331.

Floeter, M. K., & Greenough, W. T. (1979). Cerebellar plasticity: Modification of Purkinje cell structure by differential rearing in monkeys. *Science, 206,* 227–229.

Forgays, D. G., & Read, J. M. (1962). Crucial periods for free-environmental experience in the rat. *Journal of Comparative and Physiological Psychology, 55,* 816–818.

Forgus, R. H. (1954). The effect of early perceptual learning on the behavioral organization of adult rats. *Journal of Comparative and Physiological Psychology, 47,* 331–336.

Freeman, B. J., & Ray, O. S. (1972). Strain, sex, and environment effects on appetitively and aversively motivated learning tasks. *Developmental Psychobiology, 5,* 101–109.

Fuster, J. M. (1980). The prefrontal cortex: anatomy, physiology, and neuropsychology of the prefrontal lobe. New York: Raven Press.

Geller, E., Yuwiler, A., & Zolman, J. G. (1965). Effects of environmental complexity on constituents of brain and liver. *Journal of Neurochemistry, 12,* 949–955.

Goldman-Rakic, P. S., Isserof, A., Schwartz, M., Bugbee, N. M. (1983). The neurobiology of cognitive development. In M. M. Haith & J. J. Campos (Eds.), *Handbook of child psychology: Vol. 2, Infancy and Developmental Psychology,* (pp. 281–344). New York: Wiley.

Gorski, R. A., Gordon, J. H., Shryne, J. E. & Southam, A. M. (1978). Evidence for a morphological sex difference within the medial preoptic area of the rat brain. *Brain Research, 148,* 333–346.

Gottlieb, G. (1991). The experiential canalization of behavioral development: Theory. *Developmental Psychology, 27,* 4–13.

Green, E. J., Greenough, W. T., & Schlumpf, B. E. (1983). Effects of complex or isolated environments on cortical dendrites of middle-aged rats. *Brain Research, 264,* 233–240.

Greenough, W. T. (1978). Development and memory: The synaptic connection. In T. J. Teyler, (Ed.), *Brain and Learning* (pp. 127–145). Stanford, CT: Greylock Publishers.

Greenough, W. T., Carter, C. S., Steerman, C., & DeVoogd, T. J. (1977). Sex differences in dendritic patterns in hamster preoptic area. *Brain Research, 126,* 63–72.

Greenough, W. T., & Chang, F. -L. F. (1988). Dendritic pattern formation involves both oriented regression and oriented growth in the barrels of mouse somatosensory cortex. *Developmental Brain Research, 43,* 148–152.

Greenough, W. T., Fulcher, J. K., Yuwiler, A., & Geller, E. (1970). Enriched rearing and chronic electroshock: Effects on brain and behavior in mice. *Physiology and Behavior, 5,* 371–373.

Greenough, W. T., Juraska, J. M., & Volkmar, F. R. (1979). Maze training effects on dendritic branching in occipital cortex of adult rats. *Behavioral and Neural Biology, 26,* 287–297.

Greenough, W. T., Larson, J. R., & Withers, G. S. (1985). Effects of unilateral and bilateral training in a reaching task on dendritic branching of neurons in the rat motor-sensory forelimb cortex. *Behavioral and Neural Biology, 44,* 301–314.

Greenough, W. T., Madden, T. C., & Fleischmann, T. B. (1972b). Effects of isolation, daily handling, and enriched rearing on maze learning. *Psychonomic Science, 27,* 279–280.

Greenough, W. T. & Volkmar, F. R. (1973). Pattern of dendritic branching in rat occipital cortex after rearing in complex environments. *Experimental Neurology, 40,* 491–504.

Greenough, W. T., Volkmar, F. R., & Juraska, J. M. (1973a). Effects of rearing complexity on dendritic branching in frontolateral and temporal cortex of the rat. *Experimental Neurology, 41,* 371–378.

Greenough, W. T., West, R. W., & DeVoogd, T. J. (1978). Subsynaptic plate perforations: Changes with age and experience in the rat. *Science, 202,* 1096–1098.

Greenough, W. T., Wood, W. E., & Madden, T. C. (1972a). Possible memory storage differences among mice reared in environments varying in complexity. *Behavioral Biology, 7,* 717–722.

Greenough, W. T., Yuwiler, A., & Dollinger, M. (1973b). Effects of post-trial eserine administration on learning in "enriched" and "impoverished" reared rats. *Behavioral Biology, 8,* 261–272.

Grusser, O. -J. (1983). Multimodal structure of the extrapersonal space. In A. Hein & M. Jeannerod (Eds.), *Spatially oriented behavior* (pp. 327–352). New York: Springer-Verlag.

Harrelson, A. L., Bastiani, M. J., Snow, P. M., & Goodman, C. S. (1988). From cell ablation experiments to surface glycoproteins: Selective fasciculation and the search for axonal recognition molecules. In S. S. Easter., K. F. Barald, & B. M. Carlson (Eds.), *From message to mind* (pp. 96–109). Sunderland, MA: Sinauer.

Hatten, M. E., & Edmondson, J. C. (1988). Mechanisms of neuron-glia interactions in vitro. In S. S. Easter, K. F. Barald, & Bruce M. Carlson (Eds.), From message to mind (pp. 154–167). Sunderland, MA: Sinauer.

Hebb, D. O. (1949). *The organization of behavior.* New York: Wiley.

Hein, A., & Diamond, R. M. (1971). Contrasting development in kittens of visually triggered and guided movements with respect to interocular and interlimb equivalence. *Journal of Comparative and Physiological Psychology, 76,* 219–224.

Hein, A., & Diamond, R. M. (1983). Contribution of eye movement to the representation of space. In A. Hein & M. Jeannerod (Eds.), *Spatially oriented behavior* (pp. 119–134). New York: Springer-Verlag.

Hein, A., & Held, R. (1967). Dissociation of the visual placing response into elicited and guided components. *Science, 158,* 390–392.

Held, R., & Hein, A. (1963). Movement-produced stimulation in the development of visually guided behavior. *Journal of Comparative and Physiological Psychology, 56,* 872–876.

Holloway, R. L. (1966). Dendritic branching: Some preliminary results of training and complexity in rat visual cortex. *Brain Research, 2,* 393–396.

Horn, G., Bradley, P., & McCabe, B. J. (1985). Changes in the structure of synapses associated with learning. *Journal of Neuroscience, 5,* 3161–3168.

Huttenlocher, P. R. (1979). Synaptic density in human frontal cortex—developmental changes and effects of aging. *Brain Research, 163,* 195–205.

Huttenlocher, P. R., de Courten, C., Garey, L. J., & Van der Loos, H. (1982). Synaptogenesis in human visual cortex—evidence for synapse elimination during normal development. *Neuroscience Letters, 33,* 247–252.

Hymovitch, B. (1952). The effects of experimental variations on problem solving in the rat. *Journal of Comparative and Physiological Psychology, 45,* 313–321.

Ingham, P. W. (1988). The molecular genetics of embryonic pattern formation in Drosophila. *Nature, 335,* 25–34.

Juraska, J. M., Fitch, J., Henderson, C., & Rivers, N. (1985). Sex differences in the dendritic branching of dentate granule cells following differential experience. *Brain Research, 333,* 73–80.

Juraska, J. M., Fitch J. M., & Washburne, D. L. (1989). The dendritic morphology of pyramidal neurons in the rat hippocampal CA3 area. II. Effects of gender and experience. *Brain Research, 479,* 115–119.

Juraska, J. M., Greenough, W. T., Elliott, C., Mack, K. J., & Berkowitz, R. (1980). Plasticity in adult rat visual cortex: An examination of several cell populations after differential rearing. *Behavioral and Neural Biology, 29,* 157–167.

Juraska, J. M., Henderson, C., and Muller, J. (1984). Differential rearing experience, gender and radial maze performance. *Developmental Psychobiology, 17,* 209–215.

Kasamatsu, T., & Pettigrew, J. D. (1976). Depletion of brain catecholamines: failure of ocular dominance shift after monocular occlusion in kittens. *Science, 194,* 206–209.

Kasamatsu, T., & Pettigrew, J. D. (1979). Preservation of binocularity after monocular deprivation in the striate cortex of kittens treated with 6-hydroxydopamine. *Journal of Comparative Neurology, 185,* 139–162.

Keeble, S., & Maden, M. (1989). The relationship among retinoid structure, affinity for retinoic acid-binding protein, and ability to respecify pattern in the regenerating axolotl limb. *Developmental Biology, 132,* 26–34.

Kilman, V. L., Wallace, C. S., Withers, G. S., & Greenough, W. T. (1988). 4 days of differential housing alters dendritic morphology of weanling rats. *Society for Neuroscience Abstracts, 14,* 1135.

Krech, D., Rosenzweig, M. R., & Bennett, E. L. (1960). Effects of environmental complexity and training on brain chemistry. *Journal of Comparative and Physiological Psychology, 53,* 509–514.

Kuenzle, C. C., & Knusel, A. (1974). Mass training of rats in a superenriched environment. *Physiology and Behavior, 13,* 205–210.

Lander, A. D. (1987). Molecules that make axons grow. *Molecular Neurobiology, 1,* 213–245.

Landfield, P. W., Lindsey, J. D., & Lynch, G. (1978). Hippocampal aging and adrenocorticoids: quantitative correlations. *Science, 202,* 1098–1102.

Landmesser, L. (1988). Peripheral guidance cues and the formation of specific motor projections in the chick. In S. S. Easter, K. F. Barald, & B. M. Carlson (Eds.), *From message to mind* (pp. 121–133). Sunderland, MA: Sinauer.

Lauder, J. M., & Krebs, H. (1986). Do neurotransmitters, neurohumors, and hormones specify critical periods? In W. T. Greenough & J. Juraska (Eds.), *Developmental neuropsychobiology* (pp. 120–174). New York: Academic Press.

Lecanuet, J. P., Granier-Deferre, C., DeCasper, A. J., Maugeais, R., Andrieu, A. J., & Busnel, M. C. (1987). Perception et discrimination foetales de stimuli langagiers; mise en evidence a partir de la reactivite cardiaque; resultats preliminaires. *C. R. Acad. Sci. [III], 305,* 161–164.

Lee, K. S., Schottler, F., Oliver, M., & Lynch, G. (1980). Brief bursts of high-frequency stimulation produce two types of structural change in rat hippocampus. *Journal of Neurophysiology, 44,* 247–258.

Lee, K. S., Oliver, M., Schottler, F., & Lynch, G. (1981). Electron microscopic studies of brain slices: the effects of high-frequency stimulation on dendritic ultrastructure. In G. A. Kerkut & H. V. Wheal (Eds.), *Electrophysiology of isolated mammalian CNS preparations* (pp. 189–211). New York: Academic Press.

LeVay, S., Wiesel, T. N., & Hubel, D. H. (1980). The development of ocular dominance columns in normal and visually deprived monkeys. *Journal of Comparative Neurology, 191,* 1–51.

Levinthal, F., Macagno, E., Levinthal, C. (1975). Anatomy and development of identified cells in isogenic organisms. *Cold Spring Harbor Symposia on Quantitative Biology, 40,* 321–332.

Levitan, I. B., Mushynski, W. E., & Ramirez, G. (1972). Effects of an enriched environment on amino acid incorporation into rat brain subcellular fractions *in vivo. Brain Research, 41,* 498–502.

Mariani, J., & Changeux, J. P. (1981). Ontogenesis of olivocerebellar relationships. I. Studies by intracellular recordings of the multiple innervation of Purkinje cells by climbing fibers in the developing rat cerebellum. *Journal of Neuroscience, 1,* 696–702.

McClelland, J. L., & Rumelhart, D. E. (1986). *Parallel distributed processing. Explorations in the microstructure of cognition. Volume 2: Psychological and biological models.* Cambridge, MA: The MIT Press.

McMahon, A. P., & Moon, R. T. (1989). int-1 - a proto-oncogene involved in cell signalling. *Development, 1989 Supplement,* 161–167.
Meyer, J. S. (1987). Prevention of adrenalectomy-induced brain stimulation by corticosterone. *Physiology and Behavior, 41,* 391–395.
Miller, G. A. (1956). The magical number seven: Plus or minus two. Some limits on our capacity for processing information. *Psychological Review, 9,* 81–97.
Miller, K. D., Keller, J. B., & Stryker, M. P. (1989). Ocular dominance column development: analysis and simulation. *Science, 245,* 605–615.
Mollgaard, K., Diamond, M. C., Bennett, E. L., Rosenzweig, M. R., & Lindner, B. (1971). Qualitative synaptic changes with different experience in rat brain. *International Journal of Neuroscience, 2,* 113–128.
Montague, P. R., & Friedlander, M. J. (1989). Expression of an intrinsic growth strategy by mammalian retinal neurons. *Proceedings of the National Academy of Science (USA), 86,* 7223–7227.
Morgan, M. J. (1973). Effects of post-weaning environment on learning in the rat. *Animal Behaviour, 21,* 429–442.
Movshon, J. A., Eggers, H. M., Gizzi, M. S., Hendrickson, A. E., Kiorpes, L., & Boothe, R. G. (1987). Effects on early unilateral blur on the macaque's visual system. III. Physiological observations. *Journal of Neuroscience, 7,* 1340–1351.
Niki, H., & Watanabe, M. (1976). Prefrontal unit activity and delayed response relation to cue location versus direction of response. *Brain Research, 105,* 79–88.
Nottebohm, F. (1989). From bird song to neurogenesis. *Scientific American, 260,* 74–79.
Nyman, A. J. (1967). Problem solving in rats as a function of experience at different ages. *Journal of Genetic Psychology, 110,* 31–39.
Patel, S. N., Rose, S. P., & Stewart, M. G. (1988). Training induced dendritic spine density changes are specifically related to memory formation processes in the chick, *Gallus domesticus. Brain Research, 463,* 168–173.
Piaget, J. (1980). Adaptation and intelligence: Organic selection and phenocopy (S. S. Eames, Trans.). Chicago: University of Chicago Press.
Piaget, J., & Inhelder, B. (1956). The child's conception of space. (F. Langdon & J. J. Lunzer, Trans.). London: Rutledge & Kegan Paul.
Purves, D., & Lichtman, J. W. (1980). Elimination of synapses in the developing nervous system. *Science, 210,* 153–157.
Pysh, J. J., & Weiss, M. (1979). Exercise during development induces an increase in Purkinje cell dendritic tree size. *Science, 206,* 230–232.
Quick, M. W., Tigges, M., Gammon, J. A., & Boothe, R. G. (1989). Early abnormal visual experience induces strabismus in infant monkeys. *Investigative Ophthalmology & Visual Science, 30,* 1012–1017.
Raff, R. A., & Kaufman, T. C. (1983). *Embryos, genes, and evolution.* New York: Macmillan.
Raisman, G. & Field, P. M. (1973). Sexual dimorphism in the neuropil of the preoptic area of the rat and its dependence on neonatal endrogen. *Brain Research, 54,* 1–29.
Rakic, P. (1973). Kinetics of proliferation and latency between final cell division and onset of differentiation of cerebellar stellate and basket neurons. *Journal of Comparative Neurology, 147,* 523–546.
Rakic, P., & Sidman, R. L. (1973). Weaver mutant mouse cerebellum: Defective neuronal migration secondary to abnormality of Bergman glia. *Proceedings of the National Academy of Sciences (USA), 70,* 240–244.
Rakic, P., Bourgeois, J. -P., Eckenhoff, M. F., Zecevic, N., & Goldman-Rakic, P. S. (1986). Concurrent overproduction of synapses in diverse regions of the primate cerebral cortex. *Science, 232,* 232–235.
Ravizza, R. J., & Herschberger, A. C. (1966). The effect of prolonged motor restriction upon later behavior of the rat. *Psychological Record, 16,* 73–80.

Reh, T. A., & Constantine-Paton, M. (1984). Eye-specific segregation requires neural activity in three-eyed *Rana pipiens*. *Journal of Neuroscience, 4,* 1132–1143.

Riege, W. H. (1971). Environmental influences on brain and behavior of year-old rats. *Developmental Psychobiology, 3,* 151–167.

Riege, W. H. & Morimoto, H. (1970). Effects of chronic stress and differential environments upon brain weights and biogenic amine levels in rats. *Journal of Comparative and Physiological Psychology, 71,* 396–404.

Riesen, A. H. (1965). Effects of visual deprivation on perceptual function and the neural substrate. In J. DeAjuriaguerra (Ed.), *Symposium bel air II, desafferentation experimentale et Clinique* (pp. 47–66). Geneva: George & Cie.

Robertson, M. (1987). Retinoic acid receptor, towards a biochemistry of morphogenesis. *Nature, 330,* 420–421.

Rolls, E. (in press). Spatial memory, episodic memory, and neuronal network functions in the hippocampus. In L. Squire (Ed.), The biology of memory, symposia Hoechst, Frankfurt, Hoechst, AG.

Rose, S. P. R. & Sinha, A. K. (1974). Incorporation of 3H-lysine into a rapidly labelling neuronal protein fraction in visual cortex is suppressed in dark reared rats. *Life Sciences, 15,* 223–230.

Rosenzweig, M. R. (1971). Effects of environment on development of brain and of behavior. In E. Tobach, L. R. Aronson, & E. Shaw (Eds.), *The biopsychology of development* (pp. 303–342). New York: Academic Press.

Rosenzweig, M. R., & Bennett, E. L. (1978). Experiential influences on brain anatomy and brain chemistry in rodents. In G. Gottlieb (Ed.), *Studies on the development of behavior and the nervous system: Vol. 4. Early influences* (pp. 289–330). New York: Academic Press.

Rosenzweig, M. R., Bennett, E. L., Diamond, M. C. (1972a) Chemical and anatomical plasticity of brain: Replications and extensions. In J. Gaito (Ed.), *Macromolecules and behavior* (2nd ed.). New York: Appleton-Century-Crofts.

Rosenzweig, M. R., Bennett, E. L., & Diamond, M. C. (1972b). Cerebral effects of differential experience in hypophysectomized rats. *Journal of Comparative and Physiological Psychology, 79,* 56–66.

Rosenzweig, M., Krech, D., Bennett, E. L., & Diamond, M. (1962). Effects of environmental complexity and training on brain chemistry and anatomy: A replication and extension. *Journal of Comparative and Physiological Psychology, 55,* 429–437.

Rutledge, L. T., Wright, C., Duncan, J. (1974). Morphological changes in pyramidal cells of mammalian neocortex associated with increased use. *Experimental Neurology, 44,* 209–220.

Samel, M. (1968). Thyroid function during postnatal development in the rat. *General and Comparative Endocrinology, 10,* 229–234.

Sapolsky, R. M. (1987). Glucocorticoids and hippocampal damage. *Trends in neuroscience, 10,* 346–349.

Scheich, H. (1987). Neural correlates of auditory filial imprinting. *Journal of Comparative Physiology [A], 161,* 605–619.

Singer, W. (1986). Neuronal activity as a shaping factor in postnatal development of visual cortex. In W. T. Greenough & J. M. Juraska (Eds.), *Developmental Neuropsychobiology* (pp. 271–293). New York: Academic Press.

Sirevaag, A. M., & Greenough, W. T. (1985). Differential rearing effects on rat visual cortex synapses. II. Synaptic morphometry. *Developmental Brain Research, 19,* 215–226.

Sirevaag, A. M., & Greenough, W. T. (1987). Differential rearing effects on rat visual cortex synapses. III. Neuronal and glial nuclei, boutons, dendrites, and capillaries. *Brain Research, 424,* 320–332.

Sirevaag, A. M., & Greenough, W. T. (1991). Plasticity of GFAP-immunoreactive astrocyte size and number in visual cortex of rats reared in complex environments.

Sirevaag, A. M., Black, J. E., & Greenough, W. T. (1991). Astrocyte hypertrophy in the dentate gyrus of young male rats reflects variation of individual stress rather than group environmental complexity manipulations. *Experimental Neurology, 111,* 74–79.

Snider, W. D., & Johnson, E. M. Jr. (1989). Neurotrophic molecules. *Annals of Neurology, 26,* 489–506.

Sperry, R. W. (1963). Chemoaffinity in the orderly growth of nerve fiber patterns and connections. *Proceedings of the National Academy of Sciences, (USA), 50,* 703–710.

Summerbell, D., & Honig, L. S. (1986). Embryonic mechanisms. In W. T. Greenough & J. M. Juraska (Eds.), Developmental neuropsychobiology (pp. 1–32). New York: Academic Press.

Summerbell, D., & Maden, M. (1990). Retinoic acid, a developmental signalling molecule. *Trends in Neurosciences, 13,* 142–147.

Teller, D. Y., & Movshon, J. A. (1986). Visual development. *Vision Research, 26,* 1483–1506.

Thelen, E. (1980). Rhythmical behavior in infancy: an ethological perspective. *Developmental Psychology, 17,* 237–257.

Thinus-Blanc, C. (1981). Volume discrimination learning in golden hamsters: Effects of the structure of complex rearing cages. *Developmental Psychobiology, 14,* 397–403.

Thomas, T. L., Davenport, L. D. (1988). Site specificity of adrenalectomy- induced brain growth. *Experimental Neurology, 102,* 340–345.

Thompson, R. F. (1983). Neuronal substrates of simple associative learning: classical conditioning. *Trends in Neuroscience, 6,* 270–275.

Turkewitz, G., & Kenny, P. A. (1982). Limitations on input as a basis for neural organization and perceptual development: A preliminary theoretical statement. *Developmental Psychobiology, 15,* 357–368.

Turner. A. M. & Greenough, W. T. (1983). Synapses per neuron and synaptic dimensions in occipital cortex of rats reared in complex, social, or isolation housing. *Acta Stereologica, 2 (Suppl. 1),* 239–244.

Turner, A. M., & Greenough, W. T. (1985). Differential rearing effects on rat visual cortex synapses. I. Synaptic and neuronal density and synapses per neuron. *Brain Research, 329,* 195–203.

Uphouse, L. (1980). Reevaluation of mechanisms that mediate brain differences between enriched and impoverished animals. *Psychological Bulletin, 88,* 215–232.

Uphouse, L. L., & Brown, H. (1981). Effects of differential rearing on brain, liver, and adrenal tissues. *Developmental Psychobiology, 14,* 273–278.

Uylings, H. B. M., Kuypers, K. & Veltman, W. A. M. (1978). Environmental influences on neocortex in later life. In M. A. Corner, R. E. Baker, N. E. van de Poll, D. F. Swabb, & H. B. M. Uylings (Eds.), *Maturation of the nervous system: Progress in brain research, Vol. 48* (pp. 261–274). Amsterdam: Elsevier.

Vidal, J. -M. (1980). The relations between filial and sexual imprinting in the domestic fowl: Effects of age and social experience. *Animal Behaviour, 28,* 880–891.

Volkmar, F. R., & Greenough, W. T. (1972). Rearing complexity affects branching of dendrites in the visual cortex of the rat. *Science, 176,* 1445–1447.

von Noorden, G. K., & Dowling, J. E. (1970). Experimental amblyopia in monkeys. II. Behavioral studies of strabismic amblyopia. *Archives of Ophthalmology (Chicago), 84,* 215–220.

Wallhausser, E., & Scheich, H. (1987). Auditory imprinting leads to differential 2-deoxyglucuse uptake and dendritic spine loss in the chick rostral forebrain. *Brain Research, 428,* 29–44.

Warren, J. M., Zerweck, C., & Anthony, A. (1982). Effects of environmental enrichment on old mice. *Developmental Psychobiology, 15,* 13–18.

Weiss, G. M., & Pysh, J. J. (1978). Evidence for loss of Purkinje cell dendrites during late development: A morphometric Golgi analysis in the mouse. *Brain Research, 154,* 219–230.

Weisz, D. J., Clark, G. A., Yank, B., Thompson, R. F., & Solomon, P. R. (1978). Activity of dentate gyrus during NM conditioning in rabbit. In C. D. Woody (Ed.), *Conditioning: Representation of involved neural functions* (pp. 131–145). New York: Plenum.

Wenzel, J., Kammerer, E., Frotscher, M., Kirsche, W. Matthies, H., & Wenzel, M. (1980). Electron-microscopical and morphemetrical investigations on the plasticity of the synapses in the hippocampus of the rat following conditioning. *Journal Hirnforschung, 21,* 647–657.

Werker, J. F., & Tees, R. C. (1984). Cross-language speech perception: Evidence for perceptual reorganization during the first year of life. *Infant Behavior and Development, 7,* 49–63.

West, R. W., & Greenough, W. T. (1972). Effect of environmental complexity on cortical synapses of rats: Preliminary results. *Behavioral Biology, 7,* 279–284.

Wickelgren, W. A. (1977). *Learning and memory.* Englewood Cliffs, NJ: Prentice-Hall.

Wiesel, T. N., & Hubel, D. H. (1963). Single-cell responses in striate cortex of kittens deprived of vision in one eye. *Journal of Neurophysiology, 26,* 1003–1017.

Wilson, M., Warren, J. M., & Abbott, L. (1965). Infantile stimulation, activity, and learning by cats. *Child Development, 36,* 843–853.

Zolman, J. F., & Morimoto, H. (1965). Cerebral changes related to duration of environmental complexity and locomotor activity. *Journal of Comparative and Physiological Psychology, 60,* 382–387.

6 Language, Cognition, and Brain Organization in a Neurodevelopmental Disorder

Ursula Bellugi
Amy Bihrle
Helen Neville
Sally Doherty
The Salk Institute for Biological Studies

Terry Jernigan
San Diego VA Medical Center

A major goal of our research is to investigate the brain mechanisms that underlie linguistic and other cognitive domains. We are involved in comprehensive studies of Williams syndrome, a carefully selected population in which adolescents exhibit a rare fractionation of higher cortical functioning: selective preservation of complex syntax in the face of marked and severe cognitive deficits. The program of studies we have undertaken provides critical evidence bearing on the dissociability of components of language and other cognitive systems. Although it is well known that specific language deficits can exist without an accompanying cognitive deficit, the opposite pattern in which linguistic abilities are selectively spared in the face of overall cognitive deficits is rare and has been little studied. Williams syndrome, a specific neurodevelopmental disorder, may represent a well-defined population in which this pattern of marked cognitive deficits but spared linguistic functioning is observed. This metabolic disorder which results in distinctive physical characteristics (e.g., specific facial features, heart defects) also appears to give rise to a neuropsychological profile which is highly discontinuous from normal. We address the issue of the nature of the neural substrate that supports the unusual neuropsychological functioning found in Williams syndrome. The intensive evaluation of cognitive and linguistic capacities of such a homogeneous population of individuals affords an important opportunity to explore the interrelationships of cognitive domains and their underlying neural substrates.

Williams syndrome is a rare metabolic disorder (one estimate of occurrence is 1:50,000) labeled in 1961 by the British cardiologist J. C. P. Williams, who described a syndrome which includes a specific heart defect (supravalvular aortic stenosis), mental retardation, and a peculiar facial appearance (Williams, Barratt-Boyes, & Lowe, 1961). Jones and Smith (1975) documented some of the clinical features of Williams syndrome, based on 19 cases, noting that the cluster of unusual facial characteristics of the subjects is one of the consistent features in the recognition of this sporadically occurring disorder. Typical facial features include a broad forehead, medial eyebrow flare, depressed nasal bridge, a stellate pattern in the iris, widely spaced teeth, and full lips. Williams syndrome subjects also tend to have low birth weight, digestive disorders in infancy, apparent auditory sensitivity, mild microcephaly, and developmental delays. The syndrome has been associated with levels of calcium and abnormal levels of calcitonin (Culler, Jones, & Deftos, 1985; Jones, in press). Figure 6.1 shows photographs of Williams syndrome children which we have made into a collage, showing aspects of their unusual facial appearance (courtesy of the Williams Syndrome Association).

The medical/clinical symptoms of Williams syndrome have been described in some detail (See Burn, 1986; Morris, Demsey, Leonard, Dilts, & Blackburn, 1988 for recent reviews). However, to date there have been few studies of the psychological and behavioral characteristics of Williams syndrome subjects. A classical report, von Arnim and Engel (1964) gave case studies of 4 subjects with Williams syndrome, characterizing the psychological features as 'an unusual command of language combined with an unexpectedly polite, open and gentle manner.' Reports include descriptions of Williams syndrome children as loquacious and highly sociable. Jones and Smith (1975) report that the children are characterized by very friendly and socially disinhibited demeanor. Udwin, Yule, and Martin (1987) report marked friendliness towards adults, including strangers, as well as hyperactivity, anxiety, and hyperacusis. A consistent feature of Williams syndrome is reported to be some degree of mental retardation as measured by IQ tests. Mean full scale IQ scores of groups of Williams subjects fall in the mild to moderate mentally retarded range, as reported in Arnold, Yule, & Martin, 1985; Bennet, LaVeck, & Sells, 1978; Kataria, Goldstein, & Kushnick, 1984; Preuss, 1984.

Background. Most of the literature that has appeared to date on Williams syndrome children's psychological functioning is based on standard achievement tests and IQ measures rather than on specific probes of cognitive functioning. We argue that such standard tests mask the unusual profile typically exhibited by Williams syndrome adolescent subjects. Those behavioral studies that have appeared, moreover, suggest conflicting outcomes and inconsistent findings. For example, some studies report that verbal abilities surpass nonverbal performance abilities (Udwin et al., 1987) while others report different findings (Crisco &

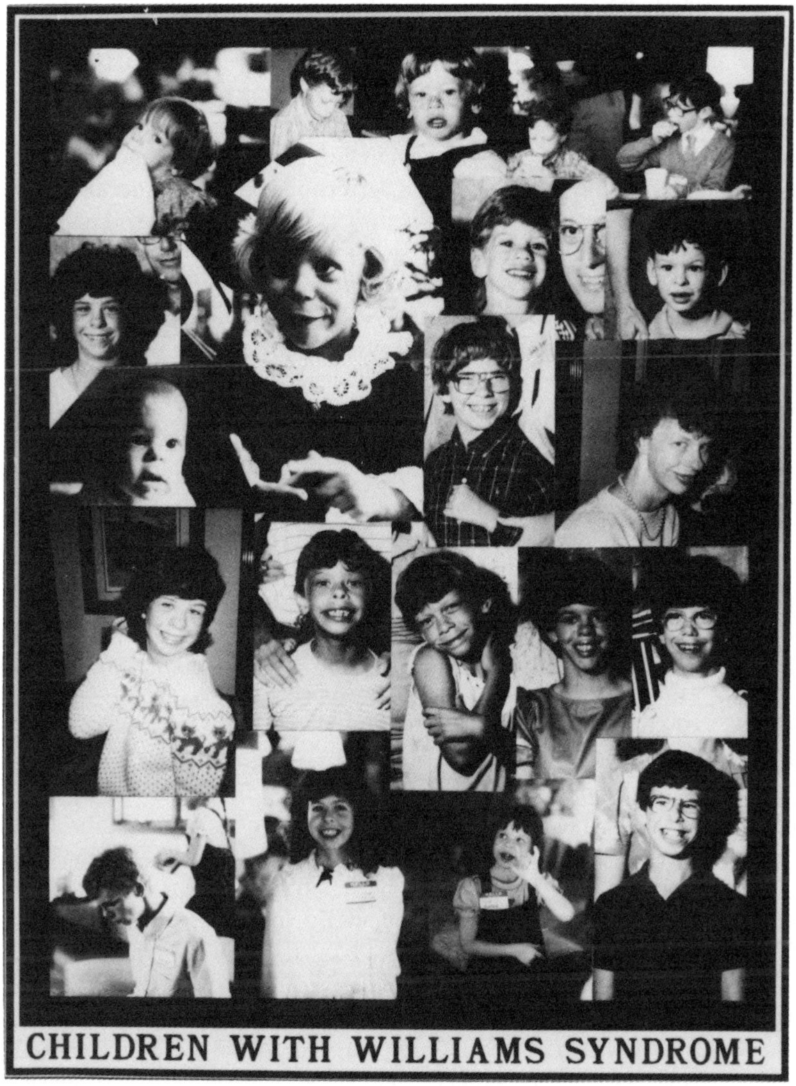

FIG. 6.1. Facial characteristics of Williams syndrome children.

Dobbs, 1988; Kataria et al., 1984; Arnold et al., 1985). A major limitation of these studies is that verbal abilities are for the most part assessed by instruments that confound linguistic with other cognitive processing, and thus do not permit assessment of domain specific functions. Another factor may be that the age of subjects differs widely across studies, and this may also be an important source of variance. Our studies to date suggest that the neuropsychological profile of younger versus older Williams syndrome children may be markedly different; language and cognitive milestones are markedly delayed (Thal, Bates, & Bellugi, 1989). We have embarked on a broad research program which seeks to provide a comprehensive approach to Williams syndrome, and to bring to bear neurobehavioral, neurophysiological, and neuroanatomic evidence to the study of this unique syndrome. Our studies are designed to provide evidence bearing on the separability and interrelationship between linguistic and nonlinguistic cognitive domains.

Previous investigations have often relied on global measures of cognitive performance which are insensitive to individual components of linguistic ability, and/or processing at different levels. IQ scores may mask important differences between linguistic and cognitive domains that make up general intelligence as Rapin (1982) points out. The Laboratory for Language and Cognitive Studies at The Salk Institute has developed a major program for investigating cognitive capacities in this unusual metabolic disorder, in concert with neuroanatomical, neurophysiological and neurobiological studies. These studies are beginning to provide new insights into the relationships between and within domains of higher cortical functioning and their underlying neural substrates (Bellugi, Bihrle, Doherty, Neville, & Damasio, 1989; Bellugi, Bihrle, Jernigan, Swanson, & Culler, 1987; Bellugi, Bihrle, Trauner, Jernigan, & Doherty, in press; Bellugi, Marks, Bihrle, & Sabo, 1988; Bellugi, Sabo, & Vaid, 1988; Bihrle, Bellugi, Delis, & Marks, 1989; Jernigan & Bellugi, 1990; Simmons, Culler, Bellugi, & Greenberg, 1990).

We report here on case studies of a small well-selected sample of matched Williams and Down syndrome subjects, across a specific battery of standard and experimental tasks. The neuropsychological battery included probes for linguistic processing at different structural levels as well as general problem solving and a battery of tasks for spatial cognition, including tasks for which the left and the right hemisphere are typically differentially specialized in hearing (and in deaf signing) subjects (Bellugi, Poizner, & Klima, 1989). In our studies to date, we have worked with over 50 Williams syndrome children and almost as many Down syndrome children, and present results here from case studies of 6 carefully selected adolescents in each group, matched on age and IQ. The Williams and Down syndrome subjects ranged from 10 to 20 years, with a mean of 14.4 years for the Williams and 15.4 years for the Down syndrome subjects. The mean Full Scale IQ was 50.8 for Williams syndrome adolescents [s.d. = 5.8] and 48.8 for Down syndrome adolescents [s.d. = 8.7]. The Williams and Down adolescents generally are in the same classrooms for the educable mentally retarded. As we shall point out, despite matching on IQ, the two groups differed markedly across many of our experimental probes. We first turn to the unusual neuropsychological profile of dissociations between linguistic and cognitive abilities in Williams syndrome, noting characteristic features which may turn out to be hallmarks of the syndrome.

A UNIQUE NEUROPSYCHOLOGICAL PROFILE IN WILLIAMS SYNDROME

In describing her future aspirations a 15-year-old adolescent states: "You're looking at a professional book writer. My books will be filled with drama, action, and excitement. And everyone will want to read them. I'm going to write books, page after page, stack after stack . . . I'll start on Monday." In view of her facility with language, proclivity for flowery, descriptive terms, and her creativity, her aspiration initially seems plausible. She describes a meal as "a scrumptious buffet," an older friend as "quite elegant," her boyfriend as "my sweet petunia" and when asked if someone could borrow her watch, replies "my watch is always available for service." Additionally, she is able to spontaneously create original stories—she weaves stories of imaginary events and recounts with vivid detail a dream in which an alien from a different planet emerges from her television set. Her creativity extends to music; she composed the lyrics to a love song. At first glance, this young woman has the makings of a novelist, but in fact, she has an IQ of 49 and has Williams syndrome. At the age of 15, she fails all Piagetian seriation and conservation tasks (normally attained by the age of 7 years), goes to a special school in classes for the mentally retarded; has reading, writing, and math skills comparable to those of a first grader, demonstrates visuospatial abilities of a 5-year-old, and requires a babysitter for supervision. The disparity between linguistic abilities and other cognitive functioning that emerges from our studies with Williams syndrome adolescents suggests that this may turn out to be characteristic of an entire population of subjects. The investigation of the unusual dissociation of language from other cognitive functions, and its underlying neural and neurobiological substrate, forms the basis for this series of studies.

Cognitive Impairment in Williams and Down Syndrome

Both the Williams syndrome subjects and the comparison group of Down syndrome subjects are mentally retarded as defined by the American Association on Mental Deficiency (AAMD): "Mental retardation refers to significantly subaverage general intellectual functioning existing concurrently with deficits in adaptive behavior, and manifested during the developmental period" (Grossman, 1978). The Williams syndrome adolescents in our studies are mentally retarded in terms of IQ test scores, as are the matched Down syndrome subjects. Furthermore, the Williams syndrome subjects' deficits in adaptive behavior are pervasive. According to parental reports, all showed marked delays in motor and language milestones. The Williams subjects we report on here, as well as matched Down subjects, are in classes for the trainable or educable mentally retarded and are unable to function in normal educational settings. Most Williams children and adolescents are unable to tie their shoes adequately, cut with a knife, or use a broom (Morris et al., 1988). Moreover, the inability of Williams syndrome adolescents and adults to lead independent lives attests to their adaptive and cognitive disability. We evaluated cognitive abilities in Williams and Down subjects by administering a series of nonverbal tasks designed to separate cognitive from linguistic factors, including problem solving, categorization, and conceptual reasoning. On a series of cognitive tasks, Williams perform poorly. For example, concept formation was assessed using the Reitan-Indiana version of the Category Test, a relatively complex test of new problem solving and concept formation requiring a number of higher order functions such as the ability to note similarities and differences in stimuli and to formulate hypotheses regarding the principle that determines the correct response. Both groups of adolescents, Williams and Down subjects alike, had mean error scores *below* that of normal 5-year-olds, the youngest age for which normative data are available, showing marked and equivalent cognitive impairment.

The unusual nature of the Williams subjects' language abilities, in contrast to their general cognitive limitations, is brought out by considering that even on some of the verbal (language related) tests of IQ, the Williams subjects scored equivalently to the Down subjects. For example, on the Vocabulary Subtest of the WISC-R, Williams and Down subjects both failed equally. Subjects are asked the meaning of words, and points are awarded based on the ability to produce a well-formed definition, a *cognitive,* not linguistic skill. On this test, the Williams and Down syndrome subjects achieved exactly the same low mean scaled scores: 3.2 for each of the groups (in the lowest percentile rank). As these scores indicate, neither the Williams nor the Down syndrome subjects were able to hone in on the most salient features of the target words to be defined. The subjects were asked to define words (e.g., "What does *hazardous* mean?"). Four of 6 Down subjects responded "I don't know" and the other two responded in sentence fragments: "Don't touch books not belong to you," and "Hassle, throw sand." Six Williams subjects, on the other hand, typically responded with long complex sentences, conjuring up the variety of situational contexts in which they might have heard the word hazardous. One Williams subject said "Turn on your hazard lights; that's an emergency. When your car broke down, you wait for a tow truck." Another responded "Hazardous. Oh, I know. Hazardous means that you have trash and the air is not clean. There's smoke coming out of chimneys. There's lots of stuff going on, like you can smell oil, and you can have terrible things happen . . . A lot of trash hanging around and you would have to clean it up and that's hazardous." Another subject responded "I'd say if you get an infection, that's hazardous and if it gets worse and worse it can turn into a red thing . . . " Still another Williams subject responded "Now, I've heard hazardous ten thousand times. It means something dangerous, like a windstorm or a fire. But there's good hazards and bad. The good ones are to prevent things from happening, like it's hazardous to smoke . . . " and on and on. We note that the Williams and Down subjects responded radically differently on this verbal task, but nonetheless scored equivalently poorly.

The Decoupling of Language from Cognition in Williams Syndrome

In order to examine the relationship between linguistic as opposed to other cognitive abilities in Williams, we have investigated cognitive abilities that have been claimed to be prerequisites for the development of specific linguistic structures. These studies have allowed us to assess the competing hypotheses: are specific linguistic abilities dependent on the development of specific cognitive prerequisites or are the two domains dissociable? One long-standing model of the relationship between language and cognitive development asserts that the two are closely intertwined and that language is one manifestation of a more general symbolic representational system whose development causes and constrains the major events of language acquisition (Bates, Benigni, Bretherton, Camaioni, & Volterra, 1979; Piaget, 1963). A second model argues for the existence of uniquely linguistic mental structures and learning mechanisms specific for language (e.g., Fodor, 1983). The relationships between linguistic and non-linguistic functions are extremely difficult to tease apart in normal development; thus, the study of abnormal populations such as Williams syndrome with selectively intact linguistic function can provide new insights into these complex issues and can provide powerful evidence to resolve long-standing theoretical debates concerning the relationship between language and cognition.

Cognitive Correlates and Linguistic Structures. To explore the relationship between linguistic and other higher cognitive abilities, we administered cognitive tasks that have been purported to be prerequisites for the development of specific linguistic structures. For example, the ability to conserve (taken to be a measure of underlying cognitive operations of reversibility and transitivity) have been argued to be an important prerequisite to the development of specific linguistic structures. Figure 6.2 shows the Williams adolescents' general inability across the board to handle standard Piagetian tests of conservation skills typically mastered by normal children well before 8 years of age, including two-dimensional space, number, substance, continuous and discontinuous quantity, and weight. Mastery of these concepts has been argued to be prerequisite to the acquisition of passive sentences in the linguistic domain (Beilin, 1975; Sinclair, 1975). How-

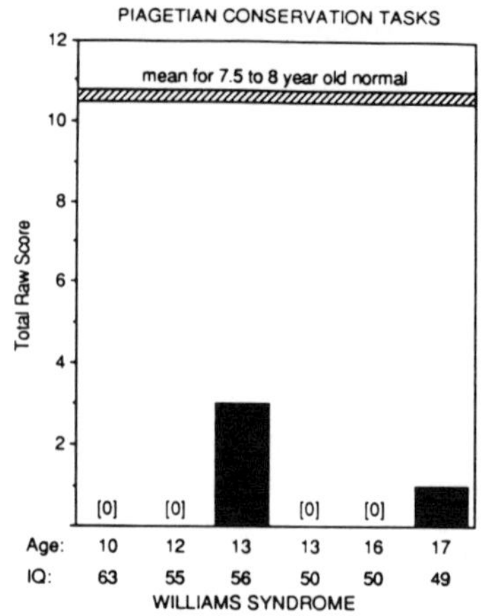

Conservation of Number, Weight, Substance and Quantity in WS Subjects

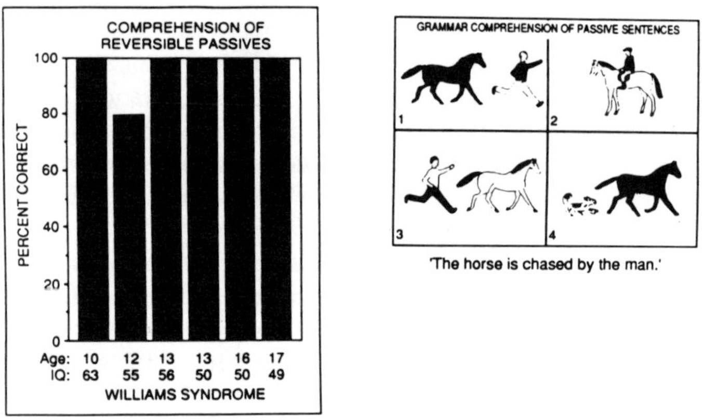

Comprehension of Passive Construction in WS Subjects

FIG. 6.2. The decoupling of language and cognition in Williams syndrome (conservation and passives).

ever, despite an inability to conserve, the Williams subjects tested do produce full passive sentences and reliably demonstrate the ability to comprehend semantically reversible possible sentences such as "The horse is chased by the man." Figure 6.2 illustrates that on comprehension of reversible passives, nearly all the Williams Syndrome subjects achieved a perfect score, whereas our studies show that the Down syndrome subjects performed at chance level or below.

Williams syndrome brings into high relief the extent to which linguistic capacities are separable from purported cognitive underpinnings. In contrast to their consistent and severe impairment across an array of conceptual reasoning tasks measuring cognitive abilities, Williams syndrome subjects (but not their matched Down counterparts) display surprisingly good performance on formal language tests. The results of the cognitive and linguistic tasks, taken together, illuminate an important and long-standing theoretical issue: specific linguistic abilities *do not* depend on the prior development of specific cognitive functions, and the two domains can be dissociable. Thus, our results with Williams syndrome subjects suggest a decoupling between linguistic and nonlinguistic abilities that challenges many contemporary theoretical positions.

Disproportionate Sparing of Linguistic Capacities in Williams Syndrome

Although there have been numerous studies of language in Down syndrome subjects (Fowler, 1990; Gleitman, 1984; Miller, 1987), until now there have been few investigations of the linguistic capacities of Williams syndrome subjects. Results of our preliminary studies suggest that although the two groups of subjects have comparable cognitive impairments (and were selected on the basis of equivalent Full Scale IQ scores), there are marked differences between them in the language domain. Analyses of expressive language and tests of language processing and comprehension indicate that, unlike in Down syndrome subjects, lexical and grammatical abilities are remarkably spared in Williams syndrome subjects (Bellugi, Marks et al., 1988). Most unusual about the cognitively impaired Williams syndrome subjects is their expressive language. Figure 6.3a gives language samples from an 18-year-old adolescent with an IQ of 49 from different contexts, e.g., she describes to her father an experience unique to her of having a Magnetic Resonance Image (MRI) scan taken of her brain ("There is a huge machine. It took a picture inside the brain . . . After it's done, they show you your brain on a computer . . . Oh, and it was very exciting!") This young woman is at the level of much younger children in cognitive tasks, yet her spontaneous language is very good, composed of grammatically complex well-formed sentences, including multiple embedded clauses, generally appropriate to the context. Clearly, the language is not what one might expect from a mentally retarded adolescent. In the description, the Williams syndrome adolescent exhibits spontaneous language that is not only phonologically and syntactically impeccable but also effective in using subordinate clauses to foreground and background information. This is in stark contrast to language samples from IQ and age matched Down syndrome subjects in our studies. This young woman's language, like that of the other adolescent Williams syndrome subjects we studied, *characteristically* shows grammatical well-formedness, even when there is grammatical complexity. Despite failure on a range of cognitive tests, Williams syndrome adolescent subjects studied so far used language that is grammatically correct, structurally rich, and morphologically elaborated, often (but by no

SPONTANEOUS LANGUAGE OF A WS SUBJECT (AGE 18, IQ 49)

1) <u>MAGNETIC RESONANCE IMAGING EXPERIENCE</u>:

"There is a huge machine. It took a picture inside the brain. You could talk but not move your head because that would ruin the whole thing and they would have to start all over again. After it's done they show you your brain on a computer. They see how large it is. And the machine on the other side of the room takes pictures from the computer. They can take pictures instantly. Oh, and it was very exciting."

2) <u>EXCERPT FROM SPONTANEOUSLY GENERATED STORY</u>:

"This is a story about chocolates. Once upon a time, in Chocolate World there used to be a Chocolate Princess. She was such a yummy princess. She was on her chocolate throne and then some chocolate man came to see her. And the man bowed to her and he said these words to her. The man said to her, "Please Princess Chocolate, I want you to see how I do my work. And it's hot outside in Chocolate World, and you might melt to the ground like melted butter. And if the sun changes to a different color, then the Chocolate World -- and you -- won't melt. You can be saved if the sun changes to a different color. And if it doesn't change to a different color, you and Chocolate World are doomed."

3) <u>AIMS IN LIFE</u>:

"You are looking at a professional book writer. My books will be filled with drama, action, and excitement. And everyone will want to read them... I am going to write books, page after page, stack after stack. I'm going to start on Monday."

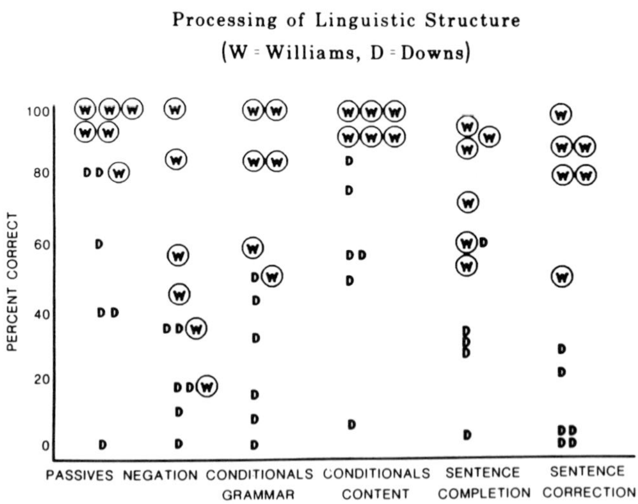

FIG. 6.3. Remarkably spared grammatical capacities in Williams syndrome.

means always) appropriate to the context. Matched Down syndrome adolescents have very different linguistic abilities, corresponding to the level of much younger normal children, markedly simplified grammatically, and with many errors and omissions.

The Autonomy of Syntax. In expressive language, there is a clear difference between the two groups of subjects, as evidenced by mean length of utterance, nounphrase complexity, verbphrase complexity, and embeddings (Bellugi, Bihrle et al., 1987; Bellugi, Marks et al., 1988). An important question, however, is whether the two groups differ in comprehension and processing of linguistic structures. Although both groups may exhibit delays in the onset and emergence of language milestones, older Williams syndrome subjects' expressive language is complex and generally grammatically correct, albeit with morphological errors. Figure 6.3b shows performance across a range of grammatical probes tapping a variety of linguistic structures including tests of Semantically Reversible Passive Sentences; tests of Negation; of Conditionals; of Sentence Completion; as well as Sentence Correction; (Bellugi, 1971; Bellugi, & Klima, 1966; Reilly, 1983). Note that the Williams syndrome subjects on the whole performed considerably better than the Down syndrome subjects. Importantly, the Williams syndrome subjects were able to manipulate, process, and comprehend complex grammatical structures; they were also able to monitor sentences for grammatical correctness, and were able to correct ungrammatical sentences, while the Down syndrome subjects failed on the same task. For example, on a metalinguistic probe for the ability to monitor and correct ungrammatical sentences, subjects are presented with sentences such as "I hope you to eat all your supper." A typical Williams subject responded "I hope that you will eat all your supper," while a matched Down subject responded "Chicken." These findings, consistent with other results of grammatical competence, suggest that syntactic functioning in Williams syndrome is relatively preserved in comparison to nonlinguistic cognitive capacities. Further, linguistic competence in Williams syndrome, both in production and comprehension, appears markedly better than in matched subjects with Down syndrome.

Unusual Semantic Organization. The Williams syndrome adolescents clearly show that they have understanding of words and are able to provide appropriate contexts of use. For example, given the word "contagious," one of the Williams syndrome subjects related being sick with the measles and unable to have visitors and provided a list of ailments such as "allergies, bleary eyes, runny nose, hay fever, cough, sore throat." None of the Williams syndrome subjects conveyed the *critical* concept of contagious required for a definition (easily spread), but they did provide appropriate associations. Williams syndrome subjects (unlike Down syndrome subjects) often used unusual words in spontaneous conversation, exhibiting considerable knowledge about words, that belied their lack of cognitive understanding of the world. When the Williams syndrome subjects were asked the meanings of spontaneously elicited words such as *surrender, saute, nontoxic, commentator,* or *brochure,* they typically provided responses such as "I wish I could surrender. That means I give up," or "It's nontoxic. That means it's not dangerous." When asked about her knowledge of a bank, a Williams subject said, "It's a place where you can put a card in a slot and money comes out." Probed further for understanding of where the money came from, what was the function of a bank or the people in it, she drew a blank. However, probed for meanings of the word *bank,* she easily provided contexts and grammatically correct sentences specifying two meanings: a place that provides money and also the side of a river.

On tests of word knowledge, such as the Peabody Vocabulary Test, we find significant differences in semantic abilities between groups of Williams syndrome and Down syndrome subjects. On this test, in which subjects hear a word and are asked to pick out the appropriate picture from an array of pictures (e.g., *abrasive*), the Williams syndrome and Down syndrome groups differ significantly in terms of their referential lexical knowledge. Five out of 6 Down syndrome subjects' receptive vocabulary scores were below their mental age equivalent, whereas all 6 of the Williams syndrome subjects performed at or above normal mental age matched individuals (see Figure 6.4). The mean receptive language mental age was 8.4 for the Williams syndrome subjects and 5.3 for Down syndrome subjects, a statistically significant difference. These findings suggest that aspects of referential lexical knowledge are considerably better than expected from mental age in Williams syndrome, while the opposite pattern is found in Down syndrome subjects.

Inferences about the organization of the mental lexicon can be gleaned from information obtained by measuring the extent to which names are accessed automatically. On a test of semantic fluency, the Williams and Down syndrome subjects performed very differently, with the Williams syndrome subjects showing a distinct advantage but a deviant organization, as Figure 6.4 shows. Subjects were asked to generate as many exemplars as possible of a semantic category (e.g., Foods and Animals) within 60 seconds (Semel, Wiig, & Secord, 1980). The Williams syndrome subjects produced significantly more words over trials than the Down syndrome subjects on this task. These results suggest that the Williams syndrome adolescents, unlike the Down syndrome subjects, have no difficulty accessing numerous members of a given semantic category. Indeed, for some of the Williams syndrome subjects tested, the number of words produced was comparable to the norms provided for their chronological age. Importantly, the results also suggest qualitative differences between the responses of the two groups of adolescent subjects. Not only did the Down syndrome subjects produce fewer words than the Williams syndrome subjects, they were more likely to include repetitions and extra category words. Predictably, within category responses generated by Down syndrome subjects were limited to highly typical

Peabody Picture Vocabulary Test
Age and IQ Matched WS and DS Subjects

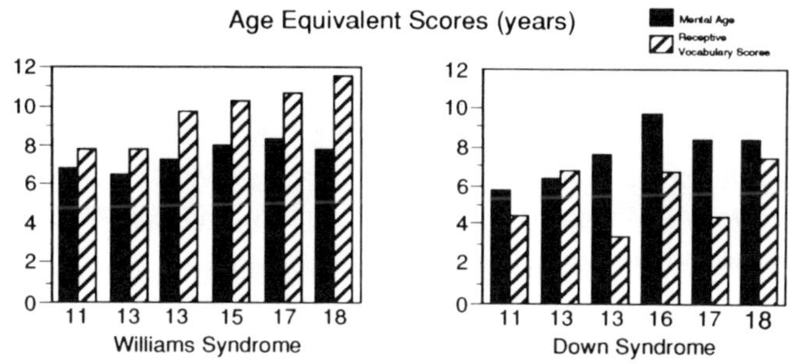

Lexical Semantics:
Age and IQ Matched WS and DS Subjects

Williams Syndrome:
The Williams Syndrome children are fluent in producing word associations on command. Asked to name all the animals they could think of in a timed test, they all responded with fluent lists, including not just typical animals (dog, cat).but also nonprototypical ones (chihuaua, yak, ibex, condor, vulture, saber tooth tiger).

Down Syndrome:
In comparison, Down Syndrome children tended to produce shorter lists and tended to name more prototypical animals. (See Appendix for scores.)

WS: BRONTOSAURUS, TYRANADON, BRONTASAURUS REX, DINOSAURS, ELEPHANT, DOG, CAT, LION, BABY HIPPOPOTAMUS, IBEX, WHALE, BULL, YAK, ZEBRA, PUPPY, KITTEN, TIGER, KOALA, DRAGON.	DS: DOGS, CATS, FISH, BIRD, FISH.
WS: TIGER, OWL SEA LION, ZEBRA, HIPPOTAMUS, TURTLE LIZARD, REPTILE, FROG, BEAVER, GIRAFFE, CHIHUAHUA.	DS: GOATS, RABBITS, BUNNIES, HORSEY, FRENCH FRIES, GOATS, MONKEYS, HORSEY, ICE CREAM.
WS: TIGERS, HORSES, DOGS, CATS, SNAILS, FISH, WORMS, UNICORN, LION SEAL, ELEPHANT, APE, COW, PIG, HENS, CHICKENS, DUCKS, ZEBRAS, GIRAFFES, ALLIGATORS, SNAKE, BEAR, WOLVES, BIRDS, CROCODILES, BILLY GOAT, FROG, SHARK, RABBIT.	DS: ELEPHANT, LION, SNAKE, DOG, FISH CAT, ELEPHANT, LION, BIRD, LION, DOG.
WS: BEAR, SNAKE, GIRAFFE, LION, BUFFALO, BULL, DOG, CAT, TIGER, LEOPARD, TURTLE, SABER TOOTH TIGER, CONDOR, VULTURE	DS: CAT, DOG, PIG, GOAT, HORSEY, ELEPHANT, GIRAFFE, ZEBRA, DONKEY, TURTLE, MONKEYS.

FIG. 6.4. Unusual lexical semantic abilities in Williams syndrome adolescents.

responses such as "dog", "cat," and "pig" for animals. In contrast, the chronological age and IQ matched Williams syndrome subjects frequently produced not just typical category members, but also unusual, low frequency, non-prototypical category members. When asked to generate animals, the Williams syndrome subjects' word choices included such oddities as "unicorn," "tyrandon," "brontosaurus," "yak," "ibex," "water buffalo," "sea lion," "saber-toothed tiger," and "vulture." The Williams syndrome subjects' surprising performance on a word fluency generation task is particularly noteworthy in that mentally retarded individuals of various etiologies are known to recognize and use the same types of lexical items and make similar semantic associations as normal subjects matched on mental age (Rondal, 1978, 1980). It has been suggested, therefore, that language in mental retardation generally represents a delay not a deviance. Our findings with Williams syndrome, by contrast, suggest that *deviance* may characterize the lexical semantic abilities of this atypical form of mental retardation.

The Williams syndrome subjects' spontaneous speech is peppered with unexpected word choices: words that are decidedly unusual, infrequent, unexpected, and often marked semantically; they are 'odd' but not contextually inappropriate. A 10-year-old Williams syndrome child gave the experimenter a drawing of a bicycle (quite unrecognizable, as is characteristic of Williams syndrome drawings), saying "Here, Doc, this is in remembrance of you." Another Williams syndrome child, age 11, before emptying the remainder of her glass of milk into the sink said, "I'll have to evacuate it." One meaning of evacuate is indeed "to cause to be empty by removing the contents," but the contents implied are more likely to be animate as in "to evacuate a building (of people)." Thus the child uses an unusual word in a context that is syntactically correct, but semantically just a little off the mark. Another Williams syndrome child, pleased at being told that she would have a computer class that day said, "Today is computer day. Victory has been accomplished!" It is again an unusual word choice; one could say "accomplish a task," or "achieve a goal," but "victory has been accomplished" is somewhat odd, a violation of selectional restrictions.

Although both Williams and Down syndrome subjects scored low on IQ definitional tests, Williams syndrome subjects obtained far higher, even sometimes normal scores on tests of referential word knowledge and semantic fluency as well as on tests of syntactic production, comprehension, and monitoring. Williams syndrome subjects are also characterized by unusual, anomalous use of words in category production and spontaneous conversation. The use of unusual lexical items by Williams syndrome subjects (that is, often more specific or *formal* than normal adults might use in comparable situations) bespeaks considerable lexical knowledge. Although these subjects' word choice and lexical semantics appears sometimes atypical, our data suggest that Williams syndrome subjects know a considerable amount about the words that they use. Unusual word choice is highly characteristic of Williams syndrome and interestingly it is unlike the semantic disturbances that accompany other clinical disorders (the aphasias, the dementias), unlike errors occasionally committed by normal subjects (e.g., slips of the tongue), and decidedly unlike semantic limitations characteristic of other mentally retarded groups. The use of unusual vocabulary is a surprising facet of Williams syndrome subjects' language ability and may turn out to be a characteristic feature which distinguishes their performance from Down syndrome subjects.

Dissociation between Language and Spatial Cognition. Our studies so far suggest that in the linguistic domain, there appears to be a striking difference between matched groups of Williams and Down syndrome subjects. We have also investigated spatial cognition because this aspect of cognition is the polar opposite of language, both in terms of processing operations that are brought into play and in terms of the basic functional organization of the brain. In the spatial domain, we are finding marked and specific spatial deficits in Williams syndrome subjects in an array of tasks including spatial construction, spatial orientation, copying geometric shapes, and all aspects of drawing (Bellugi, Sabo et al., 1988; Bihrle et al., 1989). We note that typically, the Williams syndrome subjects tend to talk their way through drawing tasks as if using their verbal skills to mediate the severely impaired act of drawing. To illustrate the dramatic contrast between visuospatial abilities and language, we present the drawing of an elephant by a Williams syndrome adolescent with an IQ of 49, juxtaposed with her verbal description of elephants (Figure 6.5). Her drawing is fractionated and extremely impoverished —the labels are added to indicate her description while she was drawing, and without the labels the drawing would be unrecognizable. Yet, her verbal description of elephants shows remarkably spared linguistic abilities. Despite their language mediation, the Williams syndrome children's drawings are grossly and severely impaired. This disparity in abilities underscores the dissociation between language and visuospatial skills in Williams syndrome.

Peaks and Valleys in Spatial Cognition in Williams Syndrome

Our studies suggest that Williams syndrome may result in a highly uneven neuropsychological profile with specific peaks and valleys of abilities even within spatial domains. Across a range of visuospatial tasks, both Williams and Down subjects are markedly impaired, but there may be differences in the nature of their deficit. The two groups of subjects performed equally poorly on a standardized visuoconstructive measure, the Developmental Test of Motor Integration (Beery & Buktenica, 1967). Williams syndrome adolescents were at the mean age equivalent of 4 years, 8 months [s.d. = 0.5] and Down syndrome subjects were at a mean age of 5 years, 6 months [s.d. = 0.7] showing marked impairment. Although the two groups were not significantly different on this visuoconstructive task, we did note that the Williams syndrome subjects showed a selective disability on items that required integration of component parts (e.g., a triangle made out of circles). This differential impairment also showed up on a drawing task from the Boston Diagnostic Aphasia Examination (Goodglass & Kaplan, 1983). Subjects are asked to draw common objects both on command from memory and copying a model (e.g., bicycle, flower, elephant, cube, cross, house). Although both groups were impaired, there were marked and characteristic differences. Note the drawings of a bicycle by age and IQ matched Down and Williams syndrome subjects (Figure 6.5b). Although the Down syndrome subject's drawing is simplified, it exhibits better spatial organization, closure, and integration of parts than does the Williams syndrome subject's drawing. In contrast, the Williams drawing completely lacks spatial organization and integration (the "person" underneath the "bike," the "chain" stretched out below the "wheels"); it is completely unrecognizable without the verbal labels. In general, Williams subjects, like right hemisphere damaged patients with lesions in the parietal lobe, often depict the parts of an object scattered on the page with no integration into functional objects, and fail to represent spatial orientation, perspective, or depth (Anderson,1988).

The processing differences which emerge between the Williams and Down syndrome subjects, even when both are equally impaired, can be highlighted by examining the Block Design subtest of the WISC-R. Subjects are asked to assemble three-dimensional blocks whose surfaces differ in design to match the pattern of a model. Both Williams and Down subjects failed equally, scoring in the lowest first percentile. Indeed, some of the children were unable to pass even the simplest items. However, when we examined the final performance on the designs, we found that the two groups failed in characteristically and distinctly *different* ways. The Down syndrome children maintained the overall configuration of the blocks, but made errors of internal detail like left hemisphere damaged patients, while the Williams syndrome subjects failed to maintain the overall configuration of the blocks, exhibiting a fragmented approach as is typical of right hemisphere damaged patients (Anderson, 1988; Bellugi, Poizner et al., 1989). Thus, although both groups are equivalently impaired on the spatial cognitive tasks, there are marked processing differences between them.

Impaired Visuospatial Processing. Despite equal impairment on a range of visuospatial tasks, performance on qualitative tasks like drawing suggests that there may be important differences in visuospatial abilities between the Williams and Down syndrome groups. We thus sought experimental means of investigating and characterizing differential visuoconstructive impairments; in particular, we were interested in how well each group integrated parts of an object to form a coherent whole. In order to explore this issue, we administered a task using hierarchical stimuli in which a larger (global) form is created by the spatial arrangement of repeated smaller (local) forms (Delis, Robertson, & Efron,

Contrast Between Visuospatial and Language Abilities in Williams Syndrome

Drawing of an Elephant

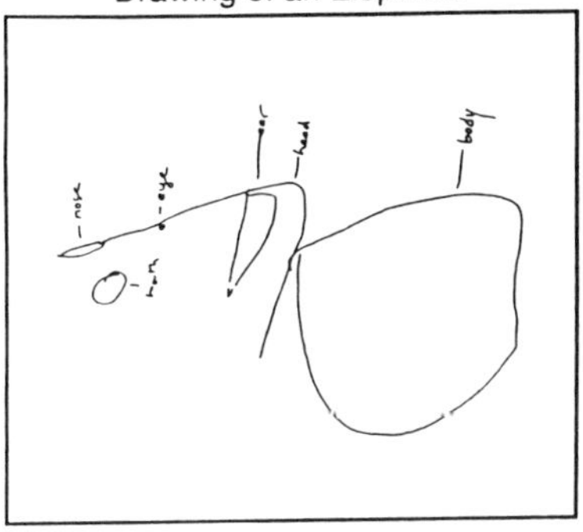

Verbal Description of Elephants

And what an elephant is, it is one of the animals. And what the elephant does, it lives in the jungle. It can also live in the zoo. And what it has, it has long gray ears, fan ears, ears that can blow in the wind. It has a long trunk that can pick up grass, or pick up hay....If they're in a bad mood it can be terrible...If the elephant gets mad it could stomp; it could charge. Sometimes elephants can charge, like a bull can charge. They have big long tusks. They can damage a car...It could be dangerous. When they're in a pinch, when they're in a bad mood it can be terrible. You don't want an elephant as a pet. You want a cat or a dog or a bird...

18 year old Williams Subject

Drawing of a Bicycle
Age and IQ Matched WS and DS Subjects

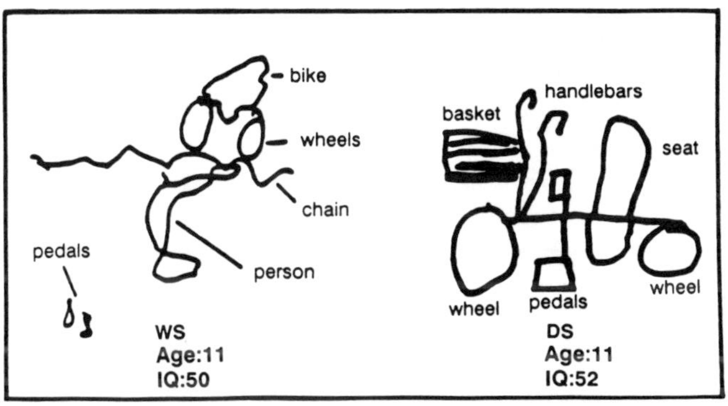

FIG. 6.5. The dissociation between language and visuospatial capacities in Williams syndrome.

1986). For example, one stimulus was a large printed letter 'D' formed out of 15 small letter 'x's. An advantage of these stimuli over standardized clinical measures is the explicit demarcation between features perceived as parts and wholes. Subjects were presented with these hierarchical stimuli for 5 seconds, then asked to reproduce the figure after a 5-sec delay. Normal age matched subjects accurately produced both the local and the global forms. Relative to normals, both the Williams and Down syndrome subjects were grossly impaired in this task of 50 items, equally low in overall accuracy. Interestingly, however, they were impaired in opposite ways (Figure 6.6). The Williams syndrome subjects were significantly more impaired than the Down syndrome subjects in accuracy for depicting the global form, whereas, the Down syndrome subjects were significantly more impaired than the Williams syndrome subjects in accuracy for depicting the local forms. In sum, the Down syndrome subjects consistently produced only the *global* figures (e.g., the large "D") using a solid line, omitting the local forms completely. In striking contrast, the Williams syndrome subjects almost invariably produced only the *local* forms (e.g., the smaller "x's") with little or no attempt to represent the global figure.

Although both groups of subjects show similar impairment in cognitive functioning generally, and both show equal impairment in some spatial cognitive tasks, we have found a marked and differential cleavage between the two groups of mentally retarded subjects for spatial constructions of parts versus construction of wholes. These clusters of spatial cognitive deficits are quite startling and potentially important as evidence for understanding the relationship between cognitive components and their representation in the brain (Bihrle et al., 1989). The findings are particularly intriguing since patients with unilateral right hemisphere lesions perform like Williams syndrome subjects, and are generally impaired in local forms, while left lesioned patients, perform like Down syndrome subjects, and show the opposite effect (Delis & Bihrle, 1989; Delis, Kiefner, & Fridlund, 1988). Whereas sharp dissociations within spatial cognition are ordinarily encountered with localized acquired lesions, mental retardation has often been considered a nonspecific pervasive disorder resulting in across the board

DELIS HIERARCHICAL PROCESSING TASK

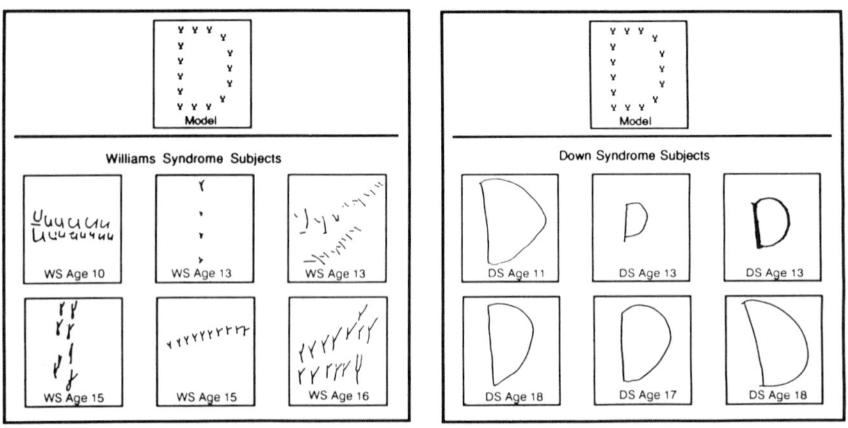

FIG. 6.6. Differential visuospatial processing in Williams and Down syndrome.

cognitive deficits. Our studies, however, suggest that Williams syndrome, even in the absence of obvious space occupying lesions, may result in a highly uneven behavioral profile with specific deficits and preservations in the visuospatial domain.

Facial Recognition: An Island of Sparing. Importantly, despite their spatial cognitive dysfunctions (Bellugi, Sabo et al., 1988; Bihrle et al., 1989), there are peaks as well as valleys of visuospatial abilities in Williams syndrome. The Williams syndrome subjects (but not the Down syndrome subjects) demonstrated a *selective* ability to discriminate unfamiliar faces on the Benton Test of Facial Recognition (Benton, Hamsher, Varney, & Spreen, 1983). Based on developmental norms with subjects of normal intelligence, Williams syndrome subjects perform at the level of normal 13-year-olds, nearly at the level of normal adults. Whereas the Down syndrome subjects demonstrated extremely severe defects on this task, the Williams syndrome subjects characteristically responded easily and correctly on this complex task involving recognition and discrimination of faces under conditions of spatial transformation. These findings suggest that preserved performance on a facial discrimination task in the context of generally impaired spatial cognition may be a unique neuropsychological marker of Williams syndrome (Bellugi, Bihrle et al., in press; Bellugi, Marks et al., 1988; Bellugi, Sabo et al., 1988; Bihrle et al., 1989).

Neuropsychological studies suggest that Williams syndrome, unlike Downs syndrome, appears to result in a highly uneven behavioral profile of specific deficits and preservations within and across domains of language and spatial cognitive functioning. Williams syndrome thus presents a rare pattern of dissociations, providing clues to underlying brain structure and function and an unusual opportunity to explore critical issues of cognitive science. We are engaged in a multi-pronged approach to these important issues, combining behavioral studies, with studies of on-line functional organization of the brain (using Event Related Potentials), and studies of the neuroanatomical basis for Williams syndrome (using Magnetic Resonance Imaging). Data from these studies are described in the following sections.

NEUROANATOMICAL MARKERS OF WILLIAMS SYNDROME

A general goal of our research is to relate cognitive functions to their underlying neural substrates. In the case of Williams syndrome our studies show that metabolic factors have produced very marked and specific alterations in behavioral development, and the resulting neuropsychological profiles of adolescent Williams subjects clearly raise the possibility of abnormal development of neural systems. The availability of noninvasive techniques for obtaining images of brain structures (Magnetic Resonance Imaging, MRI) and indices of brain function (Event-Related Potentials, ERP) allow us to investigate the possibility that abnormal profiles of neural structures and processes are related to the unique fractionation of higher cortical functions that characterizes Williams syndrome.

Unlike cruder imaging methods, MRI provides excellent neuroanatomical detail and the potential for three-dimensional reconstruction (Jernigan & Hesselink, 1987). Jernigan and Bellugi (1990) examined gross brain morphology in MRIs of Williams adolescents. We obtained images extending from the level of the pons to the vertex for 6 Williams syndrome subjects and three Down syndrome subjects, as well as for 14 normal controls ranging in age from 8 to 32 years (Bellugi, Marks, Neville, & Jernigan, 1987; Jernigan, Bellugi, & Hesselink, 1989; Jernigan & Bellugi, 1990).

Distinctive Morphological Shape. Given the unusual profile underlying Williams subjects' marked spatial deficits and spared language, one might expect to find evidence of right hemisphere abnormalities. Inspection of Williams syndrome MRI scans, however, revealed no gross abnormalities in any of the brain structures examined. Importantly, the results show no evidence of space occupying lesions in the brain parenchyma of either of the two hemispheres (Jernigan & Bellugi, 1990); however, it is possible that the two syndromes may leave their marks in distinctive morphological shape. Inspection of MRI scans contrasting Williams and Down subjects did provide suggestions of syndrome-specific differences in overall brain shape. The top portion of Figure 6.7 shows results from processed axial images resulting from computer voluming techniques for a typical Down syndrome subject, a typical Williams syndrome subject, and a matched normal control. The Down subject's brain is notable for degree of hypofrontality—relatively small frontal lobes have also been previously reported for Down subjects (Crome, Cowie, & Slater, 1966). The Williams syndrome subjects, on the other hand, appear to have relatively decreased posterior width and elongated posterior to anterior length compared to normal. Further analyses are currently underway to estimate volumes of other specific regions of the brain, including the parietal lobes, given the specific cognitive deficits exhibited by Williams syndrome subjects.

Image Analyses. Our quantification of specific brain regions involves the use of computer voluming methods recently developed by Jernigan, involving manual designation of anatomical landmarks and estimation of regional volumes (Jernigan & Hesselink, 1987). For these analyses, four classes of pixels are identified to correspond to white matter, grey matter, cerebro-spinal fluid (CSF) and signal hyperintensities. Similar methods of MRI analyses have already led to important findings bearing on the neural substrate for neurodevelopmental disorders such as Developmental Dysphasia and Autism (Courchesne, Yeung-Cour-

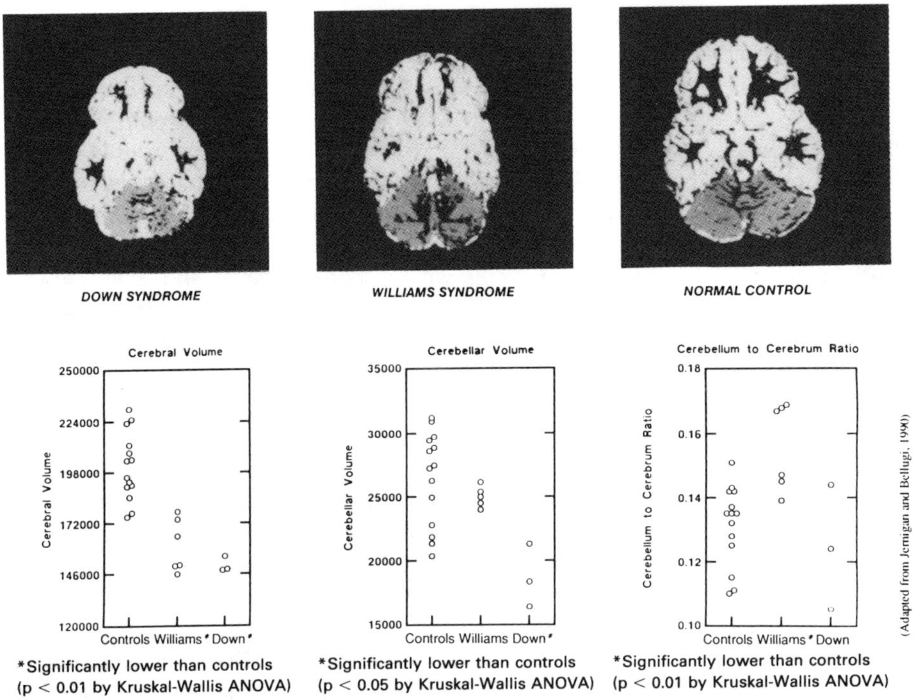

FIG. 6.7. Abnormal brain morphology on MRI in Williams syndrome.

chesne, Press, Hesselink, & Jernigan, 1988; Jernigan, Tallal, & Bellugi, 1988; Jernigan & Tallal, 1990).

Since our neurobehavioral results indicated equivalent cognitive impairment in the Down and Williams subjects, the first question we addressed was with respect to cerebral volumes. Given the different neurobehavioral profiles with respect to language and cognition, are there quantitative differences between the two groups in cerebral and cerebellar volumes? Cerebral and cerebellar volumes were estimated by summing pixels from supratentorial and infratentorial zones respectively and groups were compared using nonparametric statistical analyses. Results of these quantitative analyses of the MRI images suggest that relative to the normal control group, *both* the Williams syndrome and Down syndrome subjects have reduced cerebral volumes. In the Down syndrome subjects, the cerebrum was approximately 77% of the equivalent volume of young normal controls; the Williams syndrome cerebrum was similarly reduced to 80% of normal. The entire distribution of cerebral volume values is displayed in the bottom portion of Figure 6.7. Interestingly, although the cerebrum exhibits a significant volume reduction in both groups of subjects, the proportion of cerebral grey matter was similar to that observed in the normal controls. Moreover, no gross cerebral volume loss (as reflected in increased CSF proportion) was present in either group.

Differential Development of Cerebellar Regions. Previous studies with Down subjects (Crome et al., 1966) have found that the cerebellum and brain stem are somewhat more reduced in size than is the cerebrum. Consistent with this result, a significant reduction of the volume of the posterior fossa, as well as the cerebrum, was observed in the Down syndrome subjects in our study. In striking contrast, however, the Williams syndrome subjects showed no suggestion whatsoever of a reduction in the overall size of the cerebellar structures. Indeed, the Williams subjects had significantly *larger* cerebellar volumes than Down subjects. Whereas the volume of the cerebellum in our Down syndrome subjects was reduced to approximately 69% of that of the normal controls, the cerebellar volume in our Williams syndrome subjects was essentially *the same* as that of normal controls. This surprising finding resulted in an abnormal cerebellar-to cerebral volume in the Williams syndrome subjects. Figure 6.7 presents the distribution of these increased volume ratio values in Williams syndrome as compared to both Down syndrome and normal controls. In light of the Williams subjects' cognitive deficits, the unexpected finding of a significantly increased cerebellum-to-cerebrum ratio is an important neuroanatomical finding which may prove to be a marker of the syndrome. Such a finding is, however, puzzling since the cerebellum is often described as growing later than the cerebrum, and thus factors affecting cerebral growth would normally be expected to affect later cerebellar growth as well (Dobbing & Sands, 1973). These results are clearly provocative and they provide the first clue in our investigation to uncover the neuroanatomical basis of Williams syndrome (Jernigan et al., 1989).

Recent papers have suggested different functions in higher cognitive processing for **neocerebellar** (as opposed to **paleocerebellar**) regions; regions which are known to be ontogenetically, anatomically, and developmentally distinct (Leiner & Leiner, 1989, in press). Courchesne and his colleagues (1988) examined differential sizes of neocerebellar and paleocerebellar regions of the vermis in a group of autistic subjects. They report an aberrant pattern, with neocerebellar (but not paleocerebellar) lobules significantly smaller in autistic subjects. The unusual profile of Williams subjects, which includes remarkably preserved language, facial recognition and social affect, is in some ways opposite to that reported for autism (Courchesne et al., 1988). We compared volumes of paleocerebellar and neocerebellar regions of the cerebellar vermis, using methods adapted from Courchesne et al. We compared volumes of the neocerebellar lobules VI and VII to those of paleocerebellar lobules I to V in MRI scans of 6 Williams, 2 Down syndrome subjects, and the 14 normal controls. In a dramatic *reversal* of the pattern found in autism, we found a striking increase in neocerebellar volumes (Vermal areas VI and VII) in Williams subjects, with no significant difference in paleocerebellar volumes (Vermal areas I to V). Not only is the resulting vermal ratio of neocerebellar to paleocerebellar volumes significantly increased from controls, but in *every case* of Williams this ratio is greater than any subject in either control group, whether normal or Down (Jernigan & Bellugi, 1990). This finding of hypoplasia in autism versus hyperplasia in Williams syndrome is tantalizing, in light of the language and social differences between these groups.

Leiner, Leiner, & Dow's (1986) reexamination of neuroanatomical, neurophysiological, and neurosurgical evidence prompted these investigators to suggest that the phylogenetically new subcortical circuitry in the cerebellum participates not only in the motor but also in the *cognitive* processing of language. PET studies obtained at the Washington University Medical Center in St. Louis, Missouri, support this new assessment (Petersen, Fox, Posner, Mintum, & Raichle, 1988). We speculate that perhaps the unusual neurobehavioral profile of cognitive functions in Williams syndrome including delayed but spared language may turn out to be related to these unusual cerebellar and cerebral findings. In ongoing studies, we are probing other aspects of the neuroanatomical substrate which may be related to the distinctive neuropsychological profile of Williams syndrome (Jernigan & Bellugi, 1990). For example, given the specific spatial cognitive deficits exhibited by Williams syndrome subjects which in some ways resemble deficits typical of right parietal lesioned subjects, analyses are underway to investigate morphological abnormalities with respect to the parietal lobes. We now turn neurophysiological studies of brain activity and behavior in Williams syndrome, which may provide clues to underlying neural systems.

NEUROPHYSIOLOGICAL INDICES OF BRAIN ORGANIZATION

We have begun a series of collaborative studies of Williams syndrome with Neville and colleagues (Neville, Holcomb, & Mills, 1989) to assess the timing and organization of neural systems active during sensory, cognitive, and language processing in Williams subjects. These studies employ the event-related potential (ERP) technique, one of few noninvasive techniques that permits a millisecond by millisecond monitoring of brain activity that precedes, accompanies, and/or follows particular types of cognitive processing (for reviews, see Hillyard, & Picton, 1987; Regan, 1989). To date we have investigated just two of the notable characteristics of the Williams behavioral profile. First, we examined their auditory recovery cycle for indices that might provide clues to the basis of their hyperacousis (i.e., increased sensitivity to sounds). Is there evidence for hyperexcitability at any stage along the auditory pathway? Second, we examined auditory sentence processing. Are the relatively preserved language capabilities of these otherwise mentally retarded adolescent Williams subjects mediated by brain systems that resemble or differ in some principled manner from those that are active in normal age-matched control subjects?

Auditory and Visual Recovery Paradigm. A psychophysical result of this metabolic disorder is an unusual sensitivity to specific classes of environmental sounds, manifested in specific ways: an *awareness* of sounds before others in the environment, and an *aversion* to sounds not usually considered aversive in normal populations (Bellugi, Bihrle et al., 1989). In subjects tested to date, auditory brainstem evoked responses were normal in Williams subjects, suggesting that hyperexcitability does not occur at the brainstem level. However, the auditory recovery data suggest a possible cortical mechanism subserving the apparent sensitivity to sounds. Eight Williams subjects and 10 normal age-matched controls listened to tones presented at different repetition rates (monitoring for frequency shifts) in order to index the rate of recovery or refractory period of the auditory sensory evoked response. The overall morphology of the Event-Related Potential to tone stimuli (i.e., the N100-P200 response) was very similar in Williams and control subjects over the left and right hemisphere (Figure 6.8a). However, Williams subjects displayed larger responses at high repetition rates than did controls, suggesting that their responses were *less* refractory and, therefore, more excitable than in normals. This effect is only evident over temporal cortex and only occurs to auditory stimuli. These data suggest that although similar brain systems are activated by tones in Williams and normal subjects, Williams subjects display hyperexcitability compared with normal controls. Importantly, the same Williams subjects were run in a visual recovery cycle paradigm, and their results were indistinguishable from those of normal controls, suggesting that this effect is specific to auditory information. Taken together, these studies suggest that the hyperacousis observed in Williams subjects may be mediated by hyperexcitability specifically within the cortical areas that are utilized in processing acoustic information (Neville et al., 1989). Future studies will help to clarify the specific alteration displayed in the Williams adolescents.

Abnormal Brain Function During Language Processing. In studies with 8 Williams syndrome subjects, we recorded ERPs to auditorally presented words that formed sentences (procedures described in Holcomb & Neville, in press). Responses to open and closed class words in sentence medial position were compared. In addition, one-half of the sentences were highly contextually constrained, ending with an expected word (semantically appropriate), and the other half ended with an anomalous unexpected word (semantically inappropriate), as in "I take my coffee with cream and paper." A large number of researchers have noted that semantically primed or expected endings show a sustained positivity in normal subjects after the initial response, but that semantically anomalous information produces a large negative peak (see Neville, Kutas, Chesney, & Schmidt, 1986). Normal subjects show a large negative response at 400 msec (N400) to

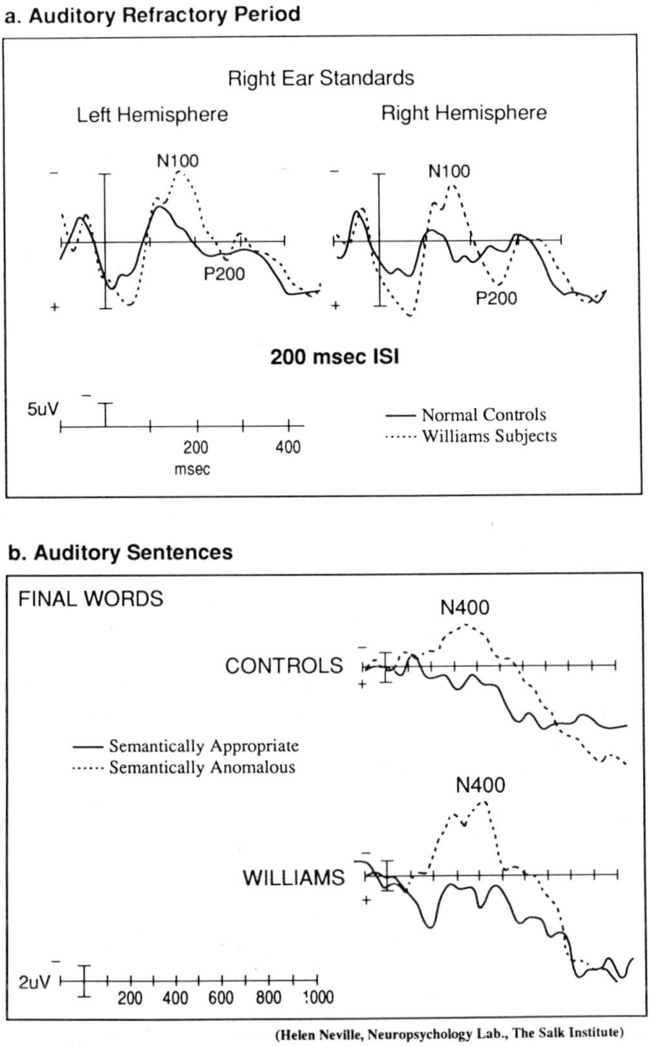

FIG. 6.8. Neurophysiological indices of auditory and language processing in Williams syndrome.

semantically unprimed words which is thought to be an index of how the mental lexicon is organized. Results from this study are highly revealing. In contrast to normal subjects, the Williams subjects displayed responses that were highly abnormal within the first 200-300 msec following word onset. The abnormality consisted of a large positivity not apparent in control subjects at any age. This effect, only apparent over temporal brain regions, may relate to the hyperacousis these subjects display. Furthermore, the Williams' responses do not display the asymmetry (left temporal regions more negative than right) that is normally apparent by about 7 years of age (Neville, in preparation), suggesting that there may be an unusual pattern of brain organization underlying language. These data suggest that the identity and/or organization of the neural systems involved in processing certain aspects of language may be different in Williams and control subjects.

Other aspects of language processing may be more similar to normal subjects. For example, the N400 response to semantically anomalous sentence endings is similar in Williams and control subjects; there is a large negative peak around 400 msec just as in the normal subjects (Figure 6.8b). However, the effect of the semantic anomaly appears to be *larger* in Williams syndrome than in controls. If upheld in future studies, an abnormally large effect of semantic priming may be related to our behavioral findings in which on tests of semantic processing many Williams subjects tend to generate low frequency and nonprototypical responses (see Figure 6.4). The effect of greater priming may indicate an abnormally large degree of activation which extends to less frequent and nonprototypical items within the mental lexicon. In order to determine whether this effect holds up and in order to rule out the possibility that it is merely a function of higher excitability of auditory temporal brain regions, in future studies we will determine whether the semantic priming effect occurs in the visual modality as well.

Taken as a whole, the neurophysiological studies raise the possibility that at least some of the brain systems that mediate the remarkably preserved language in the Williams syndrome population differ from those that mediate language in the normal population. Further studies of Williams syndrome will help to clarify the role of different factors in the development of functional differentiation in the Williams brain.

A POSSIBLE NEUROBIOLOGICAL BASIS FOR WILLIAMS SYNDROME

In collaborative research, we are initiating a program of studies which may shed light on the neurobiological basis of Williams syndrome. Williams syndrome is known to be associated with high levels of calcium and abnormal calcium metabolism and has recently been shown to include a deficiency in the synthesis or release of calcitonin (Culler et al., 1985; see Figure 6.9). We are currently exploring a hypothesis that may relate the association of central nervous system dysfunction and abnormalities of calcitonin/calcium metabolism in subjects with Williams syndrome. These studies are being conducted across laboratories at The Salk Institute, representing exciting new collaborations among disciplines from molecular biology to behavior, and form part of a broad multidisciplinary ap-

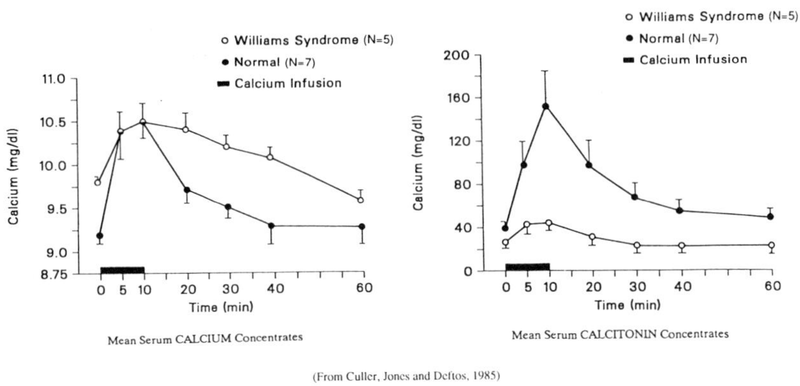

FIG. 6.9. Neurobiological correlates of Williams syndrome.

proach to this unique disorder (Bellugi, Bihrle et al., 1989; Bellugi, Bihrle et al., 1987; Bellugi & Culler, 1987; Simmons et al., 1990).

We are investigating a neurobiological marker for Williams syndrome in subjects who have a documented endocrine abnormality—calcitonin deficiency—specifically examining the hypothesis that may directly link the specific metabolic disorder and neurotransmitter imbalance with the unusual neurobehavioral profile, through an abnormality at the level of a single underlying genetic disturbance (Bellugi, Bihrle et al., 1987; Bellugi & Culler, 1987; Culler et al., 1985; Jones, in press). A defect in the alternative processing of the calcitonin gene could result in an underproduction of calcitonin and an abnormality in processing of a recently discovered neuropeptide, calcitonin gene-related peptide, producing the specific neuropsychological phenotype of Williams syndrome. Calcitonin gene-related peptide (CGRP) is a recently identified neuropeptide, discovered by scientists at The Salk Institute and the University of California at San Diego (Rosenfeld et al., 1983). Scientists in the Peptide Biology Laboratory at The Salk Institute have developed an assay for CGRP that provides accurate measurement of the amount of this neuropeptide present in a small sample. It is now possible to measure CGRP in blood samples and nerves found in small skin samples, and compare Williams syndrome and normals. These pilot studies are being undertaken in collaboration with Drs. Floyd Culler, with Donna Simmons of the Neural Systems Laboratory, and with Glen Evans of the Molecular Genetics Laboratory of The Salk Institute. We have already found that Williams syndrome subjects express levels of CGRP in skin, and are currently quantifying levels in brain tissue. Specifically, we are examining the hypothesis that there may be an underlying genetic disturbance in Williams syndrome which results in the abnormal production of calcitonin and of a neuropeptide that may play a role in the normal development and/or function of the central nervous system. In these studies, we investigate a group of unique subjects using research tools from a spectrum of disciplines ranging from molecular biology to endocrinology and behavior.

SUMMARY

Williams syndrome presents a rare decoupling of language from other cognitive capacities, providing an unusual opportunity to explore some of the central issues of cognitive neuroscience. Using a specific neurodevelopmental disorder as a model, our studies should, in the long run, illuminate brain organization for language and cognitive functioning.

In this chapter, we present a new line of investigation which forges links between a specific neurodevelopmental disorder, a specific neuropsychological profile, a pattern of abnormal brain organization, and the underlying neurobiological markers. We report on a series of studies with children with a rare metabolic disorder, Williams syndrome, which reveal an unusual fractionation of higher cortical functions: linguistic functioning is selectively preserved in the face of severe general cognitive deficits. The extreme dissociation found in Williams syndrome subjects between linguistic and other cognitive functions is rare, and its implications are important to an understanding of language and its functional organization in the human brain. Our studies show that Williams syndrome results in a fractionation even within the spatial cognitive domain; subjects exhibit selective attention to details of a configuration at the expense of the whole, while matched Down subjects show a very different pattern. Thus Williams syndrome provides a powerful vehicle for investigating the separability of functions within, as well as across, cognitive domains. In multidisciplinary studies, we investigate brain organization through a combination of neurobehavioral, neurophysiological, and neuroanatomical measures. Taken together, our findings suggest that some of the brain systems that mediate the remarkably preserved language capabilities in individuals with Williams syndrome may be different from those that mediate language in normal populations. These comprehensive studies of cognitive capacities, brain structure, and brain functioning address important questions concerning the segregation and integration of different language and other cognitive processes and the neural systems that mediate them.

ACKNOWLEDGMENTS

This research was supported in part by the National Institutes of Health, grants #NS 22343, #HD 26022, #DC 00146, and #DC 00201; the National Science Foundation, grant #BNS 88-20673; the Axe-Houghton Foundation; and the John D. and Catherine T. MacArthur Foundation Research Network. Diane Niles is parent coordinator for these studies. We are particularly grateful to subjects and their families who participated in these studies, and thank the National Williams Syndrome Association and Parents of Down Syndrome children as well.

REFERENCES

Anderson, R. A. (1988). The neurobiological basis of spatial cognition: Role of the parietal lobe. In J. Stiles-Davis, M. Kritchevsky, & U. Bellugi (Eds.), *Spatial cognition: Brain basis and development* (pp. 57–80). Hillsdale, NJ: Lawrence Erlbaum Associates.

Arnold, R., Yule, W., & Martin, N. (1985). The psychological characteristics of infantile hypercalcemia: A preliminary investigation. *Developmental Medicine and Child Neurology, 27,* 49–59.

Bates, E., Benigni, L., Bretherton, I., Camaioni, L., & Volterra, V. (1979). *The emergence of symbols: Cognition and communication in infancy*. New York: Academic Press.

Beery, K. E., & Buktenica, N. A. (1967). *Developmental test of visual-motor integration.* Cleveland, OH: Modern Curriculum Press.

Beilin, H. (1975). *Studies in the cognitive basis of language development*. New York: Academic Press.

Bellugi. U. (1971). Some language comprehension tests. In C. Lavatelli (Ed.), *Language training in early childhood* (pp. 157–169). Urbana, IL: University of Illinois Press.

Bellugi, U., Bihrle, A., Doherty, S., Neville, H., & Damasio, A. R. (1989). Neural correlates underlying dissociations of higher cortical functioning. Symposium presented at *International Neuropsychology Society,* Vancouver, BC, Canada.

Bellugi, U., Bihrle, A., Jernigan, T., Swanson, L., & Culler, F. (1987). Neuropsychological and neurobiological account of a disorder. *Society for Neurosciences,* New Orleans, LA.

Bellugi, U., Bihrle, A., Trauner, D., Jernigan, T., & Doherty, S. (1990). Neuropsychological, neurological, and neuroanatomical profile of Williams syndrome. *American Journal of Medical Genetics, 6,* 115–125.

Bellugi, U., & Culler, F. (1987). Gene coding and behavioral expression in Williams syndrome children. Colloquium presented at *UCLA Medical Center*.

Bellugi, U., & Klima, E. S. (1966). Syntactic regularities in children's speech. In J. Lyons & R. Wales (Eds.), *Psycholinguistic papers* (pp. 183–208). Scotland: Edinburgh University Press.

Bellugi, U., Marks, S., Bihrle, A., & Sabo, H. (1988). Dissociation between language and cognitive functions in Williams syndrome. In D. Bishop & K. Mogford (Eds.), *Language development in exceptional circumstances* (pp. 177–189). London: Churchill Livingstone.

Bellugi, U., Marks, S., Neville, H., & Jernigan, T. (1987). Brain organization underlying unusual language and cognitive functions. Symposium presented at *Western Psychological Association,* Long Beach, CA.

Bellugi, U., Poizner, H., & Klima, E. S. (1989). Language, modality and the brain. *Trends in Neurosciences, 10,* 380–388.

Bellugi, U., Sabo, H., & Vaid, J. (1988). Spatial deficits in children with Williams syndrome. In J. Stiles-Davis, M. Kritchevsky, & U. Bellugi (Eds.), *Spatial cognition: Brain bases and development* (pp. 273–298). Hillsdale, NJ: Lawrence Erlbaum Associates.

Bennett, F. C., LaVeck, B., & Sells, C. J. (1978). The Williams elfin faces syndrome: The psychological profile as an aid in syndrome identification. *Pediatrics, 61,* 303–305.

Benton, A. L., Hamsher, K., Varney, N. R., & Spreen, O. (1983). *Test of facial recognition, Form SL*. New York: Oxford University Press.

Bihrle, A. M., Bellugi, U., Delis, D., & Marks, S. (1989). Seeing either the forest or the trees: Dissociation in visuospatial processing. *Brain and Cognition, 11,* 37–49.

Burn, J. (1986). Williams syndrome. *Journal of Medical Genetics, 23,* 389–395.

Courchesne, E., Yeung-Courchesne, R., Press, G. A., Hesselink, J. R., & Jernigan, T. L. (1988). Hypoplasia of cerebellar vermal lobules VI and VII in Autism. *New England Journal of Medicine, 318,* 1349–1354.

Crisco, J. J., & Dobbs, J. M. (1988). Cognitive processing of children with Williams syndrome. *Developmental Medicine and Child Neurology, 5,* 650–656.

Crome, L., Cowie, V., & Slater, E. (1966). A statistical note on cerebellar and brainstem weight in Mongolism. *Journal of Mental Deficiency Research, 10,* 69–72.

Culler, F. L., Jones, K. L., & Deftos, L. J. (1985). Impaired calcitonin secretion in patients with Williams syndrome. *The Journal of Pediatrics, 107,* 720–723.

Delis, D. C., & Bihrle, A. M. (1989). Fractionation of spatial cognition following focal and diffuse brain damage. In A. Ardila & R. Ostrosky (Eds.), *Brain organization of cognitive processes* (pp. 17–35). New York: Plenum Press.

Delis, D. C., Kiefner, M. G., & Fridlund, A. J. (1988). Visuospatial dysfunction following unilateral brain damage: Dissociations in hierarchical and hemispatial analysis. *Journal of Clinical and Experimental Neuropsychology, 10,* 421–431.

Delis, D. C., Robertson, L. C., & Efron, R. (1986). Hemispheric specialization of memory for visual hierarchical stimuli. *Neuropsychologia, 24,* 205–214.

Dobbing, J., & Sands, J. (1973). Quantitative growth and development of human brain. *Archives of Disease in Childhood, 48,* 757–767.

Fodor, J. D. (1983). Phrase structure parsing and the island constraints. In *Linguistics and Philosophy, 6,* 163–223.

Fowler, A. E. (1990). Language abilities in children with Down syndrome: Evidence for a specific syntactic delay. In D. Cicchetti & M. Beeghly (Eds.), *Children with Down syndrome: A developmental perspective* (pp. 302–328). New York: Cambridge University Press.

Gleitman, L. R. (1984). Biological predispositions to learn language. In P. Marler & H. S. Terrace (Eds.), *The biology of learning* (pp. 553–584). New York: Dahlem Konferenzen.

Goodglass, H., & Kaplan, E. (1983). *Assessment of aphasia and related disorders.* Philadelphia, PA: Lea and Febiger.

Grossman, H. J. (1978). The game of the name: An examination of linguistic reference after brain damage. *Brain and Language, 6,* 112–119.

Hillyard, S. A. & Picton, T. W. (1987). Electrophysiology of cognition. In F. Plum (Ed.), *Handbook of physiology section I: The nervous system V higher functions of the brain, part II* (pp. 519–584). Baltimore, MD: American Physiology Society.

Holcomb, P. J., & Neville, H. (in press). Auditory and visual semantic priming in lexical decision: A comparison using event-related brain potentials. *Language and Cognitive Processes.*

Jernigan, T., & Bellugi, U. (1990). Anomalous brain morphology on magnetic resonance images in Williams syndrome and Down syndrome. *Archives of Neurology, 47,* 529–533.

Jernigan, T., Bellugi, U., & Hesselink, J. (1989). Structural differences on MRI between Williams and Down syndrome. *American Academic of Neurology,* Chicago, IL.

Jernigan, T. L., & Hesselink, J. (1987). Human brain-imaging: Basic principles and applications in psychiatry. In R. Michels & J. O. Cavenar (Eds.), *Psychiatry: Psychobiological foundations of clinical psychiatry* (pp. 1–9). Philadelphia, PA: Lippincott.

Jernigan, T. L., & Tallal, P. (1990). Late childhood changes in brain morphology observable with MRI. *Developmental Medicine and Child Neurology, 32,* 379–385.

Jernigan, T., Tallal, P., & Bellugi, U. (1988). Cerebral morphology of magnetic resonance imaging (MRI) in developmental cognitive disorders. Paper presented at *Society for Neurosciences,* New Orleans, LA.

Jones, K. L. (1990). Williams syndrome: A historical perspective of its evolution, natural history, and etiology. *American Journal of Medical Genetics, 6,* 89–96.

Jones, K. L., & Smith, D. W. (1975). The Williams elfin faces syndrome: A new perspective. *Journal of Pediatrics, 86,* 718–723.

Kataria, S., Goldstein, D. J., & Kushnick, T. (1984). Developmental delays in Williams elfin faces syndrome. *Applied Research in Mental Retardation, 5,* 419–423.

Leiner, H. C., & Leiner, A. L. (in press). Evolution of the cerebellum: Did it contribute to the evolution of language? In W. von Raffler-Engel (Ed.), *Studies in language origins.* Amsterdam: John Benjamins Publishing Company.

Leiner, H. C., & Leiner, A. L. (1989). Reappraising the cerebellum: What does the hindbrain contribute to the forebrain? *Behavioral Neurosciences, 103,* 998–1008.

Leiner, H. C., Leiner, A. L., & Dow, R. (1986). Does the cerebellum contribute to mental skills? *Behavioral Neurosciences, 2,* 443–454.

Miller, J. F. (1987). Language and communication characteristics of children with Down syndrome. In S. M. Pueschel, C. Tingley, J. E. Rynders, A. C. Crocker, & D. M. Crutcher (Eds.), *New perspectives on Down syndrome* (pp. 233–262). Baltimore, MD: Brookes.

Morris, C., Demsey, S. A., Leonard, C. O., Dilts, C., & Blackburn, B. L. (1988). Natural history of Williams syndrome: Physical characteristics. *Journal of Pediatrics, 113*(2), 318–326.

Neville, H. J. (in press). Neurobiology of cognitive and language processing: Effects of early experience. In K. Gibson & A. C. Peterson (Eds.), *Brain maturation and behavioral development: Biosocial dimensions.* Hawthorne, NY: Aldine Gruyter Press.

Neville, H. J., Holcomb, P. J., & Mills, D. M. (1989). Auditory sensory and language processing in Williams syndrome: An ERP study. *Journal of Clinical and Experimental Neuropsychology, 11,* 52.

Neville, H. J., Kutas, M., Chesney, G., & Schmidt, A. L. (1986). Event-related brain potentials during initial encoding and recognition memory of congruous and incongruous words. *Journal of Memory and Language, 25,* 75–92.

Petersen, S. E., Fox, P. T., Posner, M. I., Mintun, M. A., & Raichle, M. E. (1988). Positron emission tomographic studies of the cortical anatomy of single-word processing. *Nature, 331,* 585–589.

Piaget, J. (1963). *The origins of intelligence in children.* New York: Norton.

Preuss, M. (1984). The Williams syndrome: Objective definition and diagnosis. *Journal of Clinical Genetics, 25*(5), 422–428.

Rapin, I. (1982). *Children with brain dysfunction: Neurology, cognition, language, and behavior.* New York: Raven Press.

Regan, D. (1989). *Human brain electrophysiology: Evoked potentials and evoked magnetic fields in science and medicine.* New York: Raven Press.

Reilly, J. S. (1983). What are conditionals for? *Papers and Reports on Child Language Development, 22,* 1–8.

Rondal, J. (1980). Language delay and language difference in moderately and severely mentally retarded children. *Special Education in Canada, 54,* 27–32.

Rondal, J. (1978). Developmental sentence procedure and the delay-difference question in language development of Down syndrome children. *Mental Retardation, 16,* 169–171.

Rosenfeld, M. G., Mermod, J. J., Amara, S. G., Swanson, L. W., Sawchenko, P. E., Rivier, J., Vale, W. W., & Evans, R. M. (1983). Production of a novel neuropeptide encoded by the calcitonin gene via tissue-specific RNA processing. *Nature, 304,* 129–135.

Semel, E., Wiig, E. H., & Secord, W. (1980). *CELF-R: Clinical evaluation of language functions.* San Antonio, TX: The Psychological Corporation.

Simmons, D. M., Culler, F. L., Bellugi, U., & Greenberg, F. (1990). Possible clues to genetic factors in the neurological basis of Williams syndrome. Presented at the Professional Symposium, *Williams Syndrome Association National Convention,* Boston, MA.

Sinclair, H. (1975). The role of cognitive structures in language acquisition. In E. Lenneberg & E. Lenneberg (Eds.), *Foundations of language development: A multidisciplinary approach* (pp. 223–238). San Francisco, CA: Jossey-Bass.

Thal, D., Bates, E., & Bellugi, U. (1989). Language and cognition in two children with Williams syndrome. *Journal of Speech and Hearing Research, 3,* 489–500.

Udwin, O., Yule, W., & Martin, N. (1987). Cognitive abilities and behavioral characteristics of children with idiopathic infantile hypercalcaemia. *Journal of Child Psychology and Psychiatry, 28,* 297–309.

von Arnim, G., & Engel, P. (1964). Mental retardation related to hypercalcaemia. *Developmental Medical Child Neurology, 6,* 366–377.

Williams, J. C. P., Barratt, B. G., & Lowe, J. B. (1961). Supravalvular aortic stenosis. *Circulation, 24,* 1311–1318.

Author Index

N

T

U

V

Subject Index

Probability and Mathematical Statistics (Continued)

WILLIAMS • Diffusions, Markov Processes, and Martingales, Volume I: Foundations

ZACKS • Theory of Statistical Inference

Applied Probability and Statistics

ANDERSON, AUQUIER, HAUCK, OAKES, VANDAELE, and WEISBERG • Statistical Methods for Comparative Studies

ARTHANARI and DODGE • Mathematical Programming in Statistics

BAILEY • The Elements of Stochastic Processes with Applications to the Natural Sciences

BAILEY • Mathematics, Statistics and Systems for Health

BARNETT • Interpreting Multivariate Data

BARNETT and LEWIS • Outliers in Statistical Data

BARTHOLOMEW • Stochastic Models for Social Processes, *Third Edition*

BARTHOLOMEW and FORBES • Statistical Techniques for Manpower Planning

BECK and ARNOLD • Parameter Estimation in Engineering and Science

BELSLEY, KUH, and WELSCH • Regression Diagnostics: Identifying Influential Data and Sources of Collinearity

BENNETT and FRANKLIN • Statistical Analysis in Chemistry and the Chemical Industry

BHAT • Elements of Applied Stochastic Processes

BLOOMFIELD • Fourier Analysis of Time Series: An Introduction

BOX • R. A. Fisher, The Life of a Scientist

BOX and DRAPER • Evolutionary Operation: A Statistical Method for Process Improvement

BOX, HUNTER, and HUNTER • Statistics for Experimenters: An Introduction to Design, Data Analysis, and Model Building

BROWN and HOLLANDER • Statistics: A Biomedical Introduction

BROWNLEE • Statistical Theory and Methodology in Science and Engineering, *Second Edition*

BURY • Statistical Models in Applied Science

CHAMBERS • Computational Methods for Data Analysis

CHATTERJEE and PRICE • Regression Analysis by Example

CHERNOFF and MOSES • Elementary Decision Theory

CHOW • Analysis and Control of Dynamic Economic Systems

CHOW • Econometric Analysis by Control Methods

CLELLAND, BROWN, and deCANI • Basic Statistics with Business Applications, *Second Edition*

COCHRAN • Sampling Techniques, *Third Edition*

COCHRAN and COX • Experimental Designs, *Second Edition*

CONOVER • Practical Nonparametric Statistics, *Second Edition*

CORNELL • Experiments with Mixtures: Designs, Models and The Analysis of Mixture Data

COX • Planning of Experiments

DANIEL • Biostatistics: A Foundation for Analysis in the Health Sciences, *Second Edition*

DANIEL • Applications of Statistics to Industrial Experimentation

DANIEL and WOOD • Fitting Equations to Data: Computer Analysis of Multifactor Data, *Second Edition*

DAVID • Order Statistics, *Second Edition*

DEMING • Sample Design in Business Research

DODGE and ROMIG • Sampling Inspection Tables, *Second Edition*

DRAPER and SMITH • Applied Regression Analysis, *Second Edition*

DUNN • Basic Statistics: A Primer for the Biomedical Sciences, *Second Edition*

DUNN and CLARK • Applied Statistics: Analysis of Variance and Regression

ELANDT-JOHNSON • Probability Models and Statistical Methods in Genetics

ELANDT-JOHNSON and JOHNSON • Survival Models and Data Analysis

continued on back